The
Sports Medicine
Bible

The
Sports Medicine
Bible

**PREVENT, DETECT, AND TREAT
YOUR SPORTS INJURIES
THROUGH THE LATEST
MEDICAL TECHNIQUES**

Dr. Lyle J. Micheli

Former President—American College of Sports Medicine

with Mark Jenkins

A JOHN BOSWELL ASSOCIATES BOOK

HarperPerennial
A Division of HarperCollinsPublishers

To my father, Prodie Micheli, of Peru, Illinois. A promising athlete in his own right, his sports career, like that of many of his peers, was interrupted by World War II. His first road trip began on the beaches of Normandy in the summer of 1944, and ended that winter in the Ardennes with a Purple Heart and Bronze Star. He is known in our hometown for his years as a Little League baseball coach and as a doggedly local Chicago Cubs fan. My father taught me the joy of sports and the satisfaction of hard work.

FIRST EDITION

Book design by Barbara Cohen Aronica.
Illustrations by Arlene Frasca.

Library of Congress Cataloging-in-Publication Data

ISBN 0-06-273143-2

95 96 97 98 99 CW 10 9 8 7 6 5 4 3 2 1

CONTENTS

ACKNOWLEDGMENTS

No author could claim to be solely responsible for a book of this magnitude. There are several people I have to acknowledge for their assistance in researching and writing *The Sports Medicine Bible*.

My thanks first and foremost go to my co-author, Mark Jenkins, who spent many hours translating complex scientific concepts into language to be understood by the lay person. My personal assistant, Julie deserves enormous credit for being an indispensable conduit between Mark and me. For his help in fact-checking the technical content of this book, I am grateful to Dr. Ross Outerbridge, as I am to Carl Gustafson, P.T., for reviewing the rehabilitation prescriptions.

At HarperCollins I have Linda Cunningham and Robert Wilson to thank for their support of this project. The responsibility for copyediting, illustrating, and designing this book was undertaken by Anne Cherry, Arleen Frasca, Barbara Cohen Aronica, and Jan Halper Scaglia and I remain deeply impressed with the quality and thoroughness of their work. Thanks also to Dan Foust and the staff at Jackson Typsetting for their incredible speed, efficiency and care in handling the manuscript. Patty Brown and Ward Calhoun at John Boswell Associates, and especially John Boswell himself, merit a big thank you from me. Their good humor proved especially invaluable in the face of what often seemed the overwhelming task of bringing to fruition the efforts of the entire *Sports Medicine Bible* team.

And as always, I deeply appreciate the understanding of my wife, Anne, during this time-consuming project.

PREFACE

The explosion in the popularity of recreational sports and fitness during the last quarter century has rightly been described as a lifestyle revolution. Sports and fitness activities have come to provide enormous enjoyment and health benefits for millions of Americans. But it would be unwise to ignore a significant downside of the sports and fitness boom: injuries.

The sports medicine profession has responded to the rise in the injury rate by placing greater emphasis on injury prevention, developing new diagnostic and treatment techniques, and promoting rehabilitation as an indispensable aid to full recovery.

But it is not enough for athletes to rely entirely on the medical profession to take care of their sports care needs. Having personal working knowledge of the basics of sports care is essential if athletes expect to stay injury free.

In fact, the dramatic increase in the incidence of injury in recreational sports and fitness has created the need for athletes to redefine the term *fitness* to encompass freedom from injury.

In addition to redefining fitness, focusing on injury prevention and rehabilitation, and introducing a simple but effective injury management strategy, the new approach to sports medicine recognizes the specific concerns of the modern recreational athlete in another significant way.

Until recently sports medicine focused on the diagnosis and treatment of "acute" injuries, those seen most often in full- and semi-contact sports such as football, hockey, and basketball: sprains, strains, bruises, and breaks. This is an outgrowth of sports medicine's traditional concern with high-performance professional athletes.

This focus on acute injuries is not relevant anymore. The scope of sports medicine has widened dramatically. Most adult recreational athletes do not participate in the kind of rough-and-tumble sports where acute injuries are usually seen (there are notable exceptions; for instance, biking and downhill skiing). Today, the adult recreational athlete is typically a runner, swimmer, aerobic dancer, in-line skater, or racket sports player. In these sports and fitness activities the concern is not acute injuries but a relatively new injury category: "overuse" injuries. Sometimes called chronic injuries, these conditions are caused by recurrent stress to an area of the body, not a single trauma.

Overuse injuries have not been given sufficient attention in the popular literature. That is because they are a recent phenomenon, traceable in the general population to the health fitness boom that began in the sixties and gained momentum in the seventies. As such, overuse injuries are not fully understood, even by many medical professionals. Because they are misunderstood, they are often ignored in favor of more straightforward and familiar acute sports injuries.

Consider that patellar pain syndrome, pain around the kneecap, was rarely seen in Americans until a quarter century ago. Today it is the number one diagnosis in most sports medicine clinics.

Also, there is the host of new injury categories that have entered the recreational athlete's lexicon: "runner's knee" and "swimmer's shoulder," to name just two.

The new approach to sports medicine addresses the real needs and concerns of recreational athletes, namely, the sports care demands placed on their bodies by health fitness activities.

Acute sports injuries will not be ignored. They are still a factor in recreational sports, and their prevention, diagnosis and treatment, and rehabilitation will receive thorough coverage.

By following the guidelines embodied in the new approach to sports medicine, the athlete will accentuate his or her sports or fitness activity by making it safer and more successful. In doing so, he or she will pave the way for a lifetime of good health through exercise.

CHAPTER ONE

Toward a New Definition of Fitness

Exercise is "in." The evidence is everywhere. City streets and country roads teem with joggers and racewalkers. Magazine racks bend under the weight of publications dedicated to sports and fitness. The listings for health clubs and aerobics studios in our telephone directories run for pages.

The common wisdom that fitness is a passing phase is wishful thinking on the part of couch potato commentators, as exemplified by the headline in *The Wall Street Journal*, "Fitness Keeps Losing Ground with the Public." Americans are not exercising less; they are diversifying. Participation in running declined in 1992, but mountain biking increased by 16 percent, and in-line skating (RollerBlading) increased 51 percent. Health club membership remained constant, despite the economic hard times of the early 1990s. At these health clubs, members are more likely to cross-train instead of just using one feature of the club. For instance, many men who once exclusively trained with weights now do aerobic work with stairclimber machines and cross-country skiing simulators; women who once did only aerobic exercise are increasingly likely to lift weights.

A recent study done by the American Dietetic Association revealed that healthy diet and physical fitness are on the rise. Americans are more aware than ever before of the positive effects of exercise and the harmful effects of saturated fats, cholesterol, smoking, and a sedentary lifestyle.

The New Fitness

Americans have always considered themselves an athletic lot, but the explosion in the popularity of "nontraditional" exercise forms, as well as the increase in "nontraditional" participants, have been truly astonishing.

Once this nation's athletes were mostly school-age young men who played football, baseball, basketball, and hockey. Now millions of Americans of all ages—and, significantly, both sexes—participate in a broad spectrum of sports and fitness activities.

Those activities that have dramatically increased in popularity are ones now considered "good for you." Hence the emergence of jogging, aerobics, yoga, strength training with weights, cross-country skiing, sports walking, biking, and swimming, to name just a few.

This trend was caused primarily by a change in the way fitness has been defined.

In previous generations, fitness was equated with athleticism related to motor skills. However, it was discovered that motor skills have almost nothing to do with health. Just because someone is a skilled baseball player or can throw a football 50 yards does not mean he is healthy according to modern health criteria.

Fitness is now measured using norms that have a direct bearing on our short- and long-term health. The four criteria we use now are cardiovascular endurance (the ability of the heart and lungs to pump blood and deliver oxygen throughout the body); muscular fitness (the strength and endurance of our muscles); flexibility (the ability to move our joints freely and without pain through a wide range of motion); and body composition (the portion of our bodies made up of fat). By testing these factors it is possible to measure a person's health in relation to how much exercise he or she does. This has come to be known as "health fitness."

As demonstrated by the exercise boom, Americans have embraced this new definition of fitness. But is it adequate? No. It makes no reference to being injury free and, for that reason, needs to be further refined.

Origins of the Health Fitness Boom

The current interest in health fitness is traceable to the sixties and seventies.

A few generations ago, Americans did not need to jog or do aerobics. Sufficient exercise was obtained in daily life, tilling fields and stoking the furnaces of industry using old-fashioned muscle power. In general, Americans ate better: lots of complex carbohydrates, little in the way of artificial ingredients.

Urbanization, dietary changes, car culture, and couch potato syndrome all contributed to a change in the way Americans live.

By the time the sixties arrived, these sedentary ways had contributed to a dramatic increase in the incidence of conditions such as heart and lung disease, back pain, and obesity. Researchers began drawing scientific conclusions about the relationship between exercise and health. Physical activity was found to have direct medical benefits (see "Benefits of Health Fitness," at left).

It did not take long for Americans to begin heeding the exhortations of the fitness advocates. The fitness craze was born. From the fuzzy black-and-white television images of Jack La Lanne have evolved Jane Fonda videos and "cardio-funk" aerobics.

Significantly, the emergence of information linking exercise to health coincided with the increase of leisure time available to Americans.

In summary, Americans started using their increased spare time to get healthy in one of the most enjoyable ways possible—through exercise.

BENEFITS OF HEALTH FITNESS

Vigorous physical activity

- increases the number and size of blood vessels in the heart and the muscles, resulting in better and more efficient circulation

- increases the elasticity of blood vessels, lessening the likelihood of breakage under pressure

- increases the efficiency of exercising muscles, enabling the muscles and blood to better carry and utilize oxygen

- increases the efficiency of the heart, making it a better pump

- increases tolerance to stress, reducing the negative effects of the stress/pressure syndrome

- decreases cholesterol and triglycerides, lessening the chances of arterial deposits

- lowers high blood pressure, reducing the risk of heart attack and stroke

Adapted from D. F. Haydon, "The Family and Health/Fitness," *Health Values* 11, 2 (1987): 36–39.

Why Exercise?

Exercise is enjoyable. If it were not, health fitness activities would not have become so popular. Vigorous physical activity has many proven physical and psychological benefits. Studies have shown that regular, vigorous exercise can improve the body's ability to consume oxygen during exertion, lower the resting heart rate, reduce blood pressure, and increase the efficiency of the heart and lungs. It also helps burn excess calories.

Since obesity and high blood pressure are among the leading risk factors for heart attack and stroke, exercise offers protection against two of America's major killers.

Perhaps more important for motivational purposes are the immediate benefits that exercise enthusiasts experience. They almost invariably report they feel better, tire less easily, and have fewer illnesses.

Exercising also exerts a favorable influence on personal habits. For example, quite often smokers who begin exercising cut down or quit. First, it is difficult for people to exercise if they smoke, and second, improved physical condition encourages a desire to improve other aspects of life.

Rise of Injuries

One of the few downsides of the health fitness boom has been the rise of sports injuries and, more disturbingly, the emergence of a whole new genre of injury previously unseen in the general public.

Of course, it is inevitable that when more people participate in an activity with the potential for injury, the number of injuries will rise. With the fitness boom came a dramatic increase in "traditional" sports injuries: sprains, strains, bruises, and breaks. These kinds of injuries are known as acute injuries, because they are caused by a single incident—a twist or a blow, for instance.

Significantly, there is evidence that acute injuries may, proportionately speaking, be *declining*. That is partly because of improvements in areas like coaching, supervision, rules, and equipment. For instance, according to the National Ski Areas Association (NSAA), ski injuries have dropped from 6 per 1,000 skier visits to 2.5–3 per 1,000 skier visits. This reduction—attributed primarily to improved skier conduct and improved technology—is a 50 percent decline from the early 1970s. But the proportional decline in the number of "traditional" sports injuries has more to do with a dramatic increase in another category of injury, which has to do with *who* is playing *what* in America.

Now it is not only children playing the kinds of vigorous, rough-and-tumble school-based and extracurricular sports where acute injuries often take place. Many more athletes today are grown-ups participating in "health fitness" sports. Participants in these activities are less susceptible to acute injuries.

What is being seen in these sports is a dramatic rise in what is called "overuse injury." Unlike acute injuries, these injuries are not caused by a single twist or blow but from an accumulation of repetitive "microtrauma" to the tissues. Overuse injuries are prevalent in health fitness sports because those activities require prolonged, repetitive movement of large muscle groups to produce a cardiovascular workout, often associated with the pounding of the body's tissues on the training surface.

1. COMPARATIVE BENEFITS OF VARIOUS ACTIVITIES

ACTIVITY	KCAL/HOUR*
Aerobic dancing	470
Backpacking (40 lb pack)	670
Badminton	440
Basketball	630
Bowling	270
Bicycling (10 mph)	450
Circuit weight training	420
Cross-country skiing	650
Digging ditches	660
Golf	250
Mowing (push-power)	510
Racquetball	800
Rope jumping	775
Running (7 mph)	880
Sawing by hand	550
Swimming (slow crawl)	600
Table tennis	350
Volleyball	228
Walking	350
3.5 mph	
4 mph (with 5 lb hand-held weights)	590
4 mph (with 5 lb ankle weights)	540
Weeding	330

Note: Cross-country skiing, swimming, and bicycling are very forgiving activities, because they involve no impact loading. People with bad knees, bad feet, or bad hips can get a lot of exercise in these sports while sparing themselves the impact loading of running, jogging, or tennis.

* The kCal values are for a 167 lb person; they are approximations and will vary with the size of the person and the intensity of the activity. The information is compiled from R. Passmore and J. V. G. A. Durnin, "Human Energy Expenditure," 1955; 35:801–840, and J. F. Miller and B. F. A. Stamford, "Intensity and Energy Cost of Weighted Walking Vs. Running for Men and Women," *Journal of Applied Physiology*, 62 (1987): 1497–1501.

Several forms of endurance exercise—cycling, swimming, and cross-country skiing among them—are as good for health as running, but running's immense popularity is due to its unique advantages. Some of them are:

Almost everyone can do it. A person does not have to take expensive lessons to be a runner. If someone can walk, he or she can probably work up to running and learn what is needed from magazines, books, and other runners.

You can do it almost anywhere. Running doesn't require expensive facilities. It can be done in parks, on streets or country roads, in gymnasiums, or on the tracks and trails found in almost every community. (Those who run on roads or streets should stay on the shoulder or close to the curb and run facing traffic. A few localities have banned runners from roadways, so beginning runners should check to see if their community is one of them.)

You can do it almost anytime. It is not necessary to get a team together to run, so runners do not have to rely on other people's schedules. Weather does not present the same problems and uncertainties it does in many sports. Running is not a seasonal activity, except in the most extreme climates, and it can be done in daylight or darkness. (Wear light-colored or reflective clothing and use extreme care when running at night. Several runners are struck and killed each year by cars.)

It's inexpensive. Runners do not have to pay to run, and the only special equipment required is a good pair of running shoes.

Until the fitness boom, overuse sports injuries were rarely seen in the general population. Today they are commonplace in the millions who have taken up health fitness activities.

Most sports medicine doctors would agree that at some point, injuries are sustained by 60 to 70 percent of runners; 40 to 50 percent of swimmers; 40 percent of aerobic dancers; and 80 to 90 percent of serious triathletes.

What is especially troubling is that in addition to a growing epidemic of overuse injuries among recreational athletes, injury *recurrence* is also commonplace. Most athletes get injured, and once injured often get hurt again. This highlights the inadequacy of rehabilitation for recreational athletes, not only because many athletes may not take their rehabilitation seriously enough but also because not enough emphasis is given to rehabilitation.

Add to this troubling information the fact that even though the incidence of overuse injuries has dramatically risen, it is not known by how much. Because symptoms are slow to develop, athletes with overuse sports injuries generally do not visit hospital emergency rooms, where most sports injury statistics originate. Many do not even consult their primary care physician or a sports doctor; they just drop out of sports because of the nagging symptoms of injury. Not only are these people losing out on the benefits of health fitness but they may also develop long-term medical problems such as arthritis from the undiagnosed, untreated overuse injury. Certainly they are at risk of reinjury if they return to sports without proper rehabilitation.

Injury and Health Fitness: A Contradiction?

Health fitness activities, then, are responsible for the vast majority of overuse injuries. This raises the question: "If overuse injuries are such a problem, how can health fitness be considered healthy?"

When overuse sports injuries began to be perceived as an inevitable by-product of the fitness boom, this sort of question became part of a backlash against health fitness activities. Because overuse injuries appeared to be caused by athletes doing exactly what it is they were supposed to do during exercise, overuse injuries were condemned as the rule in health fitness, not an exception.

After studying millions of overuse injuries, however, sports medicine discovered a host of associated "risk factors." By isolating and addressing these risk factors, it is possible to reduce drastically the incidence of overuse injury.

What is needed is for those who participate in health fitness to take as active an interest in injury prevention as they do to established health fitness components. What is needed, in fact, is to refine the definition of health fitness.

A New Definition of Fitness

In order to develop a truly comprehensive definition of fitness that is health specific, it is necessary to elevate the concept of being injury free to the pantheon of fitness determinants.

The new fitness would encompass cardiovascular endurance, muscle fitness, flexibility, body composition, *and freedom from injury*.

By introducing this definition of the new fitness, it will be possible to look forward to a time when staying injury free will become an integral part of staying fit. Athletes will be better qualified to avoid unnecessary injury, and America will be a healthier place.

RISK FACTORS FOR OVERUSE INJURIES

Extrinsic
- Errors in training, including abrupt increases in intensity, duration, or frequency of training

- Improper equipment

- Inappropriate clothing/footwear

- Poor coaching

Intrinsic
- Previous injury

- Poor conditioning, in particular lack of strength and flexibility

- Incorrect technique

- Imbalances in strength and flexibility in the muscle-tendon units

- Anatomical abnormalities (e.g., differences in leg length, internally rotated thighbones, bowlegs, knock-knee, flat feet, high arches, and feet that roll inward when running)

- Associated disease state (arthritis, poor circulation, old fracture, etc.)

- Menstrual irregularity, which causes bone thinning

CHAPTER TWO

Preventing Sports Injuries

Injury prevention is where athletes can contribute the most to staying injury free, a prerequisite to being fully "fit."

Athletes are being helped in the area of injury prevention by new sports care initiatives. In the past, sports care was more concerned with diagnosing and treating injuries than with preventing them. Now sports doctors are shifting their focus to prevention. Injuries are prevented by identifying risk factors and addressing them with preventive measures.

The techniques discussed in the following pages represent a comprehensive program to help you prevent injury and recurrences of injuries.

Have a Presports Physical

A "physical" performed by a qualified sports doctor is one of the most effective forms of preventive sports care. Such an evaluation can detect conditions that may predispose the athlete to injury and can provide treatment to alleviate these problems.

The main goals of sports physicals are

- to assess overall health

- to detect conditions that might cause injury

- to detect conditions that may disqualify the athlete from participation in certain sports

- to assess fitness for the chosen sport

- to make recommendations for the exercise program

A physical is essential for those beginning an exercise program or sport who are over forty; who suffer from obesity, diabetes, or high cholesterol; who smoke heavily; or who have had unexplained chest pains or heart problems such as a previous heart attack.

After the physical, discuss the results with the physician. Find out about any conditions that have to be corrected or rehabilitated before beginning a fitness program.

Appropriate Clothing and Footwear

Suitable clothing contributes to making exercise safer and more enjoyable. It keeps the body temperature at a comfortable level and protects it from the stresses of sports as well as wet and wind.

The appropriately clothed athlete can withstand a wide range of temperatures. Obviously, wearing clothes that help keep the body cool is helpful. For example, light-colored clothing made of cotton is preferable to dark colors made of synthetic fibers such as nylon. In cold weather, insufficient clothing will not provide the protection necessary for a runner to keep warm, especially near the end of the race when he or she slows down and the body's heat production is less than that necessary to keep warm. On a cool day the clothing worn should consist of multiple thin layers of cotton fibers. A polypropylene garment may be worn near the skin. This clothing should be covered with an easily removed windbreaker (preferably of nylon or another man-made material). As the athlete gets warm, clothing can be removed to allow sweat to evaporate or dry. However, when the pace gets too slow for the runner to keep warm, the clothes can be put back on. In addition to being more effective at retaining body heat, *multilayering* allows athletes to remove layers when they get warm. When the clothing is nonconstricting, multilayering helps prevent sweat from freezing on the body. Appropriate headgear should not be neglected during cold weather, as the body loses most of its heat through the head. In very cold weather, the face, nose, and ears should also be covered, as these areas are the ones most likely to become frostbitten. During wet weather, waterproof clothing is essential.

It is also advisable to wear sweatsuits while warming up during cool or cold weather. The insulation provided helps muscles, ligaments, and tendons get warmer and more flexible, which contributes to preventing both acute and overuse injuries.

Men should always wear an athletic supporter ("jock strap"), and women who participate in vigorous activity should invest in good-quality sports bras. (For criteria in selecting a sports bra, see page 297.)

When running at night, wear a luminous vest.

Footwear

Runners exert a combined force of three to four times their body weight with each step. That force is absorbed by the running surface, the shoe, and the foot and leg. The less force the limb absorbs, the less risk there is of overuse injury. That explains why it is better to train on slightly softer surfaces such as clay or grass rather than cement or asphalt, which have less give. It also explains why shoes are the most important item in most athletes' wardrobes.

Shoes are especially important for runners. The right footwear makes for an enjoyable, injury-free running experience, while the wrong footwear can cause discomfort and ailments ranging from ankle sprains to heel spurs to knee cartilage tears.

Socks also count as footwear. They act as shock absorbers and protection against rubbing from shoes. Socks should be thick to maximize impact absorption, free of holes to protect against blisters, and regularly laundered to avoid skin conditions. During the last ten years a variety of heavyweight socks have helped reduce the incidence of impact- and friction-related injuries such as stress fractures, plantar fasciitis, and blisters.

Respect Your Environment

Athletes who exercise outside in hot and humid or cold and wet conditions can suffer a variety of ailments. Injuries due to overheating and overcooling are especially prevalent among runners. In fun runs, for instance, the most serious injuries are related to the inability to keep the body temperature from rising too high. This increase in temperature occurs when the body produces heat at a faster rate than it can disperse. In short races of 10 km (6.2 miles) or less, increased body temperature (known medically as hyperthermia) occurs in conjunction with the tiredness caused by the heat; fainting and dizziness can occur, even on relatively cool days. In longer races on warm days, these heat problems are common. On cool or cold days, especially when it is wet and windy, the risk to participants in running races are related to low body temperature (medically known as hypothermia).

Athletes may become too hot or too cold, depending on the prevailing temperature, humidity, and wind conditions, and the clothing worn.

Tips for Cold Weather Exercise

Exercising in cold weather can be invigorating, pleasant, and safe if the participant follows a few simple rules, including dressing appropriately and eating enough.

Proper clothing is essential, and it must be selected with the individual sport in mind. Endurance sports such as cross-country skiing and running do not require as much clothing as stop-and-start activities such as downhill skiing, sledding, and skating.

Participants in those activities that are frequently interrupted need two types of clothing: for skiers, light clothing when they are coming down the slopes, and well-insulated clothing to keep them warm while waiting for the ski lift. Multiple layers of clothing trap air between each layer (air is an efficient insulator). Also, the outer layer can be added or discarded as needed.

Most experts recommend polypropylene fabric next to the body, because it carries sweat away from the skin

EXERCISE AND AIR POLLUTION

Athletes who exercise outdoors in a smog-laden, carbon monoxide–loaded, and ozone-filled environment may be doing themselves more harm than good. Air pollution is a major health concern for athletes who exercise outdoors. And oxygen depletion brought on by breathing impure air may soon rival glycogen depletion as a major performance concern.

Until recently, air pollution was a problem mainly in congested urban areas, where automobile and industrial exhausts are primary offenders, or in cities nestled in mountain basins where these same pollutants are trapped by atmospheric inversion conditions. Now rural areas are also affected, not only by forest fires, agricultural burning, and mining operations, but by pollutants blown from cities or industrial areas.

Athletes with no choice but to exercise in polluted conditions should take these precautions to minimize health risks:

Check air quality reports on the newspaper weather page, or call the regional office of the Department of Environmental Conservation and ask for the current Pollutant Standard Index (PSI) level. Readings in the range of 100 to 199 are considered unhealthy. When pollution levels are high, exercise before 10 A.M., before ozone has the chance to build up.

Avoid exercising near heavily traveled roadways if possible; work out in open, windswept areas, where pollutants are easily dispersed. To avoid the exhaust of passing vehicles, exercise on the upwind side of the road.

Reduce exercise intensity and duration when pollution levels are high or when breathing is impaired.

When competing in a polluted area, minimize physical activity prior to the event to reduce the dose of pollutants. Reduce the intensity of the warm-up before competition.

Stop if there is difficulty breathing. Constricted air passages are a warning that air quality is poor.

When pollution levels are unacceptable, exercise indoors. Instead of doing aerobic training that places a heavy demand on breathing, emphasize weight training with reduced sets and repetitions. Make use of this time to focus on flexibility, technique, and strategies specific to the sport.

and keeps the body from cooling rapidly. Sweat-soaked clothing gets cold 200 times faster than dry clothing. Wool is best for the outer layer of clothing; even when wet, it does not draw away body heat, and it dries from the inside out, thus retaining its insulating properties.

The outer layer should protect the athlete from the wind, which can rapidly deplete body heat. Runners and cross-country skiers, on the other hand, need a vented outer shell to release trapped heat.

Mittens are better than gloves, since all the fingers can warm each other in one compartment. The circulating air also allow mittens to dry between wearing. Down is the preferred lining because it traps air. Tremendous amounts of body heat are lost from the head and face. The head should be covered with a wool cap and the face protected with a scarf or high collar.

The best foods for winter fuel are those that supply carbohydrates and fat—waffles, oatmeal, pancakes with butter and syrup, raisins, nuts, bread, and fruit. It is estimated that more than 60 percent of the calories burned during winter exercise are used to heat the body.

Alcohol should be avoided at all cost: it not only dulls judgment and decreases sensitivity but it dilates blood vessels and increases heat loss.

Avoid exercise in hazardous weather conditions. Running on ice or over snow-covered terrain can lead to tripping or falling and injury.

Warm Weather Medical Self-care for Beginning Runners*

Training and preparation: You should be able to run ————† miles at nine to eleven minutes per mile pace to finish a race comfortably. Try to train ———— † miles per week for at least four weeks before a race. Drink about 8 ounces of fluid one hour before the race and up to twice that amount ten to fifteen minutes before racetime. Start warming up—stretching and jogging—about 30 minutes before a race.

---

*Reproduced with permission from D'Ambrosia and Drez, eds., *Running Injuries,* SLACK Incorporated, from the chapter "Heat Injuries in Runners: Treatment and Prevention," by Peter G. Hanson, M.S., M.D.
†Race of 6 to 9 miles: run 3, train 18.
  Race of 12 to 22 miles: run 6, train 25.
  Race of 26 miles: run 12, train 37.

Temperature is a critical factor. Significant heat injury may occur at all temperatures from 65 to 80 degrees F. Above 80 degrees F, novice runners should reduce running pace by about one minute per mile. Wear only light athletic clothing (shorts, T-shirt, tank top, or no shirt). Body temperature will normally rise to 102 to 103 degrees F during a race due to exercise heat production. Further increases may occur due to radiant sun exposure, dehydration, and decreased sweat rate.

Fluid replacement is essential to restore sweat losses. The average-size man (140 to 160 pounds) may lose 1.5 to 2 quarts of sweat per hour. Drink 6 to 8 ounces of fluid at each aid station. Stop to drink. Even then, you may replace only 50 percent of sweat loss.

Problems during run may include muscle cramps, joint pains, blisters, fatigue. Heat symptoms are most dangerous—headache, dizziness, disorientation, nausea, decrease in sweat rate, paleness, cold skin. Don't try to run through these symptoms. Stop, walk or rest, ask for help.

After running: At finish, you may become dizzy or faint on coming to a stop due to a fall in blood pressure. To prevent this, keep moving. But, if symptoms develop, lie down, raise legs, call for help.

Chronic medical problems: If you have medical problems such as asthma, diabetes, hypertension, or other cardiovascular problems, check with your physician before entering a race. Wear a "medic alert" tag and carry identification.

Remember, running is fun but it can be stressful. Listen to your body. Walk when you are tired. There is always another race.

Use Proper Equipment

Sports equipment includes such things as golf clubs and tennis rackets as well as protective equipment such as helmets, mouth guards, and shoulder pads.

Get Proper Coaching

Qualified coaches are trained not only to improve athletes' skill level but also to prevent injuries. Proper instruction is especially important in high-risk sports such as skiing and scuba diving, but it is also important in seemingly benign sports such as tennis, aerobics, racquetball, strength training, and running, where the wrong technique can cause overuse injuries.

When learning a sport or seeking to improve skill level, always look for instructors or coaches certified in their sport by a national association.

Get in Shape

Conditioning improves health and well-being as well as reduces the risk of injury. It also enhances performance. Everyone needs "basal" fitness to be able to function well in daily life: sufficient heart-lung endurance, strength, flexibility, good body composition, and freedom from injury.

Athletes also need sports-specific conditioning. For instance, tennis players need strong shoulders with good range of motion so the demands of serving do not cause them injury.

Don't Overdo It

Training error—usually "too much too soon"—is one of the main causes of injury, especially overuse injuries. Injuries can develop when athletes suddenly increase the *frequency, duration,* or *intensity* of their workouts.

Frequency refers to *how often* the athlete trains. Duration refers to *how long* the athlete trains. Intensity refers to *how hard* the athlete trains. Intensity encompasses factors such as how far or how fast a person jogs or how heavy a weight he or she lifts; it also refers to less obvious aspects of the exercise regimen, such as the hardness of the training surface on which the athlete is exercising. Joggers can consider they have significantly increased the intensity of their workout if they switch from running on grass or clay to road running, or from running primarily on flat surfaces to running hills. Softer does not always mean less stressful; for instance, running on sand stresses the Achilles tendons and predisposes the athlete to tendinitis in that area.

Aerobic dancers who change from working out on mat floors to cement floors run the risk of overuse injuries in their knees and lower legs. Other examples of increased exercise intensity: using hand weights when jogging; using hand paddles to swim; using a heavier racket.

It is generally considered safe to increase either the frequency, duration, or intensity of the exercise regimen by 5 percent without making adjustments. But when dramatically increasing the volume of one of the three elements of the exercise regimen, it is necessary to make temporary adjustments in one or both of the other elements.

Increase in exercise duration = reduce frequency and/or intensity.
Increase in exercise frequency = reduce duration and/or intensity.
Increase in exercise intensity = reduce duration and/or frequency.

By how much, though, should athletes cut back? When athletes intensify one element of the exercise regimen, they should cut back on the other two elements of their exercise regimen by 20 percent, and then increase them by 5 percent each week until they reach their previous level. For instance, if it takes a jogger an hour to run 5 miles, and he or she does this every other day on grass, when the jogger switches from grass to concrete, he or she should reduce how long and how fast he runs.

Any pain or joint stiffness should be a warning that the exerciser is increasing the other elements too quickly, and further cutbacks should be made.

Most athletes engaged in endurance sports are primarily interested in improving their health. But many others are competitive athletes who wish to improve performance in endurance sports for personal satisfaction or competition.

The principle of improving endurance is based on "overload"—when the training load exceeds the accustomed workload. However, this works only up to a point. There comes a time when endurance athletes reach a point when no further increase in endurance takes place. In fact, when athletes continue pushing themselves to improve their performance beyond this maximal performance level, their performance may worsen. More significantly, injuries may take place.

Competitive athletes who wish to improve their perfor-

mance in an endurance sport such as running, swimming, biking, sport walking, or aerobics should follow these guidelines:

- Do not increase training frequency, duration, or intensity training by more than 5 to 10 percent per week.

- If performance stabilizes or even worsens, or any of the symptoms of staleness becomes apparent, cut back on the training routine. Symptoms of injury such as swelling, increasing discomfort, or persistent pain are signals to stop training and consult a sports doctor.

- Alternate hard workouts with easy ones. Give the body a rest between extra hard training days.

- To improve performance, do not look just to increasing distance or time; consider improvements in areas such as nutrition and technique.

- Do not begin as a competitive athlete by training for the hardest race. For instance, those who want to be competitive runners should start by training for 3 km races, not marathons.

- Use common sense to tell how much is too much.

Structure Your Workout Properly

One of the most common reasons athletes get injured is that they do not prepare their bodies for the immediate demands of exercise with a structured workout that includes warm-up and cooldown periods.

The benefits of warming up and cooling down are well established: improved performance, psychological preparation, creating a comfort zone for the activity itself, and relieving the aches and pains of vigorous athletic activity. Most important, though, the warm-up and cooldown prevent injuries from occurring.

Injuries are much more likely to occur when muscles, tendons, and ligaments are "tight" or "cold." Tissues that have not been warmed by increased blood flow and then lengthened with gradual stretches are less pliable. Thus they are at greater risk of being torn during the normal twists, turns, and stretches of sports.

Less pliable tissues are also more susceptible to overuse injuries: tiny tears may occur due to repetitive, low-intensity stretching of inflexible tissues. Overuse injuries of the joints can develop because the surrounding tissues are not warmed up and stretched, which restricts the joint's range of motion and may cause grinding of the cartilage against bone or cartilage against other cartilage.

Another important reason to prepare properly for exercise is that warm-up exercises improve coordination and minimize the risk of accidents—a slip, a fall, a trip. Furthermore, studies have shown that beginning vigorous exercise without a gradual warm-up—Sudden Strenuous Exercise (SSE)—puts athletes at risk of cardiovascular difficulties. Finally, good preparation will improve *performance*.

The intensity and duration of the warm-up and cool-down vary with each athlete. A well-conditioned athlete probably requires a longer, more intense warm-up—compared to a less well-conditioned person—in order to achieve optimal elevation in body temperature and heart rate.

Irrespective of the conditioning level of the athlete, every workout should include five stages: limbering up (five minutes); stretching (five to ten minutes); warm-up (five minutes); primary activity; and cooldown and cooldown stretching (ten minutes).

Limbering Up (five minutes)

Muscles need to be warmed before they can be safely and effectively lengthened during the stretching session.

In the limbering-up stage, athletes should raise body temperature by 1.5 or 2 degrees above normal before stretching. By raising the body's temperature those couple of degrees, the athlete is making his or her muscles and tendons more lubricated and elastic. The joints increase their secretions, and so there is less friction. The transmission of nerve impulses into the muscle fibers is more efficient, and the reflexes also improve. The limbering-up phase is complete when the athlete breaks a sweat.

Kinds of exercise that are ideal for the limbering-up session include: stationary bike riding, a light jog, a brisk walk, rope skipping, rowing machine use, stairclimbing.

It is not necessary to become tired during the limbering-up period. The goal is simply to warm the muscles in preparation for stretching.

Stretching (five to ten minutes)

After limbering up, do between five and ten minutes of stretching exercises. As the athlete gets older, flexibility decreases. The older the athlete, then, the more important it is to take the time to stretch. Also, athletes with specific trouble with injuries should focus on the appropriate areas, both before and after the activity.

Stretching improves flexibility. As seen in the section on flexibility conditioning, stretching should not be painful. During each exercise, stretch to the point of tension, known as the "action point," and hold it for between thirty and sixty seconds, depending on preexisting flexibility. By not overstretching, the exerciser can relax and hold each position longer.

"Ballistic" stretching, when the exerciser bounces up and down to create the stretch, is not recommended because of potential injury to muscles caused by stretching and contracting them too quickly.

In addition to stretching all the major muscle groups before exercising, the athlete may need to pay special attention to specific stretches for different sports demands. For instance, tennis players need to devote extra time to stretching out the upper back, shoulders, and neck, as well as the calves, Achilles tendons, and ankles. Runners need to focus on the lower back, quadriceps, hamstrings, calves, and groin muscles.

It may also be necessary to spend additional time stretching areas that are naturally tight or ones that have been previously injured.

Warm-up Prior to Vigorous Activity

The warm-up session should ideally last ten minutes. The warm-up activity should mimic the primary workout activity. This maximizes coordination for the sport, thus minimizing the risk of accidental injury. For instance, joggers should perform a walk-jog, then slowly increase to a run. Swimmers should start with a few slow laps. Racket sports players should rally with their partners or by themselves (including service), and golfers should take practice strokes.

When warming up for an endurance health fitness activity such as running, swimming, aerobics, or biking, the heart rate during the warmup should be 50 percent of maximum heart rate.

> ### THE BENEFITS OF WARMING UP AND COOLING DOWN
>
> Increased range of motion
> Relaxed muscle attachments
> Improved coordination
> More efficient movement
> Decrease in common acute injuries
> Reduced risk of overuse injuries
> Improved psychological preparation
> Improved performance
> Reduced risk of cardiovascular problems in exercise

Cooldown (five minutes) and Cooldown Stretches (five minutes)

Never end vigorous physical activity suddenly. A five-minute cool-down period helps prevent sudden changes in the cardiovascular system that can cause lightheadedness or even fainting.

Cooldown should be done in the same way as the warm-up—with gentle, easy movements that return the heart rate to normal. Joggers should gradually slow down to a walking pace. Swimmers should take their last few laps slowly. Racket sports players also need a period during which their heart rate slows gradually; squash and racquetball players who work out in fitness facilities may have the opportunity to jog, then walk on a treadmill, cycle slowly on a stationary bike, or gently use a rowing machine.

Stretching for five minutes after exercise prevents muscles from tightening too quickly. It may minimize muscle discomfort and may also be helpful in maintaining flexibility. Perform an abbreviated version of the exercises in the prestretch portion of the workout. Again, pay special attention to those specific areas that the sport stressed.

Learn Proper Technique

It is crucial to learn proper sports technique. Acute injuries often result from poor technique that leads to accidents, as in high-risk sports like downhill skiing.

More frequently, repetitive use of improper technique causes overuse injury. Tennis elbow is one of the most common overuse injuries caused by poor technique or by using the wrong equipment. This condition—felt as pain radiating from the forearm to the wrist and sometimes down to the fingers—affects golfers and squash and racquetball players as well as tennis players.

Improper technique is also the cause of overuse injuries among joggers. Runners usually strike first with the heel, then the midfoot and toes. Overuse injuries such as heel spurs and plantar fasciitis may occur when the runner strikes too hard with the heel.

In aerobics, most injuries—shinsplints, primarily—occur because the participant lands primarily on the forefoot instead of distributing the landing impact between a forefoot and heel strike.

To prevent overuse injuries caused by improper sports technique, it is important to get proper instruction, and it is always preferable to get a coach who is certified.

Following are recommendations that might mean the difference between enjoyment and injury in your chosen sport or fitness activity. The areas covered are walking, golf, biking, aerobic dance, stairclimber machine, running, skiing, hiking, and sports and the young athlete.

Proper Walking Technique

Although walking is widely recognized as an excellent form of exercise, most people walk incorrectly: slumped over, toes pointing outward, arms flailing, landing flat-footed. Gary D. Yanker, author of *The Complete Book of Exercisewalking* (Chicago: Contemporary Books, 1983), offers these tips on proper fitness walking technique.

When walking, head and back should be erect and the shoulders relaxed—easier said than done, especially after walking for a few miles. The buttocks should be tucked in slightly, even when walking. The toes should point straight ahead with the feet spaced 2–4 inches apart. The eyes should be looking 4–5 yards ahead. Walking with good posture (''walking tall'') gives the walker a higher center of gravity and a longer stride.

The arms should swing naturally in an arc from the shoulder, each arm swinging with the opposite leg to counterbalance forward motion. For a faster walking style, the participant should shorten the arc by bending elbows at a 90-degree angle to conform to quicker leg movements. The walker should exhale and inhale deeply and rhythmically, counting one breath for each one, two, or more steps, depending on walking speed. This must be done deliberately at first but soon becomes second nature.

With each step one should land on the heel first, or actually the outer edge of the heel. The sole should be placed at about a 40 degree angle to the ground, with the leg at a 90 degree angle to the foot. Then one should rock forward on the outside edge of the foot, from heel to toe. The walker should strive to eliminate up-and-down and side-to-side movements, concentrating on fluid forward movements to develop a smooth walking gait.

Preventing Golf Injuries

Most golf injuries are overuse conditions that affect the lower back, wrist, shoulder, and elbow. They can be prevented by addressing technique, conditioning, and game preparation.

Technique: Qualified instruction is a must. Focus on performing the proper weight shift, trunk rotation, and the subsequent arm movements associated with the backswing—and the reverse of these as the club head is brought forward. Otherwise, the extreme spinal rotation may result in back injuries as well as other conditions affecting the wrists, shoulders, and elbows.

Conditioning: Emphasize conditioning the hip, trunk, chest, and shoulder (especially the shoulder's rotator cuff muscles and rear shoulder muscles).

A good golf swing involves the right and left sides of the body equally. Therefore, conditioning should be done bilaterally.

Regular stretching and strengthening exercises for the hip and trunk will lessen fatigue and stress in those areas. For conditioning, the golfer must strengthen the abdominal, lower back, and hip muscles.

The recreational golfer needs enough endurance to play thirty-six holes in one day (or eighteen holes if carrying his or her own bag) without undue fatigue that may contribute to technique-related injury.

Cardiovascular endurance for golf can be achieved by doing aerobic exercise for fifteen minutes, four or five times a week. Fast walking, especially over rolling terrain similar to the courses the golfer plays, is an excellent form of golf-specific endurance training.

A cross-country ski machine is beneficial because it works both the upper and lower extremities. An aerobic workout with a video or audio tape involves more of the body than does jogging or biking. Jogging would be the next-best activity, and stationary biking after that.

Muscle endurance is developed by allowing only thirty to sixty seconds between sets when doing strength training. Strengthening exercises should not be done before a game.

Because of the unique role of the neck in golf—the head stays stationary while the neck rotates with the rest of the body—neck conditioning exercises are important.

Game Preparation: Warm-up, including exercises to promote flexibility through the full range of motion of the golf swing, will decrease the potential for injury and soreness after a golf round, and will also improve performance.

These can be done at home, if the course is a short drive away, in the clubhouse, or in an area adjacent to the course. The effects will last forty-five minutes, provided the player is dressed appropriately for the weather.

The following is a list of the exercises the golfer should perform before playing a round:

- calf stretch

- trunk rotation

- hamstring stretch

- lateral hip stretch

- lumbar stretch, both flexion and extension

- rotator cuff stretch

- posterior rotator cuff stretch

- neck stretch

These exercises are best done after a brief limbering-up period, which raise the heart rate and core body temperature and improve muscle coordination.

A typical warm-up should take five to ten minutes (less if the weather is warm). A brisk walk for a quarter or half mile is effective. If the warm-up is working, the golfer should be sweating. "Shortcut" warm-ups—induced by steam baths, saunas, or hot tubs, for instance—are not as effective as proper warm-ups.

The golfer may also use a stationary bike, a cross-

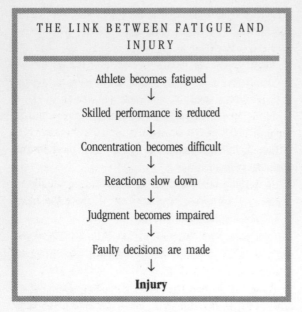

THE LINK BETWEEN FATIGUE AND INJURY

Athlete becomes fatigued
↓
Skilled performance is reduced
↓
Concentration becomes difficult
↓
Reactions slow down
↓
Judgment becomes impaired
↓
Faulty decisions are made
↓
Injury

country ski machine, jump rope, rowing machine, or any aerobic exercise routines.

Preventing Biking Injuries

The most effective ways for bikers to avoid injuries are to learn good bike-handling skills, to use common sense, to wear appropriate clothing and equipment, and to learn proper technique.

City streets are not biker friendly. One of the most common causes of urban biking injuries is getting hit by a car. Good bike-handling skills and good sense are necessary, as designated bike lanes and trails are still rare in most urban areas. Biking skills are best learned by riding with more experienced cyclists. Certain safety rules should be observed, such as riding with the flow of traffic, not against it, and staying in the right lane, obeying the same rules as the ordinary motorist.

Wearing a bike helmet is crucial. More than 75 percent of all biking fatalities are caused by head injuries, and over three-quarters of all permanently disabling injuries are due to brain damage caused by head injuries. Yet more than half of all adult recreational bikers do not wear helmets. Standards for biking helmets are now well established. Two ratings services, ANSI and Snell, approve helmets based on their safety performance. These helmets are sold through any bike store. Helmets meeting these standards have a certifying sticker inside.

Reflective vests and bike accessories are important safety measures for those who choose to ride in the dark.

For both comfort and injury prevention, a biker needs to select a bike that fits the body well. Salespeople in bike stores can be helpful in helping customers pick the *frame size* that is right for them. The upper body should be comfortable when the biker leans forward and grasps the handlebars. Lower back pain is especially common if the biker has a short torso (true for many women) and must stay in a stretched-out position for a long time because of the long top tube of many bikes.

Sustained pressure on the palms from resting on the handlebars is the cause of the most common overuse biking injury, an irritation of the median or ulnar nerves called handlebar palsy (page 258). The initial symptoms are tingling or numbness in the hands. This condition can be prevented quite easily by using biking gloves and padded handlebars.

To prevent knee overuse injuries, in particular knee-cap pain, the size of the bike needs to match the length of the biker's legs. The seat should be adjusted so that when one leg is fully extended downward and the foot is flat on the pedal, there is a 15- to 20-degree bend in the knee. If there is a question, err on the high side for the knee's sake.

Foot position on the pedal may be another cause of knee injury. Toeing in slightly will usually alleviate knee problems caused by improper foot position.

When pedaling, the biker should be able to maintain a level pelvis. If there is rocking from side to side with pedal strokes, lower the seat in small increments until it goes away. The use of toe clips or, more recently, clip-in devices attached to the shoes, optimizes pedaling efficiency by generating power not only in the push-down phase but also in the pull-up and transition phases. However, it may be difficult getting used to being tethered to the bike. In fact, a biking accident is often safer with the feet in the pedals than stuck out to the sides to protect against the impact of the fall.

Racing bike–style handlebars have traditionally been the standard on bikes, although this is changing with the advent of the "mountain bike," whose handlebars are higher and straight across, allowing the biker to adopt a more upright position. This more relaxed stance is one that is easier on the lower back.

Another important piece of safety equipment is the rearview mirror. This is especially important for urban riders. Typically, these mirrors are designed to attach to the handlebars, helmets, or even eyeglasses.

Finally, a good bicycle seat and properly padded bicycle pants help reduce "saddle soreness," although a period of conditioning is generally needed if a novice plans to spend an extended time cycling.

Preventing Injuries in Aerobic Dance

To lessen the growing incidence of injury, participants in aerobic dance should pay attention to the program structure, instructor qualifications, the dance surface, and footwear.

A well-designed aerobic dance session should include a warm-up and a cooldown.

The warm-up should include both limbering-up and stretching exercises.

Limbering-up exercises increase the metabolic rate and core temperature by elevating heart rate and increasing the flow of blood and oxygen to the working muscles. Such activities may include a slow jog, marching in place with low-level arm movements, or walking steps.

Stretching should involve static stretches, in which the participant gradually lengthens the muscle, then holds that position for between thirty and sixty seconds. The muscle should be relaxed and breathing should be normal.

To improve cardiovascular endurance during the main session, without risking injury, the following training principles should be emphasized: *progression, intensity, duration*, and *frequency*.

Progression: The aerobic dance program should start with steps that include small arm movements and foot patterns close to the floor and progress to steps with bigger arm movements and foot patterns farther from the floor. The program should begin with simple movements, then progress to where the routine becomes more complex. This stage should be maintained for at least twenty minutes to achieve cardiovascular conditioning. After this stage, the routine should return to smaller, less complicated, lower-level movements.

The progression ensures the gradual climb of the heart rate to a target zone and allows for a gradual return to the pretarget heart rate zone.

Intensity: If the aerobic dancer exercises at too low an intensity, he or she will not get the desired benefit, but exercising too hard will cause exhaustion.

Most experts suggest that most people receive the desired benefits of cardiovascular workout by exercising within their target heart rate zone, which most instructors can explain.

If working below the target heart rate, gradually increase the intensity of the workout. If above the range, gradually decrease the intensity.

Duration and frequency: How long (duration) and how often (frequency) someone participates in aerobic dance depends on fitness level and personal goals.

Most experts suggest participants train three to five times a week, keeping their heart rates within the target zone for twenty minutes each time.

Cooldown: Cooldown is as important as the warm-up, and should last five minutes.

The purpose of the cooldown is to allow the blood in the extremities to be pumped back into the central circulatory system and to gradually lower the body's core temperature and heart rate. This is generally achieved by low-level movements like walking or marching.

Cooldown is an appropriate time to do stretching exercises, such as static stretches on the floor. As the muscles are warm from the aerobic exercise, this is the most effective time to do stretching exercises.

The cooldown period should be the time to relax and stretch the muscles to help prevent injuries and to rid the body of exercise by-products thought to cause muscle soreness.

Aerobic dance classes should be taught by certified instructors trained in proper safety techniques, correct class format, and with knowledge of anatomy, physiology, and kinesiology. The instructor should be certified by one of the major aerobic dancer certification groups (IDEA, AFFA, ACSM).

The incidence of overuse injuries in aerobic dance caused by repetitive microtrauma to tissues can be lessened if the dance surface is more "forgiving." The dance surface should be a suspended wood floor. Concrete or carpet-over-concrete floors increase the risk of injuries such as shin splints, stress fractures in the foot, lower back problems, etc.

Shoes for aerobic dance should be lightweight to allow for dance movements but durable and supportive enough to absorb shock. The rear heel elevation should not be as high as in a running shoe but should still be at least one-quarter of an inch high, to allow for shock absorption.

The midsole should be cushioned to allow for shock absorption without elevating the foot too high from the ground. The outsole needs to be flexible, not as stiff as in a running shoe. This allows for the various different foot movements during aerobic dance. Aerobic shoes should have a rigid heel counter to reduce excessive foot pronation (turning). An additional heel collar may benefit those with excessive rear foot pronation who do high-impact aerobics. An additional counter may help those who weigh over 175 pounds, because of added stress on the shoe. Hightop shoes are recommended for those with ankle sprains or weak ankles. They will also stabilize the ankle during side-to-side movements.

Research has shown that more moderate, less stressful forms of exercise are safer and more effective for improving fitness. As more and more fitness professionals affirm the effectiveness of this more moderate form of exercise, exercise instructors are offering "soft workouts"—power walking, water aerobics, and high-/low-impact aerobic dance—along with the traditional high-impact aerobic dance classes.

Preventing Stairclimber Injuries

Remarkably safe because they involve no impact to the joints, stairclimber machines nevertheless do pose risks of overuse injury. These are the most effective ways to prevent stairclimber injuries:

Proper posture: Keep the back as straight as possible to prevent lower back pain or discomfort. Don't rest on the front rails for the entire workout because you will overstress the hamstrings as well as reduce the benefit of the workout.

Proper hand positioning: Inverting the wrists on the rails for long workouts may lead to carpal tunnel syndrome (page 257).

Proper foot positioning: Feet should be kept flat on the pedals. Overuse conditions such as Achilles tendinitis

(page 110) may develop when exercising with the heels extended out over the pedals for an entire workout or when continuously exercising on the balls of the feet. Do not push down with the feet or jog on the pedals, which may cause the feet to tingle and eventually become numb. To increase intensity, adjust the step height and resistance level accordingly.

Proper technique: To achieve the most benefits from the workout, keep the back as erect as possible, the feet flat on the pedals, and the fingers loose around the rails.

Preventing Running Injuries

Most running injuries are preventable. The most frequent causes of running injury are footwear problems, training errors, environmental factors, or anatomical abnormalities. By addressing these "risk factors," it is possible to reduce the risk of injury in running.

Footwear: Running shoes should provide shock absorption, motion control, and stability. When selecting a running shoe, runners should look for a brand that will provide all of the above benefits, as well as comfort. Shoes lose approximately 60 percent of their shock absorption properties after 250–500 miles of use. Someone who runs ten miles a week, therefore, should buy new shoes after nine to twelve months.

Training errors: "Too much, too fast, too soon" can sum up training errors. Every runner has a limit, and trying to exceed that limit can lead to injury. Mileage should be gradually increased or decreased, on an individual basis.

To reduce the risk of injury, runners should adhere to some of the American Running and Fitness Association's basic training principles.

Duration: Exercise for at least twenty-five to thirty-five minutes, three to four days a week, or every other day. Additional mileage depends on individual goals. Runners typically run more than the minimum to aid in weight loss, train for a race, reduce stress, or for pure enjoyment.

Ten percent rule: Do not increase mileage by more than 10 percent per week. The body grows stronger if stressed in small increments but breaks down if stressed too much. Increasing mileage by 10 percent per week helps most people grow stronger and avoid injury. Follow the ten percent rule whether increasing weekly distance from five minutes to twenty-five minutes, or from 40 miles to 60 miles. After ceasing running activity for more than two or three weeks, build mileage back slowly.

Training specificity: To run fast, the runner should incorporate fast runs into his or her training. To run long distances, he or she should incorporate long runs. It is best, though, to incorporate all types of running into a program, but allow overall goals to dictate what type of running gets the most emphasis. For example, if the runner's goal is to run the fastest mile he or she is capable of, training would include more than just running one mile a day at the fastest pace. Longer runs will provide stamina to sustain a fast pace and prevent fatigue. Shorter runs help build speed. Conversely, marathoners benefit from doing shorter, faster runs as well as longer runs.

Hard/Easy concept: A hard run one day should be followed by an easy run the next. Exercise damages muscles and they need time to repair themselves. If given time to heal, muscles come back stronger than before. If, however, muscles do not have time to repair themselves, they may get injured.

A hard run is one that includes more distance or speed than usual. A hard run means something different to each runner. For the beginner who has never run for ten minutes without stopping, a ten-minute run is hard. For the seasoned runner who has never run a seven-minute mile, then a seven-minute mile is hard. If a run feels hard, go easy the next day.

An "easy" day can mean taking an entire day or two off, or running at a distance and pace that feel comfortable, enjoyable, and relaxing. An easy day may involve vigorous training of muscles different from those used when running. Cross-training on a bicycle is a good complement to running because bicycling strengthens muscles not used much in running.

Anatomical abnormalities: A sports physical can rule out anatomical abnormalities that might predispose a runner to injury during intense training.

Preexisting structural or biochemical problems such as high arches, differences in leg length, curvature of the spine, or excessive muscle tightness may increase a runner's susceptibility to injury. The athlete can compensate for these abnormalities by following special training guidelines, incorporating a stretching regimen into the

conditioning program, and using shoe inserts (orthotics). For much more on this subject, see chapters 6 through 17.

Environmental factors: Runners are often faced with a variety of environmental factors—such as terrain, altitude, temperature, and air quality—that can adversely affect performance and physical health.

The ideal running surface is flat, smooth, resilient, and reasonably soft. Avoid concrete or rough road surfaces. If possible, use community trails that have been developed specifically for running.

Avoid hills because of the extra stress they place on joints and muscles. The ankle and foot are stressed most by running uphill, while downhill running stresses the knee and lower leg. Competitive runners cannot avoid hills, though care must be taken on such terrain.

During warm or humid weather, increase fluid intake. In cool weather, dress appropriately. Avoid running during temperature extremes—both hot and cold—or when air pollution levels are high. The entire body is stressed during those conditions and the risk of injury is increased. When running at higher altitudes, the runner should gradually acclimate to the lower oxygen levels with slow, steady increases in speed and distance.

Preventing Skiing Injuries: Experience, Ability, and Attitude

Skiing lessons are the most effective way to improve technique and enhance pleasure as well as safety. But unless skiing lessons are combined with lots of practice, there will be no improvement in skiing safety. Inexperienced skiers who learn too rapidly may be overconfident and attempt to ski terrain more difficult than they should attempt.

Inexperienced skiers should avoid skiing too fast, too long (especially on difficult terrain), and in poor snow conditions.

Well-conditioned skiers are less likely to sustain injury than those who tire significantly during the course of a skiing day. Skiing requires sustained muscle contractions (skiing in a flexed hip and knee position), quick bursts of powerful but finely coordinated muscle contractions (reaction to sudden changes in snow conditions or terrain), general flexibility, and cardiovascular (heart-lung) fitness.

To develop an individualized conditioning program, consult a sports medicine physician or a trainer at a local sports club. Popular ski magazines often feature preseason training programs.

The intangible factor in ski injuries is skier attitude. Injured skiers are often surprised when they get injured. Most admit that skiing is potentially dangerous, yet somehow they believe they are invulnerable.

Many skiers think that their bindings will magically function despite being old, worn, or mistreated. This attitude is most common in young, aggressive skiers, who have the highest injury rates.

Some skiers develop a high degree of skill but place themselves in situations that constantly challenge their abilities (e.g., skiing at high speed over challenging terrain). Although accidents are relatively rare in this group of skiers, when they do happen, they are often spectacular and frequently result in serious injury.

One of the most important ways to reduce the experienced skier's risk of injury is common sense. Being "in control" means avoiding trail and snow conditions beyond the skier's ability, resisting the temptation to join fellow skiers in reckless skiing, avoiding high speeds in crowded areas, acting with consideration toward other skiers, and constantly being alert for sudden, unexpected behavior from others.

For a thorough discussion of the role of equipment in preventing skiing injuries, see chapter 8, "Lower Leg Injuries."

Preventing Hiking Injuries

Hiking is an activity that is growing in popularity. However, it is potentially dangerous, and appropriate precautions should be taken. The most important areas of injury prevention are conditioning, planning, and clothing and equipment.

Conditioning: Hiking is not just walking. First, it involves carrying a pack. Also, when the terrain steepens or the pace quickens in order to reach a goal, it becomes an aerobic activity.

Novice hikers need to assess their prehiking aerobic condition. If not participating in regular aerobic activity, the choices are to 1) plan hikes according to current aerobic fitness, or 2) start aerobic training ahead of time.

Strength is required in hiking as well as aerobic ca-

pacity. The two most important areas to strengthen are the upper legs and the buttocks and lower back.

Sufficient aerobic endurance fur a full-day hike on moderate terrain can be achieved by running or biking three times a week for at least six weeks (make sure the heart rate is at the target level for at least twenty minutes at each session). If also doing a strength training program, it is likely a longer trip or one on steeper, more difficult terrain may be possible.

If the novice hiker does not engage in regular aerobic exercise of any kind and does not do any strength training, a full-day hike on moderate terrain may be a strain.

To test endurance, try a simple day hike on easy terrain with a light day pack.

Planning the hike: Decisions on hike *distance* cannot be made without taking into account the *elevation* and *terrain* of the hiking trail.

A five-mile hike on relatively flat terrain will be easier and faster than five miles ascending an elevation of 4,000 feet.

Elevation and terrain should probably be decided first. Then decide on distance with elevation in mind.

Elevation and terrain can be gauged using topographical maps available from the U.S. Geological Survey and at stores that specialize in hiking supplies. Be sure the map is current because trail systems change.

Trail guidebooks also include trail information not shown on maps. Rangers and other hikers are sources of firsthand information.

Plan a detailed route in advance. Note the location of campsites and shelters, as well as water holes. Assess the amount of time available and choose the distance accordingly.

Most trail guides provide travel time estimates. Keep in mind they may be slightly over- or underrepresentative.

Knowing where shelters are located is crucial in case of a storm. Also, it is essential to know where water holes are located in order to replenish water supply.

Respect the environment: Some water supplies are a source of a multitude of infections and bacteria. Several methods of water purification are available. These include boiling water, treating water with iodine, using TGHP tablets, and using the Kahn Vischer method. Nonchemical filters and pumps such as the Katadyn Pocket H20 Filter are also available.

Hikers should be prepared for all kinds of weather.

Checking the weather and forecast for the hiking site is vital. However, as demonstrated every year by tragic cases, high-altitude weather can be extremely temperamental and dangerous.

Remember that weather is different at the top of the mountain than at the bottom, so do not leave warm and/or rainproof gear behind. While this may mean carrying a heavier pack, more is better than less if a storm develops.

Proper equipment and clothing: A full review of hiking equipment and clothing is impossible here, so only the basics will be covered because they most significantly affect injury.

Appropriate clothing is crucial, whether for a day hike or a full expedition to high altitudes. Make clothing choices with two main goals in mind: keeping warm and keeping dry.

Layering is the fundamental principle when dressing for hiking. The benefit of layering is a clothing system that has been adjusted depending on weather conditions. The four layers are underwear, clothing, insulation, and the shell.

Underwear can be made of several types of fabric, including cotton, wool, or silk, depending on preference for comfort. In cold weather, keeping dry is an important criterion. Perspiration against the skin can make the hiker cold, so the underwear fabric should "wick" moisture away from the body. A light polypropylene is ideal. In especially cold weather, two layers of underwear can be worn.

Clothing includes shirts, pants, hats, and gloves. Shirts can be either short- or long-sleeved, and should be cotton. Pants include both shorts, the mainstay on the trail, and long pants, which are usually worn after the hike in camp. On cold days, long underwear can be worn under shorts, providing warmth while reserving the dry trousers for later. Clothing also includes items that cover the head and hands. Hats are extremely important because up to half of one's body heat is lost through an uncovered head. There are hats that protect against any combination of wind, rain, and cold. Not wearing mittens or gloves can cause frostbite (see page 293) due to low temperatures, which is worsened with contact against cold metal equipment.

Insulation is necessary to preserve the body's core temperature. It comprises the layer between underwear

and the shell. Insulation includes the clothing mentioned above, as well as sweaters, sweatshirts, and jackets.

The shell is the fourth and final layer. Tests have shown that with no wind, a shell can make a garment 10 to 15 degrees warmer. In more severe conditions, the difference may be up to 50 degrees—potentially the difference between life and death.

Not all shells are the same. Hikers need to assess their needs for protection and pick a shell accordingly. Features include:

- windproof, not waterproof, and breathable

- windproof, waterproof, and not breathable

- windproof, water resistant, and breathable

- windproof, waterproof, breathable, and warm

Preventing Sports Injuries in Children and Adolescents: A Summary

Recommended injury prevention strategies include attention to physical deficits, training methods, safety equipment, and psychological health. The American College of Sports Medicine has called on adults involved with youth sports to familiarize themselves with these guidelines and assist with their implementation.

- Fitness exercises should be included in children's and adolescents' training routines, rather than have all of each training session devoted to the development of specific skills required for a certain sport.

- Training sessions should include warm-up and cool-down periods.

- Flexibility exercises to stretch tight muscles should be mandatory for young athletes in rapid growth phases.

- Young people participating in organized sports should be supervised to ensure compliance with safety rules.

- Weight training to develop strength, done with *knowledgeable instruction and adequate supervision*, is safe for children and adolescents.

- Supervising adults must be knowledgeable about game rules, safety equipment, and healthy sports behaviors.

- The coach of the young athlete needs to monitor the intensity of training, the length of the daily training period, and any changes in specific techniques.

- Coaches at all levels should be required to meet a minimum level of qualification necessary to meet the responsibilities of coaching, including basic knowledge of skills development, safety rules, and equipment maintenance; competence in first aid; and an introduction to appropriate training methods and coaching behaviors for working with children and adolescents.

- Continuing education for coaches should be mandated.

- Parents and community oversight groups can influence local sports organizations to make coaching certification available.

- Have a certified athletic trainer in all high schools, at least part-time.

- Parents should show supportive, positive attitudes toward the children's athletic endeavors.

How Safe Are Children's Sports in Your Community?

- Are all the coaches in your community—those involved in after-school sports as well as volunteers who run youth leagues—trained in first aid and CPR?

- Are coaches certified?

- Is there a written rehearsed emergency?

- Is there a first aid box and ice on-site at all practices and games?

- Does the coach have the youngsters do warm-ups, stretching, and cooldown exercises?

- Does your school system have a sports injury prevention course as part of the health education program?

- Are presports physicals required?

- Does the coach hand out a conditioning program before the children go out for a team?

Grading Children's Physical Education—and Improving It

What makes for quality in a physical education class? According to the National Association for Sports and Physical Education, a good class

- is taught every day by a certified physical education teacher

- provides a logical progression in skill development, from kindergarten through twelfth grade, and encourages students to enjoy these skills

- allows them to participate and succeed at their own level

- offers a variety of aerobic exercises that improve cardiovascular fitness (at least three times a week for twenty minutes)

- offers exercises that improve strength and flexibility at least three times a week

- offers activities that teach coordination and motor skills

- gives instruction that shows how physical fitness can improve children's personal health and emotional well-being

Once parents realize what P.E. can be, they should push for funding to implement changes if necessary. Parents should take these steps to ensure high-quality physical education for their children:

Research the school's physical education requirement and how it can be expanded to include at least thirty minutes of daily physical education. Also, learn about the school's curriculum, facilities, equipment, and teacher qualifications.

Let the school administrator, board member, and national state legislators know where you stand on youth fitness. And find out where they stand.

Let P.E. teachers know that you are concerned about your child's physical education and that you would like to help improve classes. Find out what you and other parents can do to help.

Get other parents, teachers, and school administrators to help work to improve the school's physical education classes.

CHAPTER THREE

Strength and Flexibility: The Key to Injury Prevention

All components of health fitness—heart-lung endurance, strength, flexibility, appropriate ratio of muscle to fat, and freedom from injury—are vital for lifetime good health. On the whole, heart-lung endurance and muscle-fat ratio have traditionally received the most attention, which is understandable, because improving these components of health fitness is tied closely to reducing the high levels of heart and lung disease in this country. However, it is clear to many sports medicine experts that strength and flexibility have not been given sufficient attention. Though these components of health fitness do not contribute directly to combating life-threatening diseases, they make a significant difference for medical conditions that affect quality of life. Two conditions that are closely tied to declining strength and flexibility are osteoporosis and back pain. Significantly from the perspective of athletes, strength and flexibility also have a special role in preventing both acute and overuse injuries.

The Decline of Strength and Flexibility

It is well known that strength and flexibility are essential for daily living and sports injury prevention, but all the evidence suggests that Americans' levels of strength and flexibility are declining. In children the situation is no less serious—70 percent of boys and girls cannot do a single chin-up; 40 percent of boys and 70 percent of girls can do only one push-up; 40 percent of boys cannot touch their toes; and 25 percent of all children cannot do one proper sit-up.

Americans' increasingly sedentary lives mean they are not giving their muscles the workout they need. Americans' average muscle mass is declining. And while muscles and joints are getting weaker, they are also getting tighter. The human body was designed to be used, and when it is not being used, it does not work very well. This is the "use it or lose it" principle.

The Benefits of Strength and Flexibility

Strength and flexibility allow people to enjoy life more because all the body's movements are more comfortable. These components of health fitness are also important in the event of an emergency. According to the American Alliance of Health, Physical Education, Recreation, and Dance (AAHPERD), "In an emergency, the ability to apply force with the upper body can mean the difference between serious injury and escaping harm."

In sports the benefits of strength and flexibility are very clear: improved performance; reduced risk of injury; and fewer aches and pains after playing.

Improved performance is a favorable result of strength and flexibility training. Flexibility makes athletes quicker and more agile, which is useful in all sports, even those that do not depend on body-bending movements. The positive effects of strength training have been well demonstrated in sports as varied as distance running, aerobics, tennis, and golf. Strength training is especially useful in sports requiring controlled or explosive running, jumping, throwing, pushing, or pulling.

More important for the athlete is the role that strength and flexibility play in preventing injury. Most sports require sports-specific strength and flexibility in certain muscles and joints. If an athlete tries to perform the maneuvers necessary in these activities without sufficient range of motion in those muscles and joints, an injury may occur. Even the seemingly benign twists and turns of tennis can cause injury in a "tight" athlete. Increasing range of motion will minimize the chance of muscle strain or ligament sprain.

By strengthening their muscles, athletes can resist sprains and strains. Strong muscle tissue is better able to withstand the normal trauma of sports as wide-ranging as skiing, basketball, and biking. Strong muscles also lessen the jarring impact in running and jumping.

It is not as well recognized that exercise also enlarges and strengthens bones. The muscles in a tennis player's playing arm are larger than those in the nonplaying arm, and so are the bones. Not surprisingly, strong bones are a boon in later life, when bones tend to become weak and brittle.

Flexibility Training

Athletes should do some form of flexibility training daily to increase their range of motion. Flexibility exercises such as the ones in the following section can be done independently, or before and after exercise.

Although the principle is well established in elite sports circles, many recreational athletes are unaware that the stretch should not come first. Before doing flexibility exercises, athletes should warm up their muscles with a gentle, repetitive activity such as fast walking, jogging, gentle bike riding, or something similar. This activity assists the stretching phase by increasing the blood flow to muscles, ligaments, and tendons and mak-

---

THE BENEFITS OF REGULAR FLEXIBILITY TRAINING

Regular stretching can do the following:

- Reduce muscle stiffness and make the body feel more relaxed

- Help coordination by allowing freer and easier movement

- Increase joint range of motion

- Promote circulation

- Prevent injuries such as muscle strains, ligament sprains, and shinsplints

---

ing them more pliable. To understand this process better, touch your toes; then try again after a ten-minute jog. It is much easier after the muscles are warmed up.

After the initial warm-up is the stretching phase. The athlete should include at least one stretch for each of the major joint-muscle areas, including the shoulders, elbows, wrists, trunk, lower back, hips, knees, and ankles, and especially the hamstring and quadriceps muscles. After the sports activity the athlete should do a cooldown activity to let the heart rate return to normal. The final stage is stretching exercises to prevent many of the aches and pains that occur when the athlete stops exercising too quickly. Both the warm-up-then-stretch and the cooldown-then-stretch should last ten minutes, and preferably longer.

Methods of Stretching

Stretching exercises have both short-term and long-term benefits. In the short term, stretching increases the joints' range of motion, improves the ease of muscles in crossing the joints, and increases the blood supply to the soft tissues. These immediate changes, which enhance performance and help prevent injury, by themselves justify the need for stretching, both independently and in conjunction with exercise. Long-term benefits include enhanced comfort and better functioning of the whole body.

There are four main stretching techniques:

- Passive stretching, a slow stretch where the muscle is held in the stretched-out position and held

- Passive assisted stretching, where the muscle is stretched to a given position, then stretched further with the help of another person or by using gravity

- Ballistic stretching, in which the participant uses bouncing, jerky motions to stretch muscles and joints (jumping jacks or quick, repetitive toe touches are examples)

- Proprioceptive Neuromuscular Facilitation (PNF), stretching a muscle, the triceps, for instance, then tensing its opposing muscle; in this case, the biceps to relax the triceps muscle that is to be stretched, then stretching the triceps

The passive stretching technique will be the one used in the section on stretching exercises (beginning on page 25). Improvements in flexibility have been shown with passive assisted and ballistic techniques, but there is also an increased risk of injury and muscle soreness with these kinds of stretching. In using momentum or an outside force to stretch the muscle, it is possible to lose the control needed to stretch the muscle without stimulating the "stretch reflex." This reflex happens when the muscle feels itself stretching too fast and instinctively shortens, thus defeating the purpose of the stretch. For these reasons, most sports medicine experts discourage recreational athletes from using passive assisted and ballistic stretching techniques. PNF is a highly effective stretching technique, but it requires professional instruction and supervision.

Frequency, Intensity, and Duration

Whether flexibility succeeds in improving fitness depends on three factors: how often it is done (frequency), how hard it is done (intensity), and how long it is done (duration). To develop flexibility, the exercises should be done daily. If a sports physical has revealed limitations in a particular area (the hamstrings, for example) exercises should be done twice a day for that area.

Intensity in a flexibility program refers to how much the muscles stretch during each exercise. Several theories exist on intensity. The best known is the "no pain, no gain" school of thought, which holds that the muscle should be stretched until it hurts. However, this approach decreases the duration of the stretch, increases the chance of prompting the stretch reflex, and may cause a muscle strain. Instead of pushing a muscle to the point of pain, the athlete should stretch just until feeling the point of tension, known as the action point. By not overstretching the muscle, athletes can relax while stretching and thus hold each position longer.

Opinions as to how long a stretch should be held (duration) vary tremendously among different experts. Recent research points toward the most benefit from holding the stretch for a full sixty seconds. This is because it may take between twenty to forty seconds for the muscles to relax fully. By holding the stretch for sixty seconds, the athlete can be assured that tight muscles, tendons, and ligaments are being stretched slowly, with a minimal chance of injury. However, benefits can be gained with stretches between ten and thirty seconds.

Stretching Exercises

What follows is a series of flexibility exercises that can be done independently at home or in conjunction with a sports program. The recommended length of time to hold each stretch is given. If the athlete is unable to hold a position for a specified time because of fatigue, that is acceptable. A rest can be taken, or, where appropriate, one can switch to the other limb. Athletes should perform the stretch as many times as necessary to reach the recommended duration. All-around flexibility should be the goal, but some sports require extra flexibility in certain areas (refer to Table 2).

Many athletes become frustrated with flexibility programs because they do not see themselves making immediate gains. The problem is often poor technique. There are no shortcuts to achieving good flexibility; by trying to take shortcuts, athletes will not improve their flexibility and may even injure themselves in the process. It is important to pay close attention to technique and to the duration of the stretch. Do not bounce or overstretch. Athletes often overstretch because they are impatient to get the stretching phase over with. It is not necessary to be uncomfortable while stretching. A good exercise mat

2. SPORT-SPECIFIC FLEXIBILITY TRAINING

	SHOULDERS	SHOULDER ROTATOR CUFF	BACK	HIPS	GROIN	THIGH (quadriceps/hamstrings)	CALVES
Aerobic dance			X	X	X	X	X
Ballet			XX	X	X	XX	XX
Basketball	X		X	X	X	XX	X
Bowling	X		X	X	X		
Cycling	X					XX	XX
Golf	X	X	X	X	X		
In-line skating	X		X	X	X	X	X
Martial arts	X		X	XX	XX	XX	XX
Rowing	X		XX			X	X
Running			X	X	X	X	X
Skiing Downhill	X		X	X	X	X	
Cross-country	X		X	X	X	X	
Softball	X	X	X	X	X	X	X
Squash/Racquetball	XX	XX	X	X	X	X	XX
Swimming	XX	XX	X	X	X	X	X
Tennis	XX	XX	X	X	X	X	XX
Triathlon	X		X	X	X	X	X
Volleyball	XX	XX	XX	X	X	XX	X
Walking/Racewalking			X	X	XX	X	X

xx = special emphasis

can be used to increase comfort. Finally, there should be no pain during a stretch. If pain is felt, the athlete may be overstretching the muscles and should reduce the length of the stretch.

Certain stretches should be avoided because they can cause injury or are less effective than the ones described below.

Flexibility Exercises

Lying full-body stretch (relaxation)

Lie on back, arms and legs outstretched. Close your eyes, relax entire body, inhale deeply. Hold for one second, then slowly exhale completely. Repeat fifteen times.

Seated neck stretch (neck)

Sit on the floor, legs crossed Indian-style. Turn head to the right and try to look over right shoulder. Then slowly rotate head to the left and look over left shoulder. Looking forward, bend neck to the right so right ear is toward right shoulder. Do the same thing to the left. Return head to center. Bend neck forward so chin moves toward chest. Then extend neck and look at ceiling. Hold each position for thirty seconds. Do not jerk neck.

Underside cuff stretch (underside of rotator cuff)

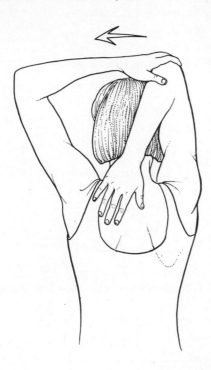

Raise right arm and bend it behind head to touch left shoulder. With free hand, clasp right elbow and gently pull it downward. Hold for sixty seconds, then switch sides.

Front cuff stretch (front of rotator cuff)

Place arms behind back, intertwine fingers, and slowly raise arms upward. Stand straight with focus remaining level. Hold for sixty seconds.

Back cuff stretch (back of rotator cuff)

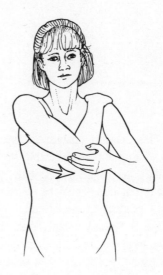

Bring right hand across front of neck and rest it on left shoulder. Place free hand on extended elbow and gently pull it so arm crosses over chest. Hold for sixty seconds, then repeat on left side.

Shoulder and side stretch (trunk)

Stand with right arm raised. Grasp right elbow with left hand behind head and gently pull right arm to ear. Bend trunk to left until stretch is felt in upper back and trunk. Hold sixty seconds, then repeat on right side.

Lunge (front of the hip)

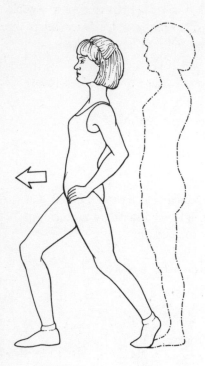

Begin with feet together, hands on hips, looking straight ahead. With right foot take big step forward. Front foot should face straight ahead. Back foot should also face forward, but heel should be off ground. Keep shoulders back, hips straight, eyes forward. Bend forward knee, moving pelvis forward toward floor until action point is felt (see page 67). Feel stretch in quadriceps of back leg and in front of that hip. Hold stretch on each side for sixty seconds. Increase exercise difficulty by placing forward foot on chair/bench.

Sitting toe touch (back of the hip)

Sit with your legs straight out. Keeping back straight, lean forward from hips and grasp toes.

Butterfly lean (inner hip)

Sit with the soles of feet together, lean forward, keeping back straight.

Standing lateral lean (outer hip)

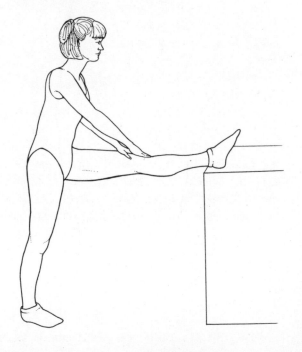

Place foot of one leg on table approximately same height as hips. Keeping both legs straight, lean forward. Repeat with other leg.

Standing ballet stretch (quadriceps)

Stand on left leg. Use left arm to balance against chair/wall. Bend right leg back and pull right ankle up toward right buttock. With right hand, pull up on ankle so that knee points down until action point is felt (see page 67). Hold sixty seconds, then change sides.

Iliotibial band stretch (outside of thigh)

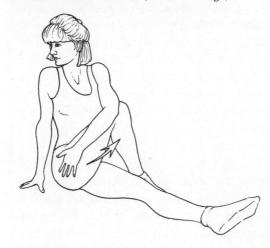

Sit on floor with left leg extended out in front. Place right foot on outside of left knee. Place left elbow on outside of right knee and push knee to left. Hold sixty seconds. Repeat with other leg.

Wall split (hamstrings and groin)

Begin by lying beside a wall. Bend knees, then swing around so body is at right angles to wall. Raise both legs so buttocks are flat against wall, legs pointing up, and feet resting against the wall. (If hamstrings are so tight that buttocks cannot reach the wall, start one or two feet away.) Straighten knees to stretch hamstrings and calf muscles. Then, keeping knees straight, gently

slide legs apart and allow gravity to pull feet toward floor. Continue to let feet slide down wall until stretch is felt in inner thigh. Hold each position sixty seconds.

Seated pike hamstring stretch (hamstrings)

Sit with legs outstretched, ankles together, toes pointed upward. Place hands on floor by thighs. Looking straight ahead, gently slide hands forward. Keeping back and knees straight, try to bring chest as close as possible to knees and thighs. When a stretch is felt behind knees and thighs, stop and hold for sixty seconds.

Wall calf stretch (calves and Achilles tendons)

Stand with feet shoulder width apart and arm's length from wall/post that can be used for balance. Slowly slide right foot directly back approximately two feet, keeping right leg fully extended and foot pointed slightly inward. Heels of both feet should stay flat on floor. Look directly forward, and keep hips and shoulders squared. Bend left knee and slowly move pelvis forward. Stop and hold for sixty seconds when stretch is felt in right Achilles tendon. Switch legs and repeat.

Toe circles (ankles)

Sit with knees straightened, toes pointing up, ankles twelve inches apart. Relax thigh and leg muscles. Begin by pointing your toes away from body. Rotate feet away from each other in opposing circles. Make largest circles possible. Perform fifteen circles, then change circle direction and do fifteen more. Repeat exercise with feet pointed back toward body.

THREE MYTHS OF STRENGTH TRAINING

Strength training with weights has been plagued by myths that persist despite scientific evidence that has invalidated them. To improve performance and guard against injury, athletes should know the reality behind the misconception.

1. *Strength training makes you muscle bound, less flexible, and slow.* Until recently, athletes in sports such as swimming, basketball, tennis, and golf were forbidden to strength train for fear it would make them "muscle bound," and thus slower and less flexible. It is now known that done properly, strength training actually increases the range of motion of joints, and makes athletes in any sport quicker and more powerful. Moreover, few people have the ability to develop very large muscles. Participants in moderate strength training programs report looking better, feeling better, and functioning better.

2. *Muscles will turn to fat if the participant stops strength training.* This is physiologically impossible. Muscle and fat are two separate and distinct tissues that are not interchangeable. Proper strength training increases the proportion of muscle to fat. Discontinuing a strength training program merely reverses this process.

3. *Strength training is dangerous for the heart and circulatory system.* A concern voiced by many beginning strength trainers, especially older persons, is that strength training may be harmful for the heart and circulatory system. As long as a person has received physician clearance, a sensible strength training program poses no harm to a healthy cardiovascular system. In fact, certain types of strength training programs, called "super circuits" (ones that incorporate into the strength training program exercises designed to increase the pulse to "target heart rate" levels), actually improve cardiovascular endurance.

STRENGTH TRAINING FOR PREPUBESCENT CHILDREN

Strength training for children has been a controversial subject for many years. Two main arguments have been made concerning the participation of children in such programs. First, critics say that because children lack adult or even adolescent levels of male sex hormones, (androgens), training with weights cannot produce gains in muscle strength or size, so there is no point in encouraging a child to go into such a program. Second, they assert that strength training for children poses the threat of injury, especially to their growth plates. However, over the past several years some important studies have shown that children in an organized strength training program can become stronger.*

In properly supervised programs, no injuries have been reported. When injuries do occur, they occur for the same reasons they do in adults—as a result of poor technique and lifting too much weight. In 1985 the National Strength and Conditioning Association stated that there had been no reports of growth plate fractures or injuries in supervised strength training. In the same year the American Orthopedic Society for Sports Medicine sponsored a conference attended by delegations from the American Academy of Pediatrics, the American College of Sports Medicine, the National Athletic Trainers Association, the President's Council on Fitness and Sports, the U.S. Olympic Committee, and the Society of Pediatric Orthopedics. The participants stated in the published proceedings that strength training for prepubescents is "beneficial as well as safe." However, they discouraged competition and maximum lifting attempts. *Under no circumstances should children attempt heavy weight–low repetition training.* Parents should exercise extra caution if their child is of very slight build or has been leading a sedentary life. Do not be fooled by size alone: a thin, active child is usually stronger than a larger, sedentary child.

With proper supervision and appropriate program design, strength training can be a safe, effective, and enjoyable activity for all young athletes, before and after puberty.

* Editor's note: The first of these groundbreaking studies was done by the author, Dr. Lyle Micheli, and his colleague, Dr. Les Sewell, at Boston Children's Hospital.

Strength Training

For years, strength training was shunned by many amateur and professional athletes. It was mistakenly believed that developing muscle strength with weights would make them muscle bound and decrease range of motion of the joints. In fact, strength training properly performed does not decrease a joint's range of motion but can actually increase it because the muscle is lengthened during the exercise. In this respect, strength training perfectly complements flexibility training. Yet the myths of strength training persist.

Proper strength training can reduce the athlete's risk of minor muscular injuries because stronger muscles are better able to resist the normal stresses of sports. In addition to strengthening soft tissues (muscles, ligaments, and tendons), training can also strengthen the athlete's bones and joints, thereby increasing their resistance to mechanical injury and helping to combat degenerative diseases such as osteoporosis. In that respect it is true preventive medicine. A strength training program should also enhance performance in any sport.

Methods of Developing Muscular Strength

Strength training exercises can be divided into two categories: static and dynamic. In static training the muscle does not change length. The most common static technique is isometrics. Isometric exercises are useful for maintaining muscle tone and can moderately improve muscle strength at the angle at which the muscle is tensed. If the athlete is recovering from a serious injury or from surgery, isometric exercises are the recommended starting point of a rehabilitation program. Isometrics can be performed by pushing against an immovable object such as a door frame, a wall, or even the nonexercising limb. Because a muscle does not lengthen during isometrics, it should be exercised at three or four different stages of flexion. A physical therapist will provide direction and education in isometric conditioning after surgery or serious injury.

In dynamic strength training, the muscles do change length. The three types of dynamic strength training are constant resistance, variable resistance, and accommodat-

---

> ### BENEFITS OF A REGULAR STRENGTH TRAINING PROGRAM
>
> A regular strength training program will improve:
>
> - "physical capacity"—your ability to perform work or exercise
> - metabolic function
> - sports performance
> - injury prevention
> - physical appearance

---

ing resistance. Constant resistance is the most widely used method of developing strength. Both accommodating resistance (isokinetics) and variable resistance involve expensive equipment not generally available to the recreational athlete. The equipment used in constant resistance strength training consists of the familiar free weights and multiexercise machines (sometimes known as home gyms). These supply resistance that remains fixed throughout the range of motion.

There has been considerable confusion in the past about the difference between strength training and weight lifting. Strength training is a method of health fitness conditioning that uses weights. Weight lifting is a sport in which the participant tries to lift the maximum weight possible. There are few health fitness benefits to be gained from weight lifting.

Developing a Strength Training Program

Frequency, intensity, and duration are the key elements of any health fitness program, including one for strength training. A good guideline for frequency is three workouts per week with one day of rest in between. Muscles need time to recover from a strength training session. A day without strength training is needed because the muscle-protein synthesis that produces increases in size and strength occurs during rest, not during the actual exercise. Athletes should not subscribe to the notion that if a little bit is good, a lot must be better.

Intensity—the effort needed to complete a particular exercise—is one of the most important and complex components of a strength training program. Intensity is measured by the size of the weight and the number of repetitions performed. A muscle develops strength by adapting to greater demands, both in daily activities and by artificial methods such as training with weights. The greater the intensity, or "overload," the greater the increase in strength. This is known as the overload principle. However, using weights that are too heavy may impair strength development and cause injury. Proper intensity is critical to achieving strength gains without pain.

Athletes will train at different levels of intensity. The general guideline is that the weight should be between 50 to 80 percent of the athlete's maximum lift, known as 1RM. Whenever the weight is increased, the number of repetitions should be decreased. If not, technique is likely to suffer because the athlete will be struggling toward the end of the set, thus increasing the risk of injuring muscles and joints. The amount of weight should be increased gradually and only when the athlete is ready. It is time to increase the weight when the athlete can perform the maximum number of sets and maximum repetitions comfortably. Athletes can increase the weight when they are able to perform three sets of twelve repetitions for two consecutive workouts.

Intensity also includes the speed at which exercises should be done. Some experts recommend high-speed training because it most closely simulates the demands of most sports. Others contend that speed is irrelevant as long as the muscles are stressed through their full range of motion. For recreational athletes, the latter is the appropriate approach to intensity. The "two-four" system is most effective: lifting the weight should take two seconds, and lowering it should take four seconds. This gives the athlete enough time for both exercising and rest periods. Between sets, the athlete should take between fifteen and sixty seconds of rest.

The two main types of equipment used for strength training are machines and free weights. Both have advantages and disadvantages. The constrained design of good strength training machines provides an added safety feature compared to free weights. While one group of muscles is being exercised, the athlete is being supported in a safe posture. Free weights can be safe for the person doing strength training, but the weight must be kept

---

TEN WEIGHT ROOM SAFETY TIPS

Those who strength train with weights at home or in a gym should adopt the following guidelines to prevent accidents:

1. Check equipment (e.g., machine cables, chains, belts, or pulleys) for wear and tear.

2. Never place hands on the chain, cam, or pulley system of the weight machine, or reach under the lifted plates supplying resistance. Make sure the selector key that sets the amount of weight is inserted all the way.

3. Do not attempt to lift too much weight.

4. Add weight a plate at a time to each end of a barbell. Carefully unload the bar after you have completed the lift.

5. Always use collars on barbells to hold weights securely in place. Make sure they are tightened.

6. Place hands or feet on resistance training machine with care, so they will not slip off pedals, rollers, or handles.

7. Use spotters for free-weight lifts. Make sure the spotters are paying attention.

8. Perform the exercise through the full range of motion in a slow, controlled manner.

9. Do not drop free weights at the end of each repetition; lower them gently to the floor, bench, or rack. This also applies to the weight stack of a weight machine.

10. Move all extra plates, barbells, and dumbbells away from the lifting area.

Source: *Penn State Sports Medicine Newsletter*

stable throughout the entire movement. This requires additional strength and muscle coordination as well as more attention to technique.

For the person not engaged in a regular exercise regimen, a total strength training program concentrating on the large muscle groups is recommended. The program should include at least one exercise for each of the major muscle groups. For most sports, strength training in the following areas will strengthen the smaller muscle groups in the major joints: quadriceps, hamstrings, lower back, abdomen, chest, upper back, shoulders, biceps, and triceps.

FREE WEIGHTS VERSUS MACHINES

Advantages of Free Weights

- Dumbbells and barbells are more effective in developing the supporting muscles around the main muscle being exercised.

- Free-weight exercises more closely resemble natural movements and, by association, the demands of most sports.

- Dumbbells and barbells are more versatile, less expensive, and take up less space.

- Dumbbells and barbells produce greater strength gains.

- Corollary aspects of fitness, including muscle bulk, flexibility, and reduced body fat are more effectively developed with dumbbells and barbells.

Disadvantages of Free Weights

- Training without the use of a spotter (someone to serve as a backup in the event control is lost) can be dangerous.

- Barbells can come apart if they are not carefully screwed to their collars.

- Changing the resistance can be time consuming and inconvenient.

- Large spaces are needed to use dumbbells and barbells; it can be hazardous for large groups of inexperienced people to use them in a confined area.

- In some cases it is difficult if not impossible to isolate specific muscles or muscle groups with dumbbells and barbells.

Advantages of Machines

- Certain machines are more effective in isolating a muscle or muscle group for maximum strength gains.

- Machines are generally safer because the weights are carefully guided through the exercise's range of movement.

- For use in limited space, some machines—especially the compact Universal "multigyms"—are more effective space savers.

- Machines are easier to use because less time is wasted changing plates and waiting for spotters; therefore, for the recreational strength trainer seeking to improve muscle tone and strength, machines might be a better option.

Disadvantages of Machines

- The vast majority of machines require the weight to be moved along a predetermined route, making it nearly impossible to exercise the supporting muscles.

- Machines that control the speed of the movement (accommodating resistance) or vary the resistance over the movement (variable resistance) are not natural because they do not effectively develop the supporting muscles around the main muscle being exercised, and therefore are not appropriate for athletes who strength train to improve sports performance.

- Most machines are constructed for the average-sized person; very tall and very short people have trouble using these machines.

- Machines are expensive.

Choosing which exercises to perform is important. The choice should be based on the muscular requirements and injury risk areas of the athlete's sport (refer to Table 3).

3. SPORT-SPECIFIC STRENGTH TRAINING

	SHOULDERS	SHOULDER ROTATOR CUFF	UPPER ARM (biceps/triceps)	LOWER ARM (forearm)	BACK	ABDOMEN	HIPS	GROIN	THIGHS (quadriceps/hamstrings)	CALVES
Aerobic dance					X	X	X	X	X	X
Ballet					XX	X	X	X	XX	XX
Basketball	X		X	X		X	X	X	XX	XX
Bowling	X	X	X	X	X	X	X	X	X	X
Cycling					X	XX	X	X	XX	XX
Golf	X	X	X	X						
In-line skating					X	X	X	X	XX	X
Martial arts	X		X		X	X	XX	XX	X	X
Rowing	XX		X	X	XX	XX	X	X	XX	X
Running							X	X	XX	XX
Skiing										
Downhill	X		X	X	X	X	X		XX	
Cross-country	X		X	X	X	X	X		XX	
Softball	XX	XX		XX	X	X	X	X	X	X
Squash/Racquetball	X	XX	X	XX	X	X	X	X	X	X
Swimming	X	XX	X		X			X		
Tennis	XX	XX	X	XX	X		X	X	XX	XX
Triathlon	XX	XX	XX	XX	XX	XX	XX	XX	XX	XX
Volleyball	XX	XX	X	X	X	X	X	X	X	X
Walking/Racewalking							XX	X	X	X

XX = special emphasis

Strength Training Exercises

The following muscle-strengthening exercises should be included in a beginning or intermediate conditioning program. When performing any strength training exercise, the athlete should

- always use proper technique

- always perform an exercise through the full range of motion

- always have total control over the weight, moving it in a smooth, fluid motion

Standing dumbbell triceps extension (triceps)

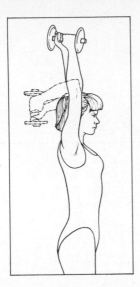

Stand with feet shoulder width apart. Hold dumbbell in both hands, with arms nearly extended overhead. Without moving elbows, slowly lower dumbbell behind neck. Pause, then raise dumbbell to original position.

Lying barbell triceps extension (triceps)

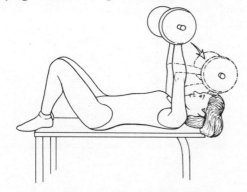

Lie on weight bench, grasping barbell with hands close together in overhand grip. Begin by holding weight with arms straight up in the air. Without moving elbows, slowly lower barbell to forehead. Pause, then slowly lift barbell to starting position.

Lying-sideways dumbbell raise (external rotator cuff)

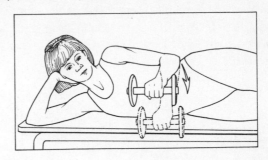

Lie sideways on bench with right hand supporting head. Hold dumbbell in left hand next to abdomen; palm should be facing inward, elbow bent at approximately ninety degrees and about one to two inches above waist. Keeping elbow stationary, lift dumbbell as far as possible. Slowly return to starting position. Do same exercise, lying on the opposite side and using left hand.

Lying-sideways dumbbell curl (internal rotator cuff)

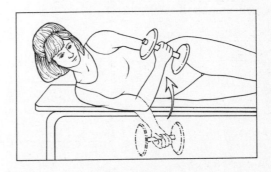

Lie sideways on bench; the right forearm should be pressed against abdomen and elbow bent at approximately ninety degrees. Lower dumbbell away from body until it extends over side of bench. Slowly raise dumbbell to starting position. Do same exercise, lying on the opposite side and using left hand.

Bar dips (triceps, chest, front shoulder)

Begin by supporting body weight with arms fully straightened. Slowly lower body until upper arms are almost parallel to floor. Slowly raise body to starting position.

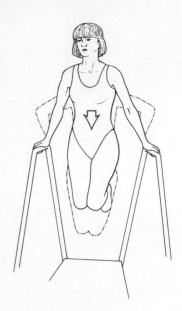

Seated dumbbell curl (biceps)

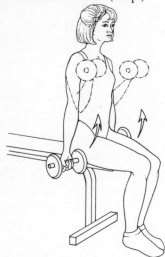

Begin by sitting on bench/chair with knees bent, feet flat on floor, arms down by sides, palms forward. Hold dumbbell in each hand. Lift weight until it reaches shoulder height. Pause, then lower dumbbell to starting position.

Barbell curl (biceps)

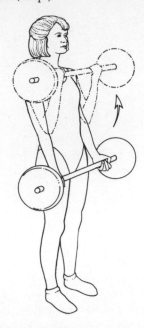

Stand with feet shoulder width apart, holding barbell at thigh level, palms upward. Keeping elbows at sides, slowly lift barbell to shoulder level. Pause. Slowly lower barbell to starting position.

Wrist curl (forearm extensors)

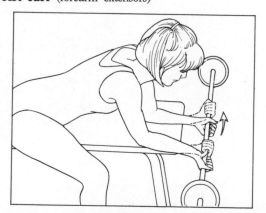

Straddle a bench, resting both forearms in front on bench, palms up, holding barbell in both hands. Wrists should be on the end of the bench, but hands must be completely off the end. Bend wrists toward body. Pause, then lower weight to starting position.

Reverse wrist curl (forearm flexors)

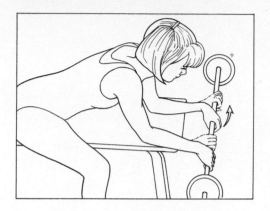

As above, except with palms facing down.

Wrist roll (forearm extensors and flexors)

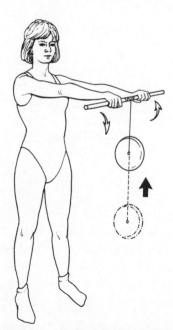

Stand with feet shoulder width apart, holding bar away from body with overhand grip. Rotate hands alternately so weight rises to top of bar (forearm flexors). Then rotate hands alternately so weight returns to starting position (forearm extensors).

Behind-the-neck press (front shoulder)

Sitting on a chair with back support, hold a barbell on top of shoulders behind head (this exercise can also be done using two dumbbells; start holding one in each hand behind the head at shoulder level). Hands should be approximately shoulder width apart on the barbell. Raise barbell above head until arms are straight. Pause, then return barbell to starting position. Do not bend back. A spotter should stand behind you to make sure weight is always under control.

Dumbbell front raise (front shoulder)

Stand with feet shoulder width apart, holding dumbbells at sides with knuckles facing forward. Slowly lift arms upward and forward until dumbbells are shoulder height. Pause. Lower dumbbells to starting position.

Bent-over dumbbell row (rear shoulder)

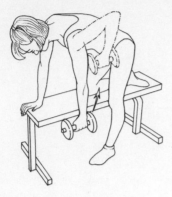

Bend at waist, placing right hand and right knee on a bench so back is parallel to floor. Hold dumbbell at arm's length with free hand. Slowly pull dumbbell up to chest height. Pause. Lower dumbbell to starting position. Do same exercise, now with left hand and knee on bench.

Shoulder shrug (upper back, neck)

Stand with feet shoulder width apart, holding barbell at thigh level, palms downward. Keeping arms straight, lift barbell a few inches by slowly elevating shoulders in shrugging motion. Pause. Lower barbell to starting position.

Upright barbell row (upper back, shoulders, and triceps)

Stand with feet shoulder width apart. Hold barbell at waist level with very narrow hand spacing. Slowly pull barbell straight up to chin. Pause. Lower barbell to starting position.

Bench press (chest, front shoulder, and triceps)

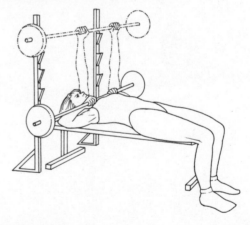

Lie on weight bench with feet on floor. Place hands evenly on barbell, slightly wider than shoulders. Lift barbell from standards. Slowly lower barbell to midchest, touching slightly. Pause. Slowly return barbell to starting position. Return barbell to standards after last repetition.

Incline barbell press (upper chest, front shoulder, triceps)

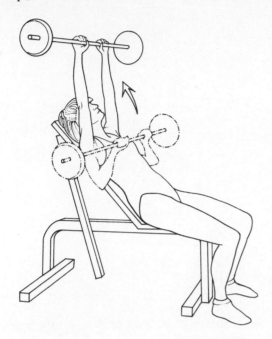

As above, with weight bench set at incline.

Dumbbell flies (chest, front shoulders)

Lie on bench with feet on floor. Hold dumbbells above chest with arms extended upward. With elbows slightly bent, slowly lower dumbbells downward and outward until at chest level. Pause. Slowly lift the dumbbells upward and inward to starting position.

Bent-knee sit-ups (abdominals)

Lie on floor with knees bent, holding weight plate behind head (or on upper chest). Slowly lift head and shoulders off floor while pressing lower back against floor. Pause, then lower head and shoulders to floor.

Dumbbell lunge (quadriceps, hamstrings, buttocks)

Stand upright with dumbbell in each hand. Step forward with right foot into "straddle" position. Step backward with right foot into beginning stance. Step forward with left foot into straddle position. Step backward with left foot to beginning stance.

Barbell squat (quadriceps, hamstrings, buttocks, lower back)

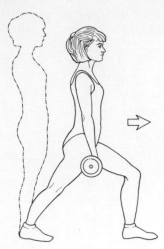

Stand with feet shoulder width apart, holding barbell across shoulders. Keeping back straight and looking straight ahead, slowly lower hips until thighs are almost parallel with floor. Pause. Return to the standing position.

Barbell heel rise (calves)

Stand with toes on raised surface, feet shoulder width apart, barbell across shoulders. Keeping back straight and looking straight ahead, slowly raise heels are high as possible. Pause. Return to starting position.

Toe raise (shins)

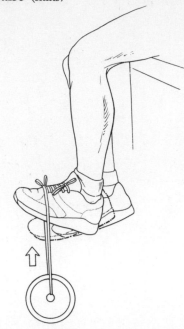

Sit on chair/bench so knees are bent at right angles. Attach weight plate to one foot with a rope. Slowly bend foot toward shin as far as possible. Pause. Return to starting position.

Tubed ankle everters/inverters*

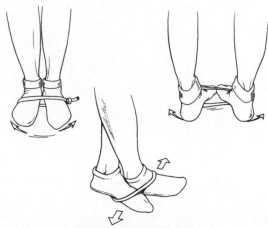

Sit with legs together and wrap tubing around feet. Pull fronts of feet apart, pushing against tubing, then pull heels apart. Next, flex one foot at a time, up and down. Cross ankles and push top foot outward and bottom foot inward. Switch feet.

Tubed leg swing* (hip flexors, extensors, abductors, adductors)

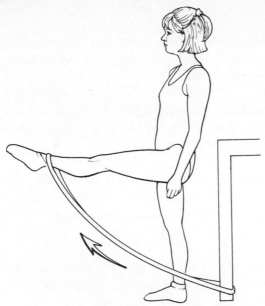

- To strengthen hip flexors, loop tubing around one ankle, attach the other to a fixed object. With back to anchor, balancing with one hand, raise leg until thigh is almost parallel to floor. Keep knee straight, back erect, and do not bend forward or back.

- To strengthen hip extensors, do same exercises as above, this time facing anchor.

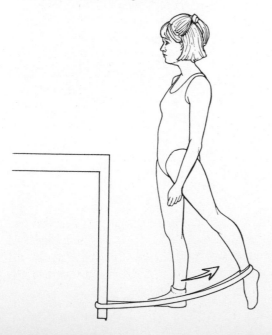

- To strengthen hip adductors, do same exercise as above, this time standing sideways to anchor, tubing attached to closer leg. Swing leg across body.

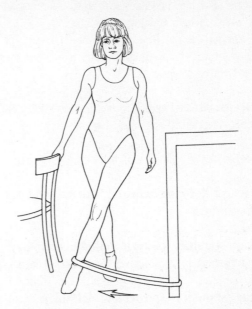

- To strengthen hip abductors, do same exercise as above, this time with tubing attached to leg farther from anchor, and raise leg away from body.

* For exercises to strengthen the hip and ankle inverters and everters, athletes will need either surgical tubing (available at surgical supply stores) or special conditioning tubing (Lifeline Gym Cord or Sports Cord are two reputable brands).

Summary of Strength Training Guidelines

The following guidelines will provide for a safe and successful strength training experience.

Selection: Do at least one exercise for each of the major muscle groups (muscle group is followed by suggested choice of exercises):

Triceps: Standing barbell triceps extension; lying barbell triceps extension; bench press; bar dips

Biceps: Seated dumbbell/barbell curl

Forearm flexors/extensors: Wrist roll; wrist curl; reverse wrist curl

Front shoulder (anterior/middle deltoids): Behind-the-neck press; dumbbell front raises; bench press

Rear shoulder (posterior deltoids): Bent-over dumbbell row

Upper back (trapezius): Shoulder shrug; upright barbell row

Back (latissimus dorsi): Bent-over dumbbell row; upright barbell row

Lower back (erectors): Straight-leg deadlift; deadlift

Buttocks (gluteals): Barbell squat; dumbbell lunge

Abdominals: Bent-knee sit-ups

Hamstrings: Barbell squat

Quadriceps: Barbell squat; dumbbell lunge

Calves: Barbell heel raise

Sets: Do one, two, or three sets of each exercise, depending on how intensive you wish the session to be.

Repetitions: Do between eight to twelve repetitions of each exercise.

Intensity: Continue each exercise until you can no longer lift the weight (usually between eight and twelve repetitions when the correct weight is used).

Progression: Increase the amount of the weight you are lifting by about 5 percent whenever you can complete twelve repetitions.

Speed: Do exercises in a slow and controlled fashion, taking about two seconds to lift the weight and four seconds to lower it.

Range: Do exercises through your full range of motion. This supplies maximum strengthening for the target muscle group and maximum stretching benefit for the opposing muscle group.

Frequency: Train every other day to let your muscles recover between workouts. An every-third-day program will produce almost the same results.

Breathing: Exhale while lifting the weight, and inhale when lowering it.

Workout Sequence: Strength trainers should exercise larger muscle groups first. Workouts should follow this sequence:

1) Hips	6) Arms
2) Legs	7) Midsection
3) Back	8) Lower back
4) Shoulders	9) Sides
5) Chest	10) Neck

NAUTILUS MACHINE ALTERNATIVES TO FREE-WEIGHT EXERCISES

The strength training exercises in this chapter are described for the use of free weights. Machines are also beneficial for building muscle strength, size, and endurance. The following are Nautilus machine alternatives to free-weight exercises.

Body part/Muscle group	Name of Exercise Machine
Neck (rotation, flexor, extensor, and lateral flexor groups)	4-way neck, neck and shoulder
Shoulders (deltoids)	Lateral raise, overhead press, reverse pullover, rotary shoulder, rowing back
Back (latissimus dorsi, teres major, and trapezius)	Torso arm, seated dip, behind neck, compound row, super pullover, rowing back, lower back, weight-assisted chin-up/dip
Chest (pectoralis major)	10-degree chest, decline press, 50-degree chest, incline press, double chest, bench press, seated dip, chest, super pullover, reverse pullover, weight-assisted chin-up/dip
Front of arm (biceps)	Multibiceps, weight-assisted chin-up/dip
Back of arm (triceps)	Multitriceps, seated dip, weight-assisted chin-up/dip
Forearm (flexor and extensor groups)	Super forearm
Sides (obliques)	Rotary torso
Midsection (rectus abdominus)	Abdominal, lower abdominal
Lower back (erector spinae group)	Lower back, rotary torso
Hips (gluteus group, iliopsoas, fascia lata)	Hip adduction/abduction, leg press, hip and back
Inner thigh (adductor group)	Hip adduction
Back thigh (hamstring)	Prone leg curl, leg press, seated leg curl
Front thigh (quadriceps)	Leg extension, leg press
Calf (gastrocnemius/soleus)	Seated calf, leg press

Recommended Workout Sequence

1. Hips
2. Legs
3. Back
4. Shoulders
5. Chest
6. Arms
7. Midsection
8. Lower back
9. Sides
10. Neck

CHAPTER FOUR

Diagnosing and Treating Your Sports Injury

Almost all athletes get injured at some time. An estimated 60 to 70 percent of runners, 40 to 50 percent of swimmers, 40 percent of aerobic dancers, and 80 to 90 percent of serious triathletes are injured at some point in their participation.

What distinguishes responsible athletes is how they respond to injuries. They recognize that prompt, proper diagnosis and treatment of all sports injuries are essential to ensure the quickest and most efficient recovery. The alternative, after all, may be pain, inconvenience, expense, long layoffs from sports and fitness activities, and, possibly, future medical conditions such as arthritis and osteoarthritis. Table 4 summarizes the general guidelines for classifying injuries according to severity, and what to do in the case of mild, moderate, and severe injuries.

Unfortunately, there is a tendency among athletes to dismiss sports injuries as "just part of the game."

Acute injuries such as ankle sprains and hamstring strains often are not treated with the seriousness they deserve. This is a surefire recipe for reinjury.

Athletes often do not respond appropriately to injuries because they are unaware of the serious consequences of their negligence. Or they may ignore the symptoms of their injury because they do not want to withdraw from their chosen activity.

Even more common than neglecting acute injuries is the tendency to underestimate overuse injuries. The symptoms of overuse injuries are slow to develop and

often difficult to pinpoint. Initially, pain may be experienced only after sports participation. Gradually the symptoms may begin to be felt during and after participation but may not be severe enough to interfere with performance. In the final stages, disabling pain is felt both during and after participation, and in daily activities.

The way overuse injuries develop can deceive an athlete into thinking the condition is not serious, until it reaches the point where aggressive treatment becomes necessary. Yet the key to efficient management of overuse injuries is "early intervention"—addressing the injury as soon as the symptoms are felt.

Whether an overuse or an acute injury, it should be treated with respect.

Self-diagnosis and Treatment

Under certain circumstances, athletes can treat their own injuries. Athletes can manage mild and moderate strains and sprains, bruises, and overuse injuries themselves—so long as they are sure of their symptoms. Refer to pages 55–59 for guidelines on what to do for common acute and overuse injuries.

If athletes are ever in doubt about the symptoms or proper care of an injury, or if self-care measures fail to improve the condition within a reasonable amount of time (two to four weeks), they should see a sports doctor.

4. INJURY CLASSIFICATION AND THE RESPONSIBLE ATHLETE'S COURSE OF ACTION

INJURY CLASSIFICATION	WHAT YOU SHOULD DO
Mild	
• Performance not affected • Pain experienced only after exercise • Usually, the area isn't tender to the touch • No or minimal swelling • No discoloration	• Reduce training schedule • Modify exercise to take stress off the injury • RICE (page 46) and OTC medication • Gradual return to full activity
Moderate	
• Performance mildly affected • Pain before and after activity • The area is mildly tender to the touch • Mild swelling • Some discoloration	• Rest the injury • Modify exercise to take stress off the injury • RICE and OTC medication • Gradual return to full activity
Severe	
• Pain before, during, and after exercise • Performance affected by pain • Daily activities affected by pain • Normal movement affected by pain • Severe pain when finger pressure is put on the area • Swelling • Discoloration	• Cease sports activities • See a doctor

The Musculoskeletal System

The foundation of the body is the musculoskeletal system, which is made up of muscles, bones, joints, and their associated tissues. These are the areas most often injured in sports:

Bones make up the skeleton, which is the body's framework. The skeleton has two main functions: supporting the body and protecting important organs.

Muscles move the bones by shortening and lengthening in response to signals from the brain. The major muscle groups are the *rotator cuff* in the shoulder, *quadriceps* in the front of the thigh, *hamstrings* behind the thigh, *biceps* in front of the upper arm, *triceps* behind the upper arm, and the *calf* muscles behind the lower leg.

Joints, where the bones meet, are the structures that enable our bodies to move. The shapes of the ends of the bones where they meet at a particular joint determine the directions in which the bones are able to move. Major joints include the shoulder, elbow, wrist, hip, knee, and ankle. Joints are made up of ligaments, tendons, cartilage, and bursae.

Ligaments hold the bones together at the joints. They are flexible but not elastic. For that reason, ligament sprains are among the most common of all sports injuries.

Cartilage is the gristly tissue found at the ends of bones. It helps absorb the impact and friction of bones bumping and rubbing against each other. It is sometimes known as "joint cartilage" or "articular cartilage." A type of cartilage found in about 10 percent of joints is

When an injury occurs, muscle, connective tissue, nerve, and/or blood vessel cells are destroyed. The cellular debris releases chemicals to signal to the body that an injury has taken place, and to initiate measures to remove the debris. The torn nerves send impulses to the brain that are interpreted as pain. Bleeding from broken blood vessels causes some swelling, but usually it is short-lived; the clotting mechanism closes damaged vessels. The mass of blood and cellular debris is known as a hematoma.

As the hematoma forms, pressure is exerted on undamaged pain fibers, causing additional pain. In addition to outward responses, such as awareness of hurting, nausea, and so on, pain causes the area to protect itself by splinting the area: some muscles go into spasm and others become inhibited, resulting in decreased muscular strength and range of motion.

Another bodily response is to remove the hematoma. A number of alterations in blood vessels on the periphery of the injured area allow the white cells to move into the area and digest the debris. This is a necessary prerequisite to healing but is not entirely positive. Slowing of blood flow on the periphery of the injury, coupled with the decreased blood flow from the damaged vasculature, decreases oxygen delivery to cells in the vicinity of (but not part of) the traumatic injury. If the oxygen supply is less than that required by the uninjured tissue, these cells die (secondary hypoxic injury). Thus the total amount of damaged tissue is increased, and more debris is added to the hematoma.

In normal tissue, the fluid portion of blood constantly passes in and out of the vascular system. As the hematoma grows, the balance of forces that control this fluid exchange is upset and fluid begins to accumulate in the tissues, increasing swelling.

a *meniscus,* a flat, crescent-shaped piece of cartilage that stablizes the joint, absorbs shock, and disperses lubrication known as synovial fluid.

Bursae are small pouches of fluid located in parts of the body where friction and stress occur. They are found between bones, muscles, tendons, and other tissues. The job of a bursa is to reduce friction between different tissue types, and protect the underlying tissue from impact.

Tendons are the tougher, narrower ends of the muscles that connect muscles to bones. Like ligaments, tendons are flexible but not elastic.

Sports Injury Terminology

Here are some common terms for conditions frequently seen among athletes. These basic definitions may help you to self-diagnose your injury; from there, you can read further about your injury. If you ultimately see a sports medicine professional, familiarity with these terms will also help you understand the treatment and rehabilitation of your injury.

Acute injuries

Fractures   A crack, break, or complete shattering of a bone. *A fracture is the same as a break.* Fractures are either *open* or *closed.* An open fracture is when the bone breaks the skin's surface. In closed fractures, the bone doesn't break through the skin.

Strains   A stretch, tear, or complete rupture of a muscle or tendon. Sprains are classified according to severity: first, second, or third degree.

Sprains   A stretch, tear, or complete rupture of a ligament. Like sprains, strains are classified according to severity: first, second, or third degree.

Bruise/contusion   A bruise, or a contusion as it is known medically, is bleeding in the muscle fibers caused by a direct blow to a muscle. If the impact is particularly severe, or if a bruise is aggravated by continued vigorous use of the muscle, it can worsen into a condition known as a *hematoma,* which is a dramatic pooling of blood in the area of the bruise.

Dislocations/subluxations   When the ball of a joint is forced out of its socket, or when the ends of two bones that meet at a joint are forced apart (the latter is sometimes called a separation).

A subluxation occurs when the ball of the joint pops out of its socket, then immediately pops back in.

Hemobursa   A bursa sac that fills with blood in response to a single, violent impact.

Acute compartment syndrome   Occurs when sudden, massive bleeding takes place in the muscles, causing them to swell within their encasements. This can be the result of a bone fracture, a complete muscle rupture, or a severe bruise in the muscle. Though less common than overuse compartment syndromes (see below, *Overuse compartment syndromes*), when they occur, acute compartment syndromes are a medical emergency and require immediate surgery.

Overuse Injuries

Tendinitis Microtears in the tendon fibers caused by repetitive stretching. This overuse condition is especially prevalent in athletes with tight or weak tendons. Tendinitis is most frequently seen in the Achilles tendon (heel), rotator cuff (shoulder), biceps, and around the kneecap.

Neuritis An irritation or inflammation of nerves caused when they are repetitively stretched or trapped against a bony surface.

Cartilage wear and tear Cartilage damage from impact or friction; can affect the cartilage at the ends of the bones that meet to form the joint, or the meniscus structures that lie between certain joints.

Osteochondritis dissecans (loose bodies in the joint) Loose bodies in the joint are created by the repetitive bumping and grinding of the ends of the bones, which may in turn cause tiny pieces of the bone and cartilage to become loose. Sometimes the piece of bone dislodges and falls into the joint, at which time it is colloquially known as a "joint mouse" because it is small, looks white on X rays, and causes havoc.

Bursitis Occurs due to repetitive microtrauma to a bursa sac, usually from the adjoining tendon. In response to these forces, the bursa sac fills with synovial fluid and becomes swollen. The bursae most frequently affected are those in the shoulder, elbow, and knee.

Overuse compartment syndrome A compartment syndrome occurs when certain muscles become too large for the fascial walls that encase them, perhaps as a result of intensive training. At rest there is no problem, but when the athlete exercises, the muscles swell with blood, causing pressure in the compartment to increase. This pressure compresses the muscles and nerves within the compartment, and therefore causes tightness, numbness, and muscle weakness. Compartment syndromes most often occur in the lower leg and are sometimes referred to as shinsplints.

Stress fractures Tiny cracks in the bone's surface caused by rhythmic, repetitive overloading. One of the most common causes of stress fractures is the pounding of the feet in running and aerobics, which can cause stress fractures in the foot and shinbone.

HOW DO STRESS FRACTURES OCCUR?

A stress fracture is a series of "microfractures" caused by repetitive, low-grade trauma seen in activities such as running, dancing, and aerobics. There have been two theories proposed to explain how stress fractures actually develop.

Fatigue theory: When tired, the muscles cannot support the skeleton as well as they can when they are not tired. During running activities that exhaust the muscles, therefore, increased load is passed on to the bones. When its tolerance is exceeded, tiny cracks appear in the bone's surface.

Overload theory: Muscles contract in such a way that they pull on the bone. For instance, the contraction of the calf muscles causes the tibia to bend forward like a drawn bow. The backward and forward bending of the bone can cause cracks to appear in the front of the tibia.

When the stress fracture takes place in the tibia, it occurs in the top two-thirds of that bone. In the fibula, stress fractures usually take place two or three inches above the lateral malleolus (the outer ankle bone).

Thinner bones are at greater risk of sustaining stress fractures, and because one of the side effects of irregular menstruation is bone thinning, girls and women with eating disorders and menstrual irregularities are at greater risk of these overuse injuries. For much more on the relationship between eating disorders, menstrual irregularities, and stress fractures, refer to chapter 19, "Sports Medicine Concerns of Female Athletes."

DEFINING STRAINS, SPRAINS, AND DEGREE OF SEVERITY

Strain: muscle and tendon tear

Sprain: ligament tear

First-degree strain/sprain (stretch or tear of less than 25 percent of the fibers). Symptoms: mild tenderness, slight swelling, no limitation of muscle mobility/joint range of motion.

Second-degree strain/sprain (tear of between 25–75 percent of the fibers). Symptoms: swelling, bruising, localized tenderness, some limitation of muscle mobility (strain)/some joint instability (sprain).

Third-degree strain/sprain (complete rupture of the fibers). Symptoms: in third-degree muscle strains, a gap in the muscle may be felt through the skin; in third-degree ligament sprains, the joint is swollen, and there will be extreme instability.

"RICE": The Cornerstone of Sports Injury Self-treatment

The most important component of self-treatment of almost all sports injuries in Rest, Ice, Compression, and Elevation, a self-treatment prescription known by the acronym RICE.

RICE self-treatment should begin as soon as an injury occurs or as soon as symptoms are felt. Do not miss the window of opportunity to self-manage an injury. Even patients in emergency rooms may have to wait several hours for treatment, and it may be days before an appointment can be secured with a family physician or sports doctor. RICE started within the first fifteen to twenty minutes after an injury occurs can make a difference of days or weeks in returning to action. Use of RICE within the first twenty-four hours after injury can reduce disability time by 50 to 70 percent.

Unless the injury is a medical emergency (see page 51, "Emergency Situations"), do not wait to be seen by a doctor before beginning RICE self-treatment.

The most important function of RICE is that it minimizes and controls inflammation and swelling, which, though they are the body's way of protecting itself by restricting movement ("natural splinting"), also delay recovery. The more inflammation and swelling are initially inhibited, the sooner motion and recovery can take place.

Rest/"Relative Rest"

Sports and exercise should cease immediately when an acute injury occurs, or when overuse injury symptoms are first felt. Continuing to exercise will only cause the injury to worsen and result in even longer layoffs.

During the first twenty-four to seventy-two hours (depending on the severity of the injury), complete immobilization is necessary to ice, compress, and elevate the injury properly.

After the initial stage of immobilization, rest does not mean total inactivity until the injured tissues have healed. Complete immobilization will only worsen the athlete's health status by encouraging muscle atrophy, joint stiffness, and a decline in cardiovascular endurance. This is known as relative rest, and will be covered in chapter 5, "Rehabilitating Your Sports Injury."

Ice

Cooling the injury—in medical terms, cryotherapy—decreases swelling, bleeding, pain, and inflammation. The most effective way to do this is to apply ice to the affected area. For maximum effect, ice needs to be applied within ten to fifteen minutes of the injury's occurrence.

Characteristic sensations experienced when using ice are cold, a burning sensation, then aching, and finally numbness.

The most common method of icing an injury is by covering the injured area with a wet towel and placing a plastic bag full of ice over it (a bandage is wrapped over the ice bag to keep it in place while simultaneously applying compression). The towel must be wet because a dry towel will serve to insulate the skin from the cooling effect.

A less common but highly efficient method of icing an injury is "ice massage." This is done by freezing water in several polystyrene coffee cups, then tearing off the upper edge of the cup. This leaves the base as an insulated grip, allowing the athlete to massage the injured area with slow, circular strokes. Ice massage combines two elements of RICE—icing and compression. Ice massage is especially effective for treating the symptoms of tennis elbow.

Although they are convenient, refrigerated commercial "gel packs" do not stay cold long enough and may leak dangerous chemicals if punctured.

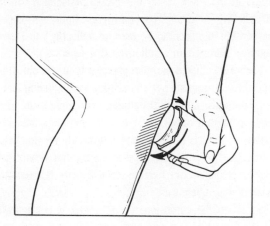

In the past, icing was recommended for only twenty-four to forty-eight hours after the injury. Evidence now suggests that intermittent icing may be beneficial for up to seven days, particularly for severe bruises. The first seventy-two hours are especially critical, and icing should be done as much as practically possible during this period. Milder injuries with less bleeding and swelling will respond more quickly, so minor injuries may need only twenty-four hours of icing. Most of the bleeding in the acute inflammatory response is resolved within one to three days after the injury.

Ice the injury for ten to thirty minutes at a time at intervals of thirty to forty-five minutes.

The duration of each icing session depends on the type of injury and how deep it lies. For example, because they lie closer to the skin's surface, injured ankle and knee ligaments require less icing time for cooling to take place than thigh or bicep muscles.

Icing duration also depends on the injured athlete's body type. In thin athletes, significant muscle cooling occurs within ten minutes, whereas fatter athletes may take thirty minutes to achieve comparable results.

Compression

To reduce swelling, gentle but firm pressure should be applied to the injury to minimize swelling. Compression can be performed while icing is being done, and also when it is not.

During icing, you can exert compression by doing ice massage with the "coffee cup" method. Alternatively, an elastic bandage can be wrapped over the ice pack and limb.

When icing is not being done, an elastic bandage should be used for compression. The following are important steps for applying the bandage:

- Start several inches below the injury.

- Wrap in an upward, overlapping spiral, starting with even and somewhat tight pressure, then gradually wrapping more loosely above the injury.

- Periodically check the skin color, temperature, and sensation of the injured area to make sure the wrap is not compressing any nerves or arteries.

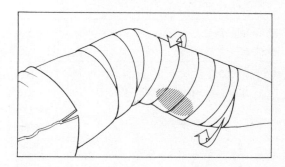

Elevation

Keeping the injury elevated is necessary to combat gravitational forces that naturally pull blood and fluids toward it, where they collect and create swelling and inflammation.

Whenever possible, the injury should be raised above heart level. An athlete with a leg injury should lie down and use a pillow to keep the injury elevated. Keep the injury elevated for twenty-four to seventy-two hours.

During the first twenty-four to forty-eight hours, DO NOT apply heat to the injured area (avoid hot showers and baths, liniments, etc.), massage the injury, exercise, or drink alcohol. All of these can cause *increased* swelling and bleeding in the injured area.

Remember, RICE is a first aid treatment only. Depending on the nature and severity of the injury, it may be necessary to seek medical treatment as soon as possible.

OVER-THE-COUNTER PAIN RELIEVERS

Over-the-counter pain relievers are an effective way to lessen the ill effects of vigorous sports activity. However, the choices can be bewildering, so it is important to learn about what is available, and what is behind the fancy packaging and high-tech television advertisements.

The majority of over-the-counter pain relievers sold in the U.S. contain one of the following ingredients: acetaminophen, ibuprofen, or aspirin. At recommended doses, all three have about the same effect on reducing pain. For reducing pain *and* inflammation, though, only ibuprofen and aspirin are effective.

Extra-strength pills *do* contain more milligrams of drug per pill. But more is not necessarily better. If you are not helped by the normal over-the-counter dose, you

should see your doctor because your sports pain may require a different medication or type of care.

There are differences among products in the kinds of supplemental ingredients some contain, including caffeine, antacids, and antihistamines. But while some evidence exists that caffeine can reduce head pain, antacids can ease stomach troubles, and antihistamines can help induce sleep, experts say there is usually not enough of these ingredients in over-the-counter pain relievers to make a real difference.

To lessen the confusion, the following is a rundown of the three types of pain relievers, and the pros and cons of each.

Active ingredient	Brand names	Pros	Cons	Consult physician before using if:
ACETAMINOPHEN (for pain caused by sports injury)	Bayer Select, Excedrin, Midol, Pamprin, Panadol, Tylenol	* Does not cause stomach upset or bleeding * Good alternative for people who suffer from peptic ulcers or who cannot tolerate aspirin * Safe to use while receiving treatment with anticoagulants * The least likely of all three types of pain relievers to have harmful interactions with other drugs	* Can cause serious liver or kidney damage if you take larger-than-recommended doses or use it over a long period of time * Larger-than-recommended doses may be toxic if consumed concurrently with more than three to four ounces of alcohol (distilled spirits) per day on a regular basis * Not recommended for use by pregnant or nursing women, unless directed by a physician	You have impaired kidney or liver function; if you are pregnant or lactating

Active ingredient	Brand names	Pros	Cons	Consult physician before using if:
IBUPROFEN (for pain, inflammation caused by sports injury)	Advil, Bayer Select Ibuprofen, Midol IB, Motrin IB, Nuprin	* Particularly effective treatment for menstrual pain and postsurgical dental pain	* Nausea, vomiting, diarrhea, constipation, and fluid retention are common side effects * Can cause stomach bleeding if taken by those with stomach problems at normal doses for more than a couple of weeks. Kidney problems can result from chronic overuse. * Not recommended for use by pregnant or nursing women, unless directed by a physician. * Should never be taken in conjunction with aspirin. * Can cause dizziness.	You have impaired kidney function, heart problems, high blood pressure, peptic ulcer, osphagitis, or acid indigestion; if you are allergic to aspirin or are taking other medications; if you are pregnant or lactating.
ASPIRIN (for pain, inflammation caused by sports injury)	Anacin, Acriptin, Bayer, Bufferin, Ecotrin, Excedrin	* In small doses, it helps prevent blood clots. * Can protect against heart disease.	* Tends to irritate stomach (although buffered and enteric-coated tablets have been shown to reduce upset). * Stomach bleeding and/or ulcers can occur when taken for several weeks by those with stomach problems. * When taken by children or adolescents with the flu, can cause Reye's syndrome, a rare brain and liver disorder. * Can prompt asthma attacks. * Not recommended for use by pregnant or nursing women.	You have impaired kidney or liver function, nasal polyps, blood clotting disorder, peptic ulcer or asthma, or are taking other medications

Seek medical attention within twenty-four to forty-eight hours in cases of persistent symptoms from injuries to muscles, tendons, joints, or ligaments, or if the pain becomes severe.

When treating an *overuse injury* with RICE, it may be helpful to take over-the-counter medications to control pain and inflammation.

Professional Diagnosis and Treatment

If unsure of the symptoms, or if they are severe (see Table 5), seek medical attention to manage the injury.

Although the family physician may be qualified to treat certain common sports injuries, he or she may not be the person best capable of treating an *athlete*. Athletes should see someone who has sports medicine training within his or her specialty. A specialist in sports medicine will be sensitive to the special needs of athletes and will try to return the athlete to full participation as quickly and safely as possible.

Who's Who in Sports Medicine

Family physicians are often the first doctors an athlete sees for a sports injury. They are qualified to treat many kinds of common sports injuries. As general practitioners, however, they frequently refer troublesome problems to specialists, and are being increasingly exposed to modern sports medicine techniques through new certification programs.

The injured athlete should try to make sure the health professional to whom he or she is referred is knowledgeable about sports and fitness activities. See someone who has sports medicine training within his or her speciality. They will be sensitive to the special needs of athletes and will get them back to full participation as quickly and safely as possible after a complete and comprehensive rehabilitation program.

Once identified solely with orthopedists, specialty sports care has branched out into several fields.

Here are the major players in the field of sports medicine:

- Chiropractors, who manipulate the spine and other bodily structures to treat a variety of conditions, can also receive additional training and certification in sports medicine.

- Orthopedists, or "bone doctors," specialize in the clinical and surgical care of injuries to the bones, muscles, and joint tissues such as cartilage, tendons, and ligaments.

- Athletic trainers are certified in conditioning, injury prevention, first aid management, rehabilitation, education and counseling. They usually work in an organized sports setting.

- Podiatrists are foot doctors. They provide clinical and surgical care for leg and foot problems. One of their most important responsibilities is to make shoe inserts ("orthotics") to correct improper alignments of the feet and legs.

- Exercise physiologists study the workings of the body and apply them to maximizing athletic performance. Some questions of interest to the exercise physiologist are: What training methods are best for athletes in different sports? What are the acute and/or chronic responses to particular forms of exercise? How does one get in shape for particular activities? How does exercise influence weight loss among dieters?

- Nutritionists provide advice on the optimum diet for individual athletes in their particular sports.

- Physical therapists are licensed health professionals who rehabilitate the sick or injured under the direction of the physician. In addition to using exercises and massage and manipulation to speed the healing process, they are also trained to use a host of "therapeutic modalities" such as ultrasound and electrical stimulation.

- Psychologists, by studying the working of the mind in sports and exercise situations, help prepare the athlete to achieve optimum performance.

Diagnosis

Despite all the high-tech diagnostic devices that have been invented, the most effective way to diagnose a sports injury is by taking a thorough *medical history* and performing a *physical examination*.

The medical history is the portion of the doctor's visit during which the physician asks the injured athlete questions about how the injury occurred. Some of the questions a doctor might ask are: Where does it hurt? On a scale of one to ten, how badly does it hurt? How did the injury happen? Did the injury happen suddenly, or did it come on slowly? Did you feel any popping, cracking, or snapping? Have you had this problem before?

During the physical examination the doctor looks for the following as signs of a possible orthopedic injury: loss of function; redness or discoloration; deformity/abnormal appearance; swelling compared to the other side; tenderness; abnormal motion; rubbing or grating; and exposed bone.

Usually the diagnosis is quite straightforward when the athlete has sustained an acute injury. Acute injuries have been dealt with by the medical profession since the beginning of time, and acute injuries in sports are no different from those that occur in daily life. The sprained ankle from falling down the stairs is really no different from one suffered on the racquetball court.

Overuse injuries are a different matter. They usually require a much more careful medical history and physical examination, because the injury is not caused by a single incident, and the pain is often unspecified. This is where the knowledge of an experienced sports doctor is crucial.

Doctors with expertise in sports medicine know that overuse injuries may be caused by certain "extrinsic" risk factors such as a too rapid increase in the frequency, intensity, or duration of the training regimen; effects of the environment (e.g., excessive heat or cold; training surface); problems in clothing and equipment (e.g., worn-out or the wrong kind of running shoes or the size of the tennis racket grip).

There are also a host of lesser-known "intrinsic" risk factors that can predispose athletes to overuse injuries in their sports or fitness activity. These include anatomical abnormalities such as tight muscles and ligaments,

---

EMERGENCY SITUATIONS

Serious sports injuries are rare, and are especially infrequent among adult recreational athletes. However, immediate medical attention is required in any of the following circumstances:

- obvious deformity in any bone

- localized tenderness or pain, especially in a joint

- any alteration in consciousness

- drowsiness

- disorientation

- persistent vomiting

- pupils of unequal size

- leakage of clear fluid from nose or ears

- eye injuries involving altered vision

- seizure

- pains in the neck after impact

- deep wound with bleeding

- breathing difficulties after blows to the head, neck, or chest

- any injury accompanied by severe pain

---

knock-knee, bowlegs, ankles that tend to "roll outward" when running, age- or gender-specific risk factors such as growing bones or brittle bones, differences in leg length (see p. 52), and unfitness.

These intrinsic risk factors often explain why some athletes incur overuse injuries whereas others following the same training regimen and using the same equipment stay injury free. Sports doctors often have to ask themselves why one runner developed shinsplints while her running partner did not, and why a ballet dancer was the only one in the class to sustain a stress fracture in his back.

In this respect, the doctor has to act like a "medical detective" to determine what caused an injury and make sure it doesn't recur.

HOW TO TELL IF YOU HAVE A SIGNIFICANT LEG LENGTH DISCREPANCY

The human body is not symmetrical. Everyone has slightly different-sized hands, feet, and legs. Usually these discrepancies do not cause problems. However, some people whose legs differ significantly in length sustain injuries because this variance puts abnormal stresses on the neck, shoulders, upper back, lower back, hips, knees, and ankles.

How can you tell if you have legs that are significantly different in length? Here are some ways:

1) Stand in front of a mirror. If one hip is higher than the other, that is an obvious sign that one of your legs is longer.

2) Use a carpenter's level to detect inequalities in leg length: put a belt around your hips and stand on an uncarpeted floor, feet together. Place the carpenter's level on your belt. If one leg is significantly longer than the other, the bubble in the level will go up toward your long leg.

3) Have someone else measure your legs. They will need a tape measure. Lie on your back, barefoot. Have the person measure each leg from the exact same spot on both sides of your pelvic girdle to the tip of your outer ankle bone. The person should do the measuring from each side.

What can you do if you have one leg longer than the other? Wear an over-the-counter heel lift of approximately one-quarter to three-eighths of an inch under your short leg. (Find the amount you need using the carpenter's level or the measurement you obtained with method 3, above.) Wearing this heel lift will alleviate any problems you have that are specifically related to your leg length discrepancy.

High-tech Diagnostic Tools

Usually the medical history and physical examination are enough to diagnose both acute and overuse injuries. There are many instances, however, when high-tech diagnostic tools are used to make or confirm a diagnosis. In sports medicine, these diagnostic tools have traditionally included X rays, arthrograms, fleuroscopy, bone scans, CAT scans, and electromyograms.

Perhaps the most exciting of the diagnostic tools is magnetic resonance imaging, or MRI. MRI has revolutionized sports medicine diagnostic techniques.

The short time it took the acronym MRI to enter the layperson's medical vocabulary is evidence of how widespread the technology's use has become since doctors started using it a mere ten years ago.

In sports medicine, magnetic resonance imaging is used to diagnose injuries by producing images of tissues inside the body. The patient lies inside a cylindrical magnet that is charged with a high-strength magnetic field. The nuclei of the hydrogen atoms in the patient's body polarize. A radio signal is pulsed at the patient, disrupting the nuclei placement. When the nuclei fall back into alignment they resonate and emit radio signals. Magnetic coils in the MRI unit "listen" to them, and a computer creates images based on the different signals produced by the various types of tissue in the body.

MRI is so important to the medical community because it enables physicians to identify injuries without physically entering the body (as in an arthroscopy) and without exposing patients to radiation (as do X rays, CAT scans, and arthrograms).

But most significantly, MRI lets doctors see soft tissues far more clearly than any other imaging medium, including CAT scans. It also allows doctors to view tissues with complex, curved, and overlapping surfaces, as well as areas where the superimposition of bone and soft tissues obscures details of underlying structures.

Patients often prefer MRIs to arthrography because there is no exposure to radiation, it involves less discomfort, and there is no need for injection of foreign substances into the body.

These features have made it a vital tool for evaluating injuries of ligaments, tendons, articular cartilage, and meniscal cartilage, especially in the joints. In sports medicine, MRI is used most often to evaluate injuries in the shoulder, wrist, hip, knee, and ankle.

In many clinics, MRI has completely replaced arthrography and CAT scans as the medium of choice for evaluating many joint injuries. MRI is especially useful for diagnosing internal problems in the knee, particularly injuries to the menisci, cruciate ligaments, and collateral ligaments, as well as disorders of the ligaments of the kneecap and the kneecap itself. In diagnosing knee injuries, arthrography has in many cases been regulated for use only in patients who cannot undergo an MRI because of its reliance on strong magnetic fields (those with metal implants, such as pacemakers and artificial joints).

An MRI machine is an extremely costly device, and it must be housed in a special facility. Therefore, it is generally only found in large medical centers. In some parts of the United States, several small hospitals share a mobile MRI unit. The major downside to this procedure is that it is extremely expensive. However, there is a strong likelihood that the cost of the test will steadily decrease over the next few years.

Treatment

It sometimes comes as a surprise to injured athletes when the treatment prescribed by the doctor is RICE, but RICE is not just a home remedy; it is the cornerstone of professional sports injury treatment, too. The importance of RICE in professional treatment reinforces the need to start initial treatment as soon as possible. To follow the doctor's treatment program better, use the RICE prescription described earlier.

There may be circumstances when more aggressive forms of treatment are necessary. The following are the most common methods of treating sports injuries.*

Prescription anti-inflammatories (NSAIDs): When over-the-counter anti-inflammatories are not sufficiently potent, the doctor may prescribe a stronger form of inflammation control available only by prescription. Nonsteroidal anti-inflammatory drugs, or NSAIDs, are very

*All the treatments described in this chapter are administered in conjunction with therapeutic modalities such as ultrasound, Transcutaneous Electrical Nerve Stimulation (TENS), and heat treatments (thermotherapy). These treatments are administered by physical therapists, and will be covered in the next chapter, "Rehabilitating Your Sports Injury."

effective when administered properly. They should never be taken except under the direct supervision of a qualified physician. Some common brand names of prescription NSAIDs: Clinoril, Naprosyn, Feldene, Motrin, Toradol, and Voltaren.

Like OTC anti-inflammatories, NSAIDs block the production of prostaglandins. NSAIDs are especially useful for treating overuse injuries, which are accompanied by inflammation.

However, athletes should not take NSAIDs to mask pain so they can participate in strenuous exercise that might worsen their condition, in particular the same activity that caused the injury. Although NSAIDs can be effective in enabling a return to action while injured, the athlete is risking the probability of aggravating the injury by overstressing the injured structure.

For the same reason that aspirin is not recommended for children, NSAIDs should not be prescribed to children. Fortunately, children respond very rapidly to RICE, so NSAIDs are not necessary.

Cortisone injections: Cortisone injections have proven very useful in treating overuse injuries, particularly tendinitis and bursitis conditions. They are never used to treat acute injuries.

The human body produces cortisone naturally to combat inflammation caused by injury. Sports doctors may inject synthetic cortisone directly into an injury if RICE, oral anti-inflammatories (OTC and prescription), and the body's natural cortisone are not successful in controlling inflammation. This injection gets a significant amount of cortisone directly into the area that needs the inflammation control.

Cortisone is never injected directly into an inflamed tendon. This may cause the tissue to weaken and eventually rupture. Instead, the cortisone is injected into the tissue *around* the tendon or the tendon sheath. Cortisone *can* be injected directly into a bursa to reduce inflammation. To be effective, injections must be administered with precision into the area.

After an injection of cortisone, do not participate for two weeks in strenuous activity that stresses the injured area. That is because as well as reducing inflammation, the cortisone also temporarily weakens the injured tissue.

For the same reason, athletes are rarely given more than two cortisone injections into the same area, and should never receive more than three. If three cortisone injections do not work, the doctor should attempt another form of treatment.

Cortisone pills are available. However, they do not go exclusively to the area that needs inflammation control, and moreover, have undesirable side effects—fluid retention, obesity, and hormonal imbalances.

Immobilization/Splinting In the case of some acute and severe overuse injuries, immobilization may be beneficial to allow unhampered healing. However, studies during the last decade or so have shown that most soft tissue injuries heal better if some motion of the affected area is allowed. For that reason, splints used to immobilize injuries should be *removable* so physical therapy can be done as soon as possible in conjunction with protecting the limb.

Immobilizing overuse injuries is rarely necessary. However, some areas where tendinitis may develop (the wrist, for instance) heal quicker if immobilized for a brief period, between three to five days. Children with Osgood-Schlatter syndrome (page 137) in the knee and osteochondritis dissecans (page 138) may require immobilization if these conditions do not respond to RICE. Some athletes with stress fractures require immobilization, usually when they do not respond well to RICE or resist complying with the doctor's relative rest prescription.

Surgery for sports medicine is generally used only as a last resort because of the inherent risks of any invasive procedure, not to mention the pain, inconvenience, and expense involved. However, it is true that surgery may be performed *more often* on athletes than on nonactive individuals. Sometimes only surgery can restore the resiliency in the injured body part that a sport demands.

Advances in surgery have had a profound effect on sports injury treatment. In addition to capitalizing on breakthroughs in general medical techniques, orthopedists have forged ahead with new surgical procedures to treat the explosion in overuse injuries that accompanied the health fitness boom.

The most common surgeries done for sports injuries are knee meniscectomies (repair of the meniscus cartilage in the joint), ligament repairs in the shoulder, elbow, knee, and ankle, tightening of the joint capsules of the shoulder and knee to prevent recurrent dislocations in those joints, and removing loose bone and cartilage chips in the elbow.

All of these surgeries are generally done using arthroscopy. This procedure, widespread for barely a decade, has revolutionized surgery for sports injuries. To perform an arthroscopy, two small punctures are usually made over the joint, one for the arthroscope, the other for pumping liquid and gas into the cavity, and then the surgical instruments are inserted.

An arthroscope is a miniature telescope—less than one-quarter inch in diameter and about eight inches long—through which a doctor can look into an injured athlete's body to assess damage, as well as watch himself repair an injury using tiny instruments.

Twenty years ago arthroscopy was a relatively crude diagnostic tool—a simple light bulb was used to illuminate the joint, and the surgeon looked through the tube with his naked eye. Nevertheless, it was regarded as a revolutionary means of physically examining the inside of a joint without having to open up the entire structure surgically (open surgery was required when X rays could not reveal damaged tissues such as ligaments and cartilage).

Arthroscopy has evolved into a highly sophisticated technique that has revolutionized many surgical procedures, especially those performed on joints. Fiber optics send a brilliant beam of light down through the arthroscope into the joint cavity, and a tiny television camera transmits pictures to a screen in the operating room. The surgeon observes himself manipulating the instruments by watching the television screen in the operating room.

A variety of tiny cutting instruments have been developed that can be inserted into the joint, as well as motorized rotating blades (shavers) that can trim off any ragged edges of tissue left during the procedure.

One of the most common sports- and exercise-related arthroscopies is the one to repair knee menisci, the pads of cartilage that lie between the bones of the knee joint and act like shock absorbers. These get worn and torn during vigorous sports activity, and eventually the roughened and ragged edges of the meniscus may start catching on the ends of the bones. The resulting pain and swelling make sports difficult, and repair is almost always required if the athlete wants to go back to sports. During this procedure, the doctor snips off the damaged portion of the crescent-shaped meniscus with a tiny scalpel, then trims the edge smooth with the shaver.

After arthroscopic surgery to repair a knee meniscus

or menisci, which takes about an hour, the patient generally leaves the hospital on crutches the same day. Usually only moderate discomfort is experienced, and that can be effectively controlled with oral painkillers. The patient is typically walking without the aid of crutches within a few days, and in a week gentle range-of-motion exercises and light strength training for the surrounding muscles can start. Stationary bicycle work begins shortly afterward, which the patient can soon alternate with a stairclimber machine. After six weeks, the athlete is usually back in action.

Until arthroscopy came into wide spread use for treating torn menisci, a much more traumatic surgical procedure was used: a large incision was made over the joint; lengthy open-knee surgery would be done to *remove the entire* meniscus; five days of in-hospital recuperation and injected narcotics were used to control the pain; and it was usually six months before the athlete could return to sports.

The specific advantages of arthroscopy over the traditional operative techniques are that the surgeon can see the inside of the joint better than through an incision, that the incisions made are smaller and the recovery in terms of pain and ability to return to action are shorter, and that it can be performed under local anesthetic, so that the risks that come from general anesthesia are eliminated.

The following pages provide a synopsis of the most common acute and overuse injuries. Once you have located the general symptoms and self-treatment described for your general type of injury, you can then go to the chapter that discusses the *particular area of the body* (chapters 6–18) for more specific information.

5. COMMON ACUTE INJURIES—SYMPTOMS AND TREATMENT

INJURY	SYMPTOMS	WHAT YOU CAN DO

Sprain: stretch or tear of a ligament.
 	
Contusion: bleeding in tissue below the skin.
 	
Strain: overstretch or tear of a muscle or tendon.
	• 1st degree—mild injury resulting from minor impact, stretching, or tearing of tissue.
	
	• Range of motion not affected. Mild tenderness. No swelling.
	
	• 2nd degree—injury causing partial tearing or moderate bleeding of tissue. Function limited. Point tenderness and probably muscle spasm. Movement causes pain.
	
	• Swelling and/or tenderness will probably occur if RICE isn't used immediately.
	
	• 3rd degree—severe or complete rupture of tissue or severe bleeding below the skin that extends deep inside the tissue. Extreme point tenderness. Immediate loss of function. Swelling and muscle spasm likely, followed by discoloration. Sometimes, obvious deformity.
		• Rest
		• Ice
		• Compression
		• Elevation
		• Icing duration:
		  Initial—30 mins
		  Later—20–30 mins
		  Or 5–7 mins ice massage.
		• Icing frequency:
		  moderate to severe—every hour or when pain is felt.
		• Less severe—as symptoms dictate.
		• Continue icing for 24–72 hours after the injury, depending on severity.
		• See a doctor if function is impaired.
		• For mild or moderate strains, sprains, and contusions, stretching within the pain threshold.

(cont. on next page)

5. COMMON ACUTE INJURIES—SYMPTOMS AND TREATMENT, *cont.*

INJURY	SYMPTOMS	WHAT YOU CAN DO

Fracture: crack, break, or complete shattering of a bone.
    Closed—bone does not penetrate the skin.
    Open—bone penetrates the skin.
	• Deformity or change in the shape of the bone; swelling; pain; tenderness to the touch
	• "Crunching" sensation when bone is moved. Eventually, discoloration.
		• Seek immediate medical attention.
		
		First aid:
		• Control bleeding—elevation, apply direct pressure to points where arteries cross joints
		• If an open fracture, control bleeding and apply a sterile dressing.
		• DO NOT MOVE BONES BACK INTO PLACE.
		• Splint above and below the joint.
		• Protect the fracture from further injury.

Laceration: tearing of skin causing an open wound with jagged edges, and exposing underlying tissues.	• Bleeding; redness; swelling. Increase in skin temperature. Tender, swollen, and painful lymph glands. Mild fever. Headache.	• Soak in antiseptic solution such as hydrogen peroxide to loosen dirt. • Clean with antiseptic soap and water, moving away from injury site. • Apply a sterile dressing. • Seek medical attention if infection seems likely. • Go to a doctor—a tetanus shot may be necessary. • If injury is severe, control bleeding, cover with thick sterile bandages, and treat for shock. See a doctor.
Incision: open wound with cleanly cut edges and exposure of underlying tissue.	• Same as for laceration.	• Clean wound with soap and water, moving away from the injury site. • Minor cuts can be closed with a butterfly stitch. • Apply a sterile dressing. • See a doctor if the wound needs stitching (large or deep cuts, or facial cuts).
Puncture: direct penetration of tissues by a pointed object.	• Same as for laceration.	• If embedded deeply, protect the area and see a doctor. • Clean around the wound and away from the injury. • Allow wound to bleed freely to minimize risk of infection. Apply a sterile dressing. Puncture wounds usually need to be seen by a doctor. A tetanus shot may be needed. • Seek medical attention if infection develops.

(cont. on next page)

INJURY	SYMPTOMS	WHAT YOU CAN DO
Abrasion: scraping off of outer skin, causing exposure of underlying tissue.		• Remove any foreign particles from the wound, flush with antiseptic solution such as hydrogen peroxide, then clean with soap and water. • Apply a petroleum-based antiseptic cream to keep wound moist (this allows healing to start at a deeper level). Cover with gauze that will not stick to the wound. • Seek medical help if infection develops.
Excessive bleeding	• From an artery Color: bright red Flow: spurts; bleeding usually profuse • From a vein Color: dark red Flow: steady • From a capillary Flow: oozing	• Elevate above heart level. • Put direct pressure over the wound using a sterile compress. • Apply a pressure dressing. • Use pressure points. • Treat for shock. • Seek medical attention.
Internal bleeding: Bleeding within the chest, abdominal, or pelvic cavity, and/or bleeding in any of the organs in these cavities.	• Usually, no external signs. However, anytime someone coughs up blood or finds blood in urine or stool, internal bleeding should be suspected. The following are other signs of internal bleeding: restlessness, thirst, faintness, anxiety. Skin temperature—cold, clammy. Dizziness. Pulse—rapid, weak, and irregular. Blood pressure—significantly lower than normal.	• Treat for shock. • Seek emergency medical attention.
Shock caused by bleeding	• Restlessness. Anxiety. Pulse—weak, rapid. Skin temperature—cold, clammy, profuse sweating. Skin color—pale, later blue/purplish. Breathing—shallow, difficult. Eyes dull. Pupils dilated. Thirst. Nausea and possible vomiting. Blood pressure significantly lower than normal.	• Maintain an open airway. • Control bleeding. • Elevate lower extremities approximately 12 inches. (exceptions: heart problems, head injury, or breathing difficulty—place in comfortable position, usually semireclining unless spinal injury suspected, in which case DO NOT MOVE.) • Splint any fractures. • Maintain normal body temperature. • Avoid further trauma. • Monitor vital signs and record at regular intervals—every 5 mins or so. • DO NOT feed or give any fluids.

6. COMMON OVERUSE INJURIES—CAUSES, SYMPTOMS, AND TREATMENT

INJURY	COMMON CAUSES	SYMPTOMS	WHAT YOU CAN DO
Tendinitis: inflammation of a tendon (a band of tough, inelastic, fibrous tissue that connects muscle to bone). Bursitis: inflammation of a bursa (a sac between a muscle and a bone, filled with fluid; facilitates motion, provides protection, and prevents abnormal function. Plantar fasciitis: inflammation of connective tissue that spans the bottom of the foot. Ostechondritis dissecans: loose bodies in the joint. Neuritis: an irritation or inflammation of nerves caused by repetitive stretching or catching on a bony surface. Epicondylitis: inflammation of muscles or tendons attaching to the bony knobs on the outside of the elbow ("Tennis elbow" is one epicondylitis condition).	• Risk factors—extrinsic: improper equipment; inappropriate clothing/footwear; improper coaching. • Risk factors—intrinsic: training errors, including abrupt increases in intensity, duration, or frequency of training; poor conditioning, in particular lack of strength and flexibility; incorrect technique; muscle-tendon imbalances in strength, flexibility, or bulk. • Anatomical malalignments (differences in leg length, abnormal hip rotation, kneecap position, bowlegs, knock-knee, flat feet). Associated disease state (arthritis, poor circulation, old fracture, etc.). Previous injury.	• Onset of symptoms gradual. Pain, swelling. Warmth over the area of pain and swelling. Tenderness. Involuntary muscle guarding. Joint locking. A crackling sensation in the tendons (crepitus). Numbness or tingling in the fingers.	• Ice and rest in the initial 24–72 hours after the symptoms are first felt. • Thereafter, heat before exercise, icing afterward. • Massage • Muscle strengthening and stretching program. • Correct the problem. • If correcting the cause doesn't relieve symptoms, see a sports doctor. • If anatomical malalignment or associated disease state is suspected, see a doctor immediately.

(cont. on next page)

INJURY	COMMON CAUSES	SYMPTOMS	WHAT YOU CAN DO
Stress fracture: tiny cracks in the bone's surface caused by repetitive pounding micro-trauma, as in pounding feet against a training surface.	• Risk factors—extrinsic: improper equipment; inappropriate clothing/footwear; improper coaching. • Risk factors—intrinsic: training errors, including abrupt increases in intensity, duration, or frequency of training; poor conditioning, in particular lack of strength and flexibility; incorrect technique; muscle-tendon imbalances in strength, flexibility, or bulk. • Anatomical malalignments (differences in leg length, abnormal hip rotation, knee-cap position, bowlegs, knock-knee, flat feet). Associated disease state (arthritis, poor circulation, old fracture, etc.). Previous injury.	Referred pain—i.e., hitting the heel causes pain in the shin. Usually extremely painful to the touch. Pain usually present at all times but increases with weight-bearing activity. Pain does not subside after warm-up.	• See a doctor for X rays. Usually, no cracks are detected in the bone. A cloudy area becomes visible when the callus begins to form. Often this doesn't show up until 2–6 weeks after the onset of pain. Early diagnosis is done with a bone scan or thermogram. • If a stress fracture is suspected but not diagnosed, treat as a stress fracture. Running and other high-stress weight-bearing activities should not be done until the fracture has healed and the bone is no longer tender to the touch. Stress fractures of the front shinbone (tibia) usually take 8–10 weeks to heal; rear shinbone (fibia) stress fractures take approximately 6 weeks. • When initial symptoms have abated, biking and swimming can usually be done to maintain cardiovascular conditioning, although this should be cleared by a sports doctor. • If the stress fracture is caused by a specific risk factor, or combination thereof, steps should be taken to correct this/these cause/s.
Mechanical lower back pain: lower back pain caused by poor sports mechanics, inflexibility of certain muscle groups, or muscle weakness. This ailment is usually brought on by activities that accentuate the curve in the lower back (e.g., hill running).	• Tight lower back and hamstring muscles. Poor posture or body mechanics habits. Weak muscles in the torso, especially the abdomen. Structural abnormality.	• Muscle spasm. Tenderness in the muscles (not the spine). Possibly a difference in pelvis height or other signs of leg length differences. Muscle tightness particularly of the hamstrings, hip flexors, and lower back.	• Any painful lower back pain accompanied by signs of a pinched nerve should be examined and X-rayed by a physician to rule out structural abnormalities such as spondylolisthesis, ruptured disc, fractures, neoplasms, or possible segmental instability.

CHAPTER FIVE

Rehabilitating Your Sports Injury

The notion that treatment and rehabilitation represent two separate phases of sports injury management is outdated. Treatment and rehabilitation should take place concurrently. How early sports doctors now start rehabilitating athletes is just one example of how sophisticated the field of rehabilitation has become. Indeed, nowhere in sports medicine have there been more advances than in rehabilitation.

Rehabilitation is the process of using exercise, manual therapy (massage and manipulation), and therapeutic modalities such as ultrasound and electrical stimulation to restore an injured athlete to sports readiness. Rehabilitation is generally supervised by a physical therapist, now an indispensable member of the sports medicine team.

Athletes who do not rehabilitate their injuries are unlikely to regain function in the injured area and are much more likely to get reinjured. The main predictor of injury is *previous injury*. The high incidence of injuries in recreational sports and the data that suggests reinjury is likely reinforce the importance of rehabilitation in injury management.

Rehabilitation can break an athlete's injury/reinjury cycle—that is, as long as the rehabilitation is appropriate for the injury and the program is geared toward restoring sports readiness, not just relieving symptoms.

Unfortunately, some physicians neglect rehabilitation when treating sports injuries, and seek only to relieve symptoms.

As well as being trained to restore full physical function, sports physicians and physical therapists watch for warning signs of poor *psychological* adjustment to the injury.

Professionally Supervised Rehabilitation

The goals of a modern sports injury rehabilitation program are to minimize the undesirable effects of immobilization on the injured area; encourage proper healing; maintain all-around conditioning (allowing for restrictions because of the injury); and restore sports-specific function.

Minimizing the Undesirable Effects of Immobilization

As seen in the previous chapter, immobilization is necessary in the initial stages of injury treatment in order to rest, ice, compress, and elevate (RICE) the injury.

However, *prolonged immobilization* may compromise recovery. Although once routine practice, there are several reasons sports doctors no longer advocate "overprotective" immobilization: muscles may lose up to 20 percent of their strength per week of immobilization; after six

PSYCHOLOGICAL ASPECTS OF REHABILITATION

Severely injured athletes may require not only physical therapy but also psychological rehabilitation. Some of the signs and symptoms of psychological distress to beware of are:

Physical

Continued pain	Muscle tension
Insomnia	Ignoring pain
Increased menstrual tension	Indigestion
	Missed menstrual cycle
Change in weight	Headaches
Change in appetite	Diarrhea/constipation

Emotional

Hyperexcitation	Depression
Boredom	Strong urge to cry
Inability to concentrate	Not enjoying the sport
Reduced body image	Denial that anything's wrong
Reduced self-esteem	
Excess concern for physical health	Desire to quit the team
	Emotional lability
Guilt	Increased feeling of depression, anger, or cynicism
Feeling life is not much fun	
Feeling ashamed	Distrust
Fear	Increased rationalization

Behavioral

Continues to train excessively, even though medically, vocationally, and socially inadvisable	Accident proneness
	Isolation
	Increased use of prescribed and/or OTC medications
Tendency to overtrain	
Difficulty training	Decay of personal relationships
Shopping for a physician	
Hypermotility	Appointments too frequently missed or scheduled
Blaming equipment for poor performance	

If an athlete experiences any of these signs or symptoms, he or she should seek the counsel of a sports psychologist. Most sports doctors will be able to make a reference to a qualified professional in the field. The sports doctor, physical therapist, and sports psychologist should work together closely.

One of the sports psychologist's most important tasks is to help the athlete develop alternative activities to fill the void created by nonparticipation in the chosen sport.

The sports psychologist may also suggest reading materials that help the athlete cope with the injury, such as *Feeling Good*, David D. Burns, New York: William Morrow & Co., 1990).

weeks of immobilization, the joint capsule stiffens to the point where ten times as much effort is needed to make it perform a given motion; after eight weeks of immobilization, vital joint cartilage at the ends of the bones may never return to normal function; and after eight weeks of immobilization, ligaments may lose 40 percent of their strength, which may take up to a year to return.

Early mobilization, conversely, has been shown to promote tissue healing, stimulate regrowth and rejoining of disrupted tissues, discourage formation of adhesions in the joint capsule, and help maintain coordination and sports-related skills. Early mobilization of injured athletes

is known as "aggressive" rehabilitation, and is especially useful for expediting safe return to full sports and fitness participation. Most sports doctors today advocate limited immobilization of injured athletes.

Casting a sprained ankle or putting a straight leg immobilizer on a knee for a medial collateral ligament sprain (page 128), for instance, though once considered routine, are now regarded as "overprotecting" an injury. Immobilizing an injury this way only increases the time necessary to restore the athlete to sports readiness, thus increasing the likelihood the athlete will return to action prematurely.

How soon should rehabilitation start? After many types of surgery, range-of-motion exercises can start *in the recovery room* immediately after the operation. Thanks to the continuous passive motion (CPM) machine, the limb that has been operated on can be maneuvered through limited ranges of motion by the CPM while the patient is still unconscious (after being discharged from the hospital, patients are often given a prescription for a CPM that they can use at home). Early motion is important for maintaining normal joint range of motion, and by stimulating the movement of synovial fluid in the joint, it may also provide much-needed nutrition to the joint cartilage. Passive motion also increases strength in the ligaments and tendons around the joint.

Within a few days of surgery, the physical therapist will help the patient move the joint through allowable ranges of motion, therapy known as "passive range of motion." This continues only until the patient can move the joint without aid, at which time "active range of motion" exercises are started. Strength training should begin as soon as possible. Even if the patient's arm is in a sling, simple isometric exercises can begin almost immediately, under the direction of a physical therapist. The advent of removable splints enables patients with serious injuries to do range of motion and strengthening exercises and then, after the session, replace the splint for protection and comfort. As quickly as possible, the physical therapist should help the athlete progress through the remainder of the rehabilitation program to eliminate pain, swelling, and stiffness, as well as restore full strength, flexibility, cardiovascular endurance, and sports-specific skills and conditioning.

For less serious injuries, rehabilitation can begin as soon as the initial pain and swelling have abated— usually within twenty-four to seventy-two hours after the injury.

The more the patient is able to stress the tissues within the pain threshold, the greater the benefit of aggressive rehabilitation. Discomfort is to be expected during the initial stages of an aggressive rehabilitation program, but any marked increase in pain, soreness, or swelling indicate the need to back off on the program.

Allowing Proper Healing

Not only does early motion minimize the undesirable consequences of protracted immobilization but it actually *promotes healing* by stimulating regrowth and rejoining of torn tissues.

Active exercise also increases blood flow to injured areas and mechanically stretches and softens fibrous scar tissue, resulting in regained range of motion, strength, and endurance.

Additionally, cardiovascular activity increases body temperature and circulation, which in turn removes damaged cells and repairs damaged tissue.

The physical therapist may use a variety of therapeutic modalities to promote healing. The most common of these are cold, heat, and electricity.

Cold treatment (cryotherapy): Besides being used to treat the immediate effects of injury by reducing pain, inflammation, and edema (swelling), cold treatment is also employed in therapy. It is especially effective in reducing tissue irritation after therapeutic exercise.

This is how cold treatments might be used to rehabilitate an ankle injury:

- Immerse foot in bucket of ice water for 20 minutes, or until it is numb, whichever comes first.

- Do exercises for three minutes, by which time the numbness will have worn off.

- Reapply ice until the foot goes numb again, or for five minutes, whichever comes first.

- Exercise a second time, then re-ice until numb.

- Repeat so exercise/numbing is done five times.

In addition to being used to develop range of motion and strength in injured joints such as the ankle, cold treatments can also be done in conjunction with muscle stretching exercises performed after strains or contusions. The icing procedure for stretching is the same, with the exception that only three series of exercises are done.

Ankle injuries are cooled most effectively in a bucket of ice water. For knee, hip, or shoulder injuries, the patient should use an ice pack.

Heat Treatment (thermotherapy): Never use heat on an injury yourself—that includes massage, hot showers, baths, or whirlpools—within seventy-two hours of injury's occurrence. At this stage, heat causes more blood to pool in the affected area, resulting in more swelling. The more swelling that occurs early on, the longer the injury takes to heal. Refer to the section on RICE for the initial treatment of soft-tissue injuries (page 46).

Heat should be used on an injury only after the first seventy-two hours, and then only under the supervision of a qualified medical professional.

Once the initial bleeding is over, increased blood flow is beneficial, stimulating blood flow and the nutrients, oxygen, and cells that help heal the injury. Heat also makes soft tissues more elastic, decreases muscle spasm, and reduces joint stiffness, all of which paves the way to earlier rehabilitation. Heat is especially useful in treating torn muscles and tendons after the immediate pain, swelling, and inflammation have abated.

There are several ways heat may be applied:

Contrast whirlpool therapy is usually done in the transition stage between therapeutic cold and heat. In this technique the athlete submerges the injured extremity in a whirlpool heated to 104 degrees F for twenty minutes, then places it immediately in ice water for twenty minutes.

Whirlpools/Immersion baths are heated to 100–105 degrees F to stimulate circulation and promote healing of injuries.

Hydrocollators, or heating pads as they are more commonly known, apply moist heat to superficial and subcutaneous tissues. Moist heat is more effective than dry heat because it penetrates deeper, increases blood supply to the area, relaxes the muscles, and "calms down" the damaged nerves. Inside the device is a gel that can retain both cold and heat. These pads are immersed in extremely hot water—160 to 176 degrees F—and then placed in a thick towel covering before being applied to the injured area for between twenty to thirty minutes per session.

Under a doctor's or physical therapist's direction, injured athletes can make their own heating pads at home by warming wet towels in a microwave. However, microwaved towels don't retain the same amount of heat heating pads do, and have to be replaced every five minutes.

Commercial moist heating pads are available, and are convenient for home use.

Electrical Nerve Stimulation: Transcutaneous electrical nerve stimulation (TENS) refers to any electrical stimulation applied to the skin to reduce pain and make exercises more comfortable.

It is most often applied using a portable, battery-operated machine that sends low-voltage electrical impulses to the nerve endings in the injured area. The nerve endings transmit these impulses to the brain in place of the pain. Also, nerve stimulation helps trigger production of endorphins, the body's "natural painkiller." Thanks to the portability of the machine, TENS can be used by patients at home.

Ultrasound is believed to be the most effective way to achieve deep heat in the tissues. In doing so it helps relieve pain and inflammation, promotes healing, reduces muscle spasms, and increases range of motion. The high-frequency sound waves created by ultrasound cause tissues deep inside to vibrate, making them more receptive to healing nutrients in the blood, and ridding the tissues of cellular waste products.

Ultrasound is frequently used to treat tendinitis, bursitis, joint sprains, and muscle strains as well as calcific tendinitis and calcaneal exostoses. In the latter two cases, ultrasound promotes calcium reabsorption.

Ultrasound is extremely safe when applied by a qualified therapist. However, it is never used around the eyes, ears, ovaries, testicles, or spinal cord. It should also not be used in an area where there is an active infection.

Microwave and short-wave diathermy are used to transmit heat up to two inches into the tissues. They may be employed to rehabilitate injuries in joints, muscles, and tendons, especially sprains, tendinitis, bursitis, osteoarthritis, and tenosynovitis.

Spinal traction is a method of separating the vertebrae in the neck and back, as well as stretching smaller neck muscles, ligaments, and joint capsules.

Traction is used for spine-related conditions such as whiplash, cervical arthritis, and cervical disc problems, such as pinched nerves.

The physical therapist may perform traction with his or her hands. Usually, this is only possible when the problem is with the neck. In the back, where the structures are much larger and more difficult to manipulate, traction is usually done mechanically. Traction most often occurs in conjunction with range of motion exercises.

The effects of cervical traction are only temporary. The cause of the problem usually has to be resolved with methods for the longer term, including exercise therapy, posture modification, and learning proper body mechanics.

Although these therapeutic modalities are very useful, exercise is the ultimate modality. Cold, heat, and electrotherapy promote healing and help the patient do exercises free of pain, but will by themselves do nothing to return the athlete to sports readiness by restoring strength, flexibility, and endurance. Only exercise can do this.

Maintaining All-around Fitness

If the patient cannot perform the chosen sport or fitness activity, the physical therapist should design a conditioning program to maintain or improve the person's preinjury fitness, including strength, flexibility, and cardiovascular endurance. Such a program decreases rehabilitation time and will expedite return to action. The patient is also less likely to be reinjured as a result of fatigue. Doing appropriate exercise while injured is known as relative rest.

The exercise prescription should take into consideration the limitations imposed by the injury. The patient should participate in fitness activities that do not overly stress the affected area. For instance, swimmers with rotator cuff tendinitis (the shoulder) can use a stationary bicycle or stairclimber, while a skier with a severe leg bruise could swim several times a week, as long as the activity did not cause pain or recurrent swelling in the injured leg.

The modern principles of relative rest are especially useful for dedicated or competitive athletes with overuse injuries. The athlete may have to withdraw from those activities that caused the condition—for instance, court time for tennis players with tennis elbow, or swimming laps for swimmers with shoulder tendinitis—but during the time of decreased activity, the injured athlete should continue to participate in as much of the regular training program as possible.

If some or all of the regular training program is deemed unsafe, the sports physician or physical therapist should help design a substitute training program that resembles the preinjury training program as closely as possible. The substitute training program prescribed during the relative rest period should exercise as many of the same muscle groups used in the regular sporting

activity and use them in a manner that duplicates that activity. For example, a tennis, squash, or racquetball player wearing an ankle brace gains more sports-specific benefit from a stairclimber machine or stationary bicycle *programmed to simulate the specific demands of his or her sport* than from a cross-country skiing machine.

During the recovery phase, the athlete should take the opportunity to improve the strength and flexibility of other, uninjured, areas. Because the injured athlete is not doing his or her usual training, uninjured muscles, tendons, and ligaments often become weak or inflexible unless a program is designed to prevent it.

The ultimate goal of the injured athlete is to return to participation in the chosen sport with *improved* all-around conditioning.

Restoring Sports-specific Function

This final stage of the rehabilitation integrates gains in strength, flexibility, cardiovascular endurance into sports-specific activities and drills.

All-around fitness is necessary for the reasons described in the previous section, but it is also true that the physical therapist should advise the athlete on regaining the skills and fitness requirements specific to a sport before okaying a full return to action.

The physical therapist will recommend activities that duplicate the sports or fitness activity. If the athlete has a knee injury and wants to return to racket sports, sports-specific training should begin with jogging in a straight line and progress to full-speed running and cutting. Before returning to competitive tennis, the player should first be able to run at full speed and "cut" 90 degrees left or right without a limp. Ideally, these activities should be practiced on the tennis court itself. Tennis players with an elbow or shoulder injury should begin with gentle practice serves and hitting against a wall, and before returning to play should be able to serve and rally without any pain or dysfunction. Do not risk overuse injury by overdoing it when practicing sports skills after a long layoff.

Return to Action

The physician and/or physical therapist should okay the athlete for return to participation and competition only if all the necessary steps of the rehabilitation program have been fulfilled and the athlete has regained painless full range of motion; normal strength and muscle size; all-around conditioning (strength, flexibility, and cardiovascular endurance); and sports-specific skills.

Return to action is based on the "95 percent rule"—that is, when the injured area has 95 percent of its function restored. If there is no record of preinjury function, this is measured by comparing the injured site with the opposing limb. For example, if there is a tear in the quadriceps muscle in the left thigh, the optimal strength of the injured muscle is measured by comparing it with the strength of the quadriceps muscle in the uninjured right leg by doing straight-leg lifts on a weight machine.

A good example of the new aggressive approach to rehabilitation is the way sports doctors manage ankle sprains. A few years ago ankle sprains were treated with plaster casts and bandaging. However, it was found that this caused persistent weakness and recurrent injury. Now the emphasis is on early mobilization after controlling the inflammation with RICE. After two days of RICE, the athlete should begin wearing a *removable* splint such as an AIRCAST. Such a splint allows up-and-down movement of the ankle joint (known as plantar flexion and dorsiflexion) without risk of rolling over on the ankle and reinjuring the joint. Within forty-eight hours of an ankle sprain, the athlete can begin physical therapy—exercises to restore range of motion, strength, and proprioception (the ability to maneuver parts of the body in a coordinated fashion without the benefit of sight). In seventy-two hours, one can commence activities such as running, cutting, and jumping while wearing a protective splint.

How Long Will It Take for My Injury to Heal?

Following are some general guidelines for healing times of common acute and overuse injuries. Keep in mind that these times can be greatly affected by factors such as all-around conditioning, rehabilitation schedule, and psychological health.

Ligament Sprain

A sprain is a stretch, tear, or complete rupture of a ligament. Sprains are classified in order of severity: first, second, or third degree. First-degree sprains are mere stretches, or tears of up to 25 percent of the ligament fibers. Second-degree sprains are tears of between 25 percent and 75 percent of the ligament. Third-degree sprains are complete ruptures of the ligaments.

Healing times for ligaments vary tremendously, depending on the particular ligament damaged and the severity of the injury. This is a rough guide:

First-degree sprains	5–14 days
Second-degree sprains	14–30 days
Third-degree sprains	anywhere from 2 months to a year

Remember, just because the ligament has healed does not mean you can go back to sports. Careful rehabilitation is needed to restore strength and flexibility to the ligament and prevent reinjury.

Fracture

When a bone is fractured, the body goes into overdrive to heal it. Within several days of the injury, the mass of blood created by the soft tissue damage around the ends of the bones starts to consolidate. This area provides fertile ground for bone healing. New bone cells start to form at the ends of the broken bones, and within two weeks, bone begins to form from these cells. Within six weeks, the bone cells at the ends of the broken bones merge to form a single bone.

Healing time for children who sustain fractures is about two-thirds that of adults.

Remember, just because the bone has healed does not mean the athlete can go back to sports. Careful rehabilitation is crucial to restore strength and flexibility to the surrounding muscles and ligaments.

This is how long it generally takes for a displaced fracture ("displaced" means the ends of the bones have separated) to heal:

FRACTURE SITE	HEALING TIME (weeks)
Finger	3–5
Hand	6
Wrist	10–12
Forearm	10–12
Upper arm	
lower	8
mid	8–12
Collarbone	6–10
Spinal column	16
Pelvis	6
Hip	10–12
Thigh	
mid	18
lower	12–15
Lower leg	12–15
upper	8–10
mid	14–20
lower	6
Heel	12–16
Foot	6
Toe	3

Stress Fracture

Healing times for stress fractures vary greatly, depending on the size of the bone and the severity of the condition. These are some general guidelines on healing times:

FRACTURE SITE	HEALING TIME (weeks)
Upper arm bone	6
Prominence of the shoulder blade	
(coracoid process)	6
Pelvic bone	3
Hipbone	12
Thighbone	
middle	12
lower	6
Shinbone	
upper	3
lower	3
Heel bone	6
Foot/toe bones	4

Home Rehabilitation for Mild Injuries

Rehabilitation prescribed by a sports doctor and supervised by a physical therapist is always preferable. In the case of mild sprains, strains, or contusions, though, the athlete may be able to self-rehabilitate an injury at home. However, if there is ever any doubt about the severity of an injury, consult a sports doctor immediately.

What is needed for a home rehabilitation program is an area to do stretching and stretching exercises (a stable, flat surface and, preferably, an exercise mat); a small backpack ("day pack"); cans or books; access to appropriate facilities to maintain cardiovascular endurance; access to facilities to practice sports-specific skills particular to the athlete's chosen activity.

As with a professionally supervised rehabilitation program, the goals of a home rehabilitation program are for the athlete to regain all-around aerobic and musculoskeletal conditioning; range of motion in the injured area; strength and endurance in the injured area; proprioception and sports skills.

Maintaining All-around Conditioning

With allowances made for the injured area, strength and flexibility training should continue as usual.

Most athletes are able to maintain their cardiovascular conditioning while injured. For instance, runners or walkers who sustain a lower extremity injury can use stairclimbers, stationary bicycles, cross-country skiing simulators, rowing machines, and swimming for cardiovascular exercise.

A mild upper extremity injury should not restrict a runner or walker, though even if the person does not use the upper body extensively during regular activity, it is still important to fully rehabilitate the injury. Athletes such as swimmers or rowers who sustain an upper extremity injury can easily find a cardiovascular exercise to do, such as the stairclimber, stationary bicycle, and so on, until they can resume their regular activity.

For endurance athletes such as runners, cross-country skiers, and power walkers, cardiovascular training during rehabilitation is quite straightforward: they should replicate the steady cardiovascular demands of their regular activity during their replacement exercise.

However, athletes in sports such as tennis, racquetball, squash, and aerobics may require a more complex approach to cardiovascular training during rehabilitation. Athletes in sports with special cardiovascular demands should tailor their cardiovascular maintenance program to replicate their activity. For instance, squash and racquetball players should use a stairclimber or stationary bicycle that can be programmed for the cardiovascular demands of those sports. The machine should be programmed for short bursts of intense activity (30–60 seconds), alternated with longer periods (90–120 seconds) of less intense work. This resembles the rhythm of high-grade squash or racquetball.

Lower body exercise calls into play a larger muscle mass and provides a greater stimulus to the cardiovascular system. Therefore, cycling, underwater running, stairclimbing, and rowing are preferable for rehabilitation to activities such as upper body ergometry and swimming.

Regaining Range of Motion

For mild injuries, range-of-motion exercises should begin at home the day after the injury occurs, or when there is no local tenderness in the affected area.

The most common type of stretching used in postinjury range-of-motion exercises is static hold. Most athletes are familiar with static hold stretching techniques. These are the ones usually done during warm-up and cooldown sessions. In static hold flexibility exercises the person stretches a joint or muscle until he or she reaches the "action point"—the point of tension—then holds that position for between 30 and 60 seconds. During each stretch the muscle should relax slightly, allowing the exerciser to extend the stretch slightly further. Each stretch should be done daily and repeated three to five times, if possible. Over several days the "action point" will gradually increase, a sign that the injured area is regaining range of motion. Refer to chapter 3 for instructions on specific static hold stretching techniques.

Regaining Muscle Endurance

There are two main categories of training used to regain muscle strength and endurance: isometric and isotonic.

Generally, isometric exercises, which involve tightening the muscles without changing their length, are used in the initial stages of rehabilitating a serious injury, under the direction of a physical therapist. Athletes with mild injuries can go straight into isotonic exercises.

One of the most effective ways to perform isotonic exercises at home is by loading books or cans of food into a small backpack and doing exercises with it hanging from the injured limb.

Start by choosing a "working weight," a load heavy enough to provide significant resistance. Then perform four sets of strengthening exercises with it, varying the working weight accordingly.

Table 7 shows how to calculate what percentage of the working weight to use, and how many repetitions to do during each set.

The number of repetitions that the injured athlete can do in the third set helps determine the "adjusted working weight." Refer to Table 8 for guidelines in determining adjusted working weight.

7. DAPRE TECHNIQUE (DAILY ADJUSTABLE PROGRESSIVE RESISTANCE EXERCISES) FOR HOME INJURY REHABILITATION

SET	WEIGHT	REPETITIONS
1	½ wkg. wt.	10
2	¾ wkg. wt.	6
3	full wkg. wt.	maximum*
4	adjusted wkg. wt.	maximum+

* Number of repetitions performed in third set used to determine adjusted working weight for fourth set according to guidelines in table below.
+ Number of repetitions performed in fourth set used to determine working weight for next session according to guidelines in table below.

Adapted with permission from K. L. Knight, "Knee Rehabilitation by the Daily Adjustable Progressive Resistive Exercise Technique," *American Journal of Sports Medicine*, 7, 6 (1979): 336–37.

8. GUIDELINES FOR ADJUSTING YOUR WORKING WEIGHT DURING HOME STRENGTH REHABILITATION

NO. OF REPETITIONS PERFORMED DURING SET	ADJUSTED WKG. WT. FOURTH SET*	NEXT SESSION⁺
0–2	Decrease 5–10 lbs	Decrease 5–10 lbs
3–4	Decrease 0–5 lbs	Keep the same
5–6	Keep the same	Increase 5–10 lbs
7–10	Increase 5–10 lbs	Increase 5–15 lbs
11 plus	Increase 10–15 lbs	Increase 10–20 lbs

* Number of repetitions performed during third set used to determine adjusted working weight for fourth set in table above. See Table 7 for earlier sets with DAPRE Technique.
⁺ Number of repetitions performed during fourth set used to determine working weight for next session (usually the next day).

Adapted from K. L. Knight, "Knee Rehabilitation by the Daily Adjustable Progressive Resistive Exercise Technique," *American Journal of Sports Medicine*, 7, 6 (1979): 336–37.

Muscle fatigue is a major cause of reinjury, so injured athletes must regain muscle endurance as part of their home rehabilitation program.

The same exercises that develop cardiovascular endurance and muscle strength also help build muscle endurance. Start muscle endurance exercises when strength in the injured side is 70 to 80 percent of the uninjured side. Athletes with upper extremity injuries such as elbow, shoulder, or wrist sprains, can use the same exercises to regain muscle endurance that they use to develop muscle strength. The difference is they should lessen the amount of weight while performing each set, and do the exercise until the muscle is tired. As the injured athlete gradually begins to regain muscle endurance, he or she will be able to do more repetitions.

Another effective way to regain muscle endurance is by doing repetitive endurance activities such as swimming, rowing, cross-country skiing, upper body cycling, and other activities that require repetitive movement of large muscle groups.

Athletes with lower extremity injuries can regain muscle endurance by using stationary bikes, stairclimbers, rowing machines, or cross-country skiing simulators.

Regaining Proprioception

Proprioception, the ability to judge where body parts are in space without the benefit of sight, is compromised by injury because of the harm done to the delicate interaction between the central nervous system and muscles, tendons, and ligaments. By regaining proprioception after injury, the athlete is able to perform his or her sports or fitness activity more efficiently without risk of injury. Poor proprioception can lead to faulty mechanics or sudden loss of coordination, which may cause both overuse and acute injuries.

For mild lower extremity injuries, straightforward balance exercises such as standing on one foot with the eyes closed are sufficient to regain proprioception. It is possible to make lower extremity proprioception training more challenging by changing the position of the non-weightbearing foot while balancing, or by training on an unstable surface such as a spring mattress.

Proprioception exercises for the upper extremities are more complex and are beyond the scope of a home rehabilitation program.

Regaining Sports Skills

The final step before going back to regular exercise is to regain the specific skills needed for the sport or fitness activity. It is important to regain these because skill deficits caused by injury and layoff time can put athletes at risk of reinjury. For example, improper technique can put tennis players at risk of sustaining tennis elbow; poor footwork can cause racket sports players to twist an ankle on the squash, racquetball, or tennis court.

When is it appropriate to begin sports-specific skills? This depends on the injury and the athlete's chosen sports or fitness activity.

With lower extremity injuries, wait until pain is minimal and there is no limping before practicing sports skills. Cut back if there is pain or swelling. Refer to the box below, "Rehabilitation Progression for Lower Limb Injuries," for guidelines on rehabilitation progression.

Racket sports players who suffer lower extremity injuries should be working on skills that do not place great demands on their legs, such as their service game, quite early in the rehabilitation process, while still building range of motion and muscle strength.

When range of motion and muscle strength reach about 80 percent but muscle endurance and proprioception are still well below par, begin hitting shots against a wall. When endurance and proprioception also reach 80 percent, practice hitting shots to a court opponent. The next step is low-key games, which should gradually increase in intensity until reaching preinjury caliber of play.

Properly done, rehabilitation gets the athlete back into action in the shortest possible time, with minimal risk of reinjury, while maintaining or even improving general conditioning. New rehabilitation tools and techniques have made rehabilitation the most dynamic area of sports care.

But no matter how sophisticated rehabilitation has become, its success comes down to the individual athlete. Far too many athletes either do not take their rehabilitation seriously enough or pay insufficient attention to warnings not to push themselves too hard. To be successful, rehabilitation needs to be done properly, and should be regarded as an integral part of injury management.

REHABILITATION PROGRESSION FOR LOWER LIMB INJURIES

- Nonweight-bearing range-of-motion exercises (up and down, side to side, circles).

- Standing up, shift the weight from foot to foot, gradually increasing amount of weight on the injured leg.

- Walk, first with small steps and then progress to bigger steps; when this becomes easy, walk around objects or in a "lazy Z."

- Jog slowly in a straight line; then jog in a "lazy Z" pattern and progress into a "sharp Z."

- Sprint 5 to 10 meters, starting and stopping slowly, then more quickly.

- Begin strengthening exercises to strengthen the joint and the muscles around it.

- Sports-specific drills with the injury protected where appropriate (ankle/knee braces, neoprene hamstring warmers), first at half speed, then three-quarters speed, and finally, full speed.

- Full workout with the injury protected where appropriate.

CHAPTER SIX

Foot Injuries

The foot is the site of numerous athletics-related injuries. Most athletes at one time or another develop a problem in their feet, whether it is a seemingly benign blister or a serious stress fracture. This should come as no surprise. Exercise that involves any running or jumping motions places enormous demands on the lower extremities, and the feet absorb the brunt of this stress.

The foot is the part of the body that must receive and distribute the weight of the body during dynamic locomotion. During running, forces two to three times the athlete's body weight have to be absorbed by the lower extremities, running shoes, and running surface. Given that runners can take more than 10,000 steps an hour, problems can develop as a result of these repetitive forces.

The feet may also *create* many sports medicine conditions between the ankle and the pelvis. Injuries to the foot may be debilitating due to the importance of the foot in any activity requiring walking, running, or jumping.

One of the most common reasons some athletes sustain overuse injuries while others do not is that they have anatomical abnormalities that place additional stress on the surrounding structures. In daily activities, these anatomical abnormalities do not cause problems, but when they are subjected to the repetitive stresses of sports, overuse injuries may occur. The four most common anatomical abnormalities of the lower extremities are flat feet, feet that excessively pronate (roll inward when the athlete runs), high arches, knock-knee, bowlegs, and turned-in thighbones (femoral anteversion).

Flat Feet *(Pes Planus)—Excessive Pronation*

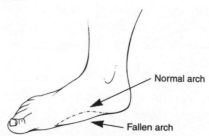

Some people have naturally flat feet or feet that excessively turn in when they run. In both cases they run on the insides of their feet. A certain amount of pronation occurs during the running cycle with each step any athlete takes. Excessive pronation, however, can be harmful. It causes increased stress on the tissues in and around the foot, and also forces the muscles to work more than they ought. In such cases, overuse injuries may occur. In the foot itself, the most common overuse injuries associated with flat feet and feet that excessively pronate are stress fractures, posterior tibial tendinitis, and compartment syndrome.

Flat feet and feet that excessively pronate not only cause problems in the foot but may also affect the entire lower extremities, including the knee and hip, because both these conditions cause inward rotation of the legs.

Problems in the lower extremities above the feet thought to be caused in part by flat feet or feet that excessively pronate are patellofemoral pain syndrome (kneecap pain), compartment syndrome in the lower leg, and trochanteric bursitis in the hip.

Shoe inserts (orthotics, page 122) may help the athlete who has flat feet or whose feet overly pronate. They support the inside of the foot so that the lower leg does not have to contort when running.

High Arches (Pes Cavus)

High arches, or clawfoot as this condition is sometimes known, make the foot inflexible. The rigidity of this kind of foot makes it susceptible to overuse injuries. It also results in overuse injuries in the lower leg because the foot's inflexibility causes the force to be transmitted to the structures above.

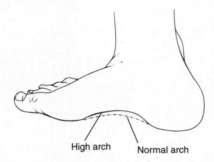

High arch   Normal arch

Athletes with high arches are susceptible to stress fractures in the foot, lower leg, upper thigh, and pelvis, plantar fasciitis (heel spurs), and Achilles tendinitis.

A person with high arches may also develop a hammertoe (the second toe buckles and cannot be straightened). A high arch makes the big toe slide under the second toe when the athlete runs, causing hammertoes to develop.

Orthotics usually do not help a person who has high arches. Sometimes "static stretching" of the arch may be of some assistance in alleviating the problem. The athlete should stand on a board inclined at a 35 degree angle 20 to 30 seconds at a time, first with the toes facing downward, then facing upward (when doing these static stretches, point the toes inward slightly).

If pain continues, the athlete may have no choice other than to take up a different sport.

Knock-Knee (Genu Valgum)

Knock-knee creates serious problems for the knee joint. Because of the inward angling of the thigh and lower leg, the athlete's weight has to be borne by the inside of the knees. During sports, this may subject the area to more stress than it can tolerate. Knock-knee is often a cause of patellofemoral pain syndrome, the most common diagnosis seen in sports clinics.

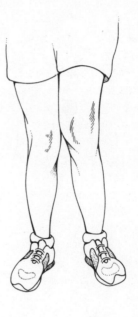

Bowlegs (Genu Varum)

Bowlegs are the opposite of knock-knees; they bend outward instead of angling inward. Athletes with bowlegs are at greater risk of sustaining problems on the outer side of the knee, especially iliotibial band syndrome. Having bowed legs creates a longer distance over which the iliotibial band must stretch, making it tighter over the outer side of the knee joint where the symptoms develop. However, it should be noted that many athletes with bowlegs participate in distance running without any problems.

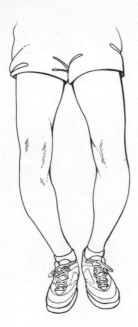

Turned-in Thighbones (Femoral Anteversion)

Some people have thighbones that turn inward. This is caused by abnormal hip joints. In this condition, the kneecaps face slightly inward. This can cause "tracking" problems in the kneecap, which is a frequent cause of patellofemoral pain syndrome, a very common overuse sports condition.

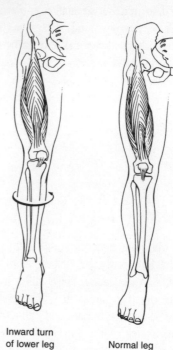

Inward turn
of lower leg   Normal leg

Injuries of the Foot

Acute foot injuries include bone fractures, muscle strains, ligament strains, and joint dislocations. These injuries usually occur when the tissues are stretched beyond their normal elasticity, or when they are subjected to direct impact. Such impact can occur when an athlete lands heavily on the foot, kicks an immovable object or stubs a toe, or is hit by another player or piece of equipment.

Overuse foot injuries are more common than acute injuries, especially among recreational athletes. Overuse foot injuries include several of the same overuse problems seen in other parts of the body, such as stress fractures, tendinitis conditions, bursitis, and, unique to the foot, irritations of the plantar fascia. There are also a host of unique disorders in the feet brought on by exercise, and whose prevalence can be explained by the complexity of the feet, the number of anatomical abnormalities often associated with them, and the extraordinary stresses to which they are subjected in sports.

Foot overuse injuries are caused by excessive sports activity, but they often have an underlying cause, known as a risk factor. Risk factors can either be internal (intrinsic) or external (extrinsic).

Internal factors usually involve deficits in strength and flexibility and, especially, the anatomical abnormalities just discussed.

Another important internal risk factor for overuse injuries is *gender,* and relates specifically to the incidence of stress fractures in women. Many women who train excessively or have eating disorders, and frequently both, may stop menstruating regularly. Irregular menstruation may cause these women's bones to lose their density. When exposed to the repetitive demands of exercise, such as jogging or aerobics, such bones are susceptible to stress fractures. The most frequent sites of these stress fractures are the bones of the foot and lower leg. The relationship between overtraining, eating disorders, and stress fractures is known as the "female athlete triad," and is covered in depth in chapter 19, "Sports Medicine Concerns of Female Athletes."

External risk factors usually involve the athlete's footwear and the training surface on which he or she exercises. Inappropriate footwear includes worn-out shoes that have lost their absorbency, shoes with insufficient arch support, and shoes with overly rigid soles. Such footwear may place excessive stress on the feet. For instance, worn-out shoes that have lost their absorbency place runners or aerobic dancers who train on a hard surface at risk of stress fractures in the feet and lower legs.

An overly hard training surface is one of the prime causes of overuse injuries in the feet, including stress fractures. Joggers can consider they have significantly increased the intensity of their workout if they switch from running on grass or clay to road running, or from running primarily on flat surfaces to running hills. (Note: Softer does not always mean less stressful; for instance, running on sand stresses the Achilles tendons and predisposes the athlete to tendinitis in that area.) Aerobic dancers who change from working out on mats to cement or unforgiving wood floors also run the risk of overuse injuries in their feet.

Preventing Foot Injuries

Acute foot injuries are often caused by freak accidents and are therefore difficult to prevent, other than by observing a strength and flexibility program for the muscles in and around the foot, warming up properly before exercise, and using common sense.

Overuse injuries of the foot are most effectively prevented by addressing the well-established risk factors associated with overuse injuries (see chapter 2).

Most importantly, before embarking on an exercise program, athletes should have a presports physical to rule out any anatomical abnormalities that may put them at risk of developing overuse injuries in the foot or elsewhere. If flat feet or high arches have caused the person any previous problems, the doctor may prescribe orthotics to relieve the stress these conditions can cause. Tightness or weakness in the muscles of the lower legs that may cause tendinitis should be detected during the physical by the doctor, who should recommend exercises to overcome these deficits. Women with menstrual irregularities are at increased risk of stress fractures, and they should seek nutritional counseling before embarking on or continuing in a vigorous exercise program.

FOOT ANATOMY

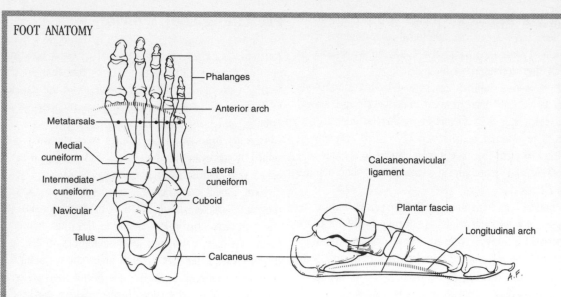

Bones and joints: The foot is made up of twenty-six bones and about thirty joints, each with separate sets of ligaments. This skeletal structure provides the foot with two arch systems—the *longitudinal arch* (the cavity under the foot that extends from the heel to the big toe) and the *anterior arch* (which passes across the front of the foot, under the fleshy ball of the foot where the long bones of the midfoot meet the toes).

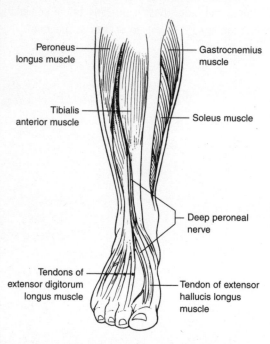

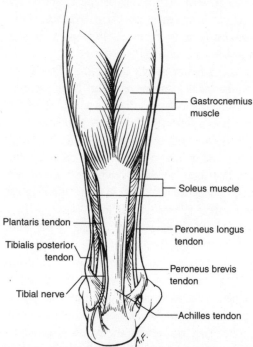

Muscles and nerves: Powerful up-and-down foot motions—which enable a person to walk, run, and jump—take place because of the strong muscles of the lower leg. Delicate foot and toe movements are possible due to the muscles in the foot itself. The two main nerves in the foot are the *tibial* and *peroneal* nerves, which are offshoots of the *sciatic* nerve that originates in the brain.

Overuse Injuries of the Foot

RETROCALCANEAL BURSITIS *("Pump Bump")*

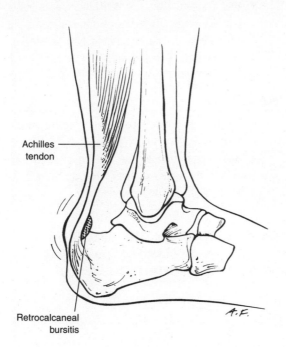

Achilles
tendon

Retrocalcaneal
bursitis

A.F.

A bursitis occurs when an irritation of a bursa sac causes fluid to flow into the sac and it becomes inflamed. One of the most common bursitis conditions in the foot affects the retrocalcaneal bursa sac, located behind the lower leg, just above where the Achilles tendon attaches to the heel bone. Because this condition is often seen in women who wear tight-fitting, high-heeled shoes, it is sometimes known as "pump bump."

Symptoms:

- Onset of symptoms is gradual; it may be two to three months before they become severe.
- Pain, irritation, redness, and swelling just above where the Achilles tendon attaches to the heel bone. Pain is elicited when the bursa is pressed.
- As the condition deteriorates, the soft bump becomes harder, making it increasingly susceptible to outside pressure.

Causes:

- This condition usually develops because of irritation of the retrocalcaneal bursa from the back of the shoe.
- Sports activity precipitates the condition, though there may be several predisposing risk factors:
- Internal: unusually shaped heel bone, flat feet, and feet with high arches, all of which cause the heel to rub against the back of the shoe.
- External: wearing high heels can cause this condition, which is aggravated during sports activities; sports shoes may also exert pressure in this area.

Athletes at risk:

- Any athlete can sustain this injury, though it primarily affects those with the anatomical abnormalities described under "Causes," women who wear high-heeled shoes, and athletes who wear shoes that rub against the back of the heel.

Concerns:

- If allowed to become chronic, surgery may be necessary to remove the bursa.
- Note: sudden onset of pain may signify an Achilles tendon tear.

What you can do:

- Caught early on, this condition responds well to self-treatment.
- Cease the activity that caused the condition for 48 to 72 hours, administer ice massage, and avoid high-heeled shoes and footwear that puts pressure on the back of the heel.
- Use a doughnut pad to take pressure off the bursitis.
- Athletes with flat feet should wear a shoe insert to correct this abnormality.
- Wear slightly larger athletic shoes with softer heel contours.
- After four to six weeks of being pain free, go back to running, working back to full activity in four to twelve weeks.

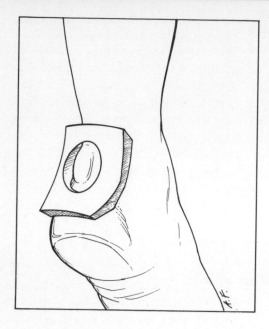

- If the condition does not resolve within two weeks, or if the bursitis has noticeably hardened, seek medical attention.

Medication:

- For relief of minor to moderate pain, take acetaminophen as directed on label, or, for the relief of pain *and* inflammation, ibuprofen or aspirin if tolerated (see page 49).

What the doctor can do:

- Follow the nonoperative measures described above ("What you can do"). If these measures are unsuccessful, physician may prescribe anti-inflammatories or administer a cortisone injection.
- If the bursitis is severe, and the walls of the bursa sac have hardened, an operation may be performed to remove the bursa.
- After surgery, the foot should be immobilized for five days; range-of-motion exercises can begin thereafter.

Rehabilitation:

- If nonoperative treatment is used, continue with exercises that do not aggravate the bursitis, especially swimming.
- After surgery, level one rehabilitation exercises can begin after six weeks of immobilization. In three weeks the athlete should have worked up to level three (see pages 88–91).

Recovery time:

- If caught in its early stages, this bursitis should clear up in four to six weeks.
- After surgery, the athlete can go back to running in six weeks, and can return to full activity within eight to twelve weeks.

STRESS FRACTURES OF THE HEEL BONE (*Calcaneus*), NAVICULAR BONE, and LONG BONES OF THE MIDFOOT (*Metatarsals*)

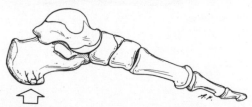

A stress fracture is a series of microfractures that develop in a bone subjected to rhythmic, repetitive, subthreshold impact, such as the kind experienced by runners and ballet or aerobic dancers. Ninety-five percent of all stress fractures occur in the lower extremities. Stress fractures are most often seen in the lower legs and the feet. The bones in the foot that are most at risk are the heel bone (calcaneus), navicular bone, and the long bones in the midfoot (metatarsals). The vast majority of stress fractures occur in the metatarsals. These were dubbed "march fractures" by doctors because they were first diagnosed on a large scale in unfit civilians drafted into the army and forced to train vigorously. Diagnosing stress fractures may be quite difficult not only because the onset of symptoms is gradual, but because X rays do not reveal the stress fracture until three to six weeks after the symptoms first occur (in medical terms, they are "occult").

Symptoms:

- Onset of symptoms is gradual.
- Pain in the affected bone during activity.
- Distinct pain and swelling over the affected bone.

Causes:

- Excessive sports activity usually precipitates the condition, especially a sudden increase in the frequency, intensity, and duration of exercise.
- There may, however, be several other predisposing risk factors:
- Internal: An athlete with bunions, flat feet, or a shorter-than-normal first metatarsal bone (Morton's foot) are more likely to sustain stress fractures, as are athletes who have tight Achilles tendons, which tend to make a person run on the inside of the feet and have inflexible plantar fascia, two conditions associated with stress fractures.
- Women who menstruate irregularly suffer from bone thinning, and are therefore at increased risk of sustaining stress fractures. (For more on the relationship between eating disorders, menstrual irregularities, and stress fractures, refer to chapter 19.)
- Poor running technique may also be to blame.
- External: Worn-out shoes or shoes with poor absorption, as well as an overly hard training surface increase the likelihood of sustaining stress fractures.

Athletes at risk:

- Primarily distance runners, ballet dancers, aerobic dancers, any athlete in running and jumping sports who has the anatomical abnormalities and flexibility deficits described above, and women with menstrual irregularities.

Concerns:

- If allowed to worsen, a complete displaced fracture may occur.

STRESS FRACTURES IN RUNNERS

These are the most common stress fractures seen in runners, based on three doctors' experiences with 1,000 runners:

TIBIA (front shinbone)		34%
upper tibia	7%	
upper-midtibia	12%	
midtibia	4%	
lower tibia	11%	
FIBULA (rear shinbone)		24%
Metatarsals (foot/toe)		18%
second	7%	
third	11%	
PELVIS		6%
OTHERS		
fourth/fifth metatarsals;		4%
pars; sesamoid; navicular;		
talus		

Courtesy of Drs. M. E. Blazine, R. S. Watanabe, A. M. McBryde, Jr.

What you can do:

- If symptoms described above are present, cease the activity that caused the condition.
- Ice massage the area of pain.
- Use a doughnut pad to relieve pressure on the area.
- Continue nonweight-bearing cardiovascular activities such as swimming and stationary biking.
- If the pain is severe, or if it does not clear up in two weeks, seek medical attention.

Medication:

- For relief of minor to moderate pain, take acetaminophen as directed on label, or, for the relief of pain *and* inflammation, ibuprofen or aspirin if tolerated (see page 49).

What the doctor can do:

- Take X rays to confirm the diagnosis. If the X rays are negative, as they are in half of all cases (stress fractures do not show up until three to six weeks after symptoms are first felt), the doctor may take another set of X rays two weeks later. If the X rays are negative, and a stress fracture is suspected, a bone scan may be taken.
- If the stress fracture is severe, the doctor may protect the injured foot by prescribing a removable cast for several weeks to prevent further stress.
- Try to determine the cause of the condition. If the underlying cause is an anatomical abnormality or flexibility deficits, the doctor may address these problems by prescribing shoe inserts (orthotics) and/or flexibility exercises. If the athlete's footwear is to blame, a better shoe would be recommended. If the athlete is a girl or woman with an eating disorder or menstrual irregularities, the person should be referred to a sports nutritionist.

Rehabilitation:

- In the initial stages, the athlete should focus on flexibility exercises, especially those of the Achilles tendons and plantar fascia (see chapter 6).
- Begin level three exercises as soon as possible, and progress to the conditioning program if pain allows (see pages 88–91).

Recovery time:

- Resume weight-bearing sports activities six to eight weeks after the onset of symptoms.

FLEXOR AND EXTENSOR TENDINITIS

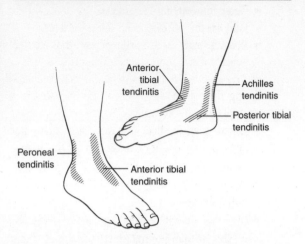

Flexor and extensor tendinitis in the foot refers to inflammations of the tendons that enable a person to straighten (extend) or bend (flex) the toes. These tendons originate in the muscles of the lower leg, cross the ankle, and run along the top of the foot.

Symptoms:

- Onset of symptoms is gradual.
- Pain and puffy swelling on top of the foot. Pain intensifies when either bending or straightening the toes, and especially when running. Pain elicited by pressing the affected tendons.
- In severe cases, a creaking sensation (crepitus) is felt.
- The athlete may walk with a limp.

Cause:

- The condition is usually seen in athletes who lace their shoes too tightly, causing pressure on the tendons from the tongue of the shoe.

Athletes at risk:

- Any athlete who does a lot of running and jumping, and who laces shoes too tightly.

Concerns:

- Tendons are notoriously poor healers, and if this condition is allowed to deteriorate, it can be difficult to overcome.

What you can do:

- Cease the activity that caused the condition for one week.
- Ice massage the painful area for forty-eight to seventy-two hours, twenty minutes at a time.
- Loosen the laces so the tongue is not compressing the top of the foot, and tie the laces in a stepladder fashion, not crisscross.
- When wearing shoes, place a foam rubber pad with a gap cut into it on top of the foot to keep direct pressure off the tendons.
- Almost always, the above self-treatment will resolve the condition.
- If the condition persists for more than two weeks, seek medical attention.

Medication:

- For relief of minor to moderate pain, take acetaminophen as directed on label, or, for the relief of pain *and* inflammation, ibuprofen or aspirin if tolerated (see page 49).

What the doctor can do:

- If the above treatment has not or does not work under the doctor's supervision, the doctor may administer a cortisone injection into the area around the tendon. Such an injection should be followed by two weeks of complete rest from running or strenuous activities using the foot.

Rehabilitation:

- Follow the conditioning program at the end of this chapter, initially avoiding upward and downward bending of the foot until pain has completely gone.

Recovery time:

- When caught in its initial stages, this condition should resolve within one to two weeks.

MORTON'S NEUROMA

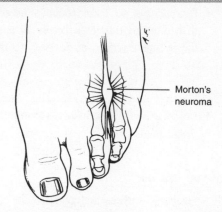

Morton's neuroma

A neuroma is a swelling of a part of a nerve caused when the nerve gets pinched. In the foot it is called a Morton's neuroma, an interdigital neuroma, or a plantar neuroma. It usually affects the nerve between the third and fourth toes or, less often, the second and third toes. The swelling, or neuroma, occurs where the two branches of the nerve intersect, which makes them thicker and more likely to be pinched between the bones of the foot.

Symptoms:

- Onset of symptoms is gradual.
- Recurrent pain from the outer side of the one toe to the inner side of the adjoining one. Usually the pain occurs between the third and fourth toes.
- The pain worsens when tight shoes are worn, and may go away entirely when the athlete is barefoot.
- The pain is often described as resembling a mild electric shock.
- There is often radiating pain and numbness in the affected toes. These symptoms can be triggered by squeezing the ball of the foot between the affected metatarsals.

Causes:

- Condition is usually precipitated by too narrow footwear, although unusually large bony prominences in the joints of the midfoot can be a contributing factor.

Athletes at risk:

- Condition is no more common in one sport than another; usually it occurs as a result of the reasons described above (see "Causes").

Concerns:

- Unless treated, the condition can result in persistent pain.

What you can do:

- Cease any activities that aggravate the condition.
- Ice massage the top of the foot.
- Wear wider, softer shoes that do not compress the bones.
- Wear a foam rubber pad in the shoes below the ball of the foot.
- If the condition does not clear up, or if it clears up and then recurs, seek medical attention.

Medication:

- For relief of minor to moderate pain, take acetaminophen as directed on label, or, for the relief of pain *and* inflammation, ibuprofen or aspirin if tolerated (see page 49).

What the doctor can do:

- If the athlete has followed the above treatment regimen, and the symptoms do not abate, or they resolve and then recur, the doctor may prescribe anti-inflammatories, administer a cortisone injection, or recommend a special shoe insert known as a metatarsal bar to help spread apart the bones pinching the nerve.
- If X rays reveal the condition is caused by overly prominent metatarsal joints, surgery may be necessary. During the procedure the nerve is removed. The patient is left with less sensation in the affected toes, though most contend this is preferable to the pain. After surgery, a dressing is worn for three weeks, during which time the athlete wears a postoperative shoe with a firm sole.

Rehabilitation:

- Level three exercises can start as soon as pain allows (see pages 88–91).

Recovery time:

- When the appropriate measures are taken, this condition may clear up within one to two weeks, though it often recurs.
- If surgery is necessary, the athlete may go back to running within six weeks of the operation.

SESAMOIDITIS

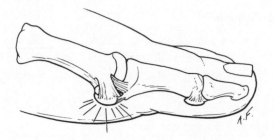

Sesamoiditis is inflammation or damage to the sesamoids, oval-shaped bones that lie within a tendon in the foot. The sesamoids both protect the underlying bones and improve their function (the largest sesamoid bone in the body is the kneecap). In the foot, sesamoiditis usually affects one or both of the sesamoid bones underneath the long bone that connects to the big toe.

Symptoms:

- Onset of symptoms is gradual.
- Pain is felt on the fleshy ball of the foot just behind the big toe, which may extend into the arch. Pain is especially acute during the toe-off phase of the running cycle. The big toe is usually stiff and weak.

Cause:

- Repetitive microtrauma to the sesamoids during the toe-off stage of the running cycle.

Athletes at risk:

- Distance runners, and baseball pitchers (because of the powerful toe-off motion involved when pitching).

Concerns:

- If allowed to deteriorate, the sesamoid may fracture completely, may "die" because of interrupted blood supply, or may develop arthritis.

What you can do:

- Cease the activity that caused the condition for one week.
- Wear a quarter-inch-thick foam pad under the sesamoids when returning to sports. How to make the pad: Obtain a piece of foam rubber from a pharmacy, trim it so it is two inches long, and one and a half inches wide; tape it in place with adhesive tape or "sticky spray" such as tincture of benzoin (available in most pharmacies).
- Stretch the toes each time before exercising.
- If the condition persists for more than two weeks, seek medical attention.

Medication:

- For relief of minor to moderate pain, take acetaminophen as directed on label, or, for the relief of pain *and* inflammation, ibuprofen or aspirin if tolerated (see page 49).

What the doctor can do:

- If the above measures fail (see "What you can do"), the doctor may prescribe anti-inflammatories. When the condition remains painful, a cortisone injection may be administered into the area around the sesamoids. A series of three injections may be necessary.
- The doctor may also prescribe a shoe insert that prevents the big toe from bending upward.
- If this fails, surgery may be done to remove the sesamoid, though this is very rare.

Rehabilitation:

- Begin level two rehabilitation exercises forty-eight to seventy-two hours after starting icing. For levels one, two, and three rehabilitation guidelines, refer to the sections on rehabilitation and conditioning at the end of this chapter.

Recovery time:

- The condition may clear up within four to twelve weeks, or may not clear up at all unless surgery is performed.

BUNIONS *(Hallux Valgus)*

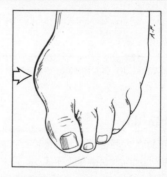

A bunion is a deformity of the big toe that causes it to angle outward by more than 10 to 15 degrees so that the tip of the toe points toward the smaller toes. When the toe is deformed this much, friction from athletic shoes or daily footwear can cause a growth of cartilage and bone (exostosis) to develop over the bone where the angle is greatest. A bursitis can develop over the exostosis, which can itself cause extreme pain.

Note: a bunionette is the same condition, but it affects the little toe.

Symptoms:

- The big toe is angled outward by an angle greater than 10 to 15 degrees; the tip of the toe points inward toward the smaller toes.
- Pain is felt directly over the bony prominence, and this area may look red and inflamed.
- As a consequence of the big toe sliding under the second toe, "hammertoe" may develop in the second toe (page 82).

- A callus may develop on the sole of the foot behind the second toe.
- Athletes with bunions have difficulty wearing shoes.

Causes:

- The bone deformity may be genetic and is exacerbated by tight footwear. It may also be caused solely by tight-fitting high-heeled shoes.
- Athletes with flat feet are predisposed to this condition because the exaggerated rolling-in action created when running exerts an angular push on the big toe.

Athletes at risk:

- See above, "Causes."

Concerns:

- If allowed to deteriorate, surgery may become necessary.

What you can do:

- Wear wider shoes for exercise, and wider, softer shoes during daily activities.
- Use ice, compression, and elevation after exercise or intensive weight-bearing activity.
- Use a toe spacer to straighten the big toe and reduce the likelihood of hammertoe in the second toe, and wear a doughnut pad over the outside of the bony prominence on the side of the big toe to reduce friction.
- If athletic activity becomes difficult, seek medical attention.

Medication:

- For relief of minor to moderate pain, take acetaminophen as directed on label, or, for the relief of pain *and* inflammation, ibuprofen or aspirin if tolerated (see page 49).

What the doctor can do:

- If self-treatment measures do not work, the doctor may prescribe anti-inflammatories.
- If flat feet are causing the condition, the doctor may prescribe a shoe insert to correct this anatomical abnormality.
- Recommend shoes that do not aggravate the condition.
- Quite frequently, surgery must be done to enable pain-free athletic activity. This procedure involves cutting into the first metatarsal, straightening it, then pinning it in place.

Rehabilitation:

- Wearing comfortable shoes, participate in the conditioning program described at the end of this chapter. Continue with cardiovascular activities that do not aggravate the condition.

Recovery time:

- Symptoms may diminish if the appropriate measures are taken, but the bunion itself will usually not heal unless surgery is done.

HAMMERTOE

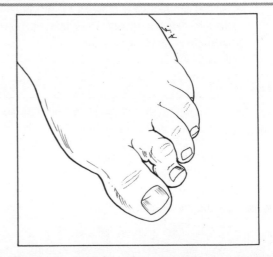

Hammertoe is the name for a condition in which the second toe, the one beside the big toe, becomes buckled under due to repetitive bumping against the front of the shoe. When buckled under, the top of the toe rubs against the inside of the shoe. Eventually, the tendons under the toe become very tight while at the same time the tendons on top of the toe loosen, which makes it very difficult for the toe to return to its normal shape.

Symptoms:

- Pain at the tip of the toe where it comes into contact with the inside of the shoe.
- Toe is usually buckled under.
- Due to friction, a callus or hard corn usually forms on top of the toe.
- Top of the toe is often red and inflamed.

Causes:

- Condition may be congenital, or may be caused by wearing shoes that are too tight or too narrow.
- A flat front arch (anterior transverse arch) is believed to be a contributing factor to hammertoe, as this condition causes the toes to spread.
- Athletes with bunions (see page 81) often develop hammertoe because the deformed big toe slides under the second toe when the forefoot is compressed by shoes, thereby lifting it and causing it to rub against the inside of the shoe.

Athletes at risk:

- Women are particularly susceptible to this condition if they wear shoes that are too tight or too narrow.
- Athletes with a flat front arch or bunions are also at increased risk of developing hammertoe or clawed toes.

Concerns:

- As a result of repetitive buckling of the toes, the flexor tendons get extremely tight and the extensor tendons stretch out. If this persists, it may be impossible to "unbuckle" the toes without resorting to surgery.

What you can do:

- Wear shoes of proper length and width.
- Apply a doughnut pad to the top of the affected toe/s to reduce friction and irritation.
- Stretch out the toe/s as often as possible. Tape the toes to maintain their symmetry.
- If pain makes athletic participation difficult, seek medical attention.

Medication:

- For relief of minor to moderate pain, take acetaminophen as directed on label, or, for the relief of pain *and* inflammation, ibuprofen or aspirin if tolerated (see page 49).

What the doctor can do:

- If the above measures do not succeed, surgery may be necessary:
  The flexor tendon may be severed so the toe can straighten.
  The toe is cut and kept in a straightened position with a wire.
  The foot is bandaged for three weeks, during which time a wooden-soled shoe is worn to protect the wound. After three weeks, the stitches are removed. For six weeks afterward, the toe is then taped so it is bent slightly upward.

Rehabilitation:

- When self-treatment is used, start level two rehabilitation exercises immediately (see pages 88–91).
- After surgery, begin level three exercises for the lower leg as soon as pain allows, taking care to avoid damaging the stitches.

Recovery time:

- After surgery, the athlete can return to sports six to twelve weeks after the procedure.

PLANTAR FASCIITIS *(Bone Spurs, Heel Spurs)*

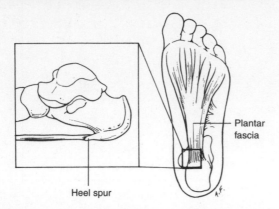

Plantar fascia

Heel spur

Plantar fasciitis is an inflammation of the plantar fascia, the thick fibrous tissue that runs the length of the long arch on the sole of the foot. The longer the inflammation lasts, the greater the possibility a bone spur will develop at the point where the plantar fascia attaches to the heel bone.

Symptoms:

- Onset of symptoms is gradual, often enabling the athlete to continue running and jumping for several weeks or months.
- Pain and tenderness on the inner side of the sole of the foot, just in front of the fleshy part of the heel. Pain is worse when getting out of bed in the morning, and diminishes during the course of the day. However, the pain may again intensify with increased weight-bearing activity. When the pain is severe, the athlete will avoid walking on the heel and will favor the forefoot. Athlete with plantar fasciitis will find that pain intensifies when walking on heels or tiptoes. In severe cases, there may be numbness on the outside of the foot.
- When a bone spur has developed, the athlete may feel a nodule at the site of pain.

Causes:

- When the athlete lifts the heel during the push-off stage of running or jumping, the plantar fascia is stretched in a way that exerts maximum tension at the point where it attaches to the heel bone.

- Intensive sports activity precipitates this condition, though there may be several predisposing factors:

    Internal: Athletes who run with their feet rolling inward (excessive pronation) are at increased risk of this condition, as are athletes with flat feet or knock-knee. All three conditions force the plantar fascia to stretch more as the athlete runs and jumps, putting increased pressure at the point where it attaches to the heel bone. High arches are also associated with plantar fasciitis, as are tightness in the calf muscle—Achilles tendon unit.

    External: Worn-out shoes, shoes with inadequate arch support, and shoes with overly stiff soles predispose athletes to plantar fasciitis because of the excessive stretching they force the plantar fascia to perform.

Athletes at risk:

- Distance runners are by far the most likely candidates for this condition, as are athletes with the anatomical abnormalities and flexibility deficits described above.

Concerns:

- If allowed to progress to the point where bone spurs develop at the attachment of the plantar fascia to the heel, a bone spur may form. In such cases, surgery may be required.

What you can do:

- As soon as symptoms are felt, cease the activity that caused the condition.
- During the first forty-eight to seventy-two hours after symptoms first develop, use ice massage as well as crutches to take the stress off the sole of the foot.
- Place a one-eighth-inch heel wedge inside the shoes to lessen stretching of the plantar fascia.
- Avoid walking in bare feet as this places excess stress on the soles of the feet.
- Continue cardiovascular activities that do not involve weight bearing—swimming and stationary biking are particularly useful.

- After the initial symptoms have abated, start gentle stretching of the calf muscle–Achilles tendon unit and the plantar fascia (see page 90).
- When there is no tenderness, no limp, and no pain in the morning (this may take six weeks), *gradually* return to running, preferably on a "forgiving" surface such as grass or dirt.
- If the athlete has any of the anatomical abnormalities described above (see "Causes"), or if the symptoms have been present for six weeks, he or she should seek medical attention.

Medication:

- For relief of minor to moderate pain, take acetaminophen as directed on label, or, for the relief of pain *and* inflammation, ibuprofen or aspirin if tolerated (see page 49).

What the doctor can do:

- The doctor should try to ascertain the exact cause of the condition (see above, "Causes"). If the underlying cause is an anatomical abnormality such as flat feet or high arches, the doctor may prescribe a shoe insert to correct the condition. If the cause is tightness and/or weakness in the calf muscle–Achilles tendon unit, the athlete should be given exercises to overcome these problems. If footwear is to blame, the doctor should recommend a better shoe.
- The doctor may prescribe anti-inflammatories and/or administer a steroid injection.
- If the condition persists for four to six months despite appropriate treatment, surgery may be necessary. In this procedure, the surgeon completely severs the plantar fascia from the heel bone. A wooden shoe is worn for four weeks, during which time the tissue will reattach to the bone.

Rehabilitation:

- If this condition is caught in its early stages, athletes can begin a conditioning program for the lower extremities after the initial pain dissipates.
- Athletes with chronic plantar fasciitis should

start level two rehabilitation exercises three to five days after beginning ice massage. For levels one, two, and three rehabilitation guidelines, refer to the sections on rehabilitation and conditioning at the end of this chapter.

Recovery time:

- Even when the condition is caught in its early stages, relative rest (see page 64) for at least six weeks is usually necessary before the foot has no pain and the athlete can return to running.
- Chronic plantar fasciitis may take several months to a year to resolve, and sometimes may not clear up at all unless surgery is done.

Nonorthopedic and Skin Conditions of the Foot

Blisters

Blisters are portions of the skin that become irritated due to friction, causing them to fill up with clear fluid, blood, or pus. They can be extremely disabling, especially when they open. They frequently occur in the foot, especially the ball of the foot and the heel.

Blisters commonly affect athletes at the beginning of the season, after a long layoff, when beginning an exercise program, or when breaking in a new pair of shoes.

To prevent blisters that may occur in the above circumstances, dust the skin with talcum powder or petroleum jelly (such as Vaseline). Wearing two pairs of socks also helps reduce friction, especially if the athlete has sensitive skin or sweats excessively. Certain types of socks have special reinforcement in high-risk areas to reduce friction. Thor*lo, for instance, makes socks to accommodate the frictional forces exerted in twelve different sports. The extra padding also helps protect against stress fractures.

If a sore spot occurs, the athlete should cover the area with a friction-reducing substance such as petroleum jelly or moleskin (available at most pharmacies).

If and when a blister does develop, the athlete should

remember the very real potential for serious infection if the blister is mismanaged. Any blister that gets infected needs to be seen by a doctor.

The surface of the blister should be kept intact because it acts as a protective barrier against bacteria. *Never break a blister deliberately.* Instead, wear a doughnut pad to protect it against further friction.

It may be necessary to break a blister "preemptively" if it is likely to tear by itself. In such cases, sterilize a needle by holding it under a flame until it turns red hot; let it cool down, then pierce the skin just inside the edge of the blister. The blister should be opened wide enough so that it does not reseal. After the fluid has been dispersed, place a pressure pad over the blister to prevent it from refilling with fluid. After five or six days, the skin should have hardened and can be cut away.

Always, the nonaggressive method of treating blisters is preferred because of the potential for infection. A blister that tears by itself should be cared for as follows:

- Clean the area with soap and water, then rinse with an antiseptic.

- Using sterile scissors, cut the torn blister halfway around perimeter so there is a ring of blistered skin around the edge.

- Apply antiseptic and a mild ointment such as zinc oxide to the exposed tissue.

- Lay the cut-off flap of skin over the exposed tissue and cover the area with a sterile dressing.

- Within two or three days, the underlying skin should have hardened sufficiently, and you can remove the dead skin.

- The athlete should wear a Band-Aid for a week afterward.

Corns

There are two types of corns: hard and soft.

Hard corns (clavus durum) are thick nodules of skin that usually develop over the middle joint of the second or third toe. They are caused by the friction created by rubbing inside the shoes, often as a result of too narrow shoes that cause the second and third toes to buckle. Hard corns are often seen in athletes with hammertoe.

The athlete can prevent symptoms by soaking the foot daily in warm, soapy water to soften the skin, wearing properly fitting shoes, and wearing a doughnut pad over the corn. However, if the underlying cause of the corn is a hammertoe, this troublesome condition will have to be corrected before the corn will go away.

Soft corns (clavus molle) are usually caused by a combination of wearing too narrow shoes and profuse sweating. This type of corn usually develops *between* the fourth and fifth toes. These small, conical-shaped growths create pain because the skin on top of the corn is always flaking, leaving a tender portion of skin underneath. To treat soft corns, wear wider shoes, keep the skin between the toes clean and dry, wear a corn pad between the toes, and apply 40 percent salicylic acid (available at pharmacies in liquid or patch form).

Calluses

A callus is a thickening of the skin caused by repetitive friction. Pain is caused by the loss of elasticity in the skin and the tightness in the shoes created by the thickened skin. Calluses may be caused by too tight or too narrow shoes, or an anatomical abnormality such as bunions/bunionettes, hammer/claw toes, or flat feet, conditions that cause the shape of the foot or the way it moves to exert increased pressure and friction inside the shoe.

In the foot, the most common sites of calluses are the heel, the ball of the foot, the top of a hammertoe, and the inner side of the big toe.

Calluses can be prevented by wearing two pairs of socks (a thin cotton or nylon pair next to the skin, a heavy athletic pair over those) or double-knit socks. Wear socks with special reinforcement and padding in high-friction areas (Thor* lo is one reputable brand).

In the initial stages, anyone who develops a callus should file it with an emery file after showering. Massaging small amounts of lanolin into the softened skin may help maintain elasticity.

Once a thick callus has formed, a keratolytic agent such as Whitehead's ointment should be used. Salicylic acid, 5 to 10 percent strength (available at pharmacies), can be applied at night and peeled off in the morning.

If the callus does not go away, and causes pain, make an appointment to see a chiropodist, who may pare off the excess skin with a sharp knife, by sanding, or by pumicing.

Warts/Verrucae

Warts, or verrucae, as they are sometimes called, are caused by a virus that is often transmitted from one athlete to another via the floor of showers and locker rooms, or anywhere people walk barefoot.

They are usually located on the sole of the foot, are round or oval, and have a crack or dark spot in the middle. This distinctive mark distinguishes warts from calluses or corns.

Warts are susceptible to infection, especially on the sole of the foot, where they are constantly irritated. The athlete should prevent this irritation by using a dough-nut pad.

After a hot foot bath, file down the wart as far as possible with an emery board, then treat it with an over-the-counter wart ointment. This may have to be continued for several months before the warts go away.

If the pain is severe, it may be preferable to see a chiropodist, who will cut or burn away the warts.

Athlete's Foot (Tinea Pedis)

Athlete's foot is a fungus that causes the skin between the toes to become soggy, cracked, scaly, and chalky-looking. The soles of the affected feet and the toes become extremely itchy. Feet that develop this condition often smell offensive.

The cause of athlete's foot is poor foot hygiene and not drying the feet thoroughly after shower or baths. As the condition is contagious, it is relatively common for athletes who walk barefoot on damp locker room floors.

As athlete's foot is a troublesome condition to overcome, the focus should be on prevention:

- Wash the feet regularly with soap and water, dry them thoroughly after showering or bathing, and use talcum powder on the feet.

- Always wear clean socks, and change them daily.

- Wear porous shoes that allow air circulation and evaporation of moisture.

- Wear slippers or flip-flops when walking around locker rooms.

If athlete's foot develops, follow the above steps, and use standard over-the-counter fungicide as directed on label. Brand names include Resenex and Tinactin.

If the condition does not clear up in two weeks, seek medical treatment from the family doctor or a podiatrist.

Black Nails (Subungual Hematoma)

Repetitive impact to the front of the big toe can cause blood to form under the nail. Usually it is seen in runners, especially those who wear shoes that are too small, or who run downhill a lot, which causes the nail to be pried upward with each step. When the nail becomes separated from the underlying tissue, pain develops under the nail, where a pooling of blood can be seen. Often, the nail falls off.

The most important measure is to wear shoes that provide the big toe with enough room to move, and to avoid running downhill too much. It may be helpful to wear padding over the nail to prevent it from being pried upward.

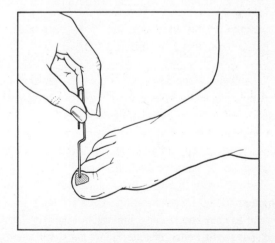

A doctor may relieve this condition by sterilizing a paper clip under a flame until it glows red, letting it cool down, then passing the hot end through the nail, allowing blood to escape and thus relieving pressure on the nail.

Ingrown Toenail

Ingrown toenail describes a condition in which the edges of a toenail grow in such a way that they dig into the surrounding skin. This condition almost always affects the big toe. Ingrown toenail may be caused by tight-fitting shoes or improper care of the nails.

To prevent ingrown toenail, wear shoes that fit comfortably, and cut the nails at least once a week, making sure to cut the nail straight across so the sharp edges of the nail do not grow into the surrounding skin.

If an ingrown toenail develops, see a chiropodist, who may use surgical or nonsurgical measures to correct the condition. Bear in mind that infections can easily develop in an ingrown toenail.

Lower Leg, Ankle, and Foot Injury Rehabilitation

Rehabilitation exercises serve to

- promote blood flow to the area, which speeds the healing process

- relieve stiffness in the joint caused by immobilization

- prevent atrophy and tightening of the surrounding muscles resulting from inactivity.*

Rehabilitation should begin as soon as possible to prevent loss of range of motion and strength. Protracted inactivity after injury causes inordinate range-of-motion and strength deficits that need to be restored before return to sports activity. Delays in rehabilitation spell delays in an athlete's return to sports readiness.

After an injury that does not require surgery or prolonged splinting, range-of-motion exercises should begin as soon as pain and swelling diminish—usually no later than forty-eight hours after the injury symptoms begin, and often as early as twenty-four hours. Even after some types of surgery, range-of-motion exercises for the knee should start after twenty-four hours.

*For more on the importance and general principles of rehabilitation, see chapter 5, "Rehabilitating Your Sports Injury."

With other types of surgery, range-of-motion exercises should begin as early as five days after the operation, and no more than two to three weeks later. The patient should be put in a splint that can be removed for physical therapy.

Exercise is the most effective way to restore an injured athlete to sports readiness. A physical therapist may also employ ice, superficial heat, deep heat, massage, electrical stimulation, and/or physical manipulation of the joints to promote healing and make performing the exercises more comfortable.

The starting intensity level of the rehabilitation depends on the severity of the injury. Postsurgery range-of-motion exercises usually begin at level one. At this level, range of motion is "active assisted"—the physical therapist helps patients use their own strength to move through allowable ranges of motion. If the injury is too severe for active assisted exercises, the patient may have to rely on "passive assisted" exercises—the physical therapist moves the injured joints through allowable ranges of motion. Continuous passive motion machines (CPMs) can be taken home by the patient so he or she can do passive range-of-motion exercises at home.

After surgery, muscle atrophy is prevented by using isometric exercises. With the direction of a physical therapist, these exercises can usually begin immediately after surgery. Isometrics help maintain strength in the important muscles surrounding the ankle and foot—especially those in the lower leg—without compromising the healing process by changing the length of the muscle.

Athletes who have sustained only mild or moderately severe foot injuries can begin with level two exercises.

In the initial stages of rehabilitation, the primary goal is to restore range of motion in the joints; the secondary goal is to prevent atrophy in the muscles. As the rehabilitation program progresses, more strengthening exercises are included.

Range-of-motion and strength exercises should always be done within the pain threshold. Any exercise that causes pain should be discontinued.

The following are the most common and effective exercises used to rehabilitate the foot, ankle, and lower leg after injury.

Level One

After surgery, active assisted or passive assisted range-of-motion therapy is used as a starting point of rehabilitation. The physical therapist should move the patient's foot, ankle, and lower leg through their major motions. The joints should be moved only through those ranges of motion that do not compromise the stability of the surgery.

Isometrics and assisted range-of-motion therapy should continue only until patients are capable of using their own strength to do level two exercises.

Level Two

When patients can move their injured joints themselves, level two exercises to develop range of motion and strength and flexibility in the muscles can start.

Level two exercises can also be used as a starting point for rehabilitating moderate to severe foot, ankle, and lower leg injuries that do not require surgery. Do the following exercises two or three times a day.

Exercise 1: Ankle range of motion and proprioception
Sit or lie with heel of injured foot suspended. ''Draw'' capital letters with foot, toes pointed. Do entire alphabet three times.

Exercise 2: Ankle and toe range of motion using foot and toe flexor and extensor muscles in lower leg and foot
Lying on back, bend foot upward while simultaneously straightening toes, then point foot downward while bending toes. Do ten repetitions, two or three times.

Exercise 3: Ankle range of motion using muscles of the lower leg
As above, but this time rotate ankle in circles. Do ten circles one way, ten circles the other, two or three times.

Exercise 4: Toe range of motion using toe extensors and flexors in the lower leg and foot
Sitting or lying down, grip and spread toes. Do ten repetitions, two or three times.

Exercise 5: Foot range of motion using ankle inversion and eversion

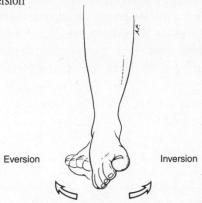

Eversion　　　　Inversion

Sitting or lying down, turn soles of feet toward each other from the ankle, then away from each other. Do ten repetitions.

Exercise 6: Static stretches for calf muscle–Achilles tendon unit

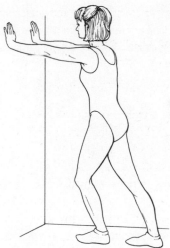

Stand with hands at chest height against a wall, one leg behind the other. Feet should be pointing straight ahead, and heels should remain on the floor throughout exercise. Supporting weight of body with hands, bend front knee and straighten back one slightly. Press back foot against floor six to ten seconds. Relax two seconds. Stretch for another six to ten seconds by moving hips forward and straightening back leg so there is a pull in calf.

Exercise 7: Ankle strengthening using foot extensors and flexors in the lower leg

Standing with toes straight ahead, raise heels slowly as far as possible, then lower yourself back down again. Also perform exercises with toes pointed inward, then outward. Do ten repetitions, two or three times.

Level Three

When the patient can do the level two exercises without difficulty or pain, level three exercises can begin.

Level three exercises can also be used as a starting point for mild lower leg, ankle, and foot injuries.

Level three involves dynamic exercises to strengthen the lower leg, ankle, and toes, as well as flexibility exercises for the muscles and joints in those areas. Perform the following exercises two or three times a day.

Exercise 1: Strengthening and stretching calf muscle–Achilles tendon unit and front-lower leg muscles, and promoting ankle range of motion (plantar flexion and dorsiflexion)

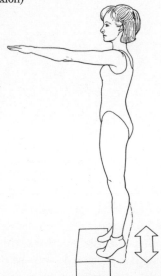

Stand on a step with heels hanging off back edge, hands straight out in front. Raise heels as far as possible, then lower them as far as you can. Perform exercise with the toes pointed inward, then pointed outward. Do ten repetitions, two or three times a day.

Exercise 2: Ankle strengthening and range of motion (eversion and inversion)

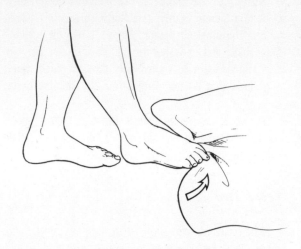

Fold a towel in half and place it on floor. Place heel firmly on floor, forefoot on end of towel. Back up exercising foot with nonexercising foot. Without lifting heel from floor, scoop towel forward with forefoot. To increase resistance, place book or similar weight on end of towel. Repeat exercise between five and ten times.

Exercise 3: Ankle and foot proprioception

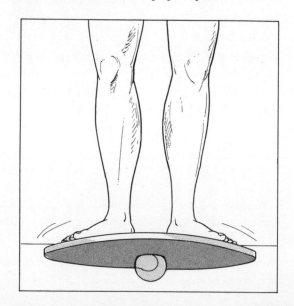

Spend three to five minutes a day on a "wobble board."

Exercise 4: Toe strengthening and range of motion

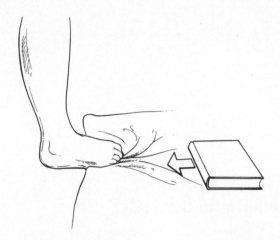

Sitting in a chair, place a towel flat on floor in front of you. Keeping heel of injured foot stationary, use toes to pull towel toward you. Do this five to ten times. To add resistance, place book or similar weight on towel and do exercises.

When the strength of your injured ankle is the same as that of the healthy side (and, by association, 95 percent of its original strength), ease back into sports.

Before going back to sports, however, the athlete who has been injured should be able to do daily activities without pain, and simulate the leg motions of his or her sport without pain or difficulty. See page 69 for progression of rehabilitation after lower limb injuries.

To reduce the chance of reinjury, begin the strength and flexibility conditioning program that follows.

Conditioning Program for the Foot, Ankle, and Lower Leg

Conditioning to prevent injuries in the muscles in and around the foot, ankle, and lower leg requires improving the strength and flexibility of all the major muscles, in particular the muscles in the lower leg. Incorporate in your workout regimen at least one set of the following exercises for each muscle group mentioned. The exercises are described in chapter 3, "Strength and Flexibility: The Key to Injury Prevention."

Make these exercises part of an overall strength and flexibility program, and do them before any activity that will stress the muscles around the foot.

Ankle, Foot, and Lower Leg Strengthening Exercises

Calves and Achilles tendons: Barbell heel raise
Front lower leg muscles: Toe raise
Calf and front lower leg muscles: Tubed ankle everters/inverters

Lower Leg and Ankle Flexibility Exercises

Calves and Achilles tendons: Wall calf stretch

CHAPTER SEVEN

Ankle Injuries

Injuries to the ankle joint are among the most common in sports. Ankle sprains occur with unfortunate regularity in athletes and nonathletes alike. It has been estimated that there is one ankle sprain per 10,000 Americans daily. That amounts to 23,000 ankle sprains every day. The ankle sprain is considered by most doctors to be the most common acute sports injury of all. Yet ankle sprains are accorded very little respect, despite the fact that they can cause chronic instability in the ankle. This reinforces the need to treat even mild ankle sprains with the seriousness they deserve.

In recent years there have been major developments in the way ankle sprains are treated, characterized by early range of motion as opposed to lengthy immobilization. This aggressive attitude toward treating ankle sprains should be of interest to all athletes, given the frequency with which this injury occurs.

Overuse ankle injuries are rivaling acute injuries for the attention of doctors. Rarely seen by doctors until the fitness boom, overuse ankle injuries are caused by the repetitive motions involved in many of the sports that have grown in popularity, especially running and aerobic dancing.

Because of the importance of the ankle joint in almost every sport, it is important to treat both overuse and acute injuries with respect.

Injuries to the Ankle

Acute ankle injuries include ligament sprains, bone fractures, and joint dislocations. By far the most common of these injuries is the ligament sprain.

Ankle sprains are usually caused by a twist of the ankle. An ankle that sprains because the athlete rolls over on the outside of the ankle is known as an *inversion* sprain; sprains caused by turn-ins are *eversion* sprains.

Inversion sprains are much more common than eversion sprains. That is because there is more bony stability on the outer side of the ankle, which makes the inner side of the ankle more likely to give way, allowing the outer side to roll over and stretching or tearing the ligament on that side.

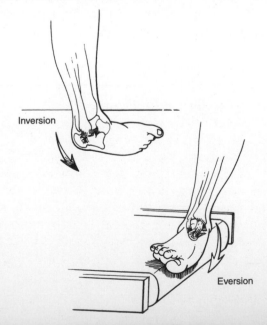

Inversion

Eversion

Most often one or two ligaments are sprained. If only one ligament is sprained, it is usually the anterior talofibular ligament, but if the ankle bends over further, the calcaneofibular ligament may also get injured.

Eversion ankle sprains are seen less frequently. This kind of sprain often occurs when the athlete steps into a hole and the ankle simultaneously bends outward and rotates outward. Usually the damage takes place in the anterior talofibular ligament, the interosseous ligament, or the deltoid ligament. Unless treated properly, the instability created by an eversion ankle sprain can cause degeneration in the talus, which may in turn lead to the onset of arthritis.

As with all sprains, ankle sprains are classified according to their severity: first, second, or third degree. Instability is one of the characteristic symptoms of an ankle sprain, and testing instability is one of the most important means of judging how bad the sprain is. However, it is important to remember that the swelling that quickly takes place may cause the joint to stiffen, thereby disguising instability and perhaps leading to a misdiagnosis as a less serious sprain. Therefore, the sooner an ankle injury is examined by a doctor, the more accurate the diagnosis can be.

Ankle fractures usually occur in one of three ways, involving a twist caused by impact or the athlete's own momentum:

1) The foot is forcefully bent one way or another

2) The lower leg is forcefully rotated one way or the other while the foot is fixed in place

3) The athlete rolls over or turns in on the ankle bone

Note: The same mechanisms that cause ankle sprains can also cause fractures. Any severe ankle sprain needs to be X-rayed to rule out a possible fracture.

Overuse injuries of the ankle are primarily tendinitis conditions of the long tendons that cross the ankle joint from the strong muscles in the lower leg.

Overuse injuries are caused by excessive sports activity, but they often have an underlying internal or external risk factor. The internal risk factors usually involve deficits of strength and/or flexibility in the muscle-tendon units and anatomical abnormalities such as flat feet, feet that roll inward (pronate) when the athlete runs, or high arches, all of which can place excessive stress on the tendons in the ankle area.

External factors may include training errors (such as excessive downhill running), inappropriate footwear, and poor technique.

Unlike most acute ankle injuries, the onset of the symptoms of overuse injuries of the ankle is gradual, and may have no obvious cause. Initially, pain may be experienced only after sports participation. Gradually the symptoms may begin to be felt during and after participation but may not be severe enough to interfere with performance. In the final stages, disabling pain is felt both during and after participation, and in daily activities.

The key to managing overuse injuries is early intervention. Anytime there is pain centering in the ankle, especially ankle pain aggravated by the same sports or fitness activity, the likelihood is that the discomfort is an overuse injury. Take immediate steps to address the condition, starting with RICE (page 46).

Preventing Ankle Injuries

Acute ankle injuries are often caused by freak accidents—tripping in a rut, for instance—and may therefore be difficult to prevent. There are, however, several preventive measures athletes can take to avoid acute ankle injuries.

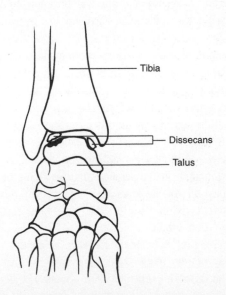

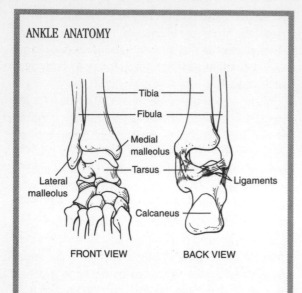

ANKLE ANATOMY

Tibia

Fibula

Medial malleolus

Tarsus

Lateral malleolus

Ligaments

Calcaneus

FRONT VIEW   BACK VIEW

Bones and joints: The large, strong bones of the ankle joint are held together by strong sets of broad ligaments, which reinforce stability.

Muscles: The muscles around the ankle are the weakest component of the joint. Because of the long tendons that cross all sides of the ankle joint from the strong muscles in the lower leg, the joint has tremendous power but little protection and support.

Most important is to engage in a conditioning program to develop strength and flexibility in the tissues around the ankle joint. Flexibility in the Achilles tendon is of particular importance. An ankle that can bend upward at least 15 degrees accommodates the forces that cause ankle sprains much more efficiently than those with less flexibility. All athletes should stretch their Achilles tendons before exercise, and those with naturally tight Achilles tendons should place extra emphasis on stretching this area. Strength and flexibility should also be developed in all the muscle-tendon units of the lower leg.

Strength in the peroneal muscles (those in the front, outer side of the lower leg) are especially important to prevent rolling over on the ankle and sustaining an inversion sprain.

Wearing appropriate footwear is another important way of preventing acute ankle injuries. Shoes not designed for a particular sport should not be used; for instance, jogging shoes designed for straight-ahead run-

ning should not be worn to play tennis or aerobics, two sports with high demands for side-to-side movements.

After an acute ankle injury such as a sprain, athletes may lose proprioceptive skills—the ability to know what different parts of the body are doing without looking at them. Coordination between the ankle and foot suffers the most, which can lead to further sprains. After sustaining a strain, it is important to regain proprioception by using a device such as wobble board.

Overuse ankle injuries can best be prevented by being aware of the risk factors associated with these conditions, which are the same for foot and knee injuries. Refer to those chapters for the most effective way to address these risk factors.

Taping Versus Bracing

Preventing an athlete from respraining an ankle during sports was once done by taping the ankle before exercise. This was quite inconvenient, especially for recreational athletes without the benefit of an athletic trainer to tape the ankle. During the last decade or so, there has been an emergence of more convenient alternatives to taping—most notably the "air brace" made by AIRCAST.

Although taping is an effective way to prevent ankle injuries, there are several disadvantages with this technique, including the following:

- Adhesive taping loses up to 50 percent of its original support after ten minutes of exercise.

- Taping cannot be done by the athlete; it requires the assistance of a skilled "taper."

- In the long run, it is more expensive to tape every time the athlete exercises than to purchase a prefabricated brace (taping also requires underwrap or skin lubricant pads for the heels or under laces, and scissors to remove the tape).

- Taping is much more time consuming than strapping on a brace.

- Studies have shown that braces are *more effective* in providing support for the ankle.

For these reasons, the use of a prefabricated brace is preferable. Braces provide an equally effective or better alternative to tape to prevent athletes from respraining an ankle, as well as providing the much needed self-confidence athletes with "bad ankles" require. These braces should not be used *in place of* conditioning but may be useful in *conjunction with* conditioning.

ANKLE SPRAINS

An ankle sprain is a stretch, tear, or complete rupture of one or more of the ligaments that hold the bones of the ankle joint together. The most common type of ankle sprain is the inversion sprain—when an athlete rolls over on the outside of his or her ankle. When this happens, the ligament that most often gets injured is the anterior talofibular ligament. In about 20 percent of cases, the calcaneofibular ligament gets injured at the same time. As with all sprains, ankle sprains are classified according to severity: first, second, or third degree.

Symptoms:

- First degree: mild pain and disability, tenderness, and localized swelling. There is no instability in the ankle, no bruising, and little loss of function.
- Second degree: a tearing sensation, pop, or snap is felt as the athlete rolls over on the ankle. There is swelling over the ankle and tenderness. Bruising begins three to four days after the injury occurs. There is some difficulty walking on the ankle.
- Third degree: in many cases, the joint "sublux-

ates" (slips out of place and then slips back in). There is swelling and tenderness over the entire outer aspect of the ankle joint, severe tenderness, and instability. It will be extremely difficult to walk using the ankle.

Causes:

- The athlete rolls over on the outside of the ankle, causing range of motion in the joint to be exceeded.
- Two common scenarios in which the ankle can get sprained are when a basketball player jumps, then lands on another player's foot, or when an athlete steps in a rut.

Athletes at risk:

- Primarily basketball players, as well as any athlete engaged in a sports involving running and jumping.

Concerns:

- Unless treated properly, sprained ankles can become chronically unstable, leading to recurrent sprains.
- The same mechanism that can cause sprains can cause fractures. Any sprain with severe swelling and pain needs to be X-rayed to rule out a fracture.
- An inversion sprain can tear the *peroneal retinaculum*, the band of tissue that holds the peroneal tendons in place, which may lead to recurrent peroneal tendon subluxations (page 99).

What you can do:

- RICE (page 46) is the cornerstone of treatment for sprains.
- If the sprain is mild, start level two rehabilitation exercises within twenty-four to forty-eight hours. For levels one, two, and three rehabilitation guidelines, refer to the section on rehabilitation and conditioning at the end of chapter 6.

- If the sprain is either second or third degree (see above, "Symptoms"), seek medical attention.
- After returning to sports, wear a brace.

Medication:

- For relief of minor to moderate pain, take acetaminophen as directed on label, or, for the relief of pain *and* inflammation, ibuprofen or aspirin if tolerated (see page 49).

What the doctor can do:

- The doctor can X-ray the joint to rule out a fracture.
- Once a fracture is ruled out, the doctor should place the athlete on a rehabilitation program to start as soon as pain allows.
- The doctor may also recommend a removable splint to prevent reinjury of the ankle. This should be worn for six weeks after the injury.

Rehabilitation:

- After a first-degree sprain, start level three rehabilitation exercises within twenty-four hours of the injury.
- After a second-degree sprain, start level two rehabilitation exercises within twenty-four to forty-eight hours.
- After a third-degree sprain in which the ligament has totally ruptured, start level one exercises one to three weeks after the injury. In addition to the exercises described, use a stationary bicycle, inversion/eversion training, and a wobble board. For levels one, two, and three rehabilitation guidelines, refer to the sections on rehabilitation and conditioning at the end of chapter 6.

Recovery time:

- First-degree sprain: four to six weeks.
- Second-degree sprain: four to eight weeks.
- Third-degree sprain: six to twelve weeks.

ANKLE FRACTURES

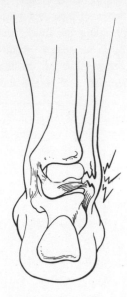

A fracture is a crack, break, or complete shattering of a bone. Ankle fractures usually affect the bottom end of the fibula on the outer side of the lower leg, and usually occur in the same way many inversion sprains do; the athlete rolls over on the ankle, and the body's momentum breaks the bone.

Symptoms:

- The signs and symptoms of an ankle fracture are much the same as those of an ankle sprain (see page 95).
- In addition, there may be pain directly over the area of the fracture, an obvious deformity, and at the moment of injury, a sharp pain like an electric shock in the ankle, followed by numbness.

Cause:

- The same mechanism that causes ankle sprains may also cause fractures. Usually, the cause is the athlete's rolling over on the outside of the ankle.

Athletes at risk:

- Primarily basketball players, as well as any athlete engaged in a sport involving running and jumping.

Concerns:

- Many ankle fractures are dismissed by athletes as sprains. A displaced fracture that goes undetected can cause wearing down of the articular cartilage, which in turn can lead to arthritis.

What you can do:

- Send for emergency medical attention.
- If there is deformity in the ankle, splint the lower leg and apply RICE (see chapter 4).
- If the fracture is "open" (the ends of the broken bones protrude through the skin), place a clean cloth over the wound to prevent dirt from entering.

What the doctor can do:

- X-ray the bones to confirm there is a fracture.
- Apply a splint that will be worn for four to eight weeks if the bones are not displaced and the ankle joint is stable.
- If the ankle joint is displaced, the doctor may operate to fix the ends of the broken bones together using pins, screws, and wires.
- The doctor will also have to operate if the bones protrude through the skin.
- After surgery, the leg is usually completely immobilized for two to three weeks, at which time level one rehabilitation exercises may start. For levels one, two, and three rehabilitation guidelines, refer to the sections on rehabilitation and conditioning at the end of chapter 6.

Rehabilitation:

- After a fracture, level one rehabilitation should begin two to eight weeks after the injury.

Recovery time:

- It usually takes two to three months before the bone heals together, but athletes should expect to be out of sports for at least four months.

CHRONIC ANKLE INSTABILITY

Chronic ankle instability was once thought to be caused simply by repetitive sprains. The more often the ankle gets sprained, it was thought, the more the ligaments got stretched. However, the cause of chronic ankle instability is more complex than that.

Even after having ankle sprains treated properly, many athletes experience chronic ankle instability. The most common symptoms are frequent "giving way" in the ankle during sports and eventually in daily activities.

New evidence suggests that chronic ankle instability is the result of injury-induced deficits in three important areas: proprioception (coordination, reflexes, and reaction time), musculature (strength, endurance, and power), and mechanical function (ligamentous laxity). Proprioception is the least well understood.

Proprioception is compromised by injury because of harm done to the delicate interaction between the central nervous system and the muscles, tendons, and ligaments. Impaired proprioception can lead to faulty technique or sudden loss of coordination; either one may cause both overuse and acute injuries.

For mild ankle sprains, straightforward balance exercises such as standing on one foot with the eyes closed are sufficient to regain proprioception. Make proprioception training more challenging by changing the position of the nonweight-bearing foot while balancing, or by training on an unstable surface such as a spring mattress or wobble board.

After an ankle sprain, athletes should work hard to regain proprioception, strengthen the muscles in the lower leg, and allow the ligaments to heal. When he or she returns to sports, the athlete should wear a brace to guard against reinjury.

Return to activity only when these criteria are met:

- The ankle must have full range of motion.

- The athlete must be able to run and walk without limping.

- The athlete must have over 90 percent strength in the injured ankle compared to the uninjured side.

Overuse Injuries of the Ankle

POSTERIOR TIBIAL TENDINITIS

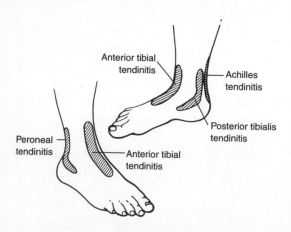

Labels:
- Anterior tibial tendinitis
- Achilles tendinitis
- Posterior tibialis tendinitis
- Peroneal tendinitis
- Anterior tibial tendinitis

Posterior tibial tendinitis is an inflammation of the tendon that runs down the back of the larger lower leg

bone (the tibia) from the tibialis posterior muscle to the inner side of the foot. The tendon runs in a narrow sheath, and inflammation causes constriction that produces the symptoms. In athletes, the pain inhibits proper running form and makes it difficult to perform any activity that requires a strong push-off.

Symptoms:

- Onset of symptoms is gradual.
- Pain occurs over the inner side of the ankle during running.
- Tenderness is felt over the point where the tendon attaches to the navicular bone on the inside of the foot, as well as where the tendon passes behind the ankle bone.
- As the condition worsens, a creaking sensation (crepitus) develops in the area.

Causes:

- Overtraining is the main reason posterior tibial tendinitis develops, especially sudden increases in the frequency, intensity, and/or duration of the athlete's training regimen. However, there are several other internal and external risk factors associated with this condition.
- Internal: anatomical abnormalities such as feet that turn inward (pronate), hypermobile feet, and flat feet; strength and flexibility deficits, especially tight posterior tibialis muscles.
- External: overly hard training surface, worn-out shoes.

Concerns:

- This condition is often mistaken by athletes for "shinsplints." Unless recognized for what it is and treated accordingly, it can become extremely troublesome to overcome.

What you can do:

- Withdraw from the activity that caused the condition for two weeks.
- Continue or begin activities that do not aggravate the tendinitis.

- Ice the tendinitis for forty-eight to seventy-two hours, then apply moist heat.
- For flat feet that may be causing the condition, obtain semirigid orthotics (page 122) that support the arch and decrease the athlete's tendency to run on the inside of the feet.
- When all symptoms are gone, gradually return to running.

Medication:

- For relief of minor to moderate pain, take acetaminophen as directed on label, or, for the relief of pain *and* inflammation, ibuprofen or aspirin if tolerated (see page 49).

What the doctor can do:

- Prescribe rest or, if the condition is severe, immobilize the ankle in a cast or plastic boot for two to three weeks.
- Prescribe anti-inflammatories.
- If the tendon sheath is constricted, surgery should be performed to make the tendon glide more smoothly inside it. After surgery, the ankle is immobilized for five days, at which time rehabilitation begins.

Rehabilitation:

- As soon as pain allows, start level two rehabilitation exercises, and proceed accordingly.
- After surgery, level one exercises can begin in five days. For levels one, two, and three rehabilitation guidelines, refer to the sections on rehabilitation and conditioning at the end of this chapter 6.

Recovery time:

- In the cases of mild to moderate cases of tendinitis, the condition can take anywhere from four to six weeks to clear up.
- After surgery, the athlete can go back to sports within twelve to fourteen weeks.

PERONEAL TENDON SUBLUXATION

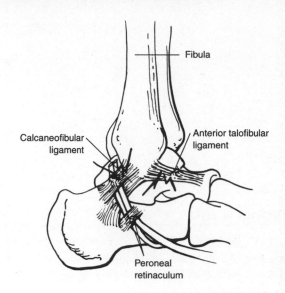

Subluxations of the tendons that run behind the outer ankle bone—the peroneal tendons—occur when the tendons slip forward in and out of the grooves through which they travel. This injury may begin after an athlete sustains an inversion sprain, because at the same time the sprain takes place, the peroneal retinaculum, the band of tissue that holds the tendons in place, may tear.

In the case of an acute dislocation, when the tendon does not return to its normal position, the injury responds well to immobilization for five to six weeks. Do not try to push the tendon back in place!

Symptoms:

- Pain behind the ankle bone when turning the foot upward and downward.
- Pain is especially acute when the tendon slips forward out of its groove and over the ankle bone.
- There may be direct pain when pressing on the tendon.
- The athlete can often make the subluxation happen by simultaneously turning the foot outward and bending upward, or by pressing the tendons from behind with the thumb.
- There should be no instability in the joint (this would signify a sprain).

Causes:

- Spending excessive time balancing on the outer edges of the feet may stretch the tendons out of shape.
- Subluxations occur more and more often as the peroneal tendons are stretched out of shape and slip back and forth over the ankle joint.
- The injury may occur because the peroneal retinaculum, the band of tissue that holds the tendons in place, get torn in an inversion strain.
- It may also be caused by a naturally shallow groove behind the outer ankle bone.

Athletes at risk:

- Primarily skiers and ice skaters, who spend an excessive amount of time balancing on the outer edges of the feet when trying to control motion.
- It is also seen in athletes who have sustained an inversion sprain, or those with a naturally shallow groove behind the ankle bone.

Concerns:

- The more often this injury occurs, the more the tendons get stretched, leading to a vicious cycle of recurrence.

What can you do:

- Seek medical attention, as surgery is usually required to correct this condition.

Medication:

- For relief of minor to moderate pain, take acetaminophen as directed on label, or, for the relief of pain *and* inflammation, ibuprofen or aspirin if tolerated (see page 49).

What the doctor can do:

- Surgery is usually required to correct a subluxing peroneal tendon.
- When the patient has a naturally narrow groove behind the ankle bone, it is surgically deepened by rasping out part of the tissue behind the ankle bone. Alternatively, the surgeon may decide to make the ankle bone larger by cutting out a portion of the bone and repositioning it so it juts out further.
- After surgery, the athlete is put in a cast or a splint for six weeks. He or she can start level three rehabilitation exercises after three weeks.

Rehabilitation:

- Three weeks after surgery, the athlete can begin level three rehabilitation exercises. For levels one, two, and three rehabilitation guidelines, refer to the section on rehabilitation and conditioning at the end of chapter 6.

Recovery time:

- The athlete can return to sports twelve to sixteen weeks after surgery.

PERONEAL TENDINITIS

Peroneal tendinitis is an inflammation of the tendon that runs behind the outer ankle bone.

Symptoms:

- Onset of symptoms is gradual.
- Pain and tenderness occur behind the outer ankle when running. Pain may radiate up the outer side of the lower leg.
- As the condition worsens, a creaking sensation (crepitus) develops in the area.

Causes:

- Overtraining is the main reason peroneal tendinitis develops, especially when there are sudden increases in the frequency, intensity, and/or duration of the athlete's training regimen. However, there are several other internal and external risk factors associated with this condition:

  Internal: anatomical abnormalities such as bowlegs or high arches that make an athlete run on the outside of the feet and therefore put excessive stress on the peroneal tendons;

strength and flexibility deficits, especially tight peroneal muscles.

External: Overly hard training surface, worn-out shoes, and shoes that rub against the tendon.

Athletes at risk:

- Runners, and especially those with anatomical abnormalities such as bowlegs and high arches.

Concerns:

- Unless treated early, this condition can deteriorate to the point where surgery becomes necessary.

What you can do:

- Withdraw from the activity that caused the condition for two weeks. Continue activities that do not aggravate the tendinitis.
- Ice the tendinitis for forty-eight to seventy-two hours, then apply moist heat.
- If high arches are causing the condition, obtain orthotics that support the arch and decrease the tendency to run on the outside of the feet.
- When all symptoms are gone, gradually return to running.

Medication:

- For relief of minor to moderate pain, take acetaminophen as directed on label, or, for the relief of pain *and* inflammation, ibuprofen or aspirin if tolerated (see page 49).

What the doctor can do:

- To correct the initial stages of pain and inflammation, the doctor should prescribe RICE, followed by a conditioning program to develop strength and flexibility in the muscles, outlined at the end of chapter 6.

Rehabilitation:

- Level three rehabilitation exercises can begin as soon as the initial pain abates—ideally, within forty-eight to seventy-two hours. For levels one, two, and three rehabilitation guidelines, refer to the sections on rehabilitation and conditioning at the end of chapter 6.

Recovery time:

- With the appropriate treatment, condition should clear up within four to six weeks.

OSTEOCHONDRITIS DISSECANS OF THE ANKLE
(Loose Bodies in the Joint)

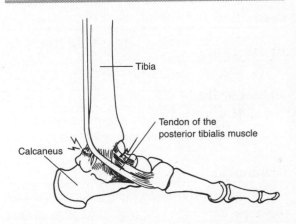

Tibia

Tendon of the posterior tibialis muscle

Calcaneus

Repetitive twists and turns of the ankle during exercise can cause the ends of the bones that form the ankle joint to bump together, particularly the larger of the lower leg bones, the tibia, and the talus bone. This can create a small crater in the talus with pieces of bone and cartilage around it—rather like a divot in the ground caused by a missed golf stroke. This condition is known as osteochondritis dissecans. Osteochondritis refers to the damage caused by the friction, while dissecans means there are loose pieces around the crater. If the stress continues, bone and cartilage may break off and fall into the joint.

In adults, the ends of the bones bumping together may cause divots, though it is rare that pieces of bone and cartilage actually dislodge and fall into the joint. But in children, whose joint surfaces are much softer because they are made up of bone that is growing and not yet hardened, there is a much greater chance that a portion of bone and cartilage can dislodge and fall into the joint. Children between the ages of twelve and sixteen are especially at risk because of the relative softness of the ends of their bones.

Symptoms:

- Onset of symptoms is gradual, usually taking place over a period of three to six months.
- Pain and swelling are felt during exercise, both of which may intensify afterward. The ankle often stiffens after sports activity.
- There is no loss of range of motion or instability.
- If the fragment has detached, the joint may occasionally lock.

Cause:

- Repetitive bumping together of the ends of the tibia and talus bones.

Athletes at risk:

- Basketball and volleyball players, as well as ballet dancers, although any athlete can be at risk.

Concerns:

- Ignoring this condition will allow a simple divot to deteriorate to the point where pieces of bone and cartilage break off and fall into the joint, which almost always requires surgery if the athlete wants to continue in sports.

What you can do:

- Cease the activity that caused the condition, or any activity that aggravates it.
- Seek medical attention.

Medication:

- For relief of minor to moderate pain, take acetaminophen as directed on label, or, for the relief of pain *and* inflammation, ibuprofen or aspirin if tolerated (see page 49).

What the doctor can do:

- Confirm the diagnosis with an X ray, CAT scan, MRI, or bone scan.
- If no fragments have detached, the doctor may immobilize the ankle for four to eight weeks to allow the damage to repair itself.

- If the symptoms continue for more than six months, surgery may be considered:

  Either an open procedure or arthroscopy is done. If the fragment is small, simple removal is sufficient, after which tiny holes are drilled in the crater to stimulate regrowth of the bone cartilage. If the fragment is larger than half an inch across, it will be necessary to pin it back in place to ensure the joint works properly.

  If drilling alone is done, the ankle is immobilized for five to seven days. When a fragment is pinned in place, the athlete should avoid weight-bearing activity for six weeks.

Rehabilitation:

- If the condition is handled nonsurgically, level two rehabilitation exercises can start as soon as pain abates.
- After surgery to remove loose fragments and/or drill holes in the crater, level one exercises can start five to seven days after the procedure. If a large fragment is pinned in place, level one exercises should begin in three weeks. For levels one, two, and three rehabilitation guidelines, refer to the sections on rehabilitation and conditioning at the end of chapter 6.

Recovery time:

- Nonoperative recovery time: six weeks or more.
- After surgical removal of fragments and/or drilling: eight to twelve weeks.
- After fixation of a large fragment: eight to twelve weeks.

Ankle Rehabilitation and Conditioning

For rehabilitation and condition of the ankle, refer to the sections on rehabilitation and conditioning at the end of chapter 6, "Foot Injuries" (pages 88–91).

CHAPTER EIGHT

Lower Leg Injuries

Considering how much stress the lower leg undergoes in sports, it is not surprising that this part of the body is the site of so many athletic injuries. Not only do the muscles of the lower leg have to generate many of the forces necessary for explosive motions in sports ranging from football to tennis, but the tissues are also subject to the repetitive microtrauma transmitted from the foot to the lower leg during activities such as distance running and aerobics.

Acute injuries to the lower leg such as fractures are common, and are frequently seen in adult recreational athletes. Fractures occur in sports with a potential for falling accidents, especially skiing, and muscle and tendon strains are frequently seen in any sport that requires powerful contractions of the calf muscles.

More common than acute leg injuries, though, are overuse conditions. Overuse injuries in the lower leg are among the most common in sports. They may also be among the most difficult injuries to treat; in large part because of misdiagnosis of many conditions as "shinsplints." Confusion over what shinsplints really are has traditionally prevented effective treatment of many conditions (see box on page 112).

Injuries to the Lower Leg

Acute lower leg injuries include bone fractures, muscle strains, and tendon strains.

Acute lower leg injuries may be caused by direct impact from an opponent, as well as a direct fall onto the leg. These may result in a fracture of the tibia, fibula,

or both. A fracture is a crack, break, or complete shattering of the bone.

The most common acute injuries in the lower leg are muscle and tendon strains caused by forceful contractions of the muscle-tendon units. A strain is a stretch, tear, or complete rupture of the muscle or tendon fibers. Strains are classified in order of severity: first degree (tearing of less than 25 percent of the fibers); second degree (tearing of between 25 and 75 percent of the fibers); or third degree (a complete rupture of the fibers—the muscle or tendon is completely torn in two).

In the lower leg, strains usually occur in either the calf muscles or the Achilles tendon; this muscle-tendon unit is especially vulnerable to strains because it spans two joints.

Lower leg overuse injuries include tendinitis of the Achilles tendon, as well as a variety of disorders traditionally lumped together under the heading "shinsplints," but which may include conditions as varied as stress fractures of the bones, compartment syndromes, tendinitis of the sheath of the tibialis interior muscle, and inflammation of the connective tissue that covers the shinbone (periostitis).

Lower leg overuse injuries are caused by excessive sports activity, especially among unconditioned athletes. In addition to overtraining, there are a host of underlying internal and external risk factors that may increase the likelihood that an athlete will develop an overuse injury.

Internal risk factors usually involve deficits in strength and/or flexibility in the muscles, tendons, and other soft tissues, such as the fascial walls of the muscle compartments and the periosteum of the tibia. For instance, a runner is much more likely to develop Achilles tendinitis if the Achilles tendons are inflexible.

Anatomical abnormalities are another internal risk factor that predispose athletes to overuse conditions in the lower leg. For instance, an athlete whose feet turn in (pronate) when he or she runs is more likely to develop pain in the front of the lower leg because of the contortions the lower leg has to perform to run in a straight line. These athletes may benefit from orthotics (see page 122). For more on anatomical abnormalities and the lower leg, see pages 70–72, 123.

Posterior tibial tendinitis, another condition grouped under the umbrella term, *shinsplints,* occurs most often in runners with flat feet. Part of the role of the posterior tibial muscle is to provide the arch of the foot with support, and in athletes with flat feet, that muscle and its tendon have to work extra hard to support the arch and prevent the heel from turning in. The pain occurs along the inner side of the shin.

External factors may include training errors—dramatically increasing the intensity of the training regimen and/or not warming up before running. The training surface also plays a major role in the incidence of overuse injury. Running on a tarmac road surface is much harder on the lower extremities than running on grass, and the runner who changes from a softer to a harder surface is often at risk of developing pain in the front of the lower leg. Running regularly on a banked surface (an indoor track or roadway), running hills, or exercising on a surface with little shock absorbency can lead to both Achilles tendinitis and pain in the front of the lower legs.

Another important external risk factor that can cause overuse injuries in the lower legs is inappropriate footwear. Worn-out athletic shoes that have lost their cushioning or shoes that allow the athlete to pronate are often to blame.

Athletes who do not structure their workouts properly are at increased risk of developing overuse injuries. Tight calf muscles and Achilles tendons behind the leg and tight muscles in front of the lower leg can cause Achilles tendinitis and pain in the front of the lower leg, respectively.

Preventing Lower Leg Injuries

Acute lower leg injuries such as muscle and tendon strains can be prevented by developing strength and flexibility in the muscles and tendons of the lower leg, and especially the calf muscles. To protect against painful contusions to the vulnerable shinbones, which frequently occur in soccer, shin guards should be worn.

A disproportionate number of lower leg fractures are seen in downhill skiers. Appropriate ski boots and bindings are essential for preventing fractures in the lower leg. Bindings are designed to release before unusual stresses are transmitted to the leg. They should not release under normal skiing forces.

The American Orthopedic Society for Sports Medicine has developed the following information to provide skiers with guidelines on skiing safety.

Ski boot bindings: The decrease in ski boot binding–related injuries (when the ski binding fails to release properly or releases at the wrong time) can be attributed to improved binding systems. However, nearly 50 percent of all injuries remain related to improper binding performance.

Bindings should release before reaching the point where excess stresses pass from the ski through the binding and boot to the leg. They should not release under normal skiing forces.

Some bindings have a multidirectional release—they open in any direction the skier might fall. But the more release flexibility created, the more likely the boot will release during normal skiing maneuvers.

Most bindings have a side-to-side, or twist, release capability at the toe and a forward-lean mechanism at the heel. They protect the leg from most falls. However, they do not protect against backward falls or those requiring twist at the heel and roll or shear from the top of the ski.

A few bindings incorporate several of these modes. But they are unpopular among many skiers because they often release inadvertently.

Beginners, who tend to fall frequently, should choose multimode release systems. This type of binding is also recommended for skiers who have sustained lower extremity injuries.

Skiers often set their bindings higher to avoid unwanted release of their bindings. This greatly increases the risk of injury. The cause of unwanted release is rarely low binding setting. Usually the cause is boot and binding incompatibility, poor binding design, mechanical failure of the binding, or failure to clear snow, ice, or mud from the boot or binding.

Binding technology has markedly improved. Skiers should avoid old or used equipment; not only is it outdated in mechanical design but often it has been poorly maintained.

Binding function changes with time and wear. Skiers should ensure that their equipment is well maintained. Before each season, have a reputable ski store give bindings a thorough mechanical check. An active skier may need more frequent evaluations.

It is important to keep boots, bindings, and skis clean. Avoid wearing ski boots on surfaces other than snow. Debris ground into the sole increases friction and, with wear, may alter the shape of the boot and impair proper binding function.

Testing bindings before skiing is a good habit. Before going to the slopes, test bindings in each release direction. Do this with slow twisting and leaning motions, using muscle control rather than sudden shocks or thrusts. If leg pain is felt before the binding releases, something is wrong. Do not ski with such bindings.

These self-release checks ensure that the binding mechanism is not jammed and that the release settings have not varied. Cycling the binding distributes lubricants and minimizes corrosion within the binding. Testing the self-release mechanism is important, but this alone is insufficient to assure proper binding function in a skiing accident.

Boots: Be certain that the boot purchased is comfortable and can be tolerated for a long time. Keep the boot tightly buckled when walking about the store, and simulate skiing motions for as long as possible. This should reveal any pressure points between foot and boot.

The usual response to pressure point pain is to loosen the boot. However, this can cause a dangerous reduction in ski control. Do not try to save money by accepting used boots that do not fit properly.

If pressure point pain occurs, go to a full-service ski shop. Shop technicians can stretch the boot's shell or modify and pad the boot's inner lining to improve fit. More experienced skiers can find instruction in popular skiing magazines on how to modify boots.

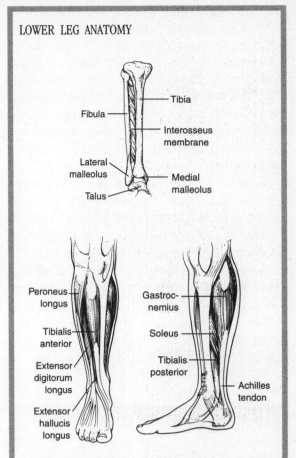

LOWER LEG ANATOMY

Bones and joints: The lower leg is made up of two bones, the *tibia* and *fibula,* which connect the ankle to the knee. These two bones are joined lengthwise by a strong sheet of fibrous tissue called the *interosseus membrane.*

Muscles: There are four muscles in the front, outer side of the lower leg. Two of these muscles bend the foot upward (foot flexion), and the other two straighten the toes (toe extension).

The five muscles behind the lower leg, known as the calf muscles, perform the opposite function—they allow one to point the foot outward (foot extension) and to curl the toes inward (toe flexion). The two largest calf muscles are the *gastrocnemius* and *soleus.*

The muscles of the lower leg are contained within four "compartments" whose walls are made up of heavy fascial tissue.

Skis: Reduce the risk of skiing injury by using ski brakes. Beginning skiers should use relatively short skis because they are easier to control than longer ones.

Ski poles: Holding on to the pole during an accident increases the likelihood of thumb injury. Consider using a ski pole that is designed to leave the hand immediately when released. Use ski poles that can be readily discarded, or avoid placing hands through the strap in a way that would keep the ski pole attached to the hand during the fall.

See chapter 2 for a discussion of the roles of coaching, experience, and attitude in preventing skiing accidents.

Overuse injuries of the lower leg are most effectively prevented by addressing the well-established internal and external risk factors associated with overuse injuries of the lower extremities (see pages 70, 123). The following measures should be taken to address these risk factors:

Have a presports physical to correct any muscle weaknesses and imbalances, as well as anatomical abnormalities that increase the risk of injury.

Engage in a strength and flexibility program for the lower legs, focusing on the muscles of the calf and the Achilles tendon.

Avoid training errors, especially rapid increases in the intensity, frequency, and duration of training, and excessive training on hard surfaces, hills, and banked surfaces.

Structure the workout properly so it includes a proper warm-up and cooldown.

Wear appropriate footwear, and change shoes when midsoles or heels lose their cushioning, typically within 500 miles. Running shoes with rigid heel counters are best for preventing Achilles tendinitis because they reduce ankle pronation and excessive pressure being placed on the heel. For a thorough discussion of athletic footwear, see chapter 6.

Refer to chapter 2, "Preventing Sports Injuries," for a comprehensive guide to addressing the risk factors associated with overuse injuries.

Acute Lower Leg Injuries

FRACTURES OF THE TIBIA AND FIBULA

A fracture of the tibia and/or fibula is a crack, break, or complete shattering of one or both of the lower leg bones. The injury is more serious if both bones get fractured, and especially if the ends of the broken bones penetrate the skin (an open fracture). For more on the different kinds of fractures, refer to pages 65–66.

Symptoms:

- Intense, immediate pain in the lower leg.
- Deformity in the area of the injury.
- Disability in the injured leg.
- Crunching sound and sensation (crepitus) when the ends of the broken bones rub together.

Cause:

- A direct blow to the lower leg, or a twist or bend when the foot is planted firmly on the ground.

Athletes at risk:

- Primarily downhill skiers, as well as athletes in contact sports.

Concerns:

- Unless treated properly, broken lower leg bones may heal in a way that causes long-term dysfunction. Even when proper techniques are used, these bones often do not heal in a stable fashion.
- Any fracture in which the ends of the broken bones pierce the surface of the skin can lead to extremely serious infections unless proper steps are taken to keep the wound clean.

What you can do:

- Send for immediate medical attention.
- Splint the lower leg in the position it was found.
- Gently apply ice over the area until medical help arrives.

What the doctor can do:

- Rule out disruption to the nerves and blood supply.
- X-ray the injury to confirm the diagnosis and the extent of injury.
- Fractures in the lower leg are managed surgically if the bones are displaced or unstable. A metal rod is inserted down the middle of the bone, which is then fixed in place with screws above and below the fracture site. A cast may not be needed for this type of surgery. If the rod is bothersome, it may be removed eighteen months later. Otherwise, it is left inside.
- After surgery, the athlete uses crutches for six weeks until full weight bearing can start. Running may start in three months.

Rehabilitation:

- Level one exercises can begin immediately after surgery, as long as pain allows. For levels one, two, and three rehabilitation guidelines, refer to the sections on rehabilitation and conditioning in chapter 6.

Recovery time:

- After fracturing the lower leg, the athlete should wait six months before returning to contact sports or those with a potential for injury.

CALF STRAIN

A strain in the calf muscles—defined as a stretch, tear, or complete rupture of the muscle fibers—usually occurs at the point where the gastrocnemius muscle (the inner calf muscle) meets the Achilles tendon.

As with all strains, calf strains are classified according to their severity: first degree (tearing of less than 25 percent of the fibers); second degree (tearing of between 25 and 75 percent of the fibers); or third degree (a complete rupture of the fibers; the muscle is completely torn in two—very rare).

Symptoms:

- Symptoms depend on the severity of the injury, and range from mild to severe.
- First degree: mild pain and tenderness in the affected area, often described as a "twinge"—frequently not felt until the day after the injury occurs.
- Second degree: a stabbing pain in the calf is felt immediately after the injury occurs. Damage to the muscle fibers may cause visible discoloration beneath the skin within twenty-four hours. It is usually difficult to use the muscle normally; the athlete may find it difficult to stand on tiptoe, and may limp when walking.

Causes:

- Massive contraction of the calf muscles, especially when decelerating. This injury frequently occurs when an athlete makes a quick stop by planting the foot flat on the ground, then suddenly straightening the knee.
- Calf strains are more likely to occur when there is:
  - inadequate warm-up
  - cold temperatures
  - previous injury—the presence of scar tissue in the muscle limits flexibility
  - flexibility deficits—the Achilles tendon is tight

Athletes at risk:

- Those engaged in sports with frequent stop-start and jumping requirements, including tennis, squash, volleyball, and basketball.

Concerns:

- Unless rehabilitated properly, excess scar tissue builds up in the calf muscle, which makes the muscle less pliable and therefore more likely to be reinjured.

What you can do:

- Athletes can treat first-degree calf strains themselves. RICE (see page 46) is the cornerstone

of self-treatment for muscle strains, and should continue for forty-eight to seventy-two hours. Return to sports only when there is absolutely no pain or tenderness when the muscle is tensed or stretched, and when there is complete and pain-free range of motion in the ankle and knee. Engage in a strength and flexibility program to reduce the risk of reinjury.
- Second- and third-degree calf strains require medical attention.

Medication:

- For relief of minor to moderate pain, take acetaminophen as directed on label, or, for the relief of pain *and* inflammation, ibuprofen or aspirin if tolerated (see page 49).

What the doctor can do:

- For second-degree muscle strains, RICE is used in the first week following injury, followed by a progressive stretching and strengthening program for the injured calf muscle. Surgery is rarely necessary for second-degree strains.

Rehabilitation:

- After first-degree calf muscle strains, begin level three rehabilitation exercises one to two days after the injury, building up quickly toward a conditioning program to develop strength and flexibility in the muscle group.
- After a second-degree muscle strain, start level one or two rehabilitation exercises, depending on pain, within a week of the injury. For levels one, two, and three rehabilitation guidelines, refer to the sections on rehabilitation and conditioning in chapter 6.

Recovery time:

- First-degree strains: three to five days.
- Second-degree strains: two to four weeks.

ACHILLES TENDON STRAIN

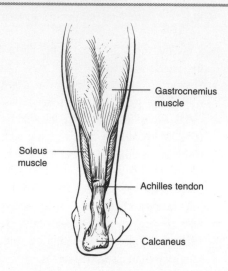

Gastrocnemius muscle

Soleus muscle

Achilles tendon

Calcaneus

A strain of the Achilles tendon is a stretch, tear, or complete rupture of the thick tendon that runs down the back of the lower leg from the calf muscles to the heel. Complete ruptures are the bane of athletes older than thirty years of age, whose muscles are naturally weaker and less flexible, especially if they are not regularly active.

Symptoms:

- A "snap" in the back of the lower leg, and then intense pain. The sensation is sometimes compared to being hit in the back of the leg. It is impossible to walk normally, stand on tiptoe, or bend the foot downward. Discoloration develops over the rupture, usually one to two inches above the heel. A gap can be felt in the tendon. The athlete will have a positive Thompson's test: while the athlete lies on the stomach, the doctor squeezes the calf muscles; a positive result is when the heel does not move.

Causes:

- Massive contraction of the calf muscles that stretches the Achilles tendon beyond its tolerance.
- Achilles tendon strains are more likely to occur when there is:
  inadequate warm-up
  cold temperature

previous injury—the presence of scar tissue limits elasticity

strength and flexibility imbalances—the tendon is weak and/or inflexible compared to the calf muscle

Athletes at risk:

- Those in sports with frequent stop-start and jumping movements.
- Complete ruptures are more common in athletes over thirty because of the natural degenerative process that takes place in the tendons beginning between the ages of twenty-five and thirty.

Concerns:

- Blood supply to the tendons is quite poor, so Achilles tendon strains are notoriously slow healers. Therefore, athletes often get frustrated with the lengthy healing process and return to sports before the injury is fully healed and rehabilitated. This predisposes them to reinjury.

What you can do:

- Athletes can treat first-degree strains themselves. RICE (see page 46) is the cornerstone of treatment.
- If pain is severe, use crutches or half-inch heel wedges to avoid stressing the tendon.
- It is advisable to seek professional treatment from a sports doctor because of the troublesome nature of tendon strains. Always seek professional treatment for second- and third-degree strains, particularly if there is difficulty standing on toes.

Medication:

- For relief of minor to moderate pain, take acetaminophen as directed on label, or, for the relief of pain *and* inflammation, ibuprofen or aspirin if tolerated (see page 49).

What the doctor can do:

- There are two ways to treat an Achilles strain: with surgery or without.

- Nonoperatively: the ankle is immobilized in a cast for six weeks with the foot in slight plantar flexion—the toes pointing downward—so the Achilles tendon has a chance to heal.
- Surgical treatment: the ends of the torn tendon are stitched together.
- Surgery may also be performed if the Achilles tendon has been repeatedly torn and there is a buildup of scar tissue.
- After surgery to stitch the ends of the tendon together, the patient may be put in a cast for six to eight weeks, and then put on a comprehensive physical therapy program.
- Studies have shown that surgery yields better results because the healing process after surgery produces less scar tissue; the tendon is less susceptible to reinjury because it is stronger and more flexible.

Rehabilitation:

- Whether immobilization or surgery is used to treat an Achilles strain, level one rehabilitation exercises should start as soon as the cast is removed after six weeks. For levels one, two, and three rehabilitation guidelines, refer to the sections on rehabilitation and conditioning in chapter 6.

Recovery time:

- After a severe Achilles tendon strain, the athlete can return to full activity after six to eight months.

Overuse Injuries of the Lower Leg

ACHILLES TENDINITIS

Achilles tendinitis is an inflammation of the thick tendon that connects the calf muscles to the heel. The inflammation is a response to the series of microtears in the tendon caused by repetitive stretching of the tendon. Because blood supply to this tendon is poor, Achilles tendinitis is extremely difficult to overcome, which reinforces the need to respect early symptoms. Too often, athletes try to "run through" the pain. Achilles tendinitis is especially common in athletes over thirty because of the degenerative changes that take place in the tendons beginning between the ages of twenty-five and thirty, which make them tighter and weaker.

Symptoms:

- Onset of symptoms is gradual.
- Pain occurs with use, and there may be swelling over the tendon.
- As the condition worsens, there may be redness over the tendon.
- There may be a creaking sensation (crepitus) in the tendon, which can be felt with the fingers when the ankle is bent backward and forward.
- If the athlete ignores the condition, the following symptoms may develop:

    Pain, aching, and stiffness before, during, and after exercise.

    The tendon may become tender to the touch.

    Pain intensifies during uphill walking or climbing stairs.

Causes:

- Repetitive contractions of the calf muscles that cause microtears in the tendon.
- Overuse is the major cause of this condition (especially sudden increases in training frequency, intensity, and/or duration), although there may be other predisposing conditions, including:

    Internal: Tight, weak calf muscles or Achilles tendons, anatomical abnormalities such as

high arches (clawfoot) or overpronating feet (excessive rolling inward).

    External: Worn-out footwear, overly hard or banked training surface, cold weather.

Athletes at risk:

- Primarily distance runners, especially those with the above risk factors.

Concerns:

- Unless caught early on, this condition is extremely difficult to overcome.

What you can do:

- Cease the activity that caused the condition, and initiate twenty-minute ice massage sessions for forty-eight to seventy-two hours.
- After seventy-two hours, begin moist heat treatments and use a neoprene heat retainer (available at most drug stores).
- Seven to ten days after the initial symptoms, begin the stretching and strengthening program outlined in chapter 6.
- Wear shoes with a half-inch heel wedge to relieve tension on the tendon (wear the lifts in both shoes to avoid problems arising from unequal leg lengths).
- Continue cardiovascular activities that do not stress the Achilles tendon, such as swimming and cycling.
- Seek medical attention if the condition does not clear up within two weeks.
- After going back to running, stretch before exercise and ice the tendon afterward if there is pain.
- Address the risk factors that may be causing the condition (see chapters 2, 6).

Medication:

- For relief of minor to moderate pain, take acetaminophen as directed on label, or, for the relief of pain *and* inflammation, ibuprofen or aspirin if tolerated (see page 49).

What the doctor can do:

- If there is any question about the diagnosis, order an MRI.
- Prescribe rest, ice for the first forty-eight to seventy-two hours, then heat treatments.
- Try to determine the exact cause of the condition (see above, "Causes"). If the cause is tightness and/or weakness in the muscles and tendon, prescribe a conditioning program to develop strength and flexibility in the tissues. If the cause is anatomical abnormalities, recommend orthotics (page 122) to correct the problem (often, store-bought leather longitudinal arch supports are all that is needed; in athletes with more severe or complex foot deformities, custom-made, rigid orthotics may be needed). If the athlete's footwear is to blame, recommend a better shoe.
- Heel wedges may be given to relieve stress on the tendon.
- If the condition is severe, the doctor may put the athlete in a cast for three to six weeks.
- If the condition persists for more than two to three months, surgery may be considered:
    The doctor will cut open the end of the tendon's sheath to give it more room, then trim off the inflamed tissue from the tendon.
- *Cortisone injections are not recommended for Achilles tendinitis, as they weaken the tendon and cause it to rupture.*

Rehabilitation:

- If the treatment is treated nonoperatively, conditioning exercises for the lower leg should begin as soon as pain allows.
- After surgery, level one rehabilitation exercises should start one week after the procedure. For levels one, two, and three rehabilitation guidelines, refer to the sections on rehabilitation and conditioning in chapter 6.

Recovery time:

- If caught early and the cause of the condition is addressed, Achilles tendinitis can clear up within one to two weeks. However, chronic con-

ditions may take up to six months to overcome, and often will not clear up at all unless surgery is performed.

MEDIAL TIBIAL PAIN SYNDROME *(Periostitis of the Shinbone)*

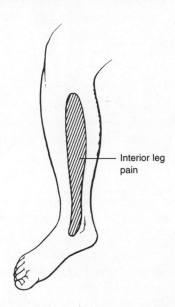

Interior leg pain

Pain in the lower leg, once diagnosed as shinsplints, is now more properly referred to as medial tibial pain syndrome. When it is not caused by compartment syndrome or stress fractures, pain on the inner side of the lower leg is usually the result of inflammation of the tissue that covers the tibia. In the lower leg, inflammation of this tissue, known as periosteum, is called tibial periostitis.

Symptoms:

- Onset of symptoms is gradual.
- Pain, tenderness, and possibly swelling on the inner side of the shin, especially pronounced over the bottom half of the lower leg.
- Pain can be triggered when the toes or ankle are bent downwards against resistance.
- Pain abates when the athlete is at rest, but returns with running and jumping activities. When allowed to deteriorate, the condition is eventually felt before, during, and after activity

SHINSPLINTS—AN OUTDATED DIAGNOSIS

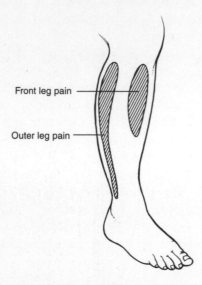

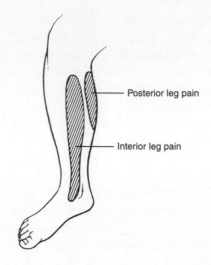

The term "shinsplints" has traditionally been used to describe any chronic, exercise-related lower leg pain. This designation may encompass several quite different conditions, including inflammation of the tissue that covers the shinbone, stress fractures of either of the lower leg bones, and compartment syndromes that may affect any of the four muscle compartments in the lower leg. Although athletes still use the term *shinsplints,* it is no longer used by sports doctors because it is too vague. Pain in the lower leg is now placed in three different categories, medial tibila (inner shinbone) pain syndrome, compartment syndromes, and stress fractures. The symptoms of these conditions may be felt in the inner side, outer side, front, or back of the lower leg.

Pain in the inner side of the leg is generally caused by inflammations of the tissue that covers the tibia (periostitis), inflammation of the tibial posterior muscle-tendon, stress fractures of the tibia or fibula, or posterior compartment syndrome.

Pain at the front of the lower leg is usually either anterior compartment syndrome or stress fracture. Pain at the outer side of the lower leg is usually lateral compartment syndrome stress fracture.

Pain behind the leg is uually posterior superficial compartment syndrome.

Depending on whether the condition is tendinitis, periostitis, a stress fracture, or a compartment syndrome, the symptoms, cause, diagnosis, treatment, and rehabilitation of each of these conditions are usually quite different.

It is important that athletes with pain in the front of the lower leg find out exactly what is causing the pain. Unless athletes can obtain an accurate diagnosis of lower leg pain, they will have difficulty overcoming their particular condition because the proper cause and treatment will be unknown.

Causes:

- Repetitive pounding of the feet.
- Overuse is the main cause of this condition, especially when there are sudden changes in the frequency, intensity, or duration of the athlete's training regimen.
- Other predisposing conditions may contribute. Internal: tight, weak calf muscles and Achilles tendons, improper running technique (running on the toes), and anatomical abnormalities (inward-rolling knees, high arches).

- External: changes in training surface (usually softer to harder), changing shoe type, and wearing worn-out shoes.

Athletes at risk:

- Those engaged in running sports, or any activities that involve the feet pounding against a hard surface, including aerobics, basketball, and volleyball.

Concerns:

- This condition can become chronic and thus difficult to clear up.

What you can do:

- Cease the activity that caused the condition. Continue or begin nonweight-bearing cardiovascular activities such as swimming, cross-country skiing simulators, and stationary biking (when cycling, the foot should be positioned so the *heel* is over the pedal, not the forefoot.)
- Use RICE (page 46) for the first forty-eight to seventy-two hours the symptoms are felt, and heat thereafter.
- Rest until there is absolutely no pain on the inner side of the lower leg when running, and no tenderness to the touch.
- When running is resumed, do so on a soft surface (ideally grass), wear appropriate footwear, and cut the frequency, intensity, and duration of the training regimen by half, building back to the original training regimen over six weeks.
- If the symptoms persist for two weeks despite the above measures, seek medical attention.

Medication:

- For relief of minor to moderate pain, take acetaminophen as directed on label, or, for the relief of pain *and* inflammation, ibuprofen or aspirin if tolerated (see page 49).

What the doctor can do:

- Prescribe RICE for forty-eight to seventy-two hours, then heat treatments with a physical therapist.
- Prescribe anti-inflammatories for two weeks.
- Rule out stress fractures and compartment syndromes.
- Try to ascertain the exact cause of the condition (see above, ''Causes''). If the cause is tightness and/or weakness in the calf muscles and Achilles tendon, prescribe a conditioning program to develop strength and flexibility in the tissues. If the cause is anatomical abnormalities, recommend orthotics (page 122) to correct the problem (often, store-bought leather longitudinal arch supports are all that is needed; for athletes with more severe or complex foot deformities, custom-made, rigid orthotics may be needed). If the athlete's footwear is to blame, recommend a better shoe.
- If the condition persists, administer a cortisone injection under the periosteum.
- If the pain does not go away, surgery may be done to separate the periosteum from the inner side of the shinbone.

Rehabilitation:

- When nonsurgical treatment is used, level three rehabilitation exercises should start as soon as pain allows.
- After surgery, level one exercises should start within twenty-four to forty-eight hours of the procedure. For levels one, two, and three rehabilitation guidelines, refer to the sections on rehabilitation and conditioning in chapter 6.

Recovery time:

- If caught early, the condition will clear up within one to two weeks. However, chronic conditions may take as long as six months to resolve, and sometimes may not clear up at all unless surgery is performed.

STRESS FRACTURES OF THE TIBIA AND FIBULA

A stress fracture is a series of microfractures caused by repetitive, low-grade trauma seen in activities such as running, dancing, and aerobics. There have been two theories proposed to explain how stress fractures actually develop.

Fatigue theory: When tired, the muscles cannot support the skeleton as well as they can when they are not tired. During running activities that exhaust the muscles, therefore, increased load is passed on to the bones. When their tolerance is exceeded, tiny cracks appear in the bone's surface.

Overload theory: Muscles contract in such a way that they pull on the bone. For instance, the contraction of the calf muscles causes the tibia to bend forward like a drawn bow. The backward and forward bending of the bone can cause cracks to appear in the front of the tibia.

When the stress fracture takes place in the tibia, it occurs in the top two-thirds of that bone. In the fibula, stress fractures usually take place two or three inches above the lateral malleolus (the outer ankle bone).

Thinner bones are at greater risk of sustaining stress fractures, and because one of the side effects of irregular menstruation is bone thinning, girls and women with eating disorders and menstrual irregularities are at greater risk of these overuse injuries. For more on the relationship between eating disorders, menstrual irregularities, and stress fractures, refer to chapter 19, "Sports Medicine Concerns of Female Athletes."

Symptoms:

- Onset of symptoms is gradual, though they may occasionally develop after a sudden increase in the intensity, frequency, or duration of an athlete's training regimen.
- When the stress fracture is in the tibia, pain and highly localized tenderness is usually felt at the top third of the front of the leg. When the stress fracture is in the fibula, the same symptoms are felt just above the ankle bone on the outside of the leg.
- Pain is especially intense during running and jumping activities, and abates at rest.
- It may be difficult to differentiate the pain from soft tissue pain such as that of a tibial periostitis

(see page 000). There are two ways to tell if the pain is caused by a stress fracture. First, firmly tap the tibia or fibula above the point of tenderness; the vibration in the bone will travel to the fracture itself and be felt only at that point (in a soft tissue injury, the pain is more spread out). Second, have someone tap the underside of the heel of the affected leg; again, the vibration will travel to the stress fracture site.

Causes:

- There are two theories to explain why stress fractures occur: the fatigue theory and the overload theory (see above).
- Overuse is the main cause of this condition, although there may be several predisposing conditions:

    Internal: tight calf muscles and Achilles tendons; anatomical abnormalities (such as feet that roll inward (pronate), flat feet, high arches, and leg length inequalities); and bone thinness brought on by menstrual abnormalities and dietary deficits.

    External: changes in training surface (usually softer to harder), changing shoe type, and wearing worn-out shoes.

Athletes at risk:

- Distance runners (who generally sustain the stress fracture in the lower third of the lower leg), ballet dancers (who generally sustain the injury in the midthird of the lower leg), and anyone who trains on hard surfaces.
- Girls and women with eating disorders and menstrual irregularities are at greater risk of sustaining stress fractures (see chapter 19).

Concerns:

- If allowed to deteriorate, stress fractures can lead to complete fractures.

What you can do:

- Cease the activity that caused the condition and use the RICE prescription (page 46).
- If the symptoms described above are present, or if pain lasts for longer than two weeks despite RICE, seek medical attention.

Medication:

- For relief of minor to moderate pain, take acetaminophen as directed on label, or, for the relief of pain *and* inflammation, ibuprofen or aspirin if tolerated (see page 49).

What the doctor can do:

- Confirm the diagnosis with X rays or a bone scan. Bone scans are more effective than X rays, as the visible changes that take place on the surface of the bone are not visible on X rays until several weeks after the actual damage occurs (in medical parlance, they are "occult").
- If the diagnosis is confirmed, the doctor may recommend six weeks' rest from activity that involves repetitive impact to the legs, especially running. The doctor should encourage nonweight-bearing cardiovascular activities such as swimming, cross-country skiing simulators, and stationary biking.
- The doctor should also try to determine if there are any predisposing factors. If training errors are the reason, a more realistic schedule should be recommended. If the underlying cause of the condition is anatomical abnormalities, the doctor may prescribe shoe inserts. If the athlete has tight calf muscles and Achilles tendons, the doctor should refer the athlete to a physical therapist for a stretching program. If the athlete is a girl or woman with an eating disorder or menstrual irregularities, she should be referred to a sports nutritionist.
- After six weeks, and at least two weeks of being pain free, the doctor can recommend the athlete resume running.

Rehabilitation:

- Level three exercises can begin immediately, with a special emphasis on stretching the calf muscles and Achilles tendons. For levels one, two, and three rehabilitation guidelines, refer to the sections on rehabilitation and conditioning at the end of chapter 6.

Recovery time:

- Stress fractures of the tibia and fibula will take three weeks to heal, although the athlete should not return to the chosen activity for at least six weeks, and two pain-free weeks.

ANTERIOR COMPARTMENT SYNDROME

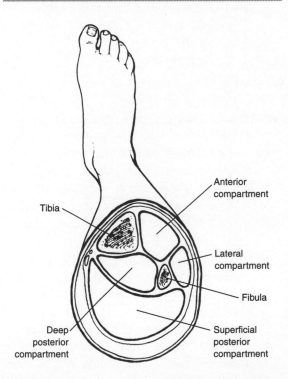

The muscles in the lower leg are encased in four different "compartments" with heavy membranous walls. Excessive training can make certain of these muscle groups too large for their compartments. At rest, there is no problem, but when the athlete uses the muscles in the lower legs during exercise, the muscles swell with blood. This causes pressure inside the compartments, which com-

presses the muscles and nerves within the compartment, and produces the characteristic symptoms of compartment syndrome. This condition can occur in any of the compartments, although it is most often seen in the anterior compartment.

Symptoms:

- Onset of consistent symptoms is gradual, though occasional symptoms may be extremely intense.
- An ache, sharp pain, or pressure in the front of the lower leg is experienced during sports activity. The symptoms completely abate when the activity is halted.
- When the condition deteriorates, there may be weakness when trying to bend the foot and toes upward, and pain when the foot and toes are bent downward using the hands. Numbness may be experienced in the top of the foot and in between the big toe and second toe. It will become impossible to exercise for extended periods.

Causes:

- Training causes muscles to enlarge, and these muscles can sometimes become too big for the membranous compartments in which they are encased. At rest, there is no problem, but when the athlete exercises, the muscles get "pumped up" and increase the pressure in the compartments.
- Overuse is the main cause, although certain athletes may be predisposed to this condition because their compartment walls are naturally tight.
- Other predisposing factors include changes in training surface (usually softer to harder), changing footwear, and wearing worn-out shoes.

Athletes at risk:

- Primarily distance runners, though condition can affect any athlete who engages in a sport with extensive demands of the lower extremities.

WHEN A COMPARTMENT SYNDROME IS AN EMERGENCY

Compartment syndrome is usually caused by overuse. However, it can also occur as a result of serious bleeding inside the muscles caused by a traumatic accident—e.g., when the tibia gets fractured, when the muscle completely ruptures, or when the leg is kicked and severely bruised. This causes the muscles to swell tremendously within the compartment, putting enormous pressure on the nerves and blood supply. The athlete will experience severe tightness, numbness, and tingling in the lower leg. This condition is a medical emergency because the consequences of an acute compartment syndrome can be long-term loss of function in the affected limb. Surgery usually involves a "fascial release" (fasciotomy) in which the membranous walls of the compartment are cut open to allow more room for the tissues within.

Concerns:

- Unless measures are taken early to manage the condition, it can deteriorate to the point where surgery may be necessary. In severe cases of overuse compartment syndromes, the muscles can exert so much pressure on the nerves in the compartment that permanent nerve damage may occur.

What you can do:

- Cease the activity that caused the condition.
- Administer RICE (page 46).
- Modify training regimen, paying particular attention to the training surface, footwear, and running technique.
- As soon as pain subsides, return to sports, though it is likely the pain will return.

Medication:

- For relief of minor to moderate pain, take acetaminophen as directed on label, or, for the relief of pain *and* inflammation, ibuprofen or aspirin if tolerated (see page 49).

What the doctor can do:

- Confirm the diagnosis with a compartment pressure test (a needle is inserted into the muscle before and after activity to measure pressure within the compartment).
- Once the diagnosis is confirmed, the doctor should advise the athlete that surgery will be necessary if he or she wishes to continue in vigorous sports.

CRAMPS

A very frequent condition in the lower leg, which can be very painful but usually does not prompt a visit to the doctor, is cramping. The most common site of muscle cramps is the calf. These sudden, powerful, involuntary contractions of the calf muscles are classified as either clonic or tonic.

Clonic cramps are intermittent contractions and relaxations of the muscles. Tonic cramps are when the muscles cramp and remain in contraction.

The cause of muscle cramps is mysterious. Contributing factors may include fatigue, dehydration due to perspiration, and poor synchronicity between the muscles.

When you get a cramp in the calf, stand up and try to relax the muscles. If the cramp does not go away, lie down and pull the foot up toward the knee while simultaneously massaging the calf (do this for six to ten seconds).

The most effective way to prevent muscle cramps is to be fit for your sport and warm up properly before activity. It is also important to make sure you drink enough water before and during exercise, and ensure that your diet contains adequate minerals, especially potassium and calcium (for more on fluid and mineral consumption, refer to chapter 21, ''Nutrition for Sports''). *Athletes should never take salt tablets.*

If the cramps are frequent and interfere with sports, consult a doctor to see if there is an underlying problem causing the condition.

- The procedure involves cutting open the membranous compartment walls, thus relieving the pressure within the compartment (fasciotomy). This procedure is done on an outpatient basis. The athlete is walking without crutches within a week, and can return to gentle running within two weeks.

Rehabilitation:

- Level three rehabilitation exercises should start immediately, with the focus on stretching the muscles in the lower leg.
- After surgery, level two rehabilitation exercises should start a week after surgery. For levels one, two, and three rehabilitation guidelines, refer to the sections on rehabilitation and conditioning at the end of chapter 6.

Recovery time:

- Unless surgery is done, this condition probably will not clear up.
- After surgery, the athlete can go back to gentle running after two weeks, working up to full activity within four to six weeks.

Rehabilitation and Conditioning Program for the Lower Leg

The muscles and tendons of the lower leg are primarily responsible for moving the ankle and foot. For guidelines and exercises to rehabilitate injuries, as well as a program to condition the musculature of the lower leg, refer to the sections on rehabilitation and conditioning in chapter 6, "Foot Injuries" (pages 88–91).

CHAPTER NINE

Knee Injuries

The knee is the single most frequently injured joint in the human body. It is susceptible to disabling acute injuries such as ligament sprains, as well as a host of overuse conditions that start off as low-grade pain but may eventually debilitate the athlete and force a withdrawal from sports.

Acute knee injuries are well known to anyone familiar with contact sports. Indeed, the words *ACL tear* strike fear in the heart of anyone who has played football, hockey, lacrosse, or rugby. Management of these injuries has improved radically, thanks to modern diagnostic techniques such as magnetic resonance imaging (MRI) and surgical procedures, including fiber optic arthroscopy. Care of acute knee injuries will continue to improve as medicine incorporates such breakthrough technologies as synthetic ligaments and meniscal alographs (tissue is taken from cadavers and used to replace the meniscus cartilage in the knee).

The most exciting recent research on knee injuries suggests that cartilage damage can be repaired with cells harvested from the patient's own body. This has enormous implications for future osteoarthritis sufferers (see page 309), as cartilage damage is a major cause of this condition which affects over 16 million Americans over fifty years old.

Overuse injuries of the knee are less well understood, and consequently are more difficult to manage. They were rarely seen in the general population until the fitness boom of the 1960s and 1970s. The explosion in the popularity of health fitness activities such as running and aerobics, which place extraordinary demands on the lower extremities, has precipitated an epidemic of overuse knee injuries among recreational athletes. In the recreational sports arena, overuse injuries of the knee are of much greater concern than acute knee injuries.

What makes knee injuries so common? And so serious?

First of all, the knee is the largest joint in the body and is subjected to an enormous workload during many sports. Yet the knee, for all its size and importance, is structurally quite weak. It is surrounded by many large muscles, which, although they provide the athlete with great mobility and strength in the legs, also subject the knee joint to massive stresses. These stresses become especially acute when there are imbalances in muscle strength and/or inflexibility. Besides these strength and flexibility imbalances, there are several anatomical abnormalities that place extra stress on the knee joint and thus increase the likelihood of an athlete's sustaining an overuse injury. These anatomical abnormalities include such common conditions as knock-knee, inequalities in leg length, turned-in thighbones, and flat feet.

Finally, because the knee is so important for sports, injuries to the joint have profound consequences for the athlete.

Prevention is always better than cure in sports medicine, but for the reasons described above, almost nowhere is it more important than in the case of knee injuries.

How Your Knee Works

Any number of the structures in the knee can get injured, including the ligaments, cartilage (both the meniscus structures that rest in the joint between the bones and the articular cartilage that covers the ends of the bones), muscle-tendon units that attach to the knee joint, the kneecap, and bursae.

The knee is one of the most complex joints in the body. Many medical scientists have made a career out of studying the "biomechanics" of this joint and how those biomechanics relate to the high incidence of injuries seen in the knee joint.

The knee lies at the junction of the thighbone (the femur) and the larger and smaller shinbones (tibia and fibula). It is a "hinge joint" that allows primarily for backward and forward movements but also some side-to-side and rotational movement.

The knee joint is held together by a complex set of ligaments. The most important of these are the cruciate, collateral, and capsular ligaments.

The cruciate ligaments—the anterior cruciate ligament (ACL) and the posterior cruciate ligament (PCL)—join the thighbone to the shinbones in the center of the knee joint. These two ligaments, which cross each other (the word *cruciate* means "crossed"), provide the knee with a large degree of its stability. The main function of the cruciate ligaments is to prevent the thighbone and shinbones from sliding and rotating against each other.

The collateral ligaments run on either side of the joint. The medial collateral ligament (MCL) is on the inner side of the joint. The lateral collateral ligament (LCL) is on the outer side of the joint. The main function of the collateral ligaments is to prevent excessive sideways bending of the thighbone and shinbones against each other.

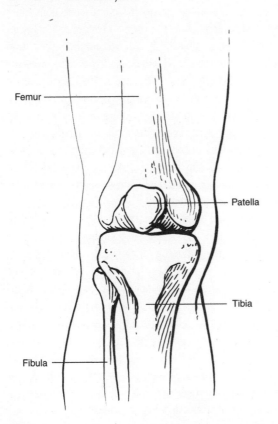

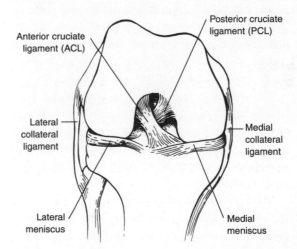

The capsular ligaments of the knee—the posterior oblique ligament, the arcuate ligament, and the oblique popliteal ligament—are actually thickenings in the joint capsule, which encases the joint like a sleeve. These capsular ligaments resemble seams in the sleeve.

The posterior oblique ligament (POL) is located just behind the MCL on the inside back corner of the knee. It is rarely injured independently. However, it frequently gets damaged when the MCL gets sprained.

The arcuate ligament is the thickening on the back outside corner of the knee joint. It is rarely injured in sports, and only when the front of the knee is subjected to a powerful blow that bends the knee backward, forcing the rear of the joint apart.

The oblique popliteal ligament is a thickening of the joint capsule in the very back of the joint. It can get injured in the same way as the arcuate ligament, when the front of the knee suffers a severe blow. Again, this is very rare.

The ligaments provide the joint with stability, and expand during sports as the knee is forced through its allowable ranges of motion. However, when the joint is forced beyond its allowable range of motion, the ligaments that hold it together will stretch, tear, or completely rupture. For example, if an athlete is running and tries to change direction, the knee may bend inward beyond its allowable range of motion, and the ligaments on the inside of the joint may get damaged.

The kneecap, or patella, rests in the V-shaped groove between the two knobs that form the bottom of the thighbone. It is located within the tendon at the bottom end of the thighbone and serves to protect the bony prominence at the bottom of the thighbone from blows to the front.

The kneecap is a critical component of the extensor mechanism, which is the combined function of the quadriceps muscle-tendon, the kneecap, the kneecap tendon, and the large shinbone (tibia). These structures, working together, provide the athlete with dynamic extension of the knee—the motion necessary to run and jump. Injuries to the kneecap greatly affect the athlete's ability to perform any motions that involve running and jumping.

Acute injuries to the kneecap area itself include fractures, dislocations, and tendon strains and ruptures.

Much more common than acute kneecap injuries are overuse injuries of the kneecap. The classic symptoms of overuse injuries of the kneecap are pain in the front of the knee, pain when bending the knee and walking downstairs and downhill, an ache when sitting for extended periods of time, and a creaking sensation (crepitus) when bending and straightening the knee.

Until recently, any knee pain with the above symptoms was usually diagnosed as chondromalachia patella. From the Greek *chondros* and *malakia,* this translates as "cartilage softness," in this case, behind the kneecap. Unfortunately, subsequent generations of doctors began assuming that any athlete with these symptoms had chondromalachia patella, but it is now clear that the diagnosis of chondromalachia patella was overused. Kneecap pain may be caused by several conditions quite unrelated to damage to the back surface of the kneecap. For this reason, athletes should beware the doctor who diagnoses knee pain as chondromalachia patella unless he or she has actually detected damage to the back surface of the kneecap through an arthrotomy, arthroscopy, CAT scan, or MRI. Doctors now diagnose problems accompanied by the classic symptoms as patellofemoral pain syndrome.

Problems associated with patellofemoral pain syndrome are usually caused by the kneecap's not "tracking" properly. Although intense sports activity usually brings on symptoms, the underlying cause is likely to be either an anatomical abnormality or a deficit of strength or flexibility in the surrounding muscles. One or more of the following anatomical abnormalities is usually present in someone who develops problems in the kneecap: leg length discrepancy, thighbones that turn inward, knock-knee, or flat feet. Athletes who develop kneecap problems often have relatively tight and strong outer quadriceps muscles, and weaker, looser muscles on the inner side of the quadriceps. As these sets of muscles are supposed to stabilize that kneecap on each side, when the outer side is stronger than the inner side, this will cause the kneecap to be pulled to the outside when the athlete runs.

Early on, and in relatively mild cases of patellofemoral pain syndrome, muscle strengthening and flexibility exercises are usually sufficient to remedy the condition. Orthotics or a knee brace often help correct the anatomical abnormality that causes damage to the kneecap.

Other problems affecting the extensor mechanism include quadriceps and patellar tendinitis, as well as osteochondritis dissecans of the kneecap, and kneecap subluxation.

There are two forms of cartilage in the knee joint—articular and meniscal—which frequently get injured in sports.

All the surfaces at the ends of the thighbone and the shinbones, as well as the back of the kneecap, are covered with a thin coating of extremely tough yet well-lubricated articular cartilage. When injured, as can happen when the ends of the bones grind together and portions of the articular cartilage are damaged, joint movement is impaired, and divots may form in the articular cartilage. The gradual erosion of articular cartilage is responsible for the condition known as degenerative arthritis. If left untreated, chips of bone can fall into the joint; this condition is called osteochondritis dissecans.

Meniscal cartilage in the knee is comprised of two *menisci*, crescent-shaped pieces of cartilage that lie in the joint and stabilize the joint, absorb shock, and disperse lubrication known as synovial fluid. The two menisci in the knee are frequently damaged in athletic activity due to the grinding that takes place between the thighbone and the larger shinbone. The medial meniscus, on the inside of the knee, is the one most often injured. The symptoms of a meniscus tear include clicking, catching, and even locking in the joint, usually accompanied by swelling. Blood supply to the menisci is very poor, and they have no nerves or lymphatic channels, making it virtually impossible for an injured meniscus to heal itself. For that reason, an athlete with an injured meniscus usually requires surgery in order to continue participating in sports.

The knee joint is also the site of eleven bursa sacs. Bursae are fluid-filled sacs located in parts of the body where friction would occur were it not for their presence.

Because of the amount of stress the knee undergoes during sports activity, the bursae in the knee often get inflamed. Inflammation of a bursa is known as bursitis. The bursa sacs most frequently inflamed are the prepatellar bursa (located between the kneecap and the skin over it), the deep infrapatellar bursa (located underneath the kneecap ligament), and the anserine bursa (located between the main shinbone and the pes anserine tendon). A bursitis is rarely serious unless it is allowed to deteriorate to the point where it is so debilitating that it needs to be aspirated or even removed.

Muscles and Nerves

The knee moves in four different directions, and it requires highly complex interaction between a number of the surrounding muscles to realize each of these separate actions. The most important actions are performed by the quadriceps (straightening) and hamstrings (bending) in the front and back of the thigh, respectively. Weakness and/or tightness in either the quadriceps or hamstrings can predispose the athlete to a number of knee conditions—most frequently, disorders affecting the kneecap.

The most common muscle imbalance causing kneecap tracking problems affects the outer quadriceps muscle, the vastus lateralis, and the muscle on the inner side of the thigh, the vastus medialis. The two muscles run down either side of the thigh and attach to the kneecap. Among their most important functions is to stabilize the kneecap. When one side is stronger than the other, the kneecap can get pulled off to one side when the athlete runs. It is very common for athletes to have comparatively tight, strong outer thigh muscles compared to the muscles on the inner side, which causes the kneecap to be pulled to the outer side of the thigh during running activities. If the athlete is a distance runner, this mechanism will likely cause patellofemoral pain syndrome.

The iliotibial band is a thick, wide band of muscle-tendon tissue running down the outside of the thigh from the hip to just below the knee. Tightness in the iliotibial band is the underlying cause of one of the most common knee overuse injuries seen in distance runners, a condition known as iliotibial band syndrome. This condition is characterized by snapping over the front outer side of the knee. Sometimes the tightness in the iliotibial band occurs when the athlete has bowlegs, because the bowed legs create a longer distance over which the iliotibial band must stretch, making it tighter against the outside of the knee joint. Treatment for iliotibial band syndrome usually includes stretching exercises for the iliotibial band and/or shoe inserts (orthotics) that make the legs less bowed.

Orthotics

Orthotics are shoe inserts designed to correct some of the abnormalities described above and, by so doing minimize the problems they cause.

Some of the most common anatomical abnormalities orthotics are used to correct are flat feet, high arches, and feet that excessively roll inward (pronate).

The overuse sports injuries that these conditions may cause include plantar fasciitis (heel spurs), Achilles tendinitis, and patellofemoral pain syndrome.

If a sports doctor determines that an athlete's overuse injury is caused by an anatomical abnormality in the foot, an orthotic may be prescribed. If the condition is mild, the doctor may recommend an over-the-counter orthotic. Otherwise, a custom-made orthotic will be recommended.

Over-the-counter Orthotics

OTC orthotics such as Dr. Scholl's may alleviate mild anatomical abnormalities, and they have the advantage of being considerably less expensive than those that are custom made.

OTC orthotics work in three different ways:

1. provide arch support for athletes with mild fallen arches

2. provide support for the long bones of the midfoot, the metatarsals

3. provide heel support through a wedge in the heel, which can help reduce the strain on the calf muscle–Achilles tendon unit

If OTC orthotics do not alleviate an overuse condition, or if the doctor deems the anatomical abnormality to be severe, custom-made orthotics may be prescribed.

Custom-made Orthotics

There are two types of custom-made orthotics, rigid and soft.

Soft orthotics are prescribed for high arches. High arches make the feet very inflexible, reducing their ability to absorb repetitive impact efficiently. That is why people with high arches who participate in endurance-type sports are susceptible to overuse conditions such as stress fractures, heel spurs, and Achilles tendinitis.

Soft orthotics are made using the "weight-bearing" method. In this technique the athlete steps into a foam-filled box and makes an imprint of the feet, from which models of the feet are made and, from those, corrective orthotics.

In addition to providing much-needed cushioning support for high arches, soft orthotics also provide impact absorption that prevents conditions such as heel spurs, plantar fasciitis, and stress fractures.

Soft orthotics are usually prescribed by orthotists and chiropractors because it requires less technical knowledge of the biomechanics of anatomical abnormalities to make them than to make rigid orthotics.

Rigid orthotics are preferable for flat feet and feet that excessively pronate. Their purpose is to restrict excessive rolling in of the foot when running, the undesirable motion associated with flat feet and feet that excessively pronate. The overuse injuries commonly seen in athletes with these kinds of feet are stress fractures, posterior tibial tendinitis, and compartment syndromes of the lower leg.

A "nonweight-bearing" technique is used to fit rigid orthotics. Using plaster of paris, an imprint of the foot is made while the athlete is sitting or lying down, legs hanging off the edge of a table. When it has dried, the negative cast is filled with wet plaster to make a model of the foot, from which an orthotic is designed to minimize the effect of the anatomical abnormality.

Having the model of the foot made when the athlete is lying down allows a much more accurate biomechanical evaluation of the athlete's foot. Because they require more skill to fit, rigid orthotics are usually made by podiatrists and physical therapists.

Injuries to the Knee

Acute knee injuries include ligament strains, kneecap dislocations, kneecap fractures, osteochondral fractures, and cartilage tears. By far the most common of these acute injuries is the ligament strain.

Acute knee injuries may be caused by a twist of the knee that forces the bones of the joint to separate. This most often happens when an athlete who is running fast changes direction or rapidly decelerates when running fast. A twist can also occur in contact sports, when one player twists another's lower leg so it rotates relative to the thighbone, or when the athlete's foot is fixed and the thighbone or body is forced in another direction. Acute knee injuries may also result from direct impact from another athlete, especially when the foot is fixed in place. Usually, the impact occurs to the outer of the knee, causing damage to the ligament on the inner side. Acute knee injuries are occasionally caused by a direct fall onto the knee.

Ligament sprains are the most common acute injuries seen in sports. Most knee sprains affect either the medial collateral ligament or the anterior cruciate ligament when damaged by a forceful bowing inward of the knee (MCL) or the thighbone sliding forward on the shinbone (ACL). As with all ligament sprains, these injuries are classified according to their severity: first, second, or third degree. The symptoms are usually obvious: immediate pain, then swelling and instability. First-degree sprains may require little more than one or two weeks of rest; complete ruptures, on the other hand, may require surgery to ensure the athlete is not subject to a lifetime of knee instability.

Overuse injuries of the knee include meniscus wear and tear, kneecap wear and tear, tendinitis conditions both above and below the kneecap, bursitis, and loose bodies in the joint.

Overuse knee injuries are caused by excessive sports activity, but they often have an underlying cause, or risk factor. Risk factors can be either internal (intrinsic) or external (extrinsic).

The internal risk factors usually involve deficits in strength and flexibility of the surrounding muscles, tendons, and ligaments, and anatomical abnormalities such as a difference in leg lengths, abnormalities in hip rotation or the position of the kneecap, bowlegs, knock-knee, or flat feet.

External risk factors may include training errors, improper footwear, and improper technique.

Unlike most acute knee injuries, the onset of the symptoms of overuse knee injuries is gradual and may have no obvious cause. Initially pain may only be experienced after sports participation. Gradually the symptoms may begin to be felt during and after participation but may not be severe enough to interfere with performance. In the final stages, disabling pain is felt both during and after participation as well as in daily activities.

The key to managing overuse injuries is early intervention. Anytime there is pain centering in the knee, especially knee pain aggravated by the same sports or fitness activity, the likelihood is that the discomfort is an overuse injury. Take immediate steps to address the condition, starting with RICE (page 46).

Proper Shoes for the Heavyweight Runner

Running shoe companies cater primarily to "lightweight" (under 145 pounds) or "middleweight" (145–175 pounds) runners. In the early years of the running boom, running shoes were designed for runners with those body types. Now companies are making shoes for runners who weigh more than 180 pounds. These shoes accommodate the extra weight, which would otherwise translate into increased impact during each step, causing problems throughout the lower extremities, the knees included.

To increase shock absorbency, heavier runners can also add a sorbothane insole.

Preventing Knee Injuries

Acute knee injuries are often caused by freak accidents and are therefore difficult to prevent. There are, however, several preventive measures athletes can take to avoid acute knee injuries.

Most importantly, athletes should engage in a conditioning program to develop strength and flexibility in the musculature surrounding the knee joint, especially the thigh muscles. Strong thigh muscles offer effective protection against forces that would ordinarily twist the knee beyond its normal range of motion. It is equally important to have *balanced* lower limb muscle strength, as imbalances in strength between one leg and another may lead to injuries when the athlete changes direction (cuts) using his stronger leg, causing the weaker leg to buckle inward.

Wearing appropriate footwear is another important factor in preventing acute knee injuries. Among athletes who wear cleated footwear (primarily football, baseball, lacrosse, and soccer players), the preference was traditionally for shoes with a small number of long cleats because these provided better traction. However, these shoes predispose athletes to injuries from twisting motions. That is because the foot can become too firmly fixed to the playing surface, while simultaneous momentum or impact form another player can force the joint beyond its normal range of motion. Athletes are now advised to wear footwear with a greater number of shorter cleats.

Ski boots, and especially their bindings, can predispose a skier to knee injuries. Bindings are designed to release before unusual stresses are transmitted to the leg. They should not release under normal skiing forces. See page 104 for a thorough discussion of ski boots and bindings.

Finally, protective braces are being used more and more frequently by athletes, not only to prevent reinjury but to prevent injuries from occurring in the first place. Such devices are called "prophylactic braces." Use of such knee braces is controversial (see page 126).

Overuse injuries of the knee are most effectively prevented by addressing the well-established internal and external risk factors associated with overuse injuries of the lower extremities (see chapter 6).

The most effective ways for athletes to avoid problems associated with these risk factors are as follows:

Have a Presports Physical

A physical examination by a qualified sports doctor is one of the most effective forms of preventive sports care. Such an evaluation can detect conditions that may predispose the athlete to knee injury and can provide measures to alleviate these problems. Two common problems that may be discovered in the presports physical are anatomical abnormalities and deficits in strength and flexibility.

Muscle imbalances: One of the most common causes of kneecap pain (patellofemoral pain syndrome) is an imbalance between the muscles in front of the thigh (quadriceps) and the muscles in back of the thigh (hamstrings). Almost always, the quadriceps muscles are much weaker and less flexible than the hamstrings.

Anatomical abnormalities: Athletes with knock-knee, thighs that turn inward from the hip joint, and flat feet that roll inward (pronate) when they run are at greater risk of sustaining kneecap pain (patellofemoral pain syndrome). Those with bowlegs are more likely to suffer from iliotibial band syndrome because the shape of their legs causes this thick band of muscle to rub against the outside of the knee joint.

Strength and flexibility deficits can be remedied through an exercise program, while anatomical abnormalities can often be corrected with orthotics (see page 122). It is better if the athlete has these conditions detected in a presports physical, and not after developing pain during exercise.

Engage in a Strength and Flexibility Program for the Lower Extremities

The stronger, more flexible athlete is at much lower risk of sustaining any knee injury. The athlete should focus on strengthening and stretching the muscles in the thigh (quadriceps and hamstrings) and the iliotibial band. For a comprehensive program on conditioning the muscles around the knee, refer to the section at the end of this chapter.

The Q-angle test was devised to establish a relationship between the vague description of knock-knee and injury rates.

Using the center of the kneecap as the meeting point, lines are drawn along the thighbone and the kneecap tendon. The angle where the lines meet in the center of the kneecap is the Q angle.

The Q angle is normally less than 10 degrees in men, and 15 degrees in women. A Q angle higher than 20 degrees increases the likelihood that the quadriceps muscles will pull the kneecap to the outer side, which can cause both patellofemoral pain syndrome and subluxations.

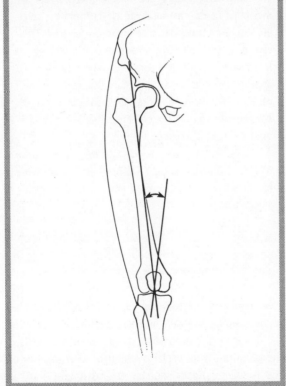

Avoid Training Errors

Training error—usually "too much too soon"—is one of the main causes of knee overuse injuries. Such injuries can develop when athletes suddenly increase the *frequency* (how often), *duration* (how long), or *intensity* (how hard) of their workouts.

Intensity encompasses not only factors such as how far or how fast one jogs or how long one does aerobic dance; it also refers to less obvious aspects of the exercise regimen, such as the hardness of the training surface or switching from a softer to a harder surface or from primarily flat surfaces to hills. Softer does not always mean less stressful; for instance, running on sand stresses the Achilles tendons and predisposes the athlete to tendinitis in that area.

Aerobic dancers who change from working out on mat floors to cement floors also run the risk of overuse injuries in their knees and lower legs.

It is generally considered safe to increase either the frequency, duration, or intensity of the exercise regimen by 10 percent without making adjustments. But when dramatically increasing one of the three elements of the exercise regimen, it is necessary to make temporary adjustments in one or both of the other elements (see formula on page 10).

Structure the Workout Properly

One of the most common reasons athletes develop overuse injuries is that they do not prepare their bodies for the immediate demands of exercise with a structured workout that includes warm-up and cooldown periods. Warming up and cooling down (sometimes called "warming down") are relatively new concepts in recreational sports. Until recently, warming up in organized team sports such as football or soccer meant doing jumping jacks in formation; in tennis, it involved easy hitting across the net; in running, the participant started out at a moderate pace in the hope that a second wind would soon happen.

Today, warming up and cooling down are commonplace. The benefits are well established: improved performance, psychological preparation, creating a comfort zone for the activity itself, and relieving the aches and pains of vigorous athletic activity. Most important, though, is that warm-ups and cooldowns prevent injuries from occurring.

Tissues that are not made more pliable before exercise are susceptible to overuse injuries; tiny tears may occur due to repetitive, low-intensity stretching of inflexible tissues, such as the tendons that attach to the kneecap. Overuse injuries of the joints can develop because the

A GUIDE TO KNEE BRACES

Many athletes with problem knees want to know if they would benefit from a brace. The benefit of wearing knee braces is hotly debated in sports medicine circles. Only in the last decade has proper research been done in the area of knee bracing. Following is a guide to the effectiveness of the three main types of knee braces available.

Prophylactic knee braces are almost never used by recreational athletes. They are primarily used by football players as a "just in case" measure. At this time, whether or not prophylactic braces are effective is extremely controversial. Some doctors say they do work, while many others argue that not only are prophylactic knee braces ineffective, they may even increase the likelihood of a knee injury. Doctors are currently trying to develop prophylactic knee braces that do work, but until such a brace comes on the market, whether or not to wear a prophylactic brace is a matter of personal preference.

Rehabilitative knee braces are prescribed by doctors to athletes who have sustained serious knee injuries, often after surgery. They allow controlled bending and straightening of the knee joint that stimulates healing, while preventing sideways or twisting motions that would compromise healing.

These types of braces are very effective in rehabilitating serious knee injuries, though expert care must be sought for fitting such a device to avoid reinjuring the knee.

Functional knee braces are designed to provide stability for unstable knees by improving the relationship between ligaments, muscles, joint structure, proprioception, and weight-bearing forces.

There are two basic designs of functional knee braces. Both use "hinges" and "posts" for support, though one design has cups that enclose the thigh and calf. Research has shown that the braces with the thigh and calf enclosures are most effective.

It is unknown whether prophylactic knee braces, rarely used by recreational athletes, prevent knee injuries in contact sports such as football. Some experts argue they may even increase the incidence of knee injuries. Rehabilitative and functional knee braces *are* effective. However, it is *extremely important* to stress that they should be employed as just one part of a comprehensive management program for a knee injury that should include correct diagnosis, aggressive rehabilitation, activity modification, and possibly surgery. Braces are not a replacement for such a program.

Finally, the most effective way to prevent knee injuries is with "natural bracing"—achieved by strengthening the muscles around the knee joint in a conditioning program.

surrounding tissues are not warmed up and stretched, which restricts the knee's range of motion and may cause cartilage to grind against bone or other cartilage. An inflexible iliotibial band may rub against the outer side of the knee joint, causing the condition known as iliotibial band syndrome.

Every workout should include five stages: limbering up (5 minutes); stretching (5–10 minutes); warm-up (5 minutes); primary activity; and cooling down and cool-down stretching (10 minutes).

Wear Proper Footwear

When running or performing high-impact aerobics, the athlete exerts with each step a combined force of three to four times body weight. That force is absorbed by the running surface, the shoe, and the foot and leg. The less force the limb absorbs, the less risk there is of overuse injury. That explains why it is better to train on slightly softer surfaces like clay or grass than cement or asphalt, which have less give. It also explains why shoes are the most important item in most athlete's wardrobe.

Shoes are especially important for runners and aerobic dancers. The right footwear makes for an enjoyable, injury-free exercise experience, while the wrong footwear can cause discomfort and overuse injuries of the knee ranging from kneecap pain to pes anserine bursitis.

Acute Knee Injuries

Knee Sprains

A knee sprain is a stretch, tear, or complete rupture of one or more of the seven ligaments that stabilize the knee joint. The particular ligament or ligaments that get damaged depends on how the injury occurs. These are the most common mechanisms of knee injuries and the specific ligaments that most often get damaged in each case:

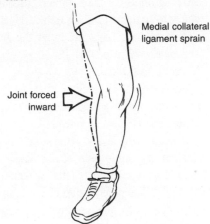

Medial collateral ligament sprain

Joint forced inward

- Impact or twisting so the joint is forced inward—medial collateral ligament sprain (sprain of the ligaments on the inner side of the joint)

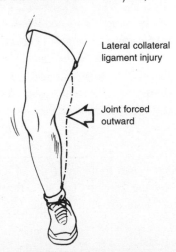

Lateral collateral ligament injury

Joint forced outward

- Impact or twisting so the joint is forced outward—lateral collateral ligament injury (sprain of the ligaments on the outer side of the joint)

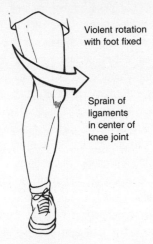

Violent rotation with foot fixed

Sprain of ligaments in center of knee joint

- Violent rotation while the foot is fixed in place—anterior cruciate ligament injury (sprain of the ligaments in the center of the joint)

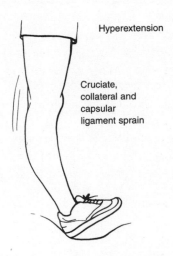

Hyperextension

Cruciate, collateral and capsular ligament sprain

- Impact or twisting causing hyperextension or hyperflexion of the cruciate, collateral, or capsular ligaments (sprain of the ligaments in the center, inner, or outer side of the joint, as well as injuries to the joint capsule)

It is absolutely essential to remember that the above mechanisms of injury are a general guide to the particular kind of sprain that might occur. Any one of these mechanisms can cause injury not just to the ligament mentioned but to other structures as well. For instance, a medial collateral ligament sprain—a sprain of the ligament on the inside of the knee—can also damage the posterior oblique ligament, as well as the meniscus on the inner side of the knee joint.

Like all sprains, knee sprains are classified according to their severity: first, second, or third degree. Instability is one of the characteristic symptoms of a moderate or severe ligament injury. However, it is important to remember that the swelling that quickly takes place may cause the joint to stiffen, thereby masking signs of instability and perhaps leading to a misdiagnosis as a less severe sprain. Therefore, the sooner a knee injury is examined by a doctor, the more accurate a diagnosis can be made.

Although any ligament can get damaged, the ligaments most often damaged are the medial collateral ligament (MCL) and the anterior cruciate ligament (ACL).

MEDIAL COLLATERAL LIGAMENT (MCL) SPRAIN

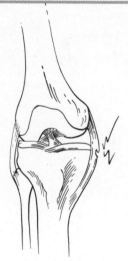

A medial collateral ligament (MCL) sprain is a stretch, tear, or complete rupture of the ligaments that join the thighbone and larger shinbone (tibia) on the inner side of the knee joint. As with all ligament sprains, MCL sprains are classified according to severity; first, second, or third degree.

Symptoms:

- Immediate pain at the time of the injury, which dissipates but then recurs when the athlete tries to use the knee.
- Swelling, stiffness, and instability.

- The level of symptoms depends on the extent of the injury.
- First degree: (stretch of the ligament or a tear of a few ligament fibers):
    Minor joint stiffness and tenderness on the inner side of the joint.
    Though the joint is stiff, there is virtually full strength and range of motion.
    The joint is stable, and there is minimal swelling.
- Second degree: (tear of a significant amount of the ligament fibers):
    Moderate to severe joint stiffness, usually inability to straighten the leg (athlete is usually unable to place heel directly on the ground and place weight on it).
    Moderate instability.
    Slight swelling, or swelling may be absent unless there is also damage to the meniscus or anterior cruciate ligament.
    Significant pain and tenderness on the joint line on the inner side of the knee joint, usually accompanied by joint weakness.
- Third degree: (complete rupture of the ligament):
    Immediate pain may be limited because the entire ligament has ruptured.
    Total loss of stability on the inner side of the knee; the knee may sometimes "give way."
    Minimal to moderate swelling.
    Pain and point tenderness on the inner side of the knee.
    The doctor will be able to detect an opening under the skin on the inner side of the knee between the thighbone and the tibia (this is because the ligament holding the two bones together has come apart).

Cause:

- Direct impact to the outer side of the knee that forces the knee inward, or a twisting motion that causes the same motion.

Athletes at risk:

- Primarily those in contact sports, skiing, or any sport where there are rapid changes of direction when running, such as tennis, basketball, soccer, baseball, etc.

- Other factors that increase the likelihood of sustaining a knee sprain:

  loose-jointedness

  muscle weakness in the thighs

  muscle imbalances between one leg and another

  previous injury

Concerns:

- Unless knee sprains are managed properly, long-term instability may result, making sports participation difficult and reinjury likely.
- A moderate or severe sprain, as well as repeated minor sprains, may damage the meniscus.

What you can do:

- First-degree sprain:

  Start RICE (page 46) as soon as possible and continue for twenty-four hours.

  Begin level two rehabilitation exercises as soon as pain abates, ideally after twenty-four hours, and pursue rehabilitation according to the regimen described in the "Knee Injury Rehabilitation" section at the end of this chapter.

  Refrain from sports that demand "cutting" motions for one to three weeks, depending on symptoms.

- Seek medical attention if there is pain during knee movement, limited range of motion, swelling in the joint, tenderness on the inner side of the joint, or instability.

Medication:

- For relief of minor to moderate pain, take acetaminophen as directed on label, or, for the relief of pain *and* inflammation, ibuprofen or aspirin if tolerated (see page 49).

What the doctor can do:

- Perform a careful examination to ascertain the extent of the damage. It may be necessary to drain the joint with a syringe to reduce swelling enough to judge instability.

- In the case of a first-degree sprain, treatment is the same as above ("What you can do"). In addition, the doctor may prescribe a brace to stabilize and protect the knee from further sprains.
- Treatment for second- and third-degree knee sprains should always include at least forty-eight to seventy-two hours of RICE. In addition, the doctor may prescribe:

  Crutches until the athlete can walk without a limp

  Hinged brace that allows limited front-and-back movement but no side-to-side motion exercises to maintain strength and flexibility in the adjoining joints (hip and ankle)

- Unless other ligaments are damaged, surgery is rarely performed on MCL sprains. It has been found that physical therapy is equally effective.

Rehabilitation:

- After a first-degree sprain, level one rehabilitation exercises should begin as soon as initial pain and inflammation abate and, ideally, within twenty-four hours after the injury occurs.
- After a second- or third-degree sprain, level two rehabilitation exercises should begin as soon as initial pain and inflammation abate and, ideally, after seventy-two hours of RICE and splinting. For levels one, two, and three rehabilitation guidelines, refer to the section on rehabilitation and conditioning at the end of this chapter.

Recovery time:

- First-degree sprain: up to six weeks before vigorous use of the knee is possible.
- Second-degree sprain: six to twelve weeks.
- Third-degree sprain: six weeks in a brace, and twelve weeks of further rehabilitation before the athlete can go back to sports.

ANTERIOR CRUCIATE LIGAMENT (ACL) SPRAIN

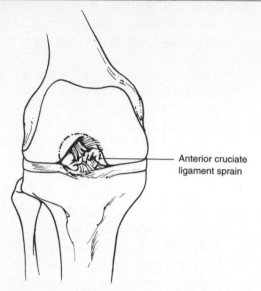

Anterior cruciate ligament sprain

An anterior cruciate ligament (ACL) sprain is a stretch, tear, or complete rupture of one of the two ligaments that lie in the center of the joint, connecting the ends of the thigh and shinbones. Unlike most ligament sprains, which are classified according to severity as first, second, or third degree, ACL sprains are almost always complete ruptures—the ligament is completely torn in two. Posterior cruciate ligament (PCL) sprains are much less common, but are sometimes seen in recreational athletes. Their treatment is similar to that for ACL sprains.

Symptoms:

- Immediate pain and a "pop" at the time the injury occurs.
- A sensation as if the knee is coming apart.
- Immediate dysfunction and instability followed in one to two hours by swelling, which reaches its peak after four to six hours.
- When the knee is fully swollen, the athlete will not be able to walk without assistance.
- Note: If the ACL alone is damaged, there will be no local tenderness around the joint.

Cause:

- A violent knee twist, usually when the foot is fixed in place (as when the cleats are stuck in grass), and the upper leg and/or body is rotated.

Athletes at risk:

- Primarily those in contact sports, skiing, or any sport where there are rapid changes of direction when running, such as tennis, basketball, soccer, baseball, etc.
- Other factors that increase the likelihood of sustaining a knee sprain:
  loose-jointedness
  muscle weakness in the thighs
  muscle imbalances between legs
  previous injury

Concerns:

- At the same time the ACl gets damaged, medial collateral ligament and meniscus damage may also occur.

What you can do:

- Use RICE (page 46) and seek medical attention as soon as possible, especially if there is pain during knee movement, limited range of motion, swelling in the joint, or instability.

Medication:

- For relief of minor to moderate pain, take acetaminophen as directed on label, or, for the relief of pain *and* inflammation, ibuprofen or aspirin if tolerated (see page 49).

What the doctor can do:

- With the patient's input, make a decision regarding surgery. The younger the patient, the more likely surgery will be performed, as these people have a longer time to develop the kinds of degenerative conditions that often result from this injury—notably, arthritis. In athletes middle-aged and older, physical therapy is more likely to be used to treat this injury, unless the athlete participates in a sport that places vigorous twisting turning forces on the knee, such as tennis or squash (see below, "Knee Injury Rehabilitation").
- Surgery to repair a torn ACL is done by replacing the ligaments with portions of tissue from other parts of the body—usually the hamstring or kneecap tendon.

- After surgery to repair an ACL, the patient has to stay in hospital for one or two days, spend three to six weeks using a brace and crutches; and perform six months to a year of rehabilitation before returning to athletic activity requiring strenuous use of the knee.

Rehabilitation:

- Early range of motion begins in the recovery room with the athlete using a continuous passive motion machine. Rehabilitation for ACL sprains is the same as for sprains of the medial collateral ligament.

Recovery time:

- When physical therapy is used to treat this condition, it usually takes three months before the athlete can return to sports that require vigorous use of the knee joint.
- After surgery, nine to twelve months of careful rehabilitation is necessary before the athlete can resume vigorous sporting activity, though it may be possible to start light running, cycling, cross-country skiing simulator, and stairclimber machine in three months.

Overuse Injuries of the Knee

ILIOTIBIAL BAND FRICTION SYNDROME

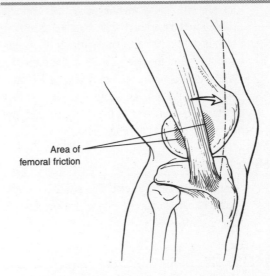

Area of femoral friction

The iliotibial band is a thick swathe of tendon tissue stretching from the outer rim of the pelvis down the side of the leg, over the outside of the knee, and attaching to the top of the outside of the large shinbone. Its job is to increase knee stability.

Inflammations of this structure can occur at the point where it rubs against the outer part of the knee joint. Often, the underlying bursa is also affected.

Symptoms:

- Onset of symptoms is gradual.
- Tightness is felt on the outer side of the knee. This sensation turns to a burning or stinging feeling during running activities.
- Discomfort will eventually cause the athlete to stop running, at which time the discomfort soon abates. Pain recurs when the athlete resumes running.
- The pain is especially acute when running downhill or walking down stairs.
- In its most severe form, pain from this condition forces the athlete to walk with the injured leg fully straightened to relieve friction of the iliotibial band over the outer side of the knee joint.

Causes:

- Repetitive bending and straightening of the knee, as in running.
- Especially at risk are athletes who do not warm up properly, those who increase their training suddenly, those who change running shoe type, and those who run on sloped surfaces (the condition will affect the downside leg of the runner).
- Anatomical abnormalities may also be to blame for this condition, especially bow legs (which increase the tightness of the iliotibial band over the outer side of the knee joint).

Athletes at risk:

- Primarily runners, though this condition is also seen in ballet dancers, skiers, aerobic dancers, and cyclists.

Concerns:

- If allowed to persist, this condition can be extremely difficult to overcome.

What you can do:

- For a mild case of iliotibial band syndrome:
  Cease the activity that caused the condition or reduce training to a pain-free level.
  Ice the knee three times a day for twenty minutes at a time.
  Continue cardiovascular activities that do not involve repetitive knee bending and straightening (especially swimming).
  Begin a strength and flexibility program for the iliotibial band, focusing on the iliotibial band stretch (page 27). Do these exercises six times a day, holding each stretch for thirty seconds at a time.
  Change running surfaces, especially avoiding sloped surfaces.
- If the condition does not clear up within two weeks, the inflammation may be severe. In such cases, consult a sports doctor.

Medication:

- For relief of minor to moderate pain, take acetaminophen as directed on label, or, for the relief of pain *and* inflammation, ibuprofen or aspirin if tolerated (see page 49).

What the doctor can do:

- Even when the condition is relatively severe, most sports doctors treat this condition non-surgically:
  Prescribe a knee immobilizer and crutches for three to five days. The knee immobilizer should be removed for icing and strengthening and strengthening exercises (see above, "What you can do").
  Prescribe anti-inflammatories.
  Rule out anatomical abnormalities, such as bowlegs, and if an abnormality exists, recommend shoe inserts to compensate for the condition (arch supports are most effective).
  Possibly administer a cortisone injection.
- Surgery is rarely required for iliotibial band syndrome, and only when all other methods fail:
  An iliotibial band release involves cutting open the back of the iliotibial band, thereby reducing the tension over the knee.

Rehabilitation:

- Rehabilitation for this condition primarily involves stretching exercises for the iliotibial band. These should be done six times a day, and the stretch should be held for at least thirty seconds.
- If the athlete has been inactive for a significant length of time due to this condition, strengthening exercises for the iliotibial band also need to be done.

Recovery time:

- Mild cases of iliotibial band syndrome may clear up within three to five days of starting rest, ice, and stretching.
- More severe cases may take up to two weeks to resolve.
- Very severe cases of iliotibial band syndrome may take up to six months to clear up.

MENISCUS INJURIES

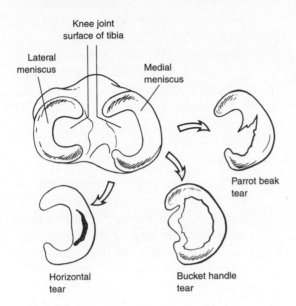

Lateral meniscus

Knee joint surface of tibia

Medial meniscus

Parrot beak tear

Horizontal tear

Bucket handle tear

A meniscus injury involves damage to one or both of the two flat, crescent-shaped pieces of cartilage that lie in the knee joint between the thighbone and large shinbone. The menisci stabilize the joint, absorb shock, and disperse lubrication known as synovial fluid. They are essential for the efficient functioning of the knee.

The meniscus most commonly injured is the one on the inner side of the knee, the medial meniscus. Injuries to the medial meniscus are about five times more common than injuries to the meniscus on the outer side of the knee, the lateral meniscus.

As blood supply to the menisci is very poor, an injury to the meniscus will almost never heal by itself. An athlete with a damaged meniscus who wants to continue in sports will have to undergo surgery.

Usually the damage to the meniscus is caused by a single episode of trauma—often a violent bend of the knee such as that associated with a medial collateral ligament sprain (page 128), which is then aggravated by repetitive twisting and turning in sports. In many cases, the symptoms do not become evident until several years later when the meniscus is significantly damaged.

Meniscus tears are named according to the shape of the tear: "bucket handle," "horizontal," and "parrot beak" to name three.

Symptoms:

- Onset of symptoms is gradual.
- Pain on the inner side of the knee joint during sports.
- Pain when pressing on the "joint line" on the inner side of the knee.
- Clicking or locking in the joint (caused by the torn portion of the meniscus catching on the end of the thighbone).
- When a sports doctor is trying to make the diagnosis of a meniscus injury, he or she will look for one or more of the signs listed below. If three or more of these signs are present, it is almost certain that the athlete has a meniscus tear:

    Point tenderness when pressure is exerted on the joint line on the inner side of the knee
    Pain in the joint line on the inner side of the knee when the knee is hyperflexed
    Pain and a "clunk" sound when the foot and lower leg are turned outward and the knee is simultaneously bent (McMurray's test)
    Weakened or atrophied quadriceps muscle

- Note: Most meniscal injuries affect the meniscus on the inner side of the knee, and in such cases pain is felt in that area. If the pain and symptoms described above are felt on the outside of the knee, then there may be a lateral meniscus tear.

Cause:

- Excessive twisting, turning, and compression of the knee joint, possibly preceded by a single small tear that worsens over time.

Concerns:

- Left untreated, a torn meniscus may worsen to the point where the entire meniscus has to be removed instead of just repaired as described below.

What you can do:

- Seek medical attention.
- If three or more of the above symptoms are

present (have a friend perform the test), begin a program of strengthening exercises to condition the quadriceps and hamstrings in anticipation of surgery and a subsequent layoff from sports. Be sure the exercises do not worsen the damage; exercise within the pain threshold.

Medication:

- For relief of minor to moderate pain, take acetaminophen as directed on label, or, for the relief of pain *and* inflammation, ibuprofen or aspirin if tolerated (see page 49).

What the doctor can do:

- Confirm the diagnosis through a physical examination and medical history (occasionally, an arthroscope may be used to look inside the joint if a definitive diagnosis cannot be made as above).
- If the injury cannot be confirmed, the doctor may order an MRI of the knee, which should provide an excellent view of the meniscus.
- Recommend surgery and prescribe a preoperative conditioning program for the quadriceps.
- Surgical options:
    To treat a torn meniscus, the doctor usually performs a partial meniscectomy. Two small puncture holes are made in the joint, an arthroscope is placed in one of the holes to look at the joint, and surgical instruments are placed in the other hole to trim off the damaged portion of the meniscus. The wound requires only two or three stitches; the patient is released from the hospital the same day as the operation and is walking the same day with the use of crutches.
    Occasionally, if the tear is small (within the 4 to 5 millimeter ''red zone'' around the edge of the meniscus), it can be repaired by microscopic stitching.
    Total surgical removal of the meniscus is no longer done, thanks to the emergence of arthroscopic technology.

Rehabilitation:

- After arthroscopic surgery to repair a meniscus, level one rehabilitation exercises can begin within one to two days.
- After one week, the patient can begin doing level two exercises, accompanied by gentle stationary biking, and progress according to the rehabilitation prescription given at the end of this chapter.

Recovery time:

- After arthroscopic surgery to repair a torn meniscus, the athlete can expect to return to activities that put rotational stress on the knee joint within four to eight weeks after the operation.
- Strengthening exercises for the muscles of the thigh should continue even after the athlete returns to sports.

BURSITIS CONDITIONS IN THE KNEE *(Prepatellar Bursitis, ''Housemaid's Knee'')*

There are several bursa sacs in the knee that can be injured in sports. In recreational athletes, injuries to bursa sacs are usually caused by repetitive stress to the bursa sac, usually in the form of friction from an overlying tendon. This repetitive stress causes bursitis— the bursa sac fills with synovial fluid to protect itself and the underlying structures from the recurrent irritation.

Note: It is also possible for a bursa sac to be injured as a result of a single blow. A single blow causes the sac to fill with blood, causing what is known as a hemobursa. Hemobursae are much less common than bursitis in recreational sports and will not be covered in this section (refer to page 44 in chapter 4, ''Diagnosing and Treating Your Sports Injury,'' for general information about hemobursae).

The bursa sac in the knee that is most frequently inflamed is the one that lies between the kneecap and the overlying skin, the prepatellar bursa.

Symptoms:

- Tenderness and swelling over the kneecap. The swelling is located in the area immediately over the knee, and nowhere else in the joint.

- Limited motion in the knee because the swelled bursa sac has made the skin over the kneecap tighten.

Causes:

- Repetitive movement and minor impacts, as well as frequent pressure (as in kneeling; hence the term "Housemaid's knee").

Athletes at risk:

- Wrestlers, ballet dancers, and trampolinists, or anyone whose knees come into repetitive contact with a hard surface.

Concerns:

- If the bursitis is allowed to become chronically inflamed, adhesions may form within the walls of the sac. In such cases, surgical removal of the entire bursa sac is the only way to resolve this condition.

What you can do:

- Rest until pain has completely abated.
- Ice the knee for forty-eight to seventy-two hours.
- Apply a bandage or doughnut pad to compress the bursa.

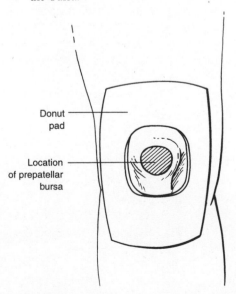

Donut pad

Location of prepatellar bursa

- After seventy-two hours, apply a moist heating pad and use a heat retainer.
- Consult a doctor if pain and swelling persist for more than two weeks or if pain and swelling become severe.

Medication:

- For relief of minor to moderate pain, take acetaminophen as directed on label, or, for the relief of pain *and* inflammation, ibuprofen or aspirin if tolerated (see page 49).

What the doctor can do:

- Treatment for prepatellar bursitis is usually nonsurgical:
  drain the bursa with a syringe
  administer a cortisone injection into the drained bursa
  prescribe RICE
- If the condition has deteriorated to the point that the bursitis does not respond to the above treatment, surgery may be necessary:
  The doctor makes an incision over the kneecap and removes the entire bursa sac.
  After surgery, range of motion exercises for the knee begin as soon as possible.
  The doctor should prescribe knee pads to protect the knee against further injury.

Rehabilitation:

- Rehabilitation for this condition primarily involves compressing the bursa with a doughnut pad and beginning level two exercises as soon as pain allows (see pages 146–51).

- If surgery is necessary, level two exercises can begin three to five days after the operation.

Recovery time:

- Nonsurgical: ten to fourteen days.
- Surgical: ten to fourteen days.

KNEE PLICA *(Synovial Plica)*

Within the knee there are several bands of tissue—known as plicae—that are tighter and less yielding in some people than in others. For people who participate in sports that require repetitive use of the knee, the plicae can cause problems. The symptoms are usually caused by a plica snapping over the end of the thighbone. Of the three to four plicae in the knee joint, the one most likely to cause the most problems is the mediopatellar plica, which lies on the inner side of the knee. An overly tight mediopatellar plica causes roughening of the ends of the thighbone and the underside of the kneecap.

Symptoms:

- This condition is difficult to identify, because the symptoms mimic the symptoms of other knee disorders.
- The athlete may experience a semilocking mechanism in the knee, and a snapping may be felt when the knee is bent past 15 to 20 degrees (these symptoms mimic those of a torn meniscus).
- There may be pain going up and down the stairs or when squatting.
- There is little or no swelling, and the joint is not loose.

Athletes at risk:

- This condition is not seen more often in any one sport than another.

Concerns:

- This condition is difficult to identify.

What you can do:

- Use RICE (page 46), and seek medical attention.

Medication:

- For relief of minor to moderate pain, take acetaminophen as directed on label, or, for the relief of pain *and* inflammation, ibuprofen or aspirin if tolerated (see page 49).

What the doctor can do:

- The doctor confirms the diagnosis through a process of elimination—by ruling out all other knee overuse condition.
- The doctor should attempt to treat the condition nonsurgically. Rest and ice are the cornerstones of treatment for this condition.
- If this course does not work, and the condition recurs, it may be necessary to intervene surgically in order to return the athlete to sports. In surgery, the plica is removed arthroscopically.

Rehabilitation:

- When physical therapy is used to correct this condition, level two rehabilitation exercises should begin as soon as pain allows.
- After surgery to remove the plica, level one rehabilitation exercises can begin within three to five days of the procedure. For levels one, two, and three rehabilitation guidelines, refer to the sections on rehabilitation and conditioning at the end of this chapter.

Recovery time:

- This condition should resolve in four to six weeks, whether it is treated nonoperatively or surgically.

OSGOOD-SCHLATTER SYNDROME

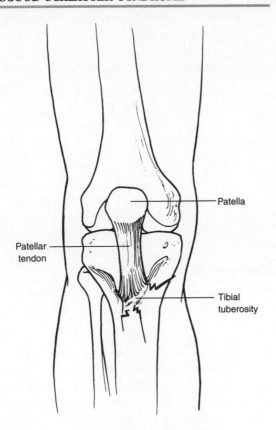

Patella

Patellar
tendon

Tibial
tuberosity

In children, repetitive knee-bending activities may cause irritation at the point where the tendon from the kneecap attaches to the top front of the larger shinbone. This is known as Osgood-Schlatter syndrome, or Osgood-Schlatter disease.

The condition occurs for two reasons. First, the ends of children's bones are still growing and have not yet fully hardened. The softness at the ends of the growing bones predisposes them to damage from the tissues that attach to these areas, which tug at this vulnerable "prebone." Second, during growth spurts, children's bones grow faster than the muscle-tendons do, which makes the muscle-tendons tighter and more likely to pull on the point where they attach to bone.

Symptoms:

- Onset of symptoms is gradual, and begins as a low-grade ache when getting out of bed in the morning, which worsens over the course of two weeks.

- Pain directly over the point where the tendon attaches to the top of the front of the shinbone.
- The child will eventually be unable to run at full speed and may walk with a limp.
- The pain is especially acute when squatting, climbing stairs, or walking uphill.

Cause:

- A combination of repetitive sports activity, tightness of the muscle-tendon units caused by a growth spurt, and the softness of the prebone to which the patellar tendon attaches.

Athletes at risk:

- Athletes nine to fourteen years old, especially those engaged in activities involving significant amounts of running.
- It was previously thought that boys were at greater risk of developing Osgood-Schlatter syndrome than girls, but with the emergence of girls in school sports, it is now believed that this condition is not seen in one gender more than the other.

Concerns:

- Ten percent of the athletes who sustain this condition develop a piece of bone in the tendon (ossicle) that can cause them pain throughout life.

What you can do:

- Use RICE (page 46), in conjunction with a horseshoe pad to relieve the pain.
- Take the child to a doctor.

What the doctor can do:

- Refer the child to a physical therapist for a comprehensive strength and flexibility program that should correct this condition.
- Recommend that the child abstain from strenuous running activities during growth spurts.
- If X rays reveal that a piece of bone has developed within the tendon, this may be removed through surgery.

Rehabilitation:

- As soon as the initial symptoms abate, the athlete should participate in a conditioning program for the knees.

Recovery time:

- This condition may take between two to four weeks or up to three years to resolve.

OSTEOCHONDRITIS DISSECANS (Loose Bodies in the Joint)

Repetitive use of the knee joint during exercise may cause grinding together of the ends of the bones that meet to form the joint. This can create a small crater with pieces of loose bone and cartilage around it—rather like a divot in the ground caused by a missed golf stroke. This condition is known as osteochondritis dissecans. If the stress continues, chips of bone and cartilage may fall into the joint.

In adults, the ends of the bones bumping together may cause divots, though it is rare that pieces of bone and cartilage actually dislodge and fall into the joint. But in children, whose joint surfaces are much softer because they are made up of growing bone that is not yet hardened, there is a much greater chance that a portion of bone and cartilage can dislodge and fall into the joint. Children between the ages of twelve and sixteen are especially at risk.

Symptoms:

- Onset of symptoms is gradual.
- Pain is caused by loosening of the bone, and is especially acute when the knee is used dynamically. The pain is nonspecific, though athletes occasionally describe it as being "inside the joint." Pain abates after sports activity.
- If a piece of bone and cartilage has dislodged and falls into the joint, the joint may occasionally lock. The athlete will be unable to straighten the injured knee fully.

Cause:

- Repetitive impact between the ends of the thighbone and the main shinbone.

Athletes at risk:

- Twelve- to sixteen-year-old sports-active children are especially susceptible to this condition.

Concerns:

- If ignored, an osteochondritis dissecans without bone and cartilage dislodgement that could heal with rest will usually deteriorate to where a piece of this hard tissue dislodges and falls into the joint, which will inevitably necessitate surgery.

What you can do:

- Anyone with the symptoms described above should seek medical attention.

Medication:

- For relief of minor to moderate pain, take acetaminophen as directed on label, or, for the relief of pain *and* inflammation, ibuprofen or aspirin if tolerated (see page 49). Aspirin *should not* be taken by children.

What the doctor can do:

- The medical history will usually reveal there is a loose or detached piece of joint cartilage.
- If the condition is severe and a piece of joint cartilage has broken off, the patient will complain of locking in the knee three or four times a day, and it will be difficult to straighten the leg fully. Just touching the joint causes pain.
- To confirm the diagnosis of osteochondritis dissecans in the knee, as well as assess its severity, X rays may be taken of *both* knee joints. The view inside the uninjured joint is needed as a comparison to tell the extent to which the bone cartilage on the injured side has been displaced. What is normally seen is either a piece of bone cartilage about to dislodge with further activity, or pieces that have already broken off.

- Because X rays do not allow doctors to see the actual joint surface, which is made of cartilage, sometimes an MRI or arthrogram is used to get a better look at the damage. These diagnostic tools allow doctors to examine the actual joint surface and, if the piece of joint cartilage has not yet detached, see the outline of the loose piece lying in its crater.
- Adults who have osteochondritis dissecans almost always require surgery to repair the damaged joint. (In children, immobilization and rest usually allow the body's healing process to help the loose chip fully rejoin the joint. Three months of limited activity is usually necessary.)
- Surgical options:

  The surgeon makes two puncture holes in the skin over the knee and, using an arthroscope, enters the joint and inspects the injury site. If the site is soft, but not unstable, the surgeon may drill holes into the cartilage and bone to stimulate healing (the blood supply created by these drilled holes creates hard scar tissue). If the piece is loose, it may be pinned back with metal or synthetic pins. Occasionally, the surgeon may pin the loose piece of bone back in place.

  If the initial diagnosis reveals that the injury has already deteriorated to where a bone chip has come loose, it may be pinned back in place or, more commonly, pieces of bone are removed arthroscopically.

  If the chip has lodged in a portion of the joint where an arthroscope cannot reach, an incision will be made over the knee and it will be removed.
- Treatment for this condition depends on whether the piece of bone and cartilage has detached. If it has not, two to three months of relative rest may enable the divot to heal.

Rehabilitation:

- If relative rest (page 64) is used to heal this condition, level two rehabilitation exercises can start after a brief rest period of between seven to fourteen days.

- If the piece of bone and cartilage is simply removed and drilling is done, level one rehabilitation exercises can start within five days of surgery.
- If a fragment of bone is pinned back in place, weight should be kept off the knee for six weeks, though range-of-motion exercises can start in three weeks. For levels one, two, and three rehabilitation guidelines, refer to the sections on rehabilitation and conditioning at the end of this chapter.

Recovery time:

- If nonoperative treatment is used, it may be three to six months before the athlete can return to full activity.
- When the fragment is removed and the crater drilled, it will be six weeks before the athlete can return to running.
- If the fragment has to be pinned in place, the athlete may return to sports in eight to twelve weeks.

Overuse Disorders of the Extensor Mechanism

Extensor mechanism is the collective name for the quadriceps muscle-tendon, kneecap, kneecap tendon, and the site where the kneecap tendon attaches to the large shinbone (tibia). These structures, working together, provide the athlete with dynamic knee extension—the motion necessary to run and jump.

Using the extensor mechanism, athletes are able to generate forces three to four times their body weight. When running and jumping, the tendon that connects the kneecap to the shinbone has to absorb forces of between 1,500 and 2,000 pounds, while the kneecap has to sustain forces of between 1,000 and 1,500 pounds. This force comes from the contraction of the quadriceps muscles necessary to push off and the impact of landing.

To generate the extremely powerful forces necessary in sports, as well as to resist the stresses of athletic activity, the extensor mechanism depends on strength and flexibility of the muscles and tendons around the knee as well as conventional alignment of the surrounding structures.

Strength and/or flexibility deficits or anatomical abnormalities may cause pain or instability in the extensor mechanism when the knee is subjected to repetitive stress. Among athletes, these conditions can be considered overuse injuries.

Overuse injuries of the extensor mechanism can be broadly defined as either those that cause pain or those that cause instability.

The most common overuse injuries associated with pain in the extensor mechanism are patellofemoral pain syndrome (damage to the kneecap itself)*, patellar tendinitis (inflammation of the tendon that attaches the larger shinbone to the kneecap), and quadriceps tendinitis (inflammation of the tendon that attaches the quadriceps muscles to the kneecap). The most common overuse injury associated with instability in the extensor mechanism is patellar subluxation (the kneecap slips out of place).

PATELLOFEMORAL PAIN SYNDROME (PFPS)

Until recently, pain in the area of the kneecap was usually diagnosed as chondromalachia patella, "cartilage softness." The term was coined at the turn of the century to describe actual damage to the back surface of the kneecap discovered during open surgery. The damage was usually caused by repetitive rubbing of the back surface of the kneecap on the thighbone (it may also be caused by degeneration associated with aging or disease).

It is now known that athletes with these classic symptoms do not necessarily have damage to the back surface of the kneecap, and furthermore, that damage to the back surface of the kneecap does not necessarily mean a person will develop knee pain. Most significant is that treating chondromalachia patella surgically often does not clear up knee pain.

Kneecap pain may be caused by several conditions quite unrelated to damage to the back surface of the kneecap, and athletes should beware the doctor who diagnoses knee pain as chondromalachia patella unless he or she has actually detected damage to the back surface of the kneecap through diagnostic testing. Unless they

have actually detected "true" chondromalachia, doctors now diagnose problems accompanied by the classic symptoms as patellofemoral pain syndrome (PFPS).

Symptoms:

- Onset of symptoms is gradual.
- Usually, there is pain in front of the kneecap, and frequently, in both kneecaps.
- Pain may be spread out, or localized along the inner or outer edge of the kneecap.
- Pain intensifies during sports activity and abates when the knee is not being used in sports.
- Typically, pain develops when the person with this condition sits for extended periods with the knee bent, as in a movie theater or during a long car ride, as well as when walking up stairs.
- Usually there is no swelling, although there may be occasional puffiness in the knee.
- There may be a crunching, crackling sensation (crepitus) in the knee that can actually be heard.
- The athlete may complain of the knee "giving way."
- The symptoms usually become progressively worse, or intensify and abate depending on sports activity levels.
- *There should be no instability of the kneecap, as this would indicate an instability syndrome, not a pain syndrome.*

Causes:

- The cause of most kneecap pain was once thought to be damage to the back surface of the kneecap—chondromalachia patella. It is now believed that the true cause of kneecap pain is problems with kneecap alignment brought on by various types of anatomical abnormality or deficits in strength and/or flexibility.

Anatomical abnormalities contributing to patellofemoral pain syndrome:

> Flat feet—foot pronation
> Thighs that turn inward from the hip (femoral anteversion)
> A thigh/lower leg Q angle greater than 15–20 degrees (see page 125)

*Pain in the kneecap *should not* be dismissed simply as chondromalachia patella, which refers specifically to wear and tear of the cartilage on the back side of the kneecap. Too often, doctors dismiss any pain in and around the kneecap as chondromalachia patella, when in fact the condition could be a completely different problem with different treatment requirements.

High-riding kneecaps (patella alta)

A shallow femoral groove in which the knee-cap lies

Looseness of the quadriceps tendon

"Miserable malalignment syndrome"—internally rotated hips, knock-knee, and flat feet

- Strength and flexibility deficits that may contribute to patellofemoral pain syndrome:

    Weakness and/or tightness in the quadriceps, hamstrings, and calves

    Weak and/or tight ankle dorsiflexors (those muscles that enable a person to point the toes upward toward the knee)

    Weak inner quadriceps muscle (vastus medialis) and a comparatively strong outer quadriceps muscle (vastus lateralis); this combination allows the kneecap to be pulled to the outside

Athletes at risk:

- Primarily those engaged in sports involving excessive amounts of running.

Concerns:

- Unless the athlete seeks the most competent sports medicine consultation available to diagnose and treat this troublesome condition, it is unlikely it will clear up.

What you can do:

- Cease the activity causing the pain.
- Seek the most expert form of sports medicine attention.

Medication:

- For relief of minor to moderate pain, take acetaminophen as directed on label, or, for the relief of pain *and* inflammation, ibuprofen or aspirin if tolerated (see page 49).

What the doctor can do:

- If detected early, surgery can almost always be avoided.

- Nonsurgical options:

    After ascertaining the exact cause of pain through physical examination in conjunction with diagnostic techniques such as X rays, arthrography, a CAT scan, an MRI, or a bone scan, the doctor has several courses of action. If the condition is caused by strength and/or flexibility deficits, exercises to overcome weakness and tightness are the cornerstone of treatment (see below, "Rehabilitation").

    If the condition is caused by anatomical abnormalities, the doctor may prescribe shoe inserts to alleviate the stresses created during sports.

    To stabilize a kneecap that is tracking erratically, the doctor may prescribe a knee brace.

Prescribe anti-inflammatories to reduce pain. Recommend alternative sports activities that maintain cardiovascular endurance but do not aggravate the pain—brisk walking, swimming, or biking instead of running.

- In about 10 to 20 percent of cases of PFPS, nonsurgical treatment fails and pain persists. Previously, it was thought that continuing pain was caused by damage to the back surface of the kneecap—chondromalachia patella—and surgery was done to smooth the area. However, it has since been discovered that it is not chondromalachia patella that is primarily responsible for the pain, and so surgery to repair the damage is not recommended. (For an in-depth discussion of diagnoses of chondromalachia patella and PFPS, see page 120).

- When surgery is done to correct pain in the kneecap, the major goal is not to repair damage to the back of the kneecap but to relieve pressure that pulls the kneecap to the outside:

    A "lateral retinacular release" is performed, in which the doctor cuts the connective tissues that are pulling the kneecap to the outside; sometimes, the muscles on the inside of the thigh that attach to the kneecap are tightened up.

Rehabilitation:

- Begin level three rehabilitation exercises immediately.
- The rehabilitation program should deemphasize the outer muscles of the quadriceps and emphasize the muscles on the inner side. For levels one, two, and three rehabilitation guidelines, refer to the sections on rehabilitation and conditioning at the end of this chapter.

Recovery time:

- Both nonoperatively and after surgery, this condition takes between six and twelve weeks to resolve.

PATELLAR TENDINITIS *("Jumper's Knee")*

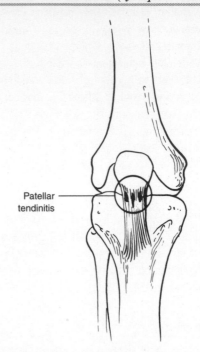

Patellar tendinitis

Patellar tendinitis, colloquially known as "jumper's knee" because of its prevalence among athletes in jumping sports, is an inflammation of the tendon that connects the larger shinbone to the kneecap. It is one of the most common—and troublesome—overuse injuries in sports. As is characteristic of most overuse conditions, patellar tendinitis develops in three phases.

Phase one (mild): Pain is felt after activity only. There is no effect on performance. Phase two (moderate): Pain is felt during and after activity. The athlete can perform at a satisfactory level. Phase three (severe): There is pain during and after activity, and it is more prolonged. Pain may be felt during daily activities. Sports performance is affected.

Symptoms:

- Onset of symptoms is gradual.
- Pain just below the kneecap, especially when sitting and straightening the leg, or when pressing the tendon.
- Pain may be felt after running or jumping activities.

- The knee may become stiff when held in the same position for extended periods.
- Little or no swelling unless the condition is extremely severe.
- The athlete experiences limitation in jumping ability.
- In the final stages, pain is felt all the time.

Causes:

- Repetitive jumping—both the muscle contraction necessary for the push-off and the impact forces of the landing stress the tendon.
- Weak or inflexible thigh muscles predispose the athlete to this condition.

Athletes at risk:

- Those engaged in sports that require dynamic jumping, such as basketball and volleyball, as well as weightlifters who perform squats.

Concerns:

- Because of the poor blood supply to tendons, healing is very slow, making this injury—one of the most common in sports—one of the most frustrating to treat.

What you can do:

- If the discomfort is felt only during and after the sports activity, the condition may be mild enough for self-treatment.
- Cease the activity that caused the condition for between two to four weeks, or until all symptoms abate.
- Ice the tendon according to the RICE (page 46) prescription for forty-eight to seventy-two hours.
- After seventy-two hours, apply a moist heating pad.
- Continue cardiovascular conditioning, especially stationary biking (set the tension on moderate, and adjust the seat so the knees are slightly bent when fully extended to the pedals).
- When the symptoms have completely abated, return to sports gradually.
- If the condition has been allowed to deteriorate

to where the pain is felt during daily activities, the athlete should seek medical attention.

Medication:

- For relief of minor to moderate pain, take acetaminophen as directed on label, or, for the relief of pain *and* inflammation, ibuprofen or aspirin if tolerated (see page 49).

What the doctor can do:

- Patellar tendinitis can almost always be treated nonsurgically:
  Four weeks of rest, in conjunction with ice during the first 72 hours, then moist heat afterward
  Anti-inflammatories
  Physical therapy to correct any deficits in tendon weakness or inflexibility
- If the condition has been allowed to deteriorate to the point where healing will likely be a long-term and possibly unsuccessful process, the doctor may recommend surgery.
- In surgery, the scar tissue on the tendon is trimmed off. Range-of-motion exercises should begin within twenty-four hours.

Rehabilitation:

- If the condition is mild, start level three rehabilitation exercises immediately.
- If moderate, start level two exercises as soon as the acute symptoms abate—no more than one week later.
- If severe, start level one exercises as soon as the acute symptoms abate—no more than one to two weeks later. For rehabilitation guidelines, refer to the sections on rehabilitation and conditioning at the end of this chapter.
- Note: Do not do full squats, which can overly stress the tendon; do quarter squats instead.

Recovery time:

- Depending on the severity of the patellar tendinitis, this condition can take anywhere from two weeks to several months to resolve.

QUADRICEPS TENDINITIS

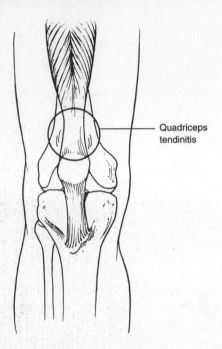

Quadriceps
tendinitis

Quadriceps tendinitis is an inflammation of the tendon that attaches the quadriceps muscle—the largest in the body—to the kneecap. This condition is seen considerably less often than patellar tendinitis and is less troublesome to resolve. However, because it affects the all-important extensor mechanism, it is of substantial concern to the athlete.

Note: Self-treatment, medication, doctor treatment, and therapeutic modalities are the same as for patellar tendinitis (page 142).

Symptoms:

- Onset of symptoms is gradual.
- Pain and tenderness in the tendon just above the kneecap. The pain intensifies when contracting the quadriceps muscles, and especially when trying to raise the leg against resistance. It is also felt when stretching the quadriceps muscle.
- Stiffness is felt after exertion.

Causes:

- Repetitive contraction of the quadriceps muscle when running or jumping.
- This condition is seen more often in athletes with weak and/or inflexible quadriceps muscles.

Athletes at risk:

- Those engaged in sports with high demands for running and jumping.

Concerns:

- Though this form of tendinitis is not as troublesome as patellar tendinitis, if allowed to deteriorate, the relative lack of blood supply to the quadriceps tendon can make it a nagging problem for athletes who place extreme demands on the extensor mechanism in their sports.

Recovery time:

- Mild and moderate cases of quadriceps tendinitis should clear up within two to four weeks.
- Severe cases of quadriceps tendinitis may take up to twelve weeks to recover.

SUBLUXING KNEECAP

An athlete whose kneecap frequently slips in and out of position is said to have a subluxing kneecap. Usually the kneecap pops over to the outside, then pops back in.

If the kneecap stays out of place, it is dislocated. Do not try to put it back in place. Seek emergency medical attention to realign the joint.

Symptoms:

- The knee feels as if it is collapsing, and the athlete may fall down.
- Pain and swelling develop, especially on the inner side of the knee, just above the kneecap.
- Difficulty bending and straightening the knee.
- The athlete may actually see the kneecap slip out and then back in.
- Athletes who have subluxing kneecaps may experience a crunching/crackling sensation (crepitus) when they fully straighten their knees, due

to wear and tear on the back surface of the kneecap.

Causes:

- When an athlete slows down, then rapidly changes direction when running, the outer quadriceps muscles may overpower the ones on the inner side, causing the kneecap to be pulled off its normal track. This is especially common in people with comparatively stronger, tighter outer quadriceps muscles and weaker, looser inner quadriceps muscles.
- Certain anatomical abnormalities may predispose an athlete to having subluxing kneecaps, including the following:
  Loose kneecaps
  Wide pelvis and thighs that turn inward from the hip
  Knock-knee
  Shallow femoral groove (the groove the kneecap lies in is too shallow)
  High-riding kneecaps (especially common in tall, thin people)
  Flat feet
  Kneecaps that face outward

Athletes at risk:

- Those with the risk factors described above, who engage in sports that require rapid changes in direction and stop-start movements.

Concerns:

- Kneecaps that frequently slip in and out of place will likely sustain damage to their back surface because of rubbing against the thigh bone.

What you can do:

- Cease those activities that cause the subluxations, especially sports involving dynamic changes in direction and stop-start running movements.
- Do exercises to strengthen the muscles on the inside of the quadriceps, and develop flexibility in the outer side of the quadriceps.

DO I HAVE LOOSE KNEECAPS?

If you have loose kneecaps, you are at increased risk of sustaining knee subluxations and/or dislocations. Following are two simple tests to determine whether you have loose kneecaps.

Sit on a table, your lower legs hanging off. Straighten one of your legs outward by extending the knee. Hold the kneecap of that knee with your thumb and index finger. Bend and straighten your knee while holding the kneecap. Does your kneecap track up and down in a straight line? If you have a loose kneecap, it will veer off track during the last 10 to 15 degrees of straightening your knee.

Now place your leg flat on the table. Completely relax your leg muscles. Again using your thumb and index finger, wiggle your kneecap sideways in both directions. Some sideways movement is desirable, but if the kneecap moves more than half an inch, you have a loose kneecap. If you can move your kneecap more than half an inch to the outside, it is likely you will sustain subluxations during dynamic "cutting" motions when running.

- Return to sports when the strength and flexibility deficits have been overcome.
- Wear a knee brace—a patellar sleeve—after returning to sports.
- If the condition persists, seek medical attention.

Medication:

- For relief of minor to moderate pain, take acetaminophen as directed on label, or, for the relief of pain *and* inflammation, ibuprofen or aspirin if tolerated (see page 49).

What the doctor can do:

- Confirm the diagnosis of subluxation with a positive apprehension test, which attempts to replicate the injury mechanism by having the doctor push the kneecap to the outside. If the athlete responds by jumping up and grasping for the doctor's hands, it can be assumed that the pain created is similar to that of the subluxation and, by association, that the athlete has suffered a subluxation.

- If deficits of muscle strength and/or flexibility are regarded as the chief cause of the subluxations, the doctor should prescribe a comprehensive exercise program primarily to develop strength on the inner side of the quadriceps, and flexibility on the outer side.
- If anatomical abnormalities such as knock-knee or flat feet are considered the main cause of the condition, the doctor may prescribe shoe inserts to correct the abnormality.
- If a loose kneecap is the cause of the subluxations, the doctor may prescribe a knee brace to stabilize the kneecap.
- If the subluxations continue despite nonsurgical treatment, the doctor may recommend surgery to correct the condition.
- Surgical options:
  Cut into the connective tissue that pulls the kneecap to the outer side
  Tighten the connective tissue that pulls the kneecap to the inner side
  Move the kneecap tendon inward
  A combination of the above procedures
- After surgery, the knee is splinted in extension for three weeks.

Rehabilitation:

- Rehabilitation exercises for a recurring subluxing kneecap are the same as those for patellofemoral pain syndrome (page 140), in which the focus is on strengthening the quadriceps, hamstrings, calf muscles, and the ankle dorsiflexors. For the quadriceps, the emphasis should be on strengthening the inner quadriceps and stretching the outer quadriceps. For levels one, two, and three rehabilitation guidelines, refer to the sections on rehabilitation and conditioning at the end of this chapter.
- The athlete can continue sports that do not involve side-to-side "cutting" motions.

Recovery time:

- If the condition is handled nonoperatively, the athlete can return to sports six to twelve weeks after rehabilitation exercises start.
- If the condition is ongoing, the athlete can return to sports six to twelve weeks after rehabilitation begins, though it's likely the condition will recur.
- After surgery, the athlete can return to vigorous sports in three to six months.

Knee Injury Rehabilitation

Rehabilitation exercises serve to
- promote blood flow to the area, which speeds the healing process

- relieve stiffness in the joint caused by immobilization

- prevent atrophy and tightening of the surrounding muscles resulting from inactivity.*

Because the knee is such a complex joint, it is essential that athletes who injure their knees take a comprehensive approach to rehabilitation. In particular, it is essential to rehabilitate fully the powerful muscles around the joint before returning to sports that place great demands on the knee. Without this support system, the knee is highly likely to be reinjured.

Rehabilitation should begin as soon as possible to prevent loss of range of motion and strength. Protracted inactivity after injury causes inordinate range of motion and strength deficits that need to be restored before return to sports activity. Delays in rehabilitation spell delays in an athlete's return to sports readiness.

After an injury that does not require surgery or prolonged splinting, range of motion exercises should begin as soon as pain and swelling diminish—usually no later than forty-eight hours after the injury symptoms begin, and often, as early as twenty-four hours. Even after some types of surgery—for instance, surgery to repair a torn meniscus—range-of-motion exercises for the knee should start after twenty-four hours.

With other types of surgery, such as a cruciate ligament repair, range-of-motion exercises should begin as

*For more on the importance and general principles of rehabilitation, see chapter 5, "Rehabilitating Your Sports Injury."

early as five days after the operation, and no later than two to three weeks later. The patient should be put in a splint that can be removed for physical therapy, or a hinged splint that allows a degree of mobility.

Exercise is the most effective way to restore an injured athlete to sports readiness. A physical therapist may also employ ice, superficial heat, deep heat, massage, electrical stimulation, and physical manipulation of the knee to promote healing and make performing the exercises more comfortable.

The starting intensity level of the rehabilitation depends on the severity of the injury. Postsurgery range-of-motion exercises usually begin at level one. At this level, range of motion is "active assisted"—the physical therapist helps the patients use their leg strength to move their knees through allowable ranges of motion. If the injury is too severe for active assisted exercises, the patient may have to rely on "passive assisted" exercises—the physical therapist moves the injured knee through allowable ranges of motion. Devices called continuous passive motion machines (CPMs) can be taken home by the patient so he or she can do passive range-of-motion exercises at home.

After surgery, muscle atrophy is prevented by using isometric exercises. With the direction of a physical therapist, exercises can usually begin immediately after surgery. Isometrics help maintain strength in the important muscles surrounding the knee without compromising the healing process by changing the length of the muscle.

Athletes who have sustained only mild or moderately severe knee injuries can begin with level two exercises.

In the initial stages of the rehabilitation program, the primary goal is to restore range of motion; the secondary goal is to prevent atrophy in the muscles. As the rehabilitation program progresses, more strengthening exercises are included.

Range-of-motion and strength exercises should always be done within the pain threshold. Any exercise that causes pain should be discontinued.

The following are the most common and effective exercises used to rehabilitate the knee after injury.

Level One

After surgery, active assisted or passive assisted range-of-motion therapy is used as a starting point of rehabilitation. The physical therapist should move the patient's knee through its major motions—flexion and extension. The knee should be moved only through those ranges of motion that do not compromise the stability of the surgery.

Isometrics and assisted range-of-motion therapy should continue only until patients are capable of using their own strength to do level two exercises.

Level Two

When patients can move their injured knees themselves, level two exercises to develop range of motion in the knee joint and strength and flexibility in the thigh muscles can start.

Level two exercises can also be used as a starting point for rehabilitating moderate to severe knee injuries that do not require surgery.

Exercise 1: Knee range of motion using the extensor muscles.

Sit on floor or mat. Place thick roll of paper toweling under injured knee. Tense thigh muscle, then raise foot until knee is fully straightened. Bad knee should stay in constant contact with the roll. Hold knee in straightened position ten seconds. Rest five seconds. Repeat.

Exercise 2: Knee range of motion using the extensor muscles

As above, but without roll of paper toweling.

Exercise 3: Knee range of motion using the flexor muscles

Sit on table or tall chair, thighs supported, lower legs hanging off. Place front of ankle of healthy leg behind heel of injured leg. Bend injured knee backward as far as possible. Hold ten seconds. Use healthy leg to guide injured leg back to starting position. Repeat.

Exercise 4: Knee range of motion using the flexor muscles

Lie facedown. Bend injured leg backward toward buttocks as far as possible. Return to starting position. Repeat.

Each of the preceding level two exercises should be done one to three times, several times a day.

Exercise 5: Strengtheners for the knee extensor muscles

Lie on back. Tense thigh muscle of injured leg; straighten knee and raise and lower leg ten times. Rest thirty seconds. Repeat ten times. Increase intensity of this exercise by increasing the number of repetitions from ten to twenty, twenty to thirty, thirty to forty, and so on.

Exercise 6: Strengtheners for the knee flexor muscles

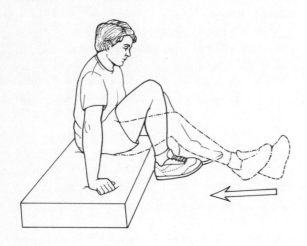

Sit on floor, knee of injured leg bent, heel flush against a low barrier so the knee is bent (sitting on mattress or thick mat best achieves this position). Straighten knee, then begin exercise by drawing heel of injured leg back until it meets barrier. Press against barrier ten seconds. Rest five seconds. Repeat exercise five to ten times.

Level Three

When the patient can do level two exercises without difficulty or pain, level three exercises can begin.

Level three exercises can also be used as a starting point for mild thigh injuries.

Level three exercises involve dynamic exercises to strengthen the thigh muscles, as well as flexibility exercises for the quadriceps, hamstrings, groin, and outer thigh muscles.

Exercise 1: Knee range of motion using the knee flexor muscles

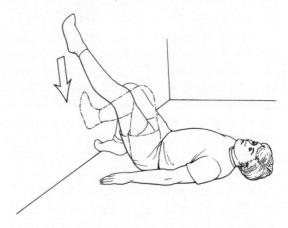

Lie on back on floor or mat, with foot of injured leg up against a wall. Let foot slide downward, at the same time bending knee. Repeat.

Exercise 2: Knee range of motion using the knee flexor muscles

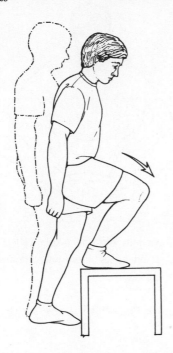

Stand with foot of injured leg on chair or bench (knee should be bent at 90 degrees). Slowly lean forward so knee of injured leg bends. Hold ten seconds. Repeat.

Exercise 3: Knee strengtheners using the extensor muscles

Attach weight cuff to ankle of injured leg. Sit on table or tall chair with thighs supported, lower legs hanging off. Straighten and lower knee ten times. Rest five seconds. Repeat.

Exercise 4: Knee strengtheners using the extensor muscles

Stand with back against a wall. Bend knees so back slides down wall. Hold position, knees bent, ten seconds. Gradually increase holding time.

Exercise 5: Knee strengtheners using the flexor muscles

Attach a piece of rubber tubing or double-thickness bandage around front legs of a chair. Sit on chair and press injured leg backward against the barrier. Hold ten seconds. Rest five seconds. Repeat.

Exercise 6: Knee strengtheners using the flexor muscles

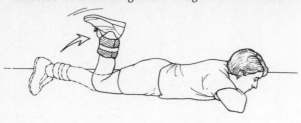

Attach weight cuff to ankle of injured leg. Lie face-down. Bend knee rapidly backward ten times. Rest five seconds. Repeat. Increase intensity of exercise by using heavier weight cuff.

Exercise 7: Flexibility for the knee extensors

Lying facedown, grasp ankle of injured leg and pull it toward buttocks (make sure thigh stays on floor). Change legs. Repeat.

Exercise 8: Flexibility for the knee flexors

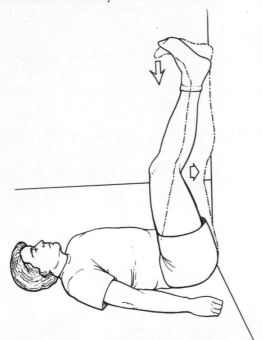

Lying on back in a doorway with buttocks as close as possible to door frame, elevate injured leg so it rests against door frame, and let healthy leg stick out through door opening. Straighten knee, while bending toes toward knee. Hold five to ten seconds. Relax three seconds. Repeat.

Exercise 9: Groin stretch

Sit on floor with knees bent, soles of feet against each other, elbows on knees. Press knees down with elbows five to ten seconds.

Exercise 10: Outer thigh muscle stretch

Sit on floor with healthy leg extended straight in front. Place foot of injured leg on outside of knee of healthy leg. Place healthy-side elbow on outside of knee of injured leg and push leg in direction of healthy leg. Hold five to ten seconds. Change legs. Repeat.

Repeat these exercises three times a day, starting at ten repetitions and gradually building up to thirty (you should be able to do ten repetitions with ease and without pain before moving on to eleven, and so on).

When you can comfortably do thirty repetitions three times a day using the starting weight, increase the weight by a pound or two, but reduce the number of repetitions back to ten, then gradually build back up to thirty.

Each time you can comfortably do thirty repetitions, increase the weight by one or two pounds and reduce the number of repetitions back to ten; then build back up to thirty.

When the strength of your injured knee is the same as that of the healthy side (and, by association, 95 percent of its original strength), ease back into sports.

Before going back to sports, however, the athlete who has been injured should be able to do daily activities without pain and simulate the leg motions of his or her sport without pain or difficulty. See page 69 for progression of rehabilitation after lower leg injuries.

To reduce the chance of reinjury, begin the strength and flexibility conditioning program that follows.

Conditioning Program for the Knee

Conditioning to prevent injuries in the muscles around the knee requires improving the strength and flexibility of all the major muscles surrounding the joint, in particular the muscles in the thigh.

Exercises to stretch and strengthen the muscles around the knee incorporate many of the exercises used to improve flexibility and strength in the hip and thigh.

Incorporate into your workout regimen at least one set of the following exercises for each muscle group mentioned. The exercises are described in chapter 3, "Strength and Flexibility: The Key to Injury Prevention."

Make these exercises part of an overall strength and flexibility program, and do them before any activity that will stress the muscles around the knee.

Knee Strengthening Exercises

Quadriceps: barbell squat, dumbbell lunge
Hamstrings: barbell squat, dumbbell lunge
Calves and Achilles tendons: barbell heel raise

Knee Flexibility Exercises

Quadriceps: standing ballet stretch
Hamstrings: seated pike hamstring stretch, wall split
Groin muscles: wall split
Outer thigh muscles: iliotibial band stretch

CHAPTER 10

Thigh Injuries

An athlete generates immense power in the thigh area. Because of the size of these muscles and their importance in any sport where explosive movement is required, it is not surprising that the thighs get injured so often.

Almost all injuries in the thigh area are *acute injuries*, those caused by a single incident. Acute thigh injuries include strains, bruises, and fractures, and may be caused by either a violent contraction of the muscle or by massive impact.

Injuries of the Thigh

Acute thigh injuries are very common in contact sports such as football, ice hockey, lacrosse, and rugby, as well as in those requiring explosive running motions. Acute thigh injuries are also seen in activities with the potential for falling accidents, such as skiing, in-line skating, and gymnastics.

Hamstring injuries, which are common in sports because they cross two joints (the hip and knee), are difficult to rehabilitate. Patience and diligence are required on the part of the athlete who sustains a hamstring injury. Hamstring injuries are especially common in athletes with more than one and a half times as much strength in their quadriceps compared to their hamstrings, because a delicate interaction between these groups of muscles is required in explosive running motions, and an imbalance can upset this synchronicity.

Strains are a problem for athletes because they tend to recur. Inelastic scar tissue forms in the area of damage, which makes the entire muscle less flexible and thus predisposes it to future injury. A vicious cycle develops; the more often the muscle gets strained, the more likely that the buildup of scar tissue will cause further injury.

Overuse injuries are not often seen in the thigh. One notable exception are stress fractures. These usually occurs at the top of the thighbone (stress fracture of the femoral neck), which, because the symptoms are felt in the hip and groin, is covered in the next chapter, "Hip, Pelvis, and Groin Injuries." Sometimes they occur at the bottom end of the thighbone, and can be confused with overuse injuries of the knee (with disastrous consequences if the bone displaces).

Preventing Thigh Injuries

Acute thigh injuries can be prevented by conditioning the thigh musculature, structuring the workout properly to include a proper warm-up and cooldown, wearing proper protective equipment, learning proper technique, and avoiding dangerous situations.

To prevent impact-type injuries, athletes engaged in contact sports such as football and hockey should wear properly fitted protective thigh pads. Those who participate in sports with the potential for falling accidents—such as skiing and mountaineering—should learn proper technique, use appropriate equipment, and avoid unnecessary risks and dangerous situations that involve skills beyond their ability.

Muscle strains are most effectively prevented by engaging in a conditioning program to develop strength and flexibility in the muscles of the thigh (the hamstrings should be 60–70 percent as strong as the quadriceps), and by performing a proper warm-up and cooldown before and after sports activity. For more on a strength and flexibility program for the thigh muscles, refer to the section at the end of this chapter. For a comprehensive guide to warming up and cooling down, refer to chapter 2, "Preventing Sports Injuries."

THIGH ANATOMY

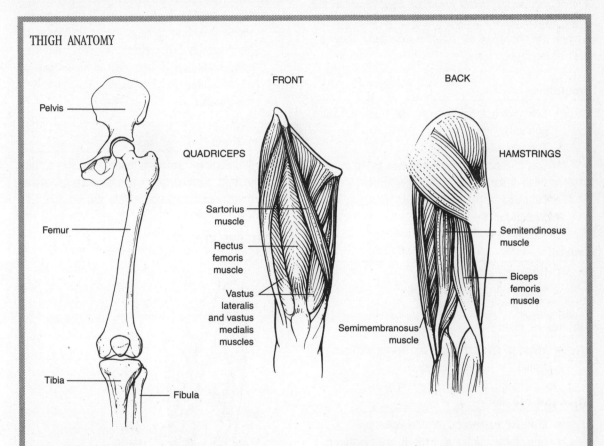

Pelvis

Femur

Tibia

Fibula

FRONT

QUADRICEPS

Sartorius muscle

Rectus femoris muscle

Vastus lateralis and vastus medialis muscles

BACK

HAMSTRINGS

Semitendinosus muscle

Biceps femoris muscle

Semimembranosus muscle

Bones and joints: The thighbone (*femur*) is the longest, strongest bone in the body. A ball at the top of the bone fits into the deep socket of the pelvis on both sides. At the bottom of each thighbone lie two flattened ball-shaped knobs with a groove in between, which attach at the knee joint to the shinbones (*tibia* and *fibula*) to form the knee joint.

Muscles: The muscle group at the front of the thigh, the quadriceps, comprises five different muscles: the *rectus femoris*, the *vastus medialis, vastus lateralis, sartorius,* and *vastus intermedius.* Behind the thigh are three hamstring muscles: the *biceps femoris, semimembranosus,* and *semitendinosus.* All three start in the buttocks bone and attach below the knee. The groin muscles on the inside of the thigh, the *adductors,* and the muscles on the outside of the thigh, the *abductors,* allow one to move the thigh inward and outward, respectively, from the hip.

Acute Thigh Injuries

THIGH FRACTURE

A thigh fracture is a crack, break, or complete shattering of the femur. Usually the bone displacement is extreme because the strength of the thigh muscles pulls apart the ends of the broken bone.

Symptoms:

- Deformity (especially when the thigh is rotated outward).
- A shortened thigh.
- Loss of function, especially when trying to move thigh inward toward the other thigh.
- Pain and acute localized tenderness.
- Swelling of the soft tissues.

Causes:

- Direct impact to the thigh.
- Violent twisting of the thigh.

Athletes at risk:

- Those in contact sports and sports with the potential for falling accidents.

What you can do:

- Send for emergency medical attention.
- Immobilize the leg and hip in the position they were found.
- Apply ice over the area.

Concerns:

- In addition to bone displacement, a fracture in the thigh also causes massive soft tissue damage, including damage to the largest quadriceps muscle (the vastus intermedius), hemorrhagings, and muscle spasm.

What the doctor can do:

- Surgery is almost always required in adults who sustain thigh fractures. The ends of the broken bones are realigned, and metal rods are inserted through an incision in the hip. These rods may be removed eighteen months after surgery, though they are often left inside the leg.

Rehabilitation:

- After a fracture, level one rehabilitation exercises should begin as soon as the athlete wakes up from surgery. For levels one, two, and three rehabilitation guidelines, refer to the sections on rehabilitation and conditioning at the end of this chapter.

Recovery time:

- Athletes can return to noncontact sports three months after surgery, and athletes in contact sports can return six months afterward.

QUADRICEPS STRAIN

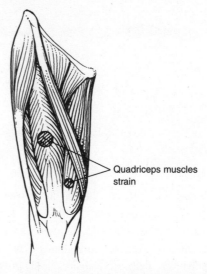

Quadriceps muscles strain

A quadriceps strain is a stretch, tear, or complete rupture of one or more of the four quadriceps muscles in front of the thigh. Though not as common as hamstring strains, strains of the quadriceps muscles are among the most common injuries in sports. This is because of the size of the quadriceps muscles—the body's largest muscles—and the amount they are used in any activity requiring dynamic locomotion. The likelihood of a quadriceps strain may be increased due to a number of intrinsic factors (see below, "Cause"). The quadriceps muscle most commonly injured is the rectus femoris, because, unlike the other three quadriceps muscles, it crosses two joints, the hip and the knee.

Symptoms:

- Sudden stabbing pain in front of the thigh.
- Possible deformity or discoloration and localized tenderness.
- In cases of mild to moderate strains, the pain may not be felt until after the sports activity, when the athlete has cooled down, at which time there is pain in the muscle in front of the thigh when trying to straighten the knee.

Cause

- Violent contraction of the quadriceps muscle, usually when trying to decelerate.

Athletes at risk:

- Those engaged in sports that require explosive stop-start running motions.

Concerns:

- Unless properly treated, a quadriceps strain is likely to recur.

What you can do:

- Start RICE (page 46) immediately and continue for forty-eight to seventy-two hours.
- Wear a heat retainer upon returning to activity, and be sure to warm up before exercising.

Medication:

- For relief of minor to moderate pain, take acetaminophen as directed on label, or, for the relief of pain *and* inflammation, ibuprofen or aspirin if tolerated (see page 49).

What the doctor can do:

- Professional treatment for a quadriceps strain follows the same prescription as above (see "What you can do").

Rehabilitation:

- In the case of a mild strain, begin level three exercises three to five days after the injury.
- In the case of a moderate or severe strain, begin level two or level one rehabilitation exercises within two weeks, depending on pain. For levels one, two, and three rehabilitation guidelines, refer to the sections on rehabilitation and conditioning at the end of this chapter.

Recovery time:

- Mild: three to five days.
- Moderate: two to three weeks.
- Severe: up to ten weeks.

HAMSTRING STRAIN

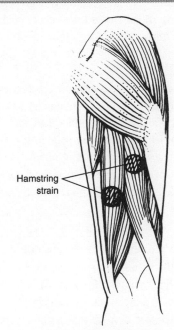

Hamstring strain

A hamstring strain is a stretch, tear, or complete rupture of one or more of the three muscles behind the thigh. It is one of the most common injuries in sports, and one of the most debilitating, given the size of the muscle group and the fact that all three muscles span two joints, the hip and the knee. The likelihood of a hamstring strain is dramatically increased if the muscles are not sufficiently warmed up (see below, "Causes"). Depending on their severity, hamstring strains are classified as first, second, or third degree.

Note: Hamstring strains are very difficult to treat and rehabilitate, so be diligent in caring for this injury. In particular, it is essential not to return to sprinting activities too soon, as reinjury—and potentially chronic recurrence of this condition—is likely.

Symptoms:

- First degree: athlete feels a slight "pull" in the muscles behind the thigh while sprinting but is able to continue the activity. The next day the muscle may be sore, but it does not inhibit walking or slow jogging, and there is no difficulty performing straight-leg raises.
- Second degree: athlete feels a "twang" while sprinting and usually has to withdraw from the activity. The muscle aches and is tender, and in three to six days bruising is noticeable under the skin, usually toward the bottom of the back of the thigh. Straight-leg raises are difficult due to pain, and bending the knee and jogging are also difficult.
- Third degree: athlete suddenly experiences severe hamstring pain while sprinting and usually collapses. Walking is impossible and even limited straight-leg raises are very painful. If not treated immediately, severe bruising occurs within four days. Crutches are usually required for one to two weeks until acute inflammation subsides.

Causes:

- A violent contraction of the hamstring muscles when the athlete increases speed when running.
- Hamstring strains can also occur when the hamstring muscles are overstretched.
- The likelihood of a hamstring strain is increased if the athlete does not warm up sufficiently, if the muscles are relatively tight and weak compared to the quadriceps muscles, or if he or she has leg length inequalities or poor posture.

Athletes at risk:

- Those engaged in sports that require explosive stop-start running motions and activities that place extreme stretching demands on the hamstrings, such as gymnastics.

Concerns:

- Unless properly treated, a hamstring strain will almost inevitably recur.

What you can do:

- The foundation of self-treatment for hamstring strains is RICE (page 46), which should begin as soon as possible after the injury occurs and continue for forty-eight to seventy-two hours.
- Wear a neoprene thigh sleeve upon return to activity.

Medication:

- For relief of minor to moderate pain, take acetaminophen as directed on label, or, for the relief of pain *and* inflammation, ibuprofen or aspirin if tolerated (see page 49).

What the doctor can do:

- Professional treatment for hamstring strains follows the prescription given above (see "What you can do"), the most important facet being RICE for forty-eight to seventy-two hours.
- If the injury is a second- or third-degree strain, the doctor may also provide the athlete with crutches or recommend bedrest. Crutches are discontinued when the athlete can walk without a limp.
- After this initial phase of treatment, the doctor should examine the patient to determine the extent of the injury. If there is little or no pain, no discoloration, and no impairment of function, the doctor should recommend level three rehabilitation exercises, followed by a relatively quick return to sports activity.
- If the injury is a second- or third-degree strain, a second phase of treatment should be undertaken for one to two weeks. This begins with level one rehabilitation exercises, and progresses accordingly. For levels one, two, and three rehabilitation guidelines, refer to the sections on rehabilitation and conditioning at the end of this chapter.

Rehabilitation:

- As scarring in the muscle usually takes place after a strain, gentle stretching exercises should be done as soon as possible after an injury to minimize the scarring. This is important because scarring makes the muscle less flexible, and therefore increases the chance of reinjury.
- After a first-degree strain, gentle stretching should begin the day after the injury, if pain allows. These stretching exercises are described under the level one rehabilitation exercises (page 159). Level two exercises to develop both strength and flexibility in the muscle should start three to five days after a first-degree strain.
- In the case of a second- or third-degree strain, level one stretching and strengthening exercises should begin within one to two weeks of the injury and progress accordingly.
- Cardiovascular conditioning should begin as soon as the initial pain abates. In the first week, upper body cardiovascular exercise such as swimming is recommended, followed the week after by cardiovascular exercise that does not overly stress the hamstrings, such as stationary biking and stairclimber machines. In addition to maintaining the athlete's cardiovascular conditioning, these activities help strengthen the hamstrings.
- When all tenderness is gone and the hamstring can be tensed fully without pain, the athlete can begin running training in conjunction with rehabilitation exercises. Start with slow jogging for twenty to thirty minutes, then perform stretching exercises for the hamstrings, then do half- to three-quarter-speed sprints over 50 to 75 yards. Explosive bursts of speed should be avoided. When sprinting can be done without pain at a three-quarters pace, full-speed sprinting can be attempted. If the athlete experiences any pain during or after any of these running activities, he or she should cut back on running intensity. During the sprinting training, it is advisable to wear a thigh sleeve that keeps the muscle warm and also acts as a support for the muscle.

Recovery time:

- First-degree strain: one to two weeks.
- Second-degree strain: three to four weeks.
- Third-degree strain: up to ten weeks.

THIGH BRUISE *(Thigh Contusion, "Charley Horse")*

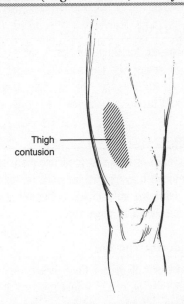

Thigh contusion

A thigh bruise, or contusion, involves bleeding in the muscle fibers caused by a blow. Usually a thigh bruise affects one or more of the quadriceps muscles. Unlike strains, which affect the superficial muscles, bruises occur deep inside the muscle, close to the bone.

Symptoms:

- Immediate pain and possible muscle spasm and discoloration.
- Difficulty bending the knee, localized pain, tenderness, and swelling.

Cause:

- Direct impact to the muscle.

Athletes at risk:

- Those engaged in contact sports and sports with a potential for falling accidents.

Concerns:

- If the bruise is severe enough, if a bruise is treated improperly or inadequately, or if the area gets reinjured, a condition known as myositis ossificans may develop in which scar tissue calcifies and bone forms in the muscle.

What you can do:

- Treatment for thigh bruises is the same as for thigh strains, with the foundation of self-treatment being RICE (page 46). A rigid thigh guard should be worn to prevent re-injury.

Medication:

- For relief of minor to moderate pain, take acetaminophen as directed on label, or, for the relief of pain *and* inflammation, ibuprofen or aspirin if tolerated (see page 49).

What the doctor can do:

- A doctor will treat a thigh bruise in much the same way he or she would treat a thigh strain. However, if myositis ossificans develops, the doctor may have to enter the joint to remove the bone surgically.

Rehabilitation:

- Rehabilitation for thigh bruises follows the same course as for thigh strains (pages 155, 157).

Recovery time:

- Mild bruise: three days to a week.
- Moderate to severe bruise: three to eight weeks (so long as a thigh guard is worn, if the athlete is engaged in a sport with the potential for contact).

Thigh Injury Rehabilitation

Rehabilitation exercises serve to

- Promote blood flow to the area, which speeds the healing process
- Relieve stiffness in the muscles and surrounding joints caused by immobilization
- Prevent atrophy and tightening of the muscles resulting from inactivity.*

Because the muscles of the thigh are so important for most sports activities, it is essential that athletes take a comprehensive approach to rehabilitation when they are injured. In particular, injuries to the hamstrings need to be carefully rehabilitated because after injury, scarring in the muscle makes the muscles less flexible and extremely susceptible to reinjury.

Rehabilitation should begin as soon as possible to prevent loss of range of motion and strength. Protracted inactivity after injury causes inordinate range-of-motion and strength deficits that need to be restored before return to sports activity. Delays in rehabilitation spell delays in an athlete's return to sports readiness.

After an injury that does not require surgery or prolonged splinting, range-of-motion exercises should begin as soon as pain and swelling diminish—usually no later than forty-eight hours after the injury symptoms begin, and often as early as twenty-four hours.

When surgery is necessary, range-of-motion exercises should begin as early as five days after surgery, and no more than two to three weeks later. The patient should be put in a splint that can be removed for physical therapy.

Exercise is the most effective way to restore an injured athlete to sports readiness. A physical therapist may also employ ice, superficial heat, deep heat, massage, electrical stimulation, and physical manipulation of the thigh to promote healing and make performing the exercises more comfortable.

The starting intensity level of the rehabilitation depends on the severity of the injury. Postsurgery range-of-motion exercises usually begin at level one. At this level, range of motion is "active assisted"—the physical

*For more on the importance and general principles of rehabilitation, refer to chapter 5, "Rehabilitating Your Sports Injury."

therapist helps the patients use their leg strength to move their legs through allowable ranges of motion. If the injury is too severe for active assisted exercises, the patient may have to rely on "passive assisted" exercises— the physical therapist moves the injured leg through allowable ranges of motion. Continuous passive motion machines (CPMs) can be taken home by the patient so he or she can do passive range-of-motion exercises at home.

After surgery, muscle atrophy is prevented by using isometric exercises. With the direction of a physical therapist, these exercises can usually begin immediately after surgery. Isometrics help maintain strength in the important muscles of the thigh without compromising the healing process by changing the length of the muscle.

Athletes who have sustained only mild or moderately severe thigh injuries can begin with level two exercises.

In the initial stages of the rehabilitation program, the primary goal is to restore range of motion; the secondary goal is to prevent atrophy in the muscles. As the rehabilitation program progresses, more strengthening exercises are included in the program.

Range-of-motion and strength exercises should always be done within the pain threshold. Any exercise that causes pain should be discontinued.

The following are the most common and effective exercises used to rehabilitate the thigh after injury.

Level One

After surgery, active assisted or passive assisted range-of-motion therapy is used as a starting point of rehabilitation. The physical therapist should move the patient's thigh through its major motions. The thigh should be moved only through those ranges of motion that do not compromise the stability of the surgery.

Isometrics and assisted range-of-motion therapy should continue only until patients are capable of using their own strength to do level two exercises.

Level Two

When patients can move their injured thighs themselves, level two exercises to stretch and strengthen the thigh muscles can start.

Level two exercises can also be used as a starting

point for rehabilitating moderate to severe thigh injuries that do not require surgery. Those low-intensity exercises develop both strength and flexibility in the thigh muscles.

Exercise 1: Quadriceps stretch

Lying facedown, grasp ankle of injured leg and pull it toward buttocks (make sure thigh stays on floor). Change legs. Repeat.

Exercise 2: Quadriceps strengthener

In same position as above, try to straighten leg against resistance of hand. Change legs. Repeat.

Exercise 3: Quadriceps stretch and strengthener

As above, except in standing position, stretch thigh by pulling ankle toward buttocks, and strengthen it by pushing against hand resistance. Change legs. Repeat. Keep hip straight or slightly back.

Exercise 4: Hamstring stretch

Lying on back in a doorway with buttocks as close as possible to door frame, elevate injured leg so it rests against door frame, and let healthy leg stick out though door opening. Straighten knee, simultaneously bending toes toward your knee. Hold five to ten seconds. Relax three seconds. Repeat.

Exercise 5: Hamstring strengthener

As above, except press heel against door frame. Hold five to ten seconds.

Exercise 6: Groin stretch

Sit on floor with knees bent, soles of feet against each other, elbows on knees. Press knees down with elbows five to ten seconds.

Exercise 7: Groin strengthener

As above, except press inward with knees against resistance of elbows.

Exercise 8: Outer thigh muscle stretch

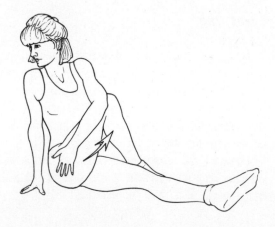

Sit on floor with healthy leg extended straight in front. Place foot of injured leg on outside of knee of healthy leg. Place healthy-side elbow on outside of knee of injured leg and push leg in direction of healthy leg. Hold for five to ten seconds. Change legs. Repeat.

Exercise 9: Outer thigh muscle strengthener

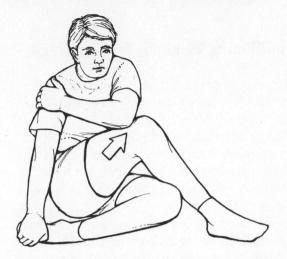

As above, except grasp outside of knee of injured leg with opposite hand, and press knee of injured leg against resistance of hand five to ten seconds. Change legs. Repeat.

Level Three

When the patient can do the level two exercises without difficulty or pain, level three exercises can begin. Level three can also be used as a starting point for mild thigh injuries.

Level three exercises involve dynamic exercises to strengthen the thigh muscles.

Flexibility for the thigh at this point should involve level two stretching exercises for the quadriceps, hamstrings, groin, and outer thigh muscles.

Exercise 1: Quadriceps strength

Attach weight cuff to ankle of injured leg. Sit in chair with thighs supported and lower legs hanging off. Straighten knee of injured leg. Hold five seconds. Lower slowly. Repeat ten to thirty times. Change legs. Repeat.

Exercise 2: Hamstring strength

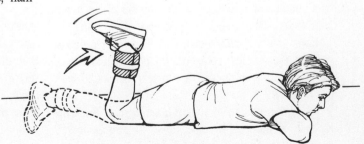

Attach weight cuff to ankle of injured leg. Lie facedown on flat surface. Curl injured leg so ankle approaches buttocks. Return slowly to starting position. Repeat ten to thirty times. Change legs. Repeat.

Exercise 3: Groin and outer thigh muscle strength

Attach weight cuff to ankle of injured leg. Placing hand against wall for balance, a) draw leg across your body, b) extend your leg away from your body. Do each exercise ten to thirty times. Change legs. Repeat.

Repeat these exercises three times a day, starting at ten repetitions and gradually building up to thirty. You should be able to do ten repetitions with ease and without pain before moving onto eleven, and so on.

When you can comfortably do thirty repetitions three times a day using the starting weight, increase the weight by a pound or two, but reduce the number of repetitions back to ten, then gradually build back up to thirty.

Each time you can comfortably do thirty repetitions, increase the weight by one or two pounds and reduce the number of repetitions back to ten; then build back up to thirty.

When the strength of your injured thigh is the same as that of the healthy side (and, by association, 95 percent of its original strength), ease back into sports.

Before going back to sports, however, the athlete who has been injured should be able to do daily activities without pain and simulate the leg motions of his or her sport without pain or difficulty.

To reduce the chance of reinjury, begin a strength and flexibility conditioning program.

Conditioning Program for the Thigh

Conditioning to prevent injuries in the muscles of the thigh requires improving the strength and flexibility of all the major muscles of the thigh.

Exercises to stretch and strengthen the muscles of the thigh incorporate many of the exercises used to improve flexibility and strength in the joints above and below the thighbone, the hip (including the pelvis and groin), and the knee.

Incorporate into your workout regimen at least one set of the following exercises for each muscle group mentioned. The exercises are discribed in chapter 3, "Strength and Flexibility: The Key to Injury Prevention."

Make these exercises part of an overall strength and flexibility program, and do them before any activity that will stress the muscles around the thigh.

Thigh Strengthening Exercises

Quadriceps: barbell squat, dumbbell lunge
Hamstrings: barbell squat, dumbbell lunge
Groin muscles and outer thigh muscles: tubed leg swing
Certain weight machines such as the ones seen in most health clubs can also help condition the muscles on the inside and outside of the thigh.

Thigh Flexibility Exercises

Quadriceps: standing ballet stretch, lying quadriceps and iliotibial band stretch
Hamstrings: seated pike hamstring stretch, wall split/stretch
Groin muscles: wall split
Outer thigh muscles: iliotibial band stretch

CHAPTER ELEVEN

Hip, Pelvis, and Groin Injuries

The hip and pelvis area is strong and stable—the "anchor" of the human body—and is not often the site of serious acute injuries such as fractures or dislocations. However, the numerous muscle-tendon units in this area are subject to strains because of the large workload they must endure in sports.

When an injury does occur in this part of the body, the consequences are often debilitating to the athlete because of the important role of the hip and pelvis muscles in any activity involving dynamic motion. The diagnosis and treatment of such injuries are quite straightforward, but the injury may be difficult to overcome because they are so integral to most sports activity. Also, complete rest of the muscle-tendons is difficult because they are necessary for daily activity. Rehabilitating muscle strains in this part of the body requires a great deal of patience and dedication on the part of the athlete. Reinjury of the muscles in this area is common.

The symptoms of injuries in this area may cause confusion because they are often vague and nonspecific, and many of the tissues that are injured lie deep inside the body. Pain from injuries in the hip area can radiate to the groin and thigh. Also, there are a variety of infections in the abdominal organs and genitals that athletes may misinterpret as a sports injury.

Injuries of the Hip, Pelvis, and Groin

Acute hip, pelvis, and groin injuries may include contusions (hip "pointers"), muscle-tendon strains, ligament sprains, fractures, avulsion fractures (tearing away of a piece of bone where the muscle-tendon attaches), and dislocations.

Acute hip, pelvis, and groin injuries can result from a fall, direct impact, twist, or extreme muscle contraction.

Dislocations of the hip and fractures of the hip and pelvis are very rare in sports, and are almost never seen in adult recreational athletes, because the bones of the hip and pelvis are strong and well protected. It requires massive trauma to cause such an injury. However, older athletes may be at increased risk of hip injuries because of the effects of bone thinning (osteoporosis). An injury may occur when the older athlete firmly plants his or her foot and the torso is twisted in another direction, as in a misstep when momentum carries the body onward.

Dislocations of the hip and fractures of the hip and pelvis are emergencies. A dislocation often damages the nerve supply to the lower extremities, with the possible result being permanent weakness and numbness. If the dislocation interferes with the blood supply of the hip, the injury may cause a condition known as avascular necrosis, resulting in the ball of the hip joint dying. This in turn may cause disabling arthritis in later life. To avoid these conditions, a hip dislocation needs to

HIP, PELVIS, AND GROIN ANATOMY

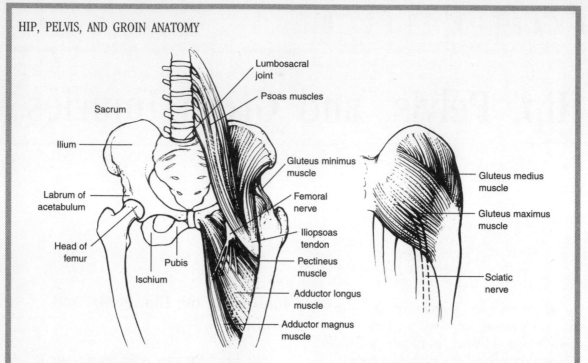

Bones and joints: The three bones of the pelvis—the *ilium, ischium,* and *pubis*—form the "pelvic ring," the unit that links the spine with the legs. The fused part of the spine and tailbone (*lumbosacrum*) connects the pelvis to the rear part of the top of the pelvic ring. The joints where the spine and pelvis meet are the *sacroiliac* joints. The legs attach to the bottom of the pelvis at the hip joints.

The hips are ball-and-socket joints that connect the thighs to the pelvis. The ball at the top of the thighbone, the *femoral head,* lies inside a socket in the pelvis, the *acetabulum.* The entire ball-and-socket structure is encased in a capsule composed of gristle-like ligaments. Several strong ligaments hold together the hip joint.

The groin is the cavity between the thigh and the abdominal area.

Muscles and nerves: The pelvis is the site of numerous muscle-tendon attachments. Most muscles in the torso and thighs attach to the pelvis. All the large *paraspinal* muscles—the muscles that run on either side of the spine and support it—and all of the muscles in the abdomen originate in the pelvis.

All of the muscles in the buttocks and upper hip, all the hamstring muscles, and some of the quadriceps muscles attach to the pelvis.

The *psoas muscles* allow for hip flexion, the ability to raise the knee toward the chest. Of these, the *iliopsoas muscle,* which runs from the lower back to the inside of the top of the thighbone, is the most important. The opposing muscle is the *gluteus maximus,* whose main function is hip extension.

The hip abductor muscles run from the pelvis down to the lower part of the thighbone and allow the leg to be drawn outward from the hip. The three main abductor muscles are the *tensor fascia latae, gluteus minimus,* and *gluteus medius.*

The hip adductor muscles are the so-called groin muscles, located on the inside of the thigh, that let one draw the leg inward. The most important of the adductor muscles are the *adductor longus, adductor magnus,* and *pectineus.*

The two main nerves in the area of the pelvis and hip are the *sciatic nerve* and the *femoral nerve.*

put back in place ("reduced"), and nerve and blood supply checked.

Unless managed properly, fractures of the hip—which primarily affect the ball of the joint at the top of the thighbone—may also cause death of the ball of the hip joint. In children, hip fractures usually damage the growth plates and can cause long-term deformity of the joint.

Hip and pelvis contusions are not often seen in recreational athletes because of the rarity of significant impact. However, they are sometimes seen when there is a fall and the crest of the iliac connects forcefully with a hard surface, known as a hip "pointer" (even though it is not the hip that is affected but rather the iliac crest of the pelvis). This injury is occasionally seen in squash or racquetball players who slam sideways into the court wall, or when tennis players slip and fall onto their sides.

Much more common than these impact-type injuries are muscle-tendon strains. A muscle-tendon strain can be either a stretch, tear, or complete rupture of the muscle-tendon unit. These injuries are so common because the pelvic area and the upper part of the leg are where many strong muscles originate and attach. It is where the abdominal muscles insert into the pelvic ring, where the gluteal muscles run from the buttocks bone to the top of the thighbone, where the groin muscles attach to the pubic bones, and where the main hip flexor attaches to the inside of the top of the thigh. Because these muscles are so important, injuries to them can be quite disabling, especially to athletes who use their lower extremities in their chosen activity.

Muscle-tendon stretches, tears, and complete ruptures are usually caused by a forceful contraction of a muscle when it is in extreme extension. A hip flexor strain may occur when sprinting: the hip is in full extension and the athlete powerfully pushes off the running surface and brings the knee toward the chest. A groin strain may occur in hockey when the leg is stretched out to the side and then the player vigorously pulls it inward.

In adults, strains affect the point where the muscle turns into tendon. This is a point of weakness. The most common muscle-tendon injuries occur in the hip flexor (iliopsoas) and groin (adductor) muscles.

Unfortunately, it is difficult to rehabilitate muscle-tendon strains in this area. It may take six to twelve weeks for them to heal completely.

POSSIBLE CAUSES OF GROIN PAIN OTHER THAN GROIN STRAIN

Too often athletes and doctors dismiss pain in the groin area as a simple "groin strain." For this reason, it is important to have prolonged groin pain checked out by a qualified physician. There are many reasons an athlete may suffer from pain in this area, including the following:

- Stress fractures of the top of the thighbone

- Avulsion injuries

- Osteitis pubis

- Tumors

- Avascular necrosis of the ball of the hip joint

- Hernias

- Lymphadenopathy

- Various forms of arthritis

The same mechanism that results in a muscle-tendon strain in an adult can cause an avulsion fracture in the younger athlete. In the growing body, the muscle-tendon unit is often stronger than the bone to which it is attached. Therefore, a forceful contraction of a muscle-tendon unit can cause a tendon to detach from the bone, pulling off a piece of bone as it does so. The most frequent sites of avulsion fractures in the hip, pelvis, and groin area are the pelvic ring, buttocks bone, and upper thighbone.

Overuse injuries of the hip, pelvis, and groin include bursitis conditions, inflammations of the tendon insertions (tendinitis), stress fractures, and a unique inflammatory condition called osteitis pubis that affects the disc of cartilage between the right and left sides of the pubic bone.

Overuse injuries develop over time from the kind of repetitive stress experienced mostly in activities where there is frequent pounding of the lower extremities on a training surface, as in running (when the impact may transmit up to the hip, pelvis, and groin), and where there is repetitive contraction of the powerful muscle-tendon units.

Athletes at greatest risk of sustaining an overuse injury in the hip, pelvis, and groin are runners and other athletes who train on hard surfaces, such as football and soccer players who practice for extended periods indoors or on AstroTurf.

The onset of symptoms in overuse injuries is gradual (unlike for most acute injuries), and may have no obvious cause. The symptoms are usually pain, changes in gait (such as a limp), and, in the cases of some bursa conditions, an audible snapping sound in the hip.

Initially, pain may be felt only after sports participation. Gradually the symptoms may be experienced during or after participation, but may not be serious enough to interfere with performance. In the final stages, disabling pain is felt both during and after participation, and in daily activities.

Bursa conditions can be caused by either repetitive trauma or massive impact. In the pelvis and hip, the most commonly injured bursa sacs are the ischial and trochanteric bursae. In recreational athletes, irritation from repetitive muscle contractions over these bursae is by far the most common cause. Fortunately, bursitis conditions in the hip and pelvis are rarely serious and seldom debilitating. They respond quite well to rest, anti-inflammatories, ice, and cortisone injections.

Inflammations of the muscle-tendon insertions into the bone are also quite common in recreational athletes. The inflammations are caused by repetitive contractions of these muscle-tendon units. Inflammation of the muscle-tendons—tendinitis—needs to be differentiated from strains because it heals very differently. Strains happen suddenly from a single trauma, and the fibers all begin healing at the same time. In tendinitis, so few fibers tear that the athlete does not notice the damage at first and continues the activity. The body begins the healing process to repair the microtears, but the next time the athlete participates in the activity, more fibers tear. Because this is a very gradual process, there may be a complex overlap of tissues in different stages of healing, which makes the healing process all the more problematic.

The most common tendinitis conditions in the hip, pelvis, and groin involve the adductor longus (the largest groin muscle), the iliopsoas (the largest hip flexor), and the rectus femoris (the main quadriceps muscle).

Stress fractures in the hip, pelvis, and groin area usually affect the pelvis or the femoral neck (the shaft of the thighbone just below the ball of the hip joint).

Pelvic stress fractures are very rare, and are seen almost exclusively in distance runners. Still, less than 2 percent of the stress fractures sustained by runners affect the pelvis.

More common are stress fractures of the femoral neck. Although this is technically an injury of the upper thigh, the pain is usually experienced in the hip and/or groin as a nonspecific ache felt during and after activities using the hip.

A growing problem among distance runners is osteitis pubis, an inflammation of the disc of cartilage where the right and left parts of the pubic bone meet. The condition is experienced as tenderness in the pubic bone that may radiate into the groin area.

Preventing Hip, Pelvis, and Groin Injuries

Acute injuries of the hip, pelvis, and groin are often caused by deficits in strength and flexibility, as well as improper preparation for vigorous athletic activity, notably inadequate warm-up and cooldown. Injuries caused by muscle-tendon weakness and inflexibility can therefore be minimized by engaging in a regular strength and flexibility program and by structuring the workout properly to include warm-up and cooldown periods. For a comprehensive conditioning program for the hip, pelvis, and groin area, refer to the section at the end of this chapter. For more information on how to structure the workout to include a proper warm-up and cooldown period, refer to chapter 2, "Preventing Sports Injuries."

In sports where there is the potential for impact from other players or from equipment, such as football, hockey, baseball, volleyball, and softball, protective hip pads should be worn to avoid impact injuries. To minimize the incidence of traumatic injuries in adventure sports such as skydiving and rock climbing, proper technique should be learned, proper equipment used, and unnecessary risks avoided.

Overuse injuries of the hip, pelvis, and groin can be minimized by following a slow, progressive training regimen and not doing "too much too soon." This is especially important for distance runners.

Anyone who participates in sports that place great demands on the lower extremities should engage in a conditioning program to develop strength and flexibility in the muscles of these areas, and do a proper warm-up and cooldown before and after their activity, as strength and flexibility deficits may contribute to overuse injuries. For example, tight muscle-tendon units are more likely to sustain inflammations where they insert into the bones. Also, tight muscles may cause excessive irritation of the underlying structures, especially bursa sacs.

It is also important for athletes involved in activities that stress the lower extremities to pay attention to external risk factors such as their training surface and the types of footwear they use. For more on addressing overuse injury risk factors, refer to chapter 2.

A presports physical may help athletes avoid overuse injuries of the hip, pelvis, and groin. Certain anatomical abnormalities may contribute to the onset of overuse injuries. For instance, excessive pronation of the foot when running is known to be one possible cause of bursitis of the hip. A presports physical can detect such anatomical abnormalities, and the doctor performing the physical can make suggestions on how to overcome these conditions (exercises or shoe inserts, for instance).

Acute Injuries of the Hip, Pelvis, and Groin

HIP FLEXOR STRAIN

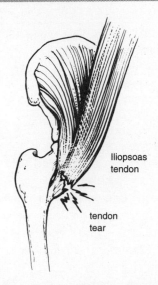

Iliopsoas
tendon

tendon
tear

A hip flexor strain is a stretch, tear, or complete rupture of the iliopsoas muscle where the tendon inserts into the inner side of the top of the thighbone.

Symptoms:

- A stab of pain in the groin area. The pain becomes acute when the athlete tries to lift the injured leg (hip flexion).
- In first- and second-degree strains the pain is felt deep inside the muscle at the top of the thighbone when the athlete tries to lift the knee against resistance. When the tear is complete, the athlete will have very little strength when attempting this maneuver.

Cause:

- A powerful contraction of the iliopsoas muscle, usually when the leg is fully extended or trapped in place.

Athletes at risk:

- Runners are at risk during the "kick" stage of the race, and the injury is common among soccer players whose legs are hit when they are kicking the ball.

- This injury is especially common among those athletes with weak or inflexible hip flexor muscles.

Concerns:

- In children, this injury may involve the tendon pulling off a portion of bone at the tendon attachment. This is known as an avulsion fracture (page 170).

What you can do:

- For first-degree strains, apply ice and begin level three exercises as soon as initial pain abates. Continue those activities that do not stress the muscle, e.g., light cycling, stairclimber machines, swimming, etc. For levels one, two, and three rehabilitation guidelines, refer to the sections on rehabilitation and conditioning at the end of this chapter.
- For second- and third-degree strains, apply ice, rest the affected limb, and make an appointment to see a sports doctor.

Medication:

- For relief of minor to moderate pain, take acetaminophen as directed on label, or, for the relief of pain *and* inflammation, ibuprofen or aspirin if tolerated (see page 49).

Rehabilitation:

- Rehabilitation for hip flexor strains follows the same pattern as for groin strains (page 169).

Recovery time:

- First-degree strains: two to seven days.
- Second-degree strains: one to two weeks.
- Third-degree strains: four to six weeks.

GROIN STRAIN *(Adductor Strain)*

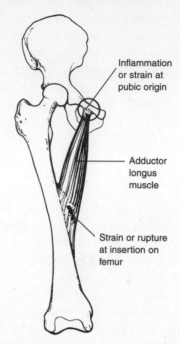

Inflammation or strain at pubic origin

Adductor longus muscle

Strain or rupture at insertion on femur

A groin strain is a stretch, tear, or complete rupture of the muscle that runs from the pubic bone to the inside of the thigh, the adductor longus. This is the main muscle that allows the athlete to draw the leg inward from the hip. The injury usually takes place where the muscle-tendon attaches to the thigh (but occasionally where it attaches to the pubic bone). As with all muscle and tendon strains, this injury is classified according to severity: first, second, or third degree.

Symptoms:

- Sudden stabbing pain in the groin.
- Inability to draw the leg inward.
- Pain when trying to draw the leg inward.
- Bruising and swelling may show up several days later.
- If the injury is severe, it may be possible to feel a deformity in the muscle.
- If the muscle is completely ruptured, it may be impossible to draw the leg inward.

Cause:

- A powerful contraction of the adductor muscles, as in forcefully drawing the leg inward.

Athletes at risk:

- Any athlete whose sport involves dynamic use of the adductor muscles, especially hockey and soccer players.
- Athletes with weak or inflexible adductor muscles are at greater risk of sustaining a groin strain.

Concerns:

- Unless fully rehabilitated, groin strains recur frequently, making participating in many sports impossible.

What you can do:

- In the case of a first-degree strain, apply RICE (page 46) and start level three rehabilitation exercises as soon as pain abates (page 179).
- If the strain is second or third degree, apply RICE and seek medical attention.
- If pain is severe, use crutches while awaiting medical attention.

Medication:

- For relief of minor to moderate pain, take acetaminophen as directed on label, or, for the relief of pain *and* inflammation, ibuprofen or aspirin if tolerated (see page 49).

What the doctor can do:

- Treatment for groin strains is almost always nonsurgical:
  Ice, rest, and immobilization, the duration of which will depend on the severity of the injury.
  Crutches may be necessary if pain and disability are severe.
  Prescribe a comprehensive, well-directed rehabilitation program to minimize buildup of scar tissue in the muscle, which will predispose the athlete to reinjury.
- In the case of a complete rupture of the adductor muscle, surgery may be necessary.

Rehabilitation:

- In cases of first-degree strains, start level three exercises as soon as pain abates.
- If the groin strain is second degree, begin level two exercises as soon as acute pain abates.
- If the groin strain is third degree, start level one exercises as soon as pain allows, and not more than one week after the injury occurs. For levels one, two, and three rehabilitation guidelines, refer to the sections on rehabilitation and conditioning at the end of this chapter.

Recovery time:

- First-degree groin strains: two weeks.
- Second-degree groin strains: four to six weeks.
- Third-degree groin strains: six to eight weeks.

HIP "POINTER" *(Contusion of the Iliac Crest)*

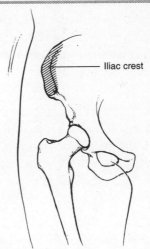

Iliac crest

A hip "pointer" is a contusion to the front part of the iliac crest, the bony portion of the pelvis that can be felt on either side of the waistline.

Symptoms:

- Immediate pain, spasms, and momentary paralysis of the muscles in the area.
- Inability to rotate the trunk or flex the hip without extreme pain.
- Possibly swelling and discoloration over the iliac crest.

Cause:

- Direct impact to the iliac crest from another athlete or from falling or running sideways into an immovable object.

Athletes at risk:

- Primarily football and hockey players.

Concerns:

- When severe, hip pointers are one of the most difficult injuries to manage because the strong muscles that attach to the hip put constant stress on the area.

What you can do:

- Apply ice and compression for at least forty-eight hours. Ice massage is especially beneficial.
- If pain is severe, seek medical attention.

Medication:

- For relief of minor to moderate pain, take acetaminophen as directed on label, or, for the relief of pain *and* inflammation, ibuprofen or aspirin if tolerated (see page 49).

What the doctor can do:

- Take X rays to rule out a pelvis fracture.
- Prescribe ice massage and, possibly, ultrasound.
- In severe cases, give a cortisone injection.
- Prescribe anti-inflammatories.

Rehabilitation:

- When pain abates, start doing level two exercises within the pain threshold. For levels one, two, and three rehabilitation guidelines, refer to the sections on rehabilitation and conditioning at the end of this chapter.

Recovery time:

- If managed correctly, this injury should resolve in one to three weeks.
- After recovery, athletes in contact sports should wear a protective hip pad in addition to normal hip protection.

AVULSION FRACTURES IN THE PELVIC AREA

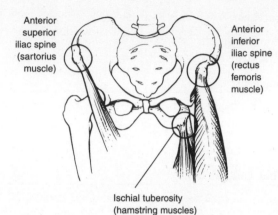

Anterior superior iliac spine (sartorius muscle)

Anterior inferior iliac spine (rectus femoris muscle)

Ischial tuberosity (hamstring muscles)

In adults, a violent contraction of a muscle may cause a muscle-tendon strain, defined as a stretch, tear, or complete rupture of the muscle-tendon unit. The damage usually occurs within the muscle-tendon unit itself. But in children, the weak point is where the muscle-tendons attach to bone. In growing children, the point at which the muscle-tendon unit attaches is actually "prebone," or bone that has not yet fully hardened. When a violent muscle-tendon contraction takes place, the muscle-tendon does not tear, but instead pulls off a portion of this prebone (known as an apophysis).

In the hip, pelvis, and groin area, the most common areas of avulsion fractures are where the hamstring muscle attaches to the buttocks bone, where the femoris rectus muscle attaches to the front of the pelvis, and where the sartorius muscle attaches to the front of the pelvis.

Symptoms:

- Severe pain and disability after a violent contraction of the muscle.

Cause:

- Violent muscle contraction.

Athletes at risk:

- Growing children, and especially sprinters, jumpers, and soccer and football players.

Concerns:

- If the athlete goes back to sports without properly rehabilitating the avulsion fracture, reinjury is inevitable.

What you can do:

- Any reports of severe pain in the pelvis area from a young athlete necessitate medical attention.

What the doctor can do:

- Take X rays to confirm the diagnosis.
- The most common treatment for an avulsion fracture is bedrest, with ice and pain medication (analgesics). Rehabilitation exercises can start ten days later.
- Very occasionally, surgery is performed when the patient is a highly competitive athlete.
- The doctor makes an incision and reattaches the portion of detached bone with pins and screws.

Rehabilitation:

- As soon as pain allows—and, ideally, within ten days of the injury—level two rehabilitation exercises should begin. For levels one, two, and three rehabilitation guidelines, refer to the sections on rehabilitation and conditioning at the end of this chapter.

Recovery time:

- The bone should have healed within four to six weeks, and the athlete can return to sports in three months.

Overuse Injuries of the Hip, Pelvis, and Groin

OSTEITIS PUBIS *(Inflammation of the Cartilage Disc in the Pubic Bone)*

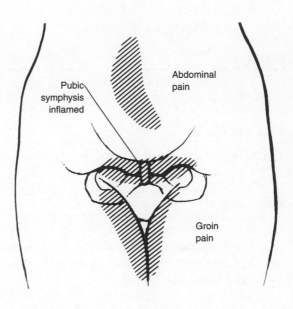

Osteitis pubis is an inflammation of the disc of cartilage (symphysis) that connects the right and left part of the pubic bone.

Symptoms:

- Onset of symptoms is gradual.
- Pain and tenderness in the front and center of the pubic bone.
- Pain may radiate into the groin and into the inside of the thighs or abdomen.
- Raising the leg outward against resistance causes specific pain.
- As the condition worsens, pain increases, causing spasm in the abdominal muscles and the muscles on the inside of the thigh.

Cause:

- Though the exact cause of this condition is unclear, it usually occurs as a result of repetitive contraction of the muscles on the inner side of the thigh that attach to the pubic bone and the pubic symphysis.

Athletes at risk:

- Mostly distance runners, but also weight lifters, and soccer and football players.
- It is also seen in persons who have recently had prostate or bladder surgery.

Concerns:

- If allowed to deteriorate, this condition will result in chronic pain in the groin.

What you can do:

- Cease the activity that caused the condition.
- Seek medical attention.

Medication:

- For relief of minor to moderate pain, take acetaminophen as directed on label or, for the relief of pain *and* inflammation, ibuprofen or aspirin if tolerated (see page 49).

What the doctor can do:

- Take X rays or bone scans to confirm the diagnosis.
- Nonsurgical treatment—rest and anti-inflammatories—is usually used to correct this condition.
- Cortisone injection
- If the condition has not resolved after two to three months, surgery may be done, namely removal of the bone spurs, or inflamed portions of the joint.

Rehabilitation:

- Level three exercises can begin as soon as pain allows, and after surgery, within three to five days. For levels one, two, and three rehabilitation guidelines, refer to the sections on rehabili-

tation and conditioning at the end of this chapter.

Recovery time:

- It may take between two to three months for this condition to resolve.
- After surgery, the athlete can return to strenuous running activities within four to six weeks.

STRESS FRACTURES AT THE TOP OF THE THIGHBONE (*Femoral Neck Stress Fracture*)

A stress fracture of the femoral neck is a series of tiny cracks in the thighbone just below the ball of the hip joint.

Symptoms:

- Onset of symptoms is gradual, but eventually, persistent pain is felt in the groin and the outside of the thigh, sometimes extending down to the knee.
- The athlete may walk with a limp.
- Limited hip motion, especially when turning the leg inward.
- Minimal tenderness because of the depth of the overlying muscle. However, pain may be felt when pushing on the hip bone.

Cause:

- Constant repetitive microtrauma in the lower extremities that transmits to the top of the thighbone.

Athletes at risk:

- Primarily distance runners, or those who train for long periods of time on hard surfaces.

Concerns:

- In children, stress fractures at the top of the thighbone may interrupt blood supply to the ball of the hip joint, causing it to "die" (avascular necrosis).
- If allowed to worsen, a stress fracture can lead to a complete fracture.

What you can do:

- Cease running activities.
- Use crutches if pain is severe.
- Seek medical attention.

Medication:

- For relief of minor to moderate pain, take acetaminophen as directed on label, or, for the relief of pain *and* inflammation, ibuprofen or aspirin if tolerated (see page 49).

What the doctor can do:

- Because of the potential for severe disability if the bone becomes displaced, the doctor must adopt a very careful and suspicious approach.
- X rays or bone scans are taken to try to confirm the diagnosis. Even if the stress fracture does not show up on X rays and symptoms persist (stress fractures often do not show up until two or four weeks after initial symptoms are felt), the doctor should assume there is a stress fracture.
- If the stress fracture cannot be seen on the initial X rays, another set of X rays should be done two to four weeks after the first ones are taken.
- Initial care for this injury is relative rest. For six weeks, the athlete should use crutches, and begin strengthening exercises as soon as possible.
- X rays should be taken weekly to monitor the injury.
- Surgery may be necessary if healing does not occur.

Rehabilitation:

- Start level two rehabilitation exercises as soon as pain allows. Avoid weight-bearing exercises. For levels one, two, and three rehabilitation guidelines, refer to the sections on rehabilitation and conditioning at the end of this chapter.

Recovery time:

- Two to three months.

Tendinitis Conditions in the Hip, Pelvis, and Groin

In addition to being suddenly strained as a result of a violent muscle contraction, muscle-tendon units are subject to irritations of the tendon fibers where they attach to the bones. Such a condition is known as a tendinitis. In the hip, pelvis, and groin area, the muscle-tendon insertions most frequently injured are the adductor and iliopsoas muscle-tendon insertions.

TENDINITIS OF THE ADDUCTOR MUSCLE *(Groin Muscle-Tendon Tendinitis)*

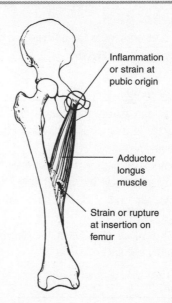

Tendinitis of the adductor muscles is an inflammation of the muscle-tendon insertion of the largest groin muscle, the adductor longus, into the pubic bone.

Symptoms:

- Onset of symptoms is gradual.
- Pain starts in the origin of the muscle-tendon unit in the groin and then radiates down into the inside of the thigh. The pain decreases after initial activity and recurs during the next exercise session with increased intensity.
- Distinct tenderness can be felt at the point where the muscle-tendon inserts into the pubic bone.
- Pain intensifies when the legs are drawn inward against resistance.

- It is difficult to run or perform any activities where drawing the hip inward is necessary (hip adduction). Activities such as biking usually do not cause discomfort.

Cause:

- Repetitive hip adduction.

Athletes at risk:

- Those whose sports require repetitive, strenuous hip adduction, especially hockey and soccer players. This condition is also seen in skiers, weight lifters, hurdlers, high jumpers, and handball players.
- Athletes with weak or inflexible adductor muscles are at greater risk.

What you can do:

- Cease the activity that caused the condition.
- Engage in a physical therapist–directed rehabilitation program.
- Continue to participate in activities that do not cause pain—cycling, stairclimber, etc.
- Gradually work back into sports when the pain goes away.
- Seek medical attention if the condition persists for more than two weeks.

Medication:

- For relief of minor to moderate pain, take acetaminophen as directed on label, or, for the relief of pain *and* inflammation, ibuprofen or aspirin if tolerated (see page 49).

What the doctor can do:

- Prescribe anti-inflammatories and refer the athlete to a physical therapist.
- If the condition is severe, administer a steroid injection, which must be followed by two weeks' rest.
- In severe cases of adductor tendinitis that do not resolve with nonsurgical treatment, may be necessary to have the doctor trim the inflamed tissue off the tendon surgically.

Rehabilitation:

- In mild cases of adductor tendinitis, begin level two exercises immediately.
- When the tendinitis condition is more severe, begin level one exercises as soon as pain allows—ideally, within one week of the initial symptoms. For levels one, two, and three rehabilitation guidelines, refer to the sections on rehabilitation and conditioning at the end of this chapter.

Recovery time:

- Mild cases: one to two weeks before the athlete can return to the activity that caused the condition.
- More severe cases may take an undetermined length of time to clear up; this can be an extremely frustrating injury to resolve.

TENDINITIS OF THE HIP FLEXOR (*Iliopsoas Tendinitis*)

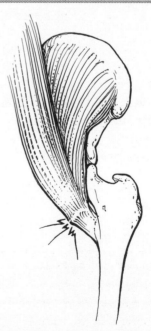

Tendinitis of the iliopsoas muscle is an inflammation of the main hip flexor muscle where the muscle-tendon inserts into the thigh muscle. Frequently the bursa beneath the tendon is also injured.

Symptoms:

- Onset of symptoms is gradual.
- Pain and tenderness where the tendon inserts into the thighbone. It may be difficult to elicit localized pain in an athlete with large muscles.
- Pain in the groin area when the athlete tries to raise the knee to the chest against resistance.
- When the bursa is also inflamed, there may be a feeling of tension and swelling in the groin area, though this may be difficult to feel with the fingers.

Cause:

- Repetitive hip flexion.

Athletes at risk:

- Those who engage in strength training, and especially those who lift weights, which involves bending into the squatting position. It may also occur in runners if they train in deep snow or water, soccer players after extended shooting practice, kickers in football after placekicking or punting practice, as well as high jumpers, long jumpers, and hurdlers.

Concerns:

- Unless managed properly, this condition can become chronic and long-term.

What you can do:

- Cease the activity that caused the condition.
- Engage in a physical therapist–directed rehabilitation program.
- Continue to participate in activities that do not cause pain—cycling, stairclimber, etc.
- Gradually work back into sports when the pain goes away.
- Seek medical attention if the condition persists for more than two weeks.

Medication:

- For relief of minor to moderate pain, take acetaminophen as directed on label, or, for the relief of pain *and* inflammation, ibuprofen or aspirin if tolerated (see page 49).

What the doctor can do:

- Prescribe anti-inflammatories and refer the athlete to a physical therapist.
- If the condition is severe, administer a steroid injection, which must be followed by two weeks' rest.
- If there is a bursitis associated with this injury, the bursa may be drained with a syringe and/or the doctor may inject cortisone into it. This measure must be followed by two weeks' rest of the injured limb.

Rehabilitation:

- In mild cases of iliopsoas tendinitis, begin level two exercises as soon as pain allows.
- When the tendinitis condition is more severe, begin level one exercises as soon as pain allows—ideally, within one week of the initial symptoms. For levels one, two, and three rehabilitation guidelines, refer to the sections on rehabilitation and conditioning at the end of this chapter.

Recovery time:

- Mild cases: one to two weeks before the athlete can return to the activity that caused the condition.
- More severe cases may take an undetermined length of time to clear up; as with a groin strain, this can be an extremely frustrating injury to resolve.

SNAPPING HIP SYNDROME

Snapping hip syndrome is not a single injury but rather describes the symptoms of a variety of disorders. Usually it is caused by snapping of the iliotibial band over the outside of the hip bone, causing trochanteric bursitis (see below).

Symptoms:

- The hip feels as if it is popping out of place.
- There may be a visible snapping over the hip (this is the inflamed bursa).

Causes:

- Repetitive movements that cause an imbalance of the muscles around the hip.
- The characteristic motions that cause this condition are lateral rotation and flexion of the hip joint as part of an exercise regimen or dance routine.

Athletes at risk:

- Primarily ballet dancers, also gymnasts, hurdlers, and distance runners.

Concerns:

- If allowed to deteriorate, this condition can become chronic.

What you can do:

- Cease the activity that caused the condition.
- Seek medical attention.

What the doctor can do:

- Prescribe physical therapy, cortisone injections, or perform surgery.

Rehabilitation:

- Rehabilitation for this condition primarily involves stretching the tight muscles and strengthening the weak ones.
- Begin with level two rehabilitation exercises as soon as pain allows. For levels one, two, and three rehabilitation guidelines, refer to the sections on rehabilitation and conditioning at the end of this chapter.

Recovery time:

- Six weeks.

TROCHANTERIC BURSITIS

Trochanteric bursitis is an inflammation of the bursa sac that lies over the hip joint. The irritation is caused by friction from the wide band of tissue that passes over the outside of the hip joint.

Symptoms:

- Onset of symptoms is gradual.
- Pain is felt over the bony prominence on the outside of the hip (at the top of the outside of the thigh).
- The pain is especially acute when attempting hip abduction (moving the leg away from the body in a sideways direction).
- Sometimes snapping is felt over the joint.
- The athlete may walk with a limp.
- As the condition worsens, pain may begin to radiate down the thigh, especially when sleeping.
- In its most severe manifestation, adhesions that develop within the bursa may create a creaking sound (crepitus) when the hip is used. These adhesions may be felt as a series of tiny bumps between the skin and bone.

Causes:

- Repetitive contraction of the muscles over the hip, as in running.
- The condition is caused by friction of the wide band of muscles that passes over the bursa on top of the hip joint. However, the likelihood of this condition is increased if the athlete has one or more of several anatomical abnormalities, including a wide pelvis (which explains why this condition is seen more often in females), excessive pronation of the foot when running, and differences in leg length.

Athletes at risk:

- Primarily runners.

Concerns:

- This condition rarely resolves by itself, so it is extremely important to seek medical attention.

What you can do:

- Cease the activity that caused the condition.
- Use ice to reduce inflammation (ice massage is especially effective).
- Seek medical attention.

Medication:

- For relief of minor to moderate pain, take acetaminophen as directed on label, or, for the relief of pain *and* inflammation, ibuprofen or aspirin if tolerated (see page 49).

What the doctor can do:

- Usually, treatment for this condition is nonsurgical. The doctor will
  Prescribe anti-inflammatories, drain the bursa with a syringe, and/or administer a cortisone injection.
  If the condition is caused by excessive foot pronation, prescribe shoe inserts.
  Refer the athlete to a physical therapist for exercises to reduce the tightness in the muscles over the hip.
- If the condition has been allowed to become severe, surgical intervention may be necessary:
  The doctor enters the joint and removes the adhesions that have developed.
  Usually, the bursa sac is removed at the same time.
  A "release" of the iliotibial band is done in which the tissue is cut open so it does not rub the bursa.
- Rehabilitation should focus on strengthening the gluteal muscles and developing flexibility in the iliotibial band.
- Begin level two exercises immediately. For levels one, two, and three rehabilitation guidelines, refer to the sections on rehabilitation and conditioning at the end of this chapter.

Recovery time:

- Without surgery: four to six weeks.
- With surgery: six weeks.

Rehabilitating Hip, Pelvis, and Groin Injuries

Rehabilitation exercises serve to

- promote blood flow to the area, which speeds the healing process

- Relieve stiffness in the joint caused by immobilization

- Prevent atrophy and tightening of the muscles resulting from inactivity.*

Rehabilitation should start as soon as possible to prevent loss of range of motion and strength. Protracted inactivity after an injury causes inordinate range-of-motion and strength deficits that need to be restored before return to sports activity. Delays in beginning rehabilitation spell delays in the athlete's return to sports readiness.

After an injury that does not require surgery or prolonged immobilization, range-of-motion exercises should begin as soon as pain abates and swelling diminishes—usually no more than forty-eight hours after the injury takes place, and often as early as twenty-four hours afterward.

When surgery is necessary, range-of-motion exercises should begin as early as five days after surgery, and no later than two to three weeks later.

Exercise is the most effective way to restore an injured athlete to sports readiness. A physical therapist may also employ ice, superficial heat, deep heat, massage, electrical stimulation, and physical manipulation of the hip joint to promote healing and make performing the exercises more comfortable.

The starting intensity level of the rehabilitation depends on the severity of the injury. Postsurgery range-of-motion exercises usually begin at level one. At this level, range of motion is "active assisted"—the physical

*For more on the importance and general principles of rehabilitation refer to chapter 5, "Rehabilitating Your Sports Injury."

therapist helps the patients use their strength to move their hip joint through allowable ranges of motion. If the injury is too severe for active assisted exercises, the patient may have to rely on "passive assisted" exercises—the physical therapist moves the injured hip through allowable ranges of motion. Continuous passive motion machines (CPMs) can be taken home by the patient so he or she can do passive range-of-motion exercises at home.

After surgery, muscle atrophy is prevented by using isometric exercises. With the direction of a physical therapist, these exercises can usually begin immediately after surgery. Isometrics help maintain strength in the important muscles around the hip joint without compromising the healing process by changing the muscle length or the angle of the joint.

Athletes who have sustained only mild or moderately severe injuries can begin with level two exercises.

In the initial stages of the rehabilitation program, the primary goal is to restore range of motion; the secondary goal is to prevent atrophy in the surrounding muscles. As the rehabilitation program progresses, more strengthening exercises are included in the program.

Range-of-motion and strength exercises should always be done within the pain threshold. Any exercise that causes pain should be discontinued.

The following are the most common and effective exercises used to rehabilitate the hip, pelvis, and groin after injury.

Level one

After surgery, active assisted or passive assisted range-of-motion therapy is used as a starting point of rehabilitation. The physical therapist should move the patient's hip through its six major motions: internal rotation, external rotation, adduction, abduction, extension, flexion, and combined internal-external circumduction. The hip should be moved only through those ranges of motion that do not compromise the stability of the surgery.

Isometrics and assisted range-of-motion therapy should continue only until patients are capable of using their own strength to do level two exercises.

Level Two

When patients are able to move their injured hips themselves, level two range-of-motion exercises can begin.

Level two exercises can also be used as a starting point for rehabilitating moderate to severe hip, pelvis, and groin area injuries that do not require surgery. They primarily develop range of motion in the joint, but through isometrics also help prevent atrophy in the important muscles around the hip.

Exercise 1: Seated leg crosses (inward and outward rotation)

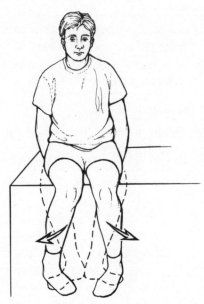

Sit on table, thighs supported, lower legs hanging off. Turn lower legs alternately a) inward, and b) outward.

Exercise 2: Lying knee to chest (flexors)
Lie on back, pulling knee toward chest, alternating between injured and healthy leg.

Exercise 3: Standing knee to chest (flexors)
Standing, pull knee toward chest, alternating between injured and healthy leg.

Exercise 4: Facedown lying leg lifts (extensors)
Lying facedown on mat or on floor, raise injured and healthy leg alternately.

Exercise 5: Advanced facedown lying leg lifts (extensors)

Lying facedown with upper part of body supported by bench or table and legs hanging off, raise injured and healthy leg alternately.

Exercise 6: Lying leg bends (abductors and adductors)

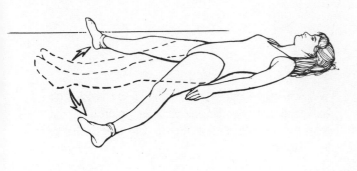

Lying on back, alternately move injured and healthy leg outward and inward.

Exercise 7: Advanced lying leg bends (abductors and adductors)

Do same exercise as above, but this time with moving leg raised two to three inches from floor or mat.

Exercise 8: Leg swings (abductors and adductors)

Placing hand against a wall for balance, a) swing leg across your body, and b) swing leg away from body.

Do these exercises three times a day, starting with ten repetitions and building up to thirty.

Level Three

When the patient can do the level two exercises without difficulty or pain, level three exercises can begin. Level three exercises can also be used as a starting point for rehabilitating mild hip, pelvis, and groin injuries.

Besides continuing to promote range of motion in the hip, pelvis, and groin, level three exercises introduce resistance to strengthen the muscles in the area.

Exercise 1: Resisted seated leg crosses (inward and outward rotators)

Sit on raised surface (such as a table) with thighs supported, lower legs hanging off, a belt around ankles. Try to force ankles outward, holding ten seconds. Repeat five to ten times.

Exercise 2: Weighted seated lateral ankle raises (inward and outward rotators)

Sit in same position as for above exercise. Attach weight cuff around ankle of injured leg. Raise ankle inward and upward and hold ten seconds. Repeat five to ten times. Change legs. Repeat.

Exercise 3: Standing weighted knee raises (flexors)

Attach weight cuff to injured leg. Standing on healthy leg, raise knee of injured leg toward chest. Hold ten seconds. Repeat five to ten times. Change legs. Repeat.

Exercise 4: Lying facedown weighted leg raises (extensors)

Attach weight cuff to injured leg. Lie on bench with body supported, legs hanging off. Raise injured leg and hold ten seconds. Repeat five to ten times. Change legs. Repeat.

Exercise 5: Weighted leg swings (abductors and adductors)

Attach weight cuff to ankle of injured leg. Placing hand against wall for balance, a) swing leg across body, and b) swing leg away from body. Do each exercise ten to thirty times. Repeat.

Repeat these exercises three times a day, starting at ten repetitions and gradually building up to thirty. You should able to do ten repetitions with ease and without pain before moving on to eleven, and so on.

When you can comfortably do thirty repetitions three times a day using the starting weight, increase the weight by one pound or so, but reduce the number of repetitions back to ten, then gradually build back up to thirty.

Each time you can comfortably do thirty repetitions, increase the weight by one or two pounds, reduce the number of repetitions to ten, then build back up to thirty.

When the strength of the injured hip, pelvis, and/or groin is 95 percent of the uninjured side (and, by association, 95 percent of its original strength), ease back into sports.

Before going back to sports, however, the athlete who has been injured should be able to do daily activities without pain and simulate the lower extremity motions of his or her sports without pain.

To reduce the chance of reinjury, begin the strength and flexibility conditioning program that follows.

Conditioning Program for the Hip, Pelvis, and Groin

Conditioning to prevent hip, pelvis, and/or groin injuries involves improving the strength and flexibility of the major muscles in the area. This includes the main muscles that enable hip flexion, extension, abduction, adduction, and internal and external rotation.

Exercises to stretch and strengthen the muscles in this area overlap with exercises to improve strength and flexibility in the lower back, abdominals, and thighs.

Incorporate into your workout at least one set of the following exercises for each muscle group mentioned. The exercises are described in chapter 3, "Strength and Flexibility: The Key to Injury Prevention."

Make these exercises part of an overall strength and flexibility program, and do them before any activity that will stress the muscles around the hip, pelvis, and groin.

Hip, Pelvis, and Groin Strengthening Exercises

Lower back: barbell squat, dumbbell lunge
Quadriceps: barbell squat, dumbbell lunge
Hamstrings: barbell squat, dumbbell lunge
Abdominals: bent-knee sit-ups
Hip flexors: tubed leg swing
Hip extensors: tubed leg swing
Hip adductors: tubed leg swing
Hip adductors: tubed leg swing

Hip, Pelvis, and Groin Flexibility Exercises

Lower back: alternate knee to chest, double knee to chest
Quadriceps: standing ballet stretch
Hamstrings: wall split
Front of the hip: lunge
Rear hip: sitting toe touch
Inner hip: butterfly lean
Outer hip: standing lateral lean

CHAPTER TWELVE

Back (Thoracic and Lumbar Spine) Injuries

Acute back injuries can be among the most serious in sports, because they pose the threat of long-term disability or even death. They have the potential to be catastrophic because they may involve the brain, spinal cord, or surrounding nerves, which are responsible for thought, movement, and sensation. Fortunately, traumatic back injuries are extremely rare in sports, and are even rarer in the sports in which most adult recreational athletes participate. Much more common than catastrophic back injuries, which require immediate medical care, are non-emergency acute conditions such as sprains, strains, and bruises (contusions).

Chronic back conditions, however—those that develop over an extended period—are a major medical problem among Americans. At some point in their lives, 60 to 80 percent of all Americans have lower back pain. The condition is disabling for 1 to 5 percent of Americans. After colds, back pain is the condition responsible for the greatest number of lost work days in the United States.

Chronic back problems may be caused by overuse (especially repetitive forward and backward bending), congenital anatomical abnormalities, faulty posture, improper body mechanics, and the degenerative processes associated with aging. Frequently, chronic back pain is brought on by a combination of one or more of these factors.

The Relationship Between Fitness and Lower Back Health

Most athletes know there is a relationship between fitness and lower back health. Until recently, the solution to solving lower back pain was to "strengthen the abs."

In fact, as the most modern sports medicine research reveals, lower back health is determined by numerous fitness factors, including

- cardiovascular endurance

Those who do plenty of cardiovascular exercise provide the discs in their back with nutrients and dispose of undesirable wastes through the elevated blood supply created by exercise. Conversely, someone who does not get enough cardiovascular exercise may suffer from premature disc degeneration.

- body composition

A high ratio of muscle to fat means a person has strong enough muscles for proper back function as well as good support of the vertebrae. Someone who is overfat increases the stress on the spine, which in turn increases the pressure on the discs and other vertebral structures.

- lower back flexibility

  Someone with a flexible lower back can bend forward fully because the lumbar curve almost reverses when the person bends forward. Without flexibility in the lower back, forward and lateral movements are disrupted, which in turn places excessive strain on the hamstrings, leading to lower back and hamstring pain.

- hamstring flexibility

  Flexibility in the hamstrings allows anterior rotation (tilt) of the pelvis in forward flexion and posterior rotation in the sitting position. Without adequate hamstring flexibility, anterior pelvic rotation is restricted and increases posterior tilt, both of which exacerbate disc compression.

- hip flexor flexibility

  A person with good flexibility in the hip flexors can achieve neutral pelvic position. Someone with "tight" hip flexors has an exaggerated anterior pelvic tilt, thereby increasing disc compression, unless it is counteracted by strong abdominal muscles.

- abdominal strength/endurance

  Strong abdominal muscles maintain the proper pelvic position; they also reinforce the back extensor fascia and pull them sideways when the person bends forward, thus providing support. Weak, easily fatigued muscles exaggerate anterior (forward) pelvic tilt, increasing strain on the back extensor muscles.

- back extensor strength/endurance

  Strong back extensor muscles provide stability for the spine, maintain erect posture, and control forward flexion (bending). Weak, easily fatigued back extensor muscles increase stress on the spine and cause increased disc compression.

For exercises to improve fitness in all the above neuromuscular areas, refer to the conditioning section at the end of the chapter.

Injuries to the Back

Acute injuries to the back include sprains, fractures, contusions, and strains. Although rare, each can result in serious injury to the spinal cord.

The mechanisms and types of back injuries are the same as those of neck injuries (see page 276).

Any back injury that results in loss of sensation, numbness, or weakness in the lower extremities needs to receive immediate emergency medical attention. The athlete should not be moved except by qualified emergency medical personnel.

Fortunately, few acute back injuries involve damage to the neurological system. More often they are nonemergency ligament sprains, muscle strains, and bruises (contusions). These can usually be treated with RICE (page 46), heat, anti-inflammatories, and pain relievers.

Overuse injuries of the back include conditions caused by repetitive microtrauma (especially excessive forward and backward bending), congenital anatomical abnormalities, bad posture, poor physical conditioning, and degenerative conditions associated with aging.

Although evidence suggests that being inactive contributes to lower back pain, it is also true that many athletes who consider themselves "in shape" are susceptible to back problems precisely because of their activity. The cause of most back problems in athletes is weak muscles (especially the abdominal muscles and hip flexors) or lack of flexibility (especially in the hamstrings and hip flexor muscles). During intensive training top athletes often neglect training parts of their bodies (especially the back, abdomen, and hip flexors) that do not seem to require development for success in their sport. In one notable study of Canadian Olympic athletes, it was discovered that several could not perform more than two sit-ups. Deficits and imbalances in strength and flexibility are especially prevalent in runners. Usually, runners have tight, strong quadriceps and weak hamstrings.

Back Injury Prevention

Acute back injuries caused by freak accidents are difficult to prevent. However, many acute back injuries such

BACK ANATOMY

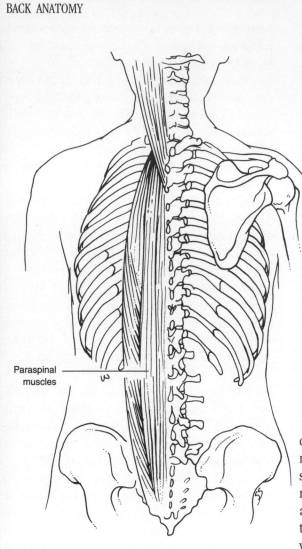

Paraspinal muscles

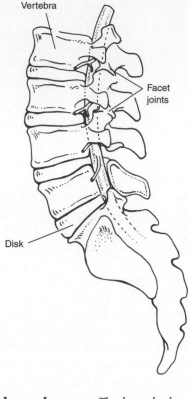

Vertebra

Facet joints

Disk

Muscles and nerves: The lower back can be described as a pole held erect by four guy-wire muscle groups: the *abdominals, extensors,* and two sets of *paraspinal* muscles. In addition to these muscles that are actually located in the back, there are other very important muscles, in particular, those that control hip motion. The hip muscles, by virtue of their relationship to the pelvis and thus the spine, have a significant influence on the back.

The spinal cord is a massive trunk of nerves that runs down the length of the spinal column from the brain to the tailbone. It is protected from superficial outside forces because it runs through a canal in the spinal column. At each vertebra, smaller nerves branch out from the main trunk. These nerves travel to the arms, the torso, and the legs. Through these nerves the brain can send out electrical impulses to the various tissues to make them function. The brain also receives feedback from the tissues through the nerves.

Bones and joints: The spine is a vertical column of twenty-four movable blocks of bone, called *vertebrae,* connected by "facet joints." Between each of these vertebrae lies a disc with a gristle-like lining and a center filled with a gelatinous substance. The discs act as shock absorbers and provide the spinal column with its flexibility. When an athlete runs and jumps, the discs absorb the impact as well as prevent the vertebrae from grinding against one another.

as muscle strains and ligament sprains are caused by deficits or imbalances in strength and flexibility. These can be remedied with an appropriate strengthening and stretching program, as well as a proper warm-up and cooldown as part of the sports activity.

In adventure sports such as skydiving and mountain climbing, where the potential for catastrophic back injuries is higher than in so-called "safe" sports, it is absolutely essential that athletes learn proper technique and safety measures, use modern, well-maintained equipment, and do not put themselves in unnecessary danger.

Overuse injuries of the back, including those brought on by poor posture and degenerative conditions, are best minimized by observing a slow, progressive training regimen and not doing "too much too soon."

Because many chronic back conditions are brought about by deficits and imbalances in strength and flexibility, it is important to participate in a conditioning program to address any such problems. It is especially important to pay attention to any potential deficits in abdominal strength and hamstring and lower back tightness and weakness. As a rough guide, all athletes should be able to do twenty bent-knee sit-ups (for abdominal strength), bend down and touch the fingers to the floor while keeping the knees straight (for hamstring flexibility), lie on the stomach with the arms and legs raised for twenty seconds (for lower back strength), and lift a weight with the hamstrings at least 60 percent of the weight they can lift with the quadriceps (for hamstring strength). In other words, the hamstrings should be two-thirds as strong as the quadriceps. Otherwise, there is the chance of developing chronic lower back pain.

Having a presports physical is a good way to detect strength and flexibility deficits, as well as postural problems, that might predispose an athlete to back injuries.

Finally, it is important to treat all back pain with respect. Nagging back pain should be regarded as a potential overuse injury of the back, and a sports physician should be consulted.

SPORTS LIKELY TO CAUSE CHRONIC LOWER BACK PAIN

High Risk
Football (especially linemen)
Gymnastics
Weight lifting (especially those who do overhead military press and the clean-and-jerk)
Tennis
Shotput
Pole vaulting
Snow/water ski jumping
Downhill skiing
Sledding
Hang gliding
Windsurfing

Moderate Risk
Baseball
Basketball
Bowling
Golf
Figure skating
Softball
Table tennis (Ping-Pong)
Water-skiing
Canoeing
Rowing
Fencing
Cross-country skiing
Badminton
Archery
In-line skating

Low Risk
Biking
Hiking
Swimming
Fishing
Curling
Darts
Scuba diving
Boccie
Billiards
Pool
Sailing

Preventing Lower Back Pain

In addition to doing a regular strength and conditioning program for the appropriate musculature, lower back pain can be combated by maintaining good posture at all times.

Dr. Robert Cantu, a past president of the American College of Sports Medicine, provides these common everyday tips for avoiding the occurrence of lower back pain:

Standing and walking

• Stand with the lower back erect and as flat as possible. By squeezing the buttocks and sucking in and tensing the abdomen, the lower back is straightened. Walk, stand, and sit as tall as possible.

• Bend the knees when leaning, as when over a sink. Avoid leaning whenever possible and squat with a straight lower back.

• Avoid high-heeled shoes. They shorten the Achilles tendons and increase "swayback."

• Avoid standing for long periods of time, but if it is necessary, alternate leaning on the left and right feet and if possible, use the bent-knee position—by putting one foot on a stool, for example. This stance flattens the lower back.

• When standing, do not lean back and support the body with the hand. Keep the hands in front of the body and lean forward slightly.

• When turning to walk from a standing position, move the feet first and then the body.

• Open doors wide enough to walk through comfortably.

• Carefully judge the height of curbs before stepping up or down.

Sitting

• Sit so that the lower back is flat or slightly convex, never hunched over.

• Sit so that the knees are higher than the hips. This may require a footstool, especially for a small person.

• Hard seat backs that begin contact with the back four to six inches above the seat and provide a flat support over the entire lower back area are preferable.

• Do not sit in soft or overstuffed chairs or sofas.

• Avoid sitting in swivel chairs or chairs on rollers.

• Do not sit with legs out straight on an ottoman or footstool.

• Never sit in the same position for prolonged periods; get up and move around.

Driving

• Push the front seat forward so that the knees are higher than the hips and the pedals are easily reached without stretching.

• Sit back with the back flat; do not lean forward; sit tall.

• Add a flat backrest if the car seat is soft or if traveling a long distance.

• If on a long trip, stop every thirty to sixty minutes, get out of the car, and walk around, tensing buttocks and abdomen to flatten the back for several minutes.

• Always fasten the seatbelt and shoulder harness.

• Be sure the car has a properly adjusted headrest.

Lying down

• Sleep or rest only on a flat, firm mattress. If one is not available, place a plywood bedboard no less than three-quarters of an inch thick under the mattress. A thinner board will sag, preventing spine alignment.

• When sleeping, the preferred position is on the side, both arms in front, the knees slightly drawn up to the chest.

• Do not sleep on the stomach.

• When lying on the back, place a pillow under the knees; raising the legs flattens the lower back curve.

• When lying in bed, do not extend the arms above the head; relax them at the sides.

• If the doctor prescribes absolute bedrest, do stay in bed. Raising the body or twisting and turning can strain the back.

- Sleep alone or in an oversize bed.

- When getting out of bed, turn over on your side, draw up your knees, and then swing your legs over the side of the bed.

Lifting

- When lifting, let the legs do the work, using the large muscles of the thighs instead of the smaller muscles of the back.

- Do not twist the body; face the object.

- Never lift with the legs straight.

- Do not lift heavy objects from car trunks.

- Do not lift from a bending-forward position.

- Do not reach over furniture to open and close windows.

- Tuck in the buttocks and pull in the abdomen when lifting.

- Always lift holding the object close to the body.

- Lift a heavy load no higher than the waist and a light load no higher than the shoulders, as greater height increases swayback.

- To turn while lifting, pivot the feet, and turn the whole body at one time.

Acute Injuries to the Back

BACK MUSCLE STRAIN/BACK LIGAMENT SPRAIN

This condition involves a stretch or tear of one or more of the back muscles and/or ligaments.

Symptoms:

- A sudden "pull" and sharp pain in the back.
- Often, the athlete is able to complete the activity, though two to three hours later the pain may become severe.
- Localized pain, tenderness, and swelling. The area may be tender to the touch, though only on one side of the spine. There should be no pain radiating down the buttocks into the legs, or pain directly over the bony prominences on the spine.
- Muscle spasm.

Cause:

- A violent twist in the back, or overexertion of any of the muscles during bending or lifting movements.

Athletes at risk:

- Those involved in contact sports such as football and ice hockey, where violent twists and turns are done.
- Back strains and sprains are also seen in weight lifters, figure skaters, dancers, and baseball and basketball players—any athlete who performs quick rotations and powerful motions.

Concerns:

- If extremely severe, a muscle strain or ligament sprain can cause serious injury to the spinal cord by affecting the stability of the spinal column.
- Unless it is fully rehabilitated, an athlete with a moderate to severe back sprain or strain runs a high risk of recurrence or of chronic lower back pain.

What you can do:

- Apply ice for forty-eight to seventy-two hours.
- As soon as severe pain dissipates, start using moist heating pads and doing range-of-motion exercises.

Medication:

- For relief of minor to moderate pain, take acetaminophen as directed on label, or, for the relief of pain *and* inflammation, ibuprofen or aspirin if tolerated (see page 49).

What the doctor can do:

- Professional treatment for this condition follows much the same course as self-treatment: ice, heat, pain relievers, and early range-of-motion exercises.
- If the injury is severe, the doctor may recommend physical therapy to ensure complete recovery.

Rehabilitation:

- If the injury is mild, start level three exercises as soon as initial pain dissipates—within forty-eight hours.
- If the injury is moderate, start level two exercises as soon as initial pain dissipates.
- If the injury is severe, start level one exercises, with the doctor's approval, as soon as pain allows. For levels one, two, and three rehabilitation guidelines, refer to the sections on rehabilitation and conditioning at the end of this chapter.

Recovery time:

- Mild strain/sprain: three to five days.
- Moderate strain/sprain: one to two weeks.
- Severe strain/sprain: three weeks or more.

BACK CONTUSION

The large surface area of the back offers the potential for bruises in sports when direct impact causes bleeding in the muscle fibers.

Symptoms:

- Local pain, tenderness, and discoloration.
- Possibly swelling.

Cause:

- Direct impact.

Athletes at risk:

- Those in contact sports or sports with the potential for falling accidents, and those where there is the possibility of being hit with a piece of equipment.

Concerns:

- An extremely severe bruise to the back can cause bleeding and swelling that can in turn constrict or pinch the spinal cord or nerves.

What you can do:

- Ice the bruise for the first forty-eight to seventy-two hours.
- Use a moist heating pad after the initial pain dissipates.
- If the bruise inhibits movement, seek medical attention.

Medication:

- For relief of minor to moderate pain, take acetaminophen as directed on label, or, for the relief of pain *and* inflammation, ibuprofen or aspirin if tolerated (see page 49).

What the doctor can do:

- Professional treatment for this condition follows much the same course as self-treatment: ice, heat, pain relievers, and early range-of-motion exercises.

- If the injury is severe, the doctor may recommend physical therapy to ensure complete recovery.

Rehabilitation:

- If the injury is mild, start level three exercises as soon as initial pain dissipates—within twenty-four hours.
- If the injury is moderate, start level two exercises as soon as initial pain dissipates.
- If the injury is severe, start level one exercises, with the doctor's approval, as soon as pain allows. For levels one, two, and three rehabilitation guidelines, refer to the sections on rehabilitation and conditioning at the end of this chapter.

Recovery time:

- Mild: two weeks.
- Moderate: four weeks.
- Severe: six weeks.

Overuse/Chronic Injuries

INTERVERTEBRAL DISC DISEASE (Slipped Disc, Herniated Disc, Ruptured Disc)

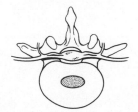
Normal disc

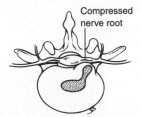
Herniated disc

Compressed nerve root

The discs in the lower back are subject to enormous stress in daily life and sports, and in later years they can degenerate and exert pressure on the nerves. Symptoms are felt not in the back but in the buttocks and legs. This condition is commonly known as a slipped disc.

Symptoms:

- "Sciatica": pain, tingling, and numbness radiating from the buttocks down the leg and, in severe cases, all the way to the little toe.
- There is muscle weakness in the affected limb, and the leg may "give way."
- The pain worsens with coughing, and straining.

Causes:

- Degeneration causes cracks in the shell of the disc, which allows the pulpy center of the disc to leak out and exert pressure on the nerve root.
- Although disc degeneration is a gradual process, a single event usually causes a portion of the pulp inside the disc to spurt out suddenly and compress a nerve root.
- Disc degeneration can cause chronic lower back pain.

Athletes at risk:

- Any athlete can sustain this condition, although it usually affects only athletes over twenty years of age.

What you can do:

- Ice the back for the first forty-eight to seventy-two hours.
- Rest in bed in the *psoas* (with the knees bent) position until the pain dissipates.
- Use a moist heating pad to control muscle spasm.
- Begin an exercise program as soon as possible to strengthen the abdominal and lower back muscles.

Medication:

- For relief of minor to moderate pain, take acetaminophen as directed on label, or, for the relief of pain *and* inflammation, ibuprofen or aspirin if tolerated (see page 49).

What the doctor can do:

- Nonsurgical treatment is most often used to manage this condition:
    Continued rest for eight to twelve weeks.
    Prescribe anti-inflammatories, traction, and TENS (see chapter 4).
- Administer a cortisone injection into the disc area.
- If, after nonsurgical treatment and a three- to six-month "wait-and-see" period, the condition does not resolve itself, surgery may be considered:
    An incision is made, and the piece of disc that is compressing the nerve is removed. This procedure is known as a discectomy. No bracing is necessary after such surgery. The athlete remains in the hospital for several days, and is encouraged to begin walking as soon as possible.
- A discectomy is an extremely safe and successful method of correcting this troublesome problem, but it should only be done when the disc does not heal by itself, or in an emergency situation.

Rehabilitation:

- As soon as initial pain dissipates, begin an overall program to condition the back and other important structures.
- After surgery, begin level one exercises as soon as pain allows, preferably within three to five days after surgery. For levels one, two, and three rehabilitation guidelines, refer to the sections on rehabilitation and conditioning at the end of this chapter.

Recovery time:

- Unless surgery is done to alleviate this problem, the condition often recurs. Episodes may last anywhere between a day or so to several months.
- After surgery, the athlete should wait six to eight weeks before returning to full activity, and three months before returning to contact sports.

SPONDYLOLISIS AND SPONDYLOLISTHESIS
(Stress Fracture of the Vertebra and Stress Fracture with Slippage of a Portion of the Vertebra)

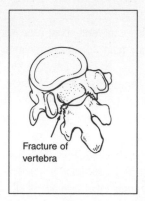

Fracture of vertebra

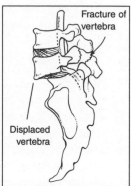

Fracture of vertebra

Displaced vertebra

Repetitive stress to a particular area in the lower back, especially frequent forward and backward bending, can cause a stress fracture in a portion of the vertebra known as spondylolisis. If the condition is not treated, the weakened vertebra may fracture completely and dislodge from its normal position. This is spondylolisthesis.

Symptoms:

- Onset of symptoms is usually gradual, but may occur after one sudden extension of back (bending backward).
- General lower back pain and stiffness on one or both sides.
- Bending backward is difficult and painful.
- Sometimes, the athlete may develop "sciatica": pain, tingling, and numbness radiating from the buttocks down the leg and, in severe cases, all the way to the little toe. Sciatica may involve muscle weakness in the affected limb, which may cause the leg to "give way."

Cause:

- Frequent bending of the back.
  Certain athletes are predisposed to this condition because they have an abnormally large front-to-back curvature in their spine, or, in medical terms, lordosis (sometimes known as "swayback").

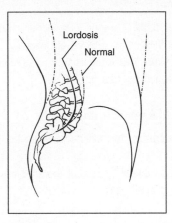

Athletes at risk:

- This condition is seen most often in athletes who must perform frequent back-bending movements, such as the back arch in gymnastics, weight lifting, blocking in football, serving in tennis, spiking in volleyball, and the butterfly stroke in swimming.
- It is especially common in adolescents and those who are genetically predisposed to the condition because of bone thinness in the vertebrae.

Concerns:

- Unless spondylolisis is caught in its early stages and treated properly, it is likely to deteriorate into full-blown spondylolisthesis. Sometimes, this condition is misdiagnosed as a back strain. Beware this diagnosis, especially if the symptoms come on slowly.

What you can do:

- Stop the activity that caused the condition, as well as any other activities involving backward bending (sit-ups, weight lifting, etc.).
- Seek medical attention.

Medication:

- For relief of minor to moderate pain, take acetaminophen as directed on label, or, for the relief of pain *and* inflammation, ibuprofen or aspirin if tolerated (see page 49).

What the doctors can do:

- The doctor should try to make the correct diagnosis as soon as possible and to do so, a special bone scan may have to be done (X rays are not nearly as effective at detecting stress fractures in their early stages).
- Treatment for this condition is usually nonsurgical:
  Rest, painkillers, heat retainer, back brace, and physical therapy.
  Bracing to prevent bending that will aggravate the condition.
  A different sport or fitness activity. Gymnastics and dance are high-risk sports for someone predisposed to this condition.
- In rare cases, when a vertebra has slipped more than 50 percent of the width of the vertebrae above and below it, and/or there is severe pain, surgery may be necessary:
  A bony bridge is created between the solid sacrum at the bottom of the spine and the area of slippage. This "fusion" effectively prevents further slippage.
- Spinal fusion is an extremely safe and successful way to correct this condition.

Rehabilitation:

- The focus on rehabilitation for this condition is exercise to correct lordosis, or curvature of the spine. This is done by strengthening the abdominal muscles and stretching the extensor muscles in the back, and by improving the overall flexibility of the spine.

Recovery time:

- Spondylolisis (stress fracture of the vertebra without slipping): one week of rest to resolve.
- Mild to moderate spondylolisthesis (25–50 percent slippage of the vertebra): one to three months to resolve.
- Without surgical treatment, the symptoms will probably recur.
- Severe spondylolisthesis: after a surgical spinal fusion, it will be six months before the athlete can return to full activity. At this time, however, the back is stronger than before.

MECHANICAL LOWER BACK PAIN

The precise cause of lower back pain is unknown, but it is a frequent condition in athletes as well as the general population. It is thought to be brought on by a combination of factors, including muscle strains, anatomical abnormalities, faulty posture, and poor physical conditioning.

Symptoms:

- General pain and stiffness in the lower back, sometimes accompanied by muscle spasm.
- Restricted motion, particularly bending forward.
- Pain does not radiate into the buttocks or legs.

Causes:

- A combination of factors is probably involved, including previous injury (sprains and strains), anatomical abnormalities, faulty posture, and poor physical conditioning.

Concerns:

- As the athlete with lower back pain consciously or unconsciously avoids using the back, the muscles important to maintaining lower back health weaken and tighten, creating a vicious cycle.

What you can do:

- Rest and ice the back in the initial stages of pain.

- Pay attention to "Preventing Lower Back Pain" (page 186).
- Participate in a conditioning program to develop strength and flexibility necessary for preventing lower back pain.

Medication:

- For relief of minor to moderate pain, take acetaminophen as directed on label, or, for the relief of pain *and* inflammation, ibuprofen or aspirin if tolerated (see page 49).

What the doctor can do:

- Determine the exact cause of the lower back pain.
- Recommend a physical therapist who specializes in rehabilitating the condition.

Rehabilitation:

- Do the exercises at the end of the chapter to relieve initial pain.
- After pain dissipates, begin the strength and flexibility program described at the end of this chapter. For levels one, two, and three rehabilitation guidelines, refer to the sections on rehabilitation and conditioning at the end of this chapter.

Recovery time:

- Although episodes of pain may recur, the initial symptoms usually dissipate after several days.

Back Rehabilitation

For more on the general principles of rehabilitation, refer to chapter 5, "Rehabilitating Your Sports Injury." Rehabilitation exercises serve to

- promote blood flow to the area, which speeds the healing process.

- relieve stiffness in the joint caused by immobilization.

- prevent atrophy and tightening of the surrounding muscles resulting from inactivity.

Rehabilitation should begin as soon as possible to prevent loss of range of motion and strength. Delays in rehabilitation spell delays in an athlete's return to sports readiness.

After an injury that does not require surgery or prolonged splinting, range-of-motion exercises should begin as soon as pain and swelling diminish—usually no more than forty-eight hours after the injury symptoms begin, and often, as early as twenty-four hours. Even after some types of surgery—for instance, surgery to repair a slipped disc—range-of-motion exercises for the back should start three to five days after the procedure.

Exercise is the most effective way to restore an injured athlete to sports readiness. A physical therapist may also employ ice, superficial heat, deep heat, massage, electrical stimulation, and physical manipulation of the back to promote healing and make performing the exercises more comfortable.

At what intensity level should exercises start?

The starting intensity level of the rehabilitation depends on the severity of the injury. Postsurgery range-of-motion exercises usually begin at level one. At this level, range of motion is "active assisted"—the physical therapist helps the patients use their own strength to move their backs through allowable ranges of motion. If the injury is too severe for active assisted exercises, the patient may have to rely on "passive assisted" exercises—the physical therapist moves the injured back through allowable ranges of motion.

After surgery, muscle atrophy is prevented by using isometric exercises. With the direction of a physical therapist, these exercises can usually begin immediately after surgery. Isometrics help maintain strength in the important muscles in the back without compromising the healing process by changing the length of the muscle.

Athletes who have sustained only mild or moderately severe back injuries can begin with level two exercises.

In the initial stages of the rehabilitation program, the primary goal is to restore range of motion; the secondary goal is to prevent atrophy in the muscles. As the rehabilitation program progresses, more strengthening exercises are included in the program.

Range-of-motion and strength exercises should always be done within the pain threshold. Any exercise that causes pain should be discontinued.

The following are the most common and effective exercises used to rehabilitate the back after injury.

Level One

After surgery, active assisted or passive assisted range-of-motion therapy is used as a starting point of rehabilitation. The physical therapist should move the patient's back through its major motions. The back should be moved only through those ranges of motion that do not compromise the stability of the surgery.

Isometrics and assisted range-of-motion therapy should continue only until patients are capable of using their own strength to do level two exercises.

Level Two

When patients can move their injured backs themselves, level two exercises to develop range of motion in the spine and strength and flexibility in the back muscles can start.

Level two exercises can also be used as a starting point for rehabilitating moderate to severe back injuries that do not require surgery.

Start by doing three repetitions of each exercise. Do the exercises every day, adding one repetition until ten repetitions can be performed. When a stretch is being done, hold it for five seconds.

Exercise 1: Lower back strengthening

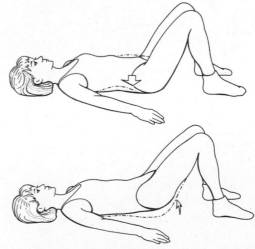

Lie on back, knees bent and feet flat on floor. Tighten abdominal muscles and push back flat to floor. After ten repetitions, raise pelvis three or four inches and hold five seconds. Repeat ten times.

Exercise 2: Lower back flexibility

Lie on back with legs extended. Grasp one knee and pull gently to chest, keeping other leg straight. Hold position five seconds, then relax. To increase effectiveness of exercise, pull both knees to chest.

Level Three

When the patient can do the level two exercises without difficulty or pain, level three exercises can begin. Level three exercises can also be used as a starting point for mild back injuries.

Level three exercises involve dynamic exercises to strengthen the lower back muscles, as well as flexibility exercises for the hip flexors, hamstrings, abdominals, and the trunk.

Start by doing three repetitions of each exercise. Do the exercises every day, adding one repetition until ten repetitions can be performed. When doing a stretch, hold it for five seconds.

Exercise 1: Lower back flexibility

Lie on back on mat and bring both legs upward so tops of feet are approximately over face. Swing feet overhead and try to touch toes to mat. Keep upper back on floor.

Exercise 2: Hip flexor flexibility

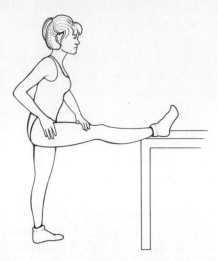

Place one leg on bench or chair, keeping other leg straight. Slowly lean forward, feeling stretch in iliopsoas muscle in front of hip.

Exercise 3: Abdominal strengthener

Lie on back with knees bent and feet flat on ground. Put hands behind head, elbows straight out to sides. Raise shoulders off floor, less than halfway to knees. Lower slowly, then relax.

Exercise 4: Hamstring flexibility

Sit with one leg straight out, the other bent inward. Bend forward, keeping back straight. Change sides.

To reduce the chance of reinjury, begin the following conditioning program for the back and maintain good posture at all times.

Exercise 5: Trunk flexibility

Stand with feet shoulder width apart. Keeping left leg straight, bend right knee so you feel a stretch in side of trunk. Change legs. As flexibility improves, increase intensity of stretch by bending knee more.

Conditioning Program for the Back

Once initial pain dissipates, it is essential to begin an exercise program to condition the musculature necessary for lower back health. In addition to doing exercises to strengthen the lower back and abdominals, it is important to develop flexibility in the lumbar extensor and pelvic rotator muscles, and the hamstring and hip flexor muscles.

The conditioning program below goes beyond the traditional sit-ups for abdominal strength and modified hurdler's stretch for the hamstrings. It includes exercises for all five major anatomical areas that affect the back. The exercises should be regarded as an all-around program, because ignoring any anatomical area may lead to imbalances.

The following exercises for the five anatomical areas are presented in three different degrees of difficulty: beginner, intermediate, and advanced. Selections can be made from each group, depending on fitness level.

The exercises should be done at least once a day.

Lower Back Flexibility

Beginner: Knee to chest

Lying on back, bring one or both knees to chest, grasping leg under thigh(s). Raise and lower head slowly. Do stretch slowly and hold ten to sixty seconds.

Intermediate: "Mad cat"

Kneeling on all fours, look up with back dipped, then look down and hunch back. Do stretch slowly and hold ten to sixty seconds.

Advanced: Crossed leg flexion

Sit with knees flexed and ankles crossed. Slowly bend forward so head approaches floor. Do stretch slowly and hold ten to sixty seconds.

Hamstring Flexibility

Beginner: Modified hurdler's stretch

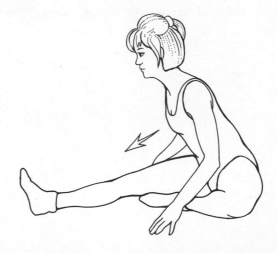

Sit with one leg straight out, the other flexed. Move flexed knee to the side and bend forward. Do stretch slowly and hold ten to sixty seconds. Change sides. Repeat.

Intermediate: PNF supine position

Lying down, place jump rope around foot or ankle, then raise leg straight into the air. Contract hamstring muscle against tension of rope, relax, then pull leg straighter. Do stretch slowly and hold ten to sixty seconds. Change sides. Repeat.

Advanced: Standing stretch

Stand with one leg on support so hip is flexed at 90 degrees. Keeping back straight and shoulders back, lean forward. Do stretch slowly and hold ten to sixty seconds.

Hip Flexor Flexibility

Beginner: Hip extension

Stand with pelvis in a neutral position. Extend leg backward from hip. Do stretch slowly and hold ten to sixty seconds. Change sides. Repeat.

Advanced: Lying stretch

Lie on bench with knees over edge and back flat. Pull one leg to chest to stretch opposite hip. Do stretch slowly and hold ten to sixty seconds. Change sides. Repeat.

Abdominal Strength/Endurance

Beginner: Pelvic tilt

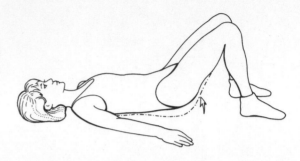

Lying down or standing with back against wall, press pelvis to floor/wall. Repeat in controlled manner five to twenty-five times.

Intermediate: Partial curl ("crunch")

Lying down with knees flexed, curl up while sliding hands by sides 3 to 4 inches. Repeat in controlled manner five to twenty-five times.

Advanced: Oblique curl

Advanced: Hyperextension III

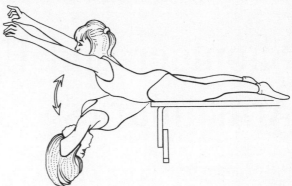

Lying on side, twist torso and curl up, reaching for top leg with opposite arm. Repeat in controlled manner five to twenty-five times.

Back Extensor Strength/Endurance

Beginner: Hyperextension I

Lie on stomach with hands by sides, Keeping neck and chin in neutral position, raise shoulders off ground. Repeat in controlled manner five to twenty-five times.

Intermediate: Hyperextension II

Lie on stomach with arms and hands extended forward. Keeping neck and head in a neutral position, raise shoulders off floor. Repeat in controlled manner five to twenty-five times.

Lie on stomach on bench, positioning yourself so body is supported from pelvis down. Bend waist to 90 degrees so head is moving toward floor, then bend upward to several inches above horizontal. Repeat in controlled manner five to twenty-five times.

CHAPTER THIRTEEN

Shoulder and Upper Arm Injuries

Injuries to the shoulder joint, and in particular overuse injuries caused by repetitive throwing and pushing motions, are quite common in sports. Due to the long-standing popularity of baseball, overuse ailments such as "pitcher's shoulder" have been known to doctors for many years. But with the emergence of interest in health fitness activities such as swimming and weight lifting, as well as the explosion in the popularity of tennis and golf, a variety of other overuse injuries of the shoulder are now being seen. Shoulder injuries account for about one in ten of all sports injuries.

Shoulder injuries, both acute and overuse, are among the most frequently misunderstood and poorly diagnosed sports medicine conditions. This is chiefly due to the complexity of the shoulder anatomy and the many functions of the joint. Even with modern diagnostic techniques such as MRI (magnetic resonance imaging), it is often difficult for a physician to establish an exact diagnosis. In many cases, shoulder pain is not related to just one injured part but may stem from a combination of bone, muscle, tendon, and ligament damage. Given how the symptoms of shoulder injuries overlap, it is not unusual for an athlete to get three different diagnoses for a shoulder ailment—and all of them would be correct.

Of all the joints in the body, the shoulder is the hardest to rehabilitate after an injury. Because of the wide range of intricate motions and the various muscle interactions that must be restored to facilitate proper function, it takes time and determination on the part of the athlete to return to original form after a shoulder injury.

Injuries to the Shoulder and Upper Arm

Acute shoulder injuries include fractures, dislocations, separations (sprains), and contusions.

Acute shoulder injuries can result from a fall onto an outstretched arm or from direct impact to the shoulder itself, especially the tip of the shoulder blade, the acromion. The symptoms of acute shoulder injuries are usually quite obvious—immediate, intense pain and tenderness, swelling, lack of mobility, and deformity.

Acute shoulder injuries are very common in contact sports such as football, ice hockey, lacrosse, and rugby. The injuries are caused by the athlete's striking a shoulder on the ground or by being hit in the shoulder by an opponent's elbow, foot, thigh, or head. Lacrosse and ice hockey sticks can also inflict serious shoulder damage. Acute shoulder injuries are also seen in activities where there is the potential for falling, such as biking, skiing, in-line skating, and gymnastics.

Thanks to the rich blood supply to the bones of

SHOULDER ANATOMY

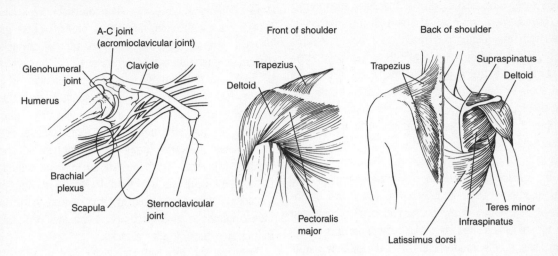

Bones and joints: The shoulder structure lies at the junction of three major bones: the collarbone (*clavicle*), shoulder blade (*scapula*), and the upper arm bone (*humerus*).

The ball at the top of the upper arm bone and the socket of the shoulder blade form the *glenohumeral* joint.

The shoulder blade is connected to the collarbone by a small joint called the *acromioclavicular* joint or, more commonly, the "A-C joint."

In addition to these two main joints, there is a minor joint called the *sternoclavicular* joint, which joins the collarbone and the breastbone.

The bones in the shoulder structure are held together by relatively weak ligaments, a structural problem that reinforces the importance of the muscles for stability.

Muscles and nerves: The bones and joints of the shoulder are in fact less important than the surrounding muscles. For example, the ball-and-socket glenohumeral joint has no bony stability and is totally dependent for its stability as well as its complex function on the surrounding muscles. Whenever the shoulder muscles are damaged, the joint will usually dislocate downward with the ball of the upper arm bone falling out of the socket.

Four powerful muscles that originate in the neck and torso provide the shoulder with the ability to perform dynamic tasks such as lifting and throwing: the *deltoid, trapezius, pectoralis major,* and *latissimus dorsi.*

Another set of four smaller muscles—the *subscapularis, supraspinatus, infraspinatus,* and *teres minor*—are known collectively as the rotator cuff muscles and have the specific job of holding the ball of the joint tightly against the socket. Damage to the rotator cuff muscles has a devastating effect on the function of this joint.

To operate our shoulder muscles, instructions go through a complex set of nerves called the *brachial plexus.* This set of nerves starts off as five major nerves—the fifth, sixth, seventh, and eighth cervical nerves and first thoracic nerve—which split off into many smaller nerves that serve the many different shoulder muscles. In addition to servicing the shoulder muscles, the brachial plexus is also the origin of three major nerves—the *radial, ulnar,* and *median* nerves—that travel down the arm to the hand.

the shoulder, fractures heal relatively quickly. Shoulder ligaments and tendons, on the other hand, have a poor blood supply and healing time is therefore much longer.

Overuse shoulder injuries almost all stem from problems with the rotator cuff mechanism (see page 213). They include supraspinatus tendinitis, subacromial bursitis, biceps tendinitis, and chronic rotator cuff tears. "Frozen shoulder" describes a condition caused by favoring the shoulder when there is an overuse condition.

Rarely do any of these conditions occur in isolation; usually they develop in conjunction. The classic case of this is the "impingement syndrome," in which weakness in the rotator cuff leads to, first, subacromial bursitis and supraspinatus tendinitis, then wear and tear on the rotator cuff, followed by the formation of a bony spur on the lip of the shoulder socket, whose presence causes tiny tears in the rotator cuff, which eventually causes the biceps tendon that attaches to the shoulder to become inflamed.

Overuse injuries in the shoulder develop gradually and usually occur as a result of a combination of internal and external factors. The internal factors are primarily weakness or damage in the rotator cuff, which makes the ball of the shoulder joint move around unnaturally in the joint, causing damage in the process. The external factors are the repetitive stress of vigorous overarm actions necessary in throwing and racket sports, swimming, rowing, and weight lifting.

Unfortunately, most athletes neglect to strengthen their rotator cuff muscles, even when their sports place enormous demands on these structures.

The onset of the symptoms of overuse shoulder injuries—unlike most acute injuries—is gradual and may have no obvious cause. Initially, pain may be experienced only after sports participation. Gradually the symptoms may begin to be felt during and after participation but may not be severe enough to interfere with performance. In the final stages, disabling pain is felt both during and after participation and in daily activities.

The key to managing overuse injuries is early intervention. Anytime there is pain centering in the shoulder, especially shoulder pain aggravated by the same sports activity, chances are there is an overuse injury. Take immediate steps to address the condition, starting with RICE (page 46).

Shoulder Injury Prevention

Acute shoulder injuries are often caused by freak accidents, and are therefore difficult to prevent. There are, however, several preventive measures athletes can take. The most important is to learn how to fall properly in a "tuck and roll" fashion, not on the shoulder or an outstretched arm. Skiers should be taught to tuck their arms in as they fall and roll over on their torsos. Similarly, in bicycling and in all contact sports, athletes need to be taught to avoid falling on an outstretched arm. Landing with body weight driven up into the shoulder is the most common way to dislocate or fracture the shoulder. Unfortunately, even in heavy contact sports, too little emphasis is given to proper techniques of falling, rolling, and tucking after a tackle.

Protective shoulder pads should be worn in all sports where there is the potential for direct impact to the shoulders, especially football, ice hockey, and lacrosse.

Although shoulder padding is not seen in most recreational sports, it has been adopted by safety-conscious participants in sports such as skiing, horseback riding, in-line skating, and biking, and has been seen to decrease the severity of falling-type shoulder injuries in those sports.

Overuse injuries of the shoulder can be minimized by observing a slow, progressive training regimen and not doing "too much too soon." This holds true especially for athletes in throwing and racket sports, as well as swimmers.

Anyone who participates in sports that stress the shoulder should participate in a conditioning program that develops strength and flexibility in the structures around the joint.

For cosmetic reasons, there is a tendency to overemphasize conditioning the four large muscles around the shoulder: the deltoid, trapezius, pectoralis major, and latissimus dorsi. The assumption is that because these muscles are more prominent, strengthening them is a surefire way to prevent injuries. However, it is just as important—if not more so—to condition the rotator cuff muscles, which provide crucial support for the shoulder joint and are exposed to extreme stress during activities that involve dynamic pulling, pushing, and throwing motions.

For more on strength and flexibility exercises for the

shoulder, refer to the conditioning program at the end of this chapter.

Proper technique also has a role to play in preventing overuse injuries of the shoulder. Incorrect form is a common cause of overuse injuries in overarm sports such as tennis and swimming.

Acute Injuries of the Shoulder and Upper Arm

FRACTURED COLLARBONE (*Clavicle Fracture*)

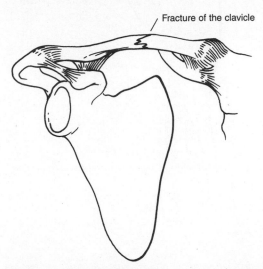

Fracture of the clavicle

A fracture is a crack, break, or complete shattering of the bone. Fractures in the shoulder area almost always affect the collarbone, and usually occur in the middle portion of the bone.

Symptoms:

- Severe pain as well as swelling and tenderness over the fracture.
- Upon movement, a crunching sensation (crepitus) produced by the broken ends of the bones rubbing together.

- A pseudoparalysis that prevents shoulder movement for the first few hours after the injury.
- In severe fractures, a bony prominence under the skin at the fracture site.

Causes:

- A fall onto the collarbone.
- Direct impact to the collarbone from another athlete.
- Falling onto an outstretched arm/s.

Athletes at risk:

- Fractured collarbones are most often seen in athletes in contact sports or in activities with the potential for falling accidents—skiing, biking, and in-line skating, for instance.

Concerns:

- At the same time the collarbone is fractured, ribs can get broken, which can in turn cause a punctured lung. The symptoms of a punctured lung are shortness of breath and pain when coughing or breathing deeply.

What you can do:

- Send for medical assistance.
- Immobilize the arm in a sling in the most comfortable position.
- Secure the arm to the body with an elastic bandage.
- Gently apply ice over the area for twenty minutes at a time until medical attention is available.

What the doctor can do:

- Rule out damage to the main nerve supply that travels just below the collarbone, as well as possible injuries to the ribs and lungs.
- Perform a physical examination and take X rays to confirm the fracture diagnosis.
- Nonoperative treatment options:
    If the collarbone is only cracked, and there is no displacement of the ends of the broken bones, a sling is used to provide support and

comfort while the bone heals. The sling is usually worn for two to three weeks.

When there is a clear break in the bone, the patient is given a cloth to keep the broken collarbone from sloping forward. The brace crisscrosses the back and front of the chest, applying steady pressure that allows the ends of the broken bones to heal together.

Adults need to wear the brace for six weeks, while children under twelve—whose bones heal faster—need to wear it only two to three weeks.

After the brace is removed, the patient should wear a sling for several days for comfort and support.

- Surgery is rarely used to repair a fractured collarbone. It may be necessary, however, if, for instance, the fracture is "open" (the bone penetrates through the skin); if, despite nonoperative treatment, the bone does not heal together; or if the fracture is in the outer third of the collarbone.
- With surgery, an "open" reduction is done in which the ends of the bones are placed end to end, then held together with a plate and screws. Because the blood supply here is poor, a bone graft is also usually done to promote bone rejoining at the ends of the broken bones.

Rehabilitation:

- Once pain symptoms have gone, level two range-of-motion exercises should begin.
- After four to six weeks, X rays are taken to check on bone healing. If the X rays show the bone is healing together, level three rehabilitation exercises can commence, and the program should progress as described in the section "Shoulder Rehabilitation."

Recovery time:

- A fractured collarbone generally takes six weeks to heal (three weeks for children under twelve), at which time conditioning exercises can begin and the athlete can return to noncontact sports.

Contact sports should not be resumed until the bone union is solid, usually four to six months after the injury.

SHOULDER DISLOCATION
(Glenohumeral Dislocation)

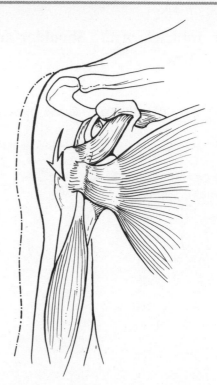

A shoulder dislocation occurs when the ball at the top of the upper arm bone comes out of the socket in the shoulder blade. Shoulder dislocations are relatively common because of the structure of the shoulder joint. Unlike all other joints in the body, the socket has almost no bony support, and although this provides the joint with its unique mobility, it also makes it susceptible to dislocations in sports.

Symptoms:

- Obvious deformity—the outside of the shoulder looks flat, not rounded.
- Extreme pain on movement.
- Muscle spasm.
- Loss of mobility—the arm hangs limply by the side.
- Top of the humerus can be felt in the underarm.

Causes:

- A fall onto an outstretched arm when the arm is forced upward and backward.
- Impact to the outside of the shoulder, either from a fall, or contact from another athlete.

Athletes at risk:

- Dislocated shoulders are most often seen in athletes in contact sports or activities with a potential for falling accidents—skiing, biking, and in-line skating, for instance.

Concerns:

- Once an athlete has dislocated a shoulder, the chances of redislocating it in sports are extremely high. After two or three dislocations, surgery is usually necessary to prevent the shoulder from redislocating during daily activities.
- In rare cases, shoulder dislocations may disrupt nerve function and blood supply to the arm.

What you can do:

- Send for medical attention (the sooner the shoulder joint is realigned, the shorter the recovery time and the fewer the complications).
- Put the arm in a sling.
- Do not let an unqualified person try to realign the joint.
- Gently apply ice over the area for twenty minutes at a time until medical help arrives.

Medication:

- For relief of minor to moderate pain, take acetaminophen or ibuprofen as directed on label, or, for the relief of pain *and* inflammation, aspirin if tolerated (see page 49).

What the doctor can do:

- Rule out damage to nerve function and blood supply to the arm.
- Take X rays to rule out a fracture.
- Treatment of shoulder dislocations is controversial. Some doctors advocate surgery to repair the ligaments after the first dislocation, as further dislocations are inevitable. However, this is appropriate only when the patient is a high-performance athlete whose sport puts inordinate stress on the shoulder. In recreational athletes, or athletes whose sport does not normally stress the shoulder, nonoperative measures are best. Surgery may be done if the shoulder does dislocate again.
- Nonoperative treatment options:
  Realign the joint under anesthetic.
  Take X rays to check that proper realignment has been achieved and rule out associated injuries, possibly fractures of the upper arm and shoulder blade.
  Immobilize the arm against the body to allow the damaged ligaments and joint capsule to heal. Premature use of the shoulder joint will stretch the ligaments and predispose the patient to redislocations.
  Two to three weeks in a sling is required for adults who dislocate a shoulder, six weeks for children. (Adults are at risk of long-term dysfunction if their joints are immobilized too long, and are less likely to redislocate their shoulders again because of the nature of their sports participation).
- Surgery is generally done when the athlete suffers recurrent dislocations. The doctor makes an incision over the joint, then tightens up the rotator cuff muscles over the ball of the joint to prevent further dislocations.

Rehabilitation:

- As soon as pain permits—usually within twenty-four to forty-eight hours of the dislocation—the patient can begin isometric strengthening exercises and range-of-motion exercises that do not threaten the stability of the joint.
- After the two- to three-week immobilization period, the patient should be able to lift the arm to shoulder height and make circular motions without pain, at which time rehabilitation with weights can begin. For levels one, two, and three rehabilitation guidelines, refer to the sections on rehabilitation and condition at the end of this chapter.

Recovery time:

- After a dislocation that is realigned without the use of surgery, two to three months of rehabilitation is necessary before a return to sports is possible.
- The same amount of time is needed to rehabilitate a dislocated shoulder after surgery.

SHOULDER SUBLUXATION

A subluxation occurs when the ball of the shoulder joint slips out of the socket, then slips back in. Subluxations can happen in isolation, or, as is more often the case, they happen regularly with particular shoulder motions because the front lip of the socket has deteriorated.

Symptoms:

- Sensation of the joint popping out, then popping back in again.
- Severe pain that subsides after a minute or so.
- Pain is especially acute when trying to bring arm across the chest.
- Arm numbness and weakness after dynamic activity, such as throwing a ball.

Causes:

- Vigorous overarm activities; sidearm motions with rotation.

Athletes at risk:

- Participants in throwing and racket sports, as well as swimmers.
- Athletes who have previously sustained one or more shoulder dislocations.

Concerns:

- Recurrent subluxations indicate significant damage to the lip of the front of the shoulder joint, which may be corrected only through surgery.

What you can do:

- Seek medical attention.

Medication:

- For relief of minor to moderate pain, take acetaminophen or ibuprofen as directed on label, or, for the relief of pain *and* inflammation, aspirin if tolerated (see page 49).

What the doctor can do:

- During the medical history, listen carefully to the athlete's description of how and when the shoulder pops out.
- To confirm the diagnosis, perform the "apprehension test": the patient lies on the examination table and the arm is pulled away from the body at the same time as it is forcefully rotated outwards. As the ball at the end of the upper arm is lifted out of the socket in the shoulder blade, extreme pain is felt in the athlete with damage to the front lip of the joint socket.
- After an isolated episode of subluxation, nonoperative treatment consists of icing the damaged shoulder for ten minutes on, twenty minutes off, as frequently as possible for the first two days following the injury. Heat treatment can begin two days after the injury occurs. Range-of-motion exercises can start one week after the injury, and strengthening with weights should commence after two weeks (see below, "Shoulder Rehabilitation").
- If nonoperative measures are unsuccessful and further subluxations occur, or if recurrent subluxations of the shoulder had already severely damaged the front lip of the shoulder socket, further diagnostic tests may be ordered. MRI (magnetic resonance imaging) or arthroscopy of the shoulder may be performed to ascertain the extent of the damage. The results may indicate that surgery is required.
- Surgery consists of tightening up the structures that hold the ball of the shoulder joint against the socket. After the operation, patients wear a sling for two weeks.
- Surgery is a successful means of preventing further subluxations. However, to stabilize the joint, the ligaments are tightened, and this can cause a slight decrease in shoulder mobility.

Rehabilitation:

- As soon as pain permits—usually twenty-four to forty-eight hours after the subluxation—level one exercises should be done in conjunction with icing.
- Level two exercises with weights can begin two weeks after the injury. For levels one, two, and three rehabilitation guidelines, refer to the sections on rehabilitation and conditioning at the end of this chapter.

Recovery time:

- Anywhere between eight weeks to six months of rehabilitation and strengthening and flexibility exercises may be necessary before athletes can return to contact sports or activities that require strenuous use of the shoulder.

A-C SHOULDER SEPARATION *(Acromioclavicular Separation)*

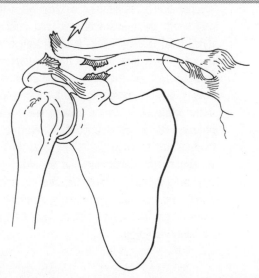

The shoulder injuries referred to as separations are actually sprains—stretches or tears of the ligaments that hold the shoulder bones together. The most common of these separations is the one that affects the ligaments of the acromioclavicular joint, the one that connects the shoulder blade to the collarbone. This injury is commonly referred to as an A-C separation.

Shoulder separations are classified according to sever-ity and are divided into first degree (mild), second degree (moderate), or third degree (complete), depending on the extent of damage to the ligaments and soft tissue around the joint.

Symptoms:

- First-degree separation (the ligaments are only stretched): Pain and tenderness over the outer tip of the collarbone. Pain intensifies when the arm is moved across the body. Pain is not severe but is sufficient to disturb sleep. There is no bone displacement, and the shoulder is stable.
- Second-degree separation (partial tearing of the ligaments): Significant pain and tenderness over the outer tip of the collarbone. The shoulder will ache constantly. Mild deformity—the outer end of the collarbone will stick up.
- Third degree (the ligaments are completely ruptured): Obvious deformity—the outer tip of the collarbone is raised and seems unstable. Extreme pain and tenderness over the outer end of the clavicle. Pain intensifies when trying to lift arm above the head. Swelling and bruising.

Causes:

- A fall onto the tip of the shoulder.
- Direct impact to the top or side of the shoulder from another athlete or when a hockey player slams into the boards, for example.

Athletes at risk:

- Shoulder separations are most often seen in athletes in contact sports and participants in activities with the potential for falling accidents—skiing, biking, and in-line skating, for instance.

Concerns:

- If a shoulder separation is not treated, the displaced collarbone will cause long-term pain, weakness, and loss of mobility in the shoulder that can be corrected only with surgery.

What you can do:

- First- and second-degree separations can be treated conservatively by the injured athlete:

Apply ice twenty minutes on, twenty minutes off, as often as possible, for the first week.

For seven to ten days, when not applying ice, keep the arm in a sling.

When pain diminishes, begin the shoulder rehabilitation program at the end of the chapter.

When strength and mobility have returned, gradually resume sports activities.

- Athletes should contact a physician if:

They are unable to lift the arm over the head

After ten days, the shoulder is still painful with decreased range of motion

During the first ten days after the injury, shoulder mobility is decreasing or pain is increasing

- For third-degree separations, follow these steps:

Send for medical assistance.

Immobilize the arm in a sling.

Secure the arm to the body with an elastic bandage.

Gently apply ice to the area for twenty minutes at a time until medical help arrives.

Medication:

- For relief of minor to moderate pain, take acetaminophen or ibuprofen as directed on label, or, for the relief of pain *and* inflammation, aspirin if tolerated (see page 49).

What the doctor can do:

- Perform range-of-motion tests and order X rays to determine the severity of the injury. X rays are taken with the patient holding a light weight because the resistance more accurately reveals the extent of the separation.
- Nonoperative treatment options:

Treatment for first-degree separations:

Immobilization in a sling for seven days.

Apply ice for twenty minutes at a time, as often as possible, for seventy-two hours after the injury, and ideally, seven days.

- Treatment for second-degree separations:

Immobilization in a sling for seven to ten days to prevent further tearing of the ligaments.

For the first forty-eight hours, icing for twenty minutes at a time to reduce pain, swelling, and inflammation.

Because pain is often severe, painkillers are prescribed.

After forty-eight hours, heat treatments should begin—hot packs, heating pads, or hot showers.

A week after the injury, the patient can begin a program to regain range of motion.

After mobility has returned to normal, strength and flexibility exercises should start. As soon as strength and mobility have returned, and the shoulder is pain free, the athlete can be okayed for gradual return to sports activity.

- Treatment for third-degree separations:

The doctor should place the athlete in a shoulder immobilizer for six weeks, then a carefully directed rehabilitation program begins. Often, nonsurgical management of A-C separation is as effective as surgery.

- Most sports doctors will offer a trial period of nonsurgical management for third-degree separations. If this fails because the shoulder stays painful and dysfunctional, surgery may be done. Surgery is also chosen for athletes in contact or throwing sports, tennis players, and for elite athletes with a vested interest in returning to absolute full function.
- In surgery, the collarbone and shoulder blade may be wired or pinned together to achieve effective realignment. Alternatively, synthetic ligaments may be used to replace ligaments that are badly damaged.

Rehabilitation:

- For rehabilitation of first- and second-degree separations, refer to the section "What you can do."
- Level one rehabilitation exercises for nonsurgically treated third-degree separations should begin two weeks after the injury occurs (the athlete should remove the immobilizer to do the exercises). Range-of-motion exercises should

be done until full mobility returns, at which time more strenuous strength and flexibility exercises can start.

- After surgery, range-of-motion exercises should start after two weeks of immobilization in a sling. Strength training with weights can begin approximately six weeks later, with more than a month generally needed to regain full shoulder strength. Once the doctor and physical therapist have determined that full strength and flexibility in the shoulder have returned, the patient can return to sports. For levels one, two, and three rehabilitation guidelines, refer to the sections on rehabilitation and conditioning at the end of this chapter.

Recovery time:

- First-degree separation: seven to ten days, or when pain is gone.
- Second-degree separations: healing should have taken place within two to three weeks, and the athlete can return to impact sports when he or she can perform all the rehabilitation exercises, usually six weeks later.
- Third-degree separations: healing is usually complete in three months, at which time the athlete is okayed to return to full sports participation by the doctor and physical therapist.

S-C SHOULDER SEPARATION (*Sternoclavicular Separation*)

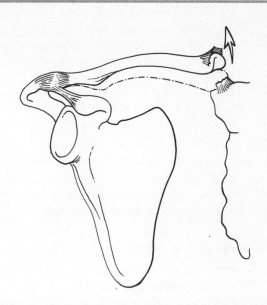

The second most common shoulder separation is a sprain of the ligaments of the sternoclavicular joint, which connects the collarbone with the breastbone. These injuries are commonly referred to as S-C separations.

S-C separations are classified in the same way as A-C separations (see above).

Symptoms:

- If the collarbone separates in a forward direction, a deformity over the area where the collarbone meets the breastbone.
- Pain over the injury.

Causes:

- A fall onto an outstretched hand or a direct blow from behind that drives the shoulder forward, as in a fall backward onto the ground or a tackle from the rear.

Athletes at risk:

- S-C separations are usually seen in athletes in contact sports and in activities with the potential for falling accidents. It happens frequently among wrestlers when they are slammed to the mat.

Concerns:

- Usually the collarbone separates forward. But if it moves backward toward major blood vessels, it may be *life threatening* because of the potential for respiratory problems or cardiac arrest.

What you can do:

- Be alert to any alterations in consciousness.
- Send for medical assistance.
- Immobilize the arm in a sling.
- Secure the arm to the body with an elastic bandage.
- Gently apply ice to the area for twenty minutes at a time until medical help arrives.

What the doctor can do:

- Perform a physical examination and take X rays to confirm the diagnosis.
- Rule out a "backward" (posterior) separation of the collarbone.
- Nonsurgical treatment options:

  If the separation is partial, the doctor will put the athlete in a sling for two weeks. Immobilization will usually allow the partially damaged ligaments to heal.

  More severe separations may be put in a figure-eight brace for six weeks to encourage healing.
- If the ligaments are completely ruptured, surgery may be required to ensure effective realignment of the joint. Surgery is done more frequently for S-C separations than for A-C separations. The same procedure is used.

Rehabilitation:

- Rehabilitation for S-C separations is the same as for A-C separations (page 206).

Recovery time:

- If the separation is first degree, the athlete can usually return to sports when he or she has regained full pain-free range of motion and the joint is not tender. This is usually in seven to fourteen days.

- If the separation is second degree, the athlete can return to noncontact sports when there is no pain on moving the joint and full range of motion has been regained. Contact sports should be avoided for four to six weeks.
- In the case of a complete separation, between six to eight weeks is needed before the athlete can go back to contact sports, and as little as four weeks before noncontact sports can be done.

RUPTURE OF THE LONG HEAD TENDON OF THE BICEPS

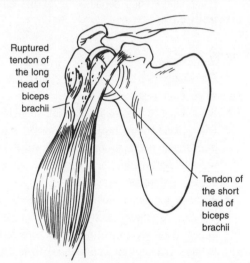

Ruptured tendon of the long head of biceps brachii

Tendon of the short head of biceps brachii

A rupture of the long head tendon of the biceps is a complete tear of the muscle tendon that attaches the biceps to the shoulder. Because of degenerative changes that occur over a lifetime, complete ruptures are especially prevalent in athletes over forty years old. In younger athletes, the likely result of stress to the tendon is inflammation.

Symptoms:

- A "snap" and intense pain at the front of the shoulder the moment the rupture occurs.
- Difficulty bending the elbow and rotating the forearm outward. Shoulder motion is not affected.
- A "Popeye" muscle that appears when the bicep is tensed—the muscle balls up because it has come free of its attachment at the upper end.

Cause:

- Forceful pushing motions.

Athletes at risk:

- Those in sports that require explosive pushing movements—weight lifters, rowers, tennis players, gymnasts, and those in throwing sports (discus, shot put, and javelin).
- Athletes who use anabolic steroids, because these substances weaken the soft tissues.

What you can do:

- Follow the RICE prescription (page 46).
- Seek medical attention.

Medication:

- For minor discomfort, take acetaminophen as directed on label or, for the relief of pain *and* inflammation, ibuprofen or aspirin if tolerated (see page 49).

What the doctor can do:

- Nonsurgical treatment: For comfort, immobilize the arm in a sling for three to five days. Prescribe a strength and flexibility program to begin as soon as pain diminishes.
- Surgery is rarely needed but may be done if the injury is causing loss of mobility; if the patient is a young and particularly active athlete or, if the patient is concerned about the appearance of the "Popeye" muscle.
- Surgery involves making an incision in the front of the shoulder, finding the detached biceps tendon, and reattaching it with stitches to the front of the upper arm bone. Following a complete and comprehensive rehabilitation, athletes who have this operation experience almost no loss of strength or flexibility, and usually return to their preinjury level of play.
- After surgery, the arm is immobilized for four weeks.

Rehabilitation:

- Isometric strengthening and physical therapist–assisted range-of-motion exercises can begin as soon as pain permits—usually within twenty-four to forty-eight hours of the injury.
- Gentle *active* range-of-motion exercises can begin within a week. In the initial stages, rehabilitation should focus on regaining the ability to bend the elbow (elbow flexion), which is compromised by damage to the biceps tendon.
- After full range of motion is restored—usually within four weeks—strengthening exercises with weights should begin.
- If surgery is performed, isometrics and physical therapist–assisted range-of-motion exercises can start as soon as pain permits. Active range-of-motion exercises begin after the four-week immobilization period, followed in two weeks by strengthening exercises. For levels one, two, and three rehabilitation guidelines, refer to the sections on rehabilitation and conditioning at the end of this chapter.

Recovery time:

- When surgery is not required, activity can resume as soon as pain is gone—usually within three to six weeks.
- After surgery, eight weeks of rest and rehabilitation is needed before vigorous arm activities can be resumed, and twelve to fourteen weeks before the athlete can participate in contact sports.

BICEPS BRUISE *(Biceps Contusion)*

A biceps bruise, medically known as a biceps contusion, is caused by damage to the tissues and capillaries of the muscle, which causes loss of fluid and blood beneath the skin.

Symptoms:

- Immediate pain upon impact.
- Initial pain diminishes with continued activity but resumes once the athlete has cooled down.
- Severe bruises in the biceps may also cause swelling in the upper arm, and the area around

the bruise may feel tight, making elbow motion difficult.

- Within twenty-four hours, discoloration beneath the skin that changes over the course of several days from an initial dark red or purple to greenish yellow.

Cause:

- Direct impact to the biceps muscle.

Athletes at risk:

- Biceps bruises are usually seen in athletes in contact sports and in activities with the potential for falling accidents.

Concerns:

- Severe bruising can cause a pooling of blood in the area, known as a hematoma. Hematomas can occur if the athlete continues to use the bruised arm, or if the impact that causes the bruise is especially hard. The greatest concern with biceps contusions is a condition called myositis ossificans, in which bone cells start forming in the muscle.

What you can do:

- For mild to moderate biceps bruises, apply RICE (page 46) as soon as possible.
- Avoid any activity that will promote bleeding, especially further sports activity using the bruised arm.
- Despite stiffness, never massage a bruise in the initial stages, as the warming effect will increase bleeding.
- If the bruise is causing significant limitation of motion, or if, after forty-eight to seventy-two hours, the bruising continues to spread and swelling does not go down, seek medical attention.

Medication:

- For relief of minor to moderate pain, take acetaminophen as directed on label, or, for the relief of pain *and* inflammation, ibuprofen or aspirin if tolerated (see page 49).

What the doctor can do:

- Prescribe icing twenty minutes on, twenty minutes off, as often as possible, for three to five days, in conjunction with a gentle compressive bandage. If the pain is severe, recommend a sling for comfort.
- If after two to three weeks pain and swelling return, and the area feels warm, myositis ossificans may be the reason. X rays are usually ordered, and though initial X rays are usually negative, after two or three weeks a dark mass shows up on the pictures.
- Anti-inflammatories and gentle range-of-motion therapy are used to control the condition.

Rehabilitation:

- For the first fourteen days after sustaining moderate to severe bruises, athletes should focus on icing the area and doing gentle range-of-motion exercises for the shoulder and elbow.
- After fourteen days, the physical therapist may prescribe moist heat massage to stimulate the healing process. At the same time, the intensity of the range-of-motion exercises will be increased, and strengthening exercises with weights may be worked into the rehabilitation program. For levels one, two, and three rehabilitation guidelines, refer to the sections on rehabilitation and conditioning at the end of this chapter.

Recovery time:

- Mild and moderate bruises should heal within five days.
- A hematoma may take between three to six weeks to clear up.
- Myositis ossificans usually takes six months to heal.

FRACTURES OF THE UPPER AND MIDDLE SHAFT OF THE UPPER ARM

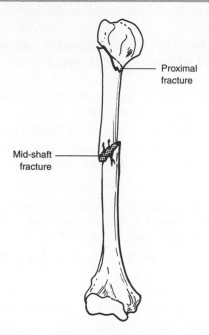

Proximal fracture

Mid-shaft fracture

A fracture is a crack, break, or complete shattering of a bone. Fractures of the upper arm, the humerus, usually present themselves as shoulder injuries.

Symptoms:

- A "crack" may be felt at the moment of injury.
- Immediate pain and swelling over the damaged bone, and the area will be tender to the touch.

Causes:

- A fall onto an outstretched arm or a fall onto the shoulder.
- Direct impact to the upper arm.

Athletes at risk:

- Fractures of the upper arm bone are usually seen in athletes in contact sports and in activities with the potential for falling accidents.

Concerns:

- Fractures of the upper arm bones can usually be treated with splinting and aggressive rehabilitation. Because there is a large area of bone

on either side of the break, splinting facilitates efficient rejoining of the broken ends.

What you can do:

- Send for medical assistance.
- Immobilize the arm in a splint.
- Secure the arm to the body with an elastic bandage.
- Gently apply ice over the area for twenty minutes at a time until medical attention is available.

Medication:

- For relief of minor to moderate pain, take acetaminophen as directed on label, or, for the relief of pain *and* inflammation, ibuprofen or aspirin if tolerated (see page 49).

What the doctor can do:

- After ruling out nerve and blood vessel damage, and performing a physical examination, order X rays to confirm the diagnosis.
- Nonsurgical treatment options:
  Realign the ends of the broken bones.
  Apply a support bandage for two to four weeks, after which rehabilitation can begin.
  In general, doctors prefer not to perform surgery on fractures of the upper arm because they are rarely successful—the bones do not heal together very well. However, surgery may be necessary if the ball or shaft at the top end of the upper arm is badly displaced, or if fragments of bone have drifted into the joint. An operation is also necessary if the patient is a child, and the fracture has broken the growth plate at the end of the upper arm bone. In such cases, surgery is necessary to prevent long-term dysfunction in the arm.
- Surgical option:
  An incision is made over the fracture, then internal fixation is done with screws or metallic bands that are wound around the ends of the broken bones.
  If fragments have entered the joint, these are removed through an incision over the joint.

Rehabilitation:

- After a brief period of immobilization, preferably as short as ten days, level one rehabilitation exercises can begin. At this stage, the physical therapist moves the patient's joints through allowable ranges of motion—"active assisted" or "passive assisted" exercise.
- As soon as patients are able to do range-of-motion exercises using their own strength, level two exercises can begin, and thereafter the rehabilitation program can progress accordingly. For levels one, two, and three rehabilitation guidelines, refer to the sections on rehabilitation and conditioning at the end of this chapter.
- Rehabilitation after surgery follows the same pattern.

Recovery time:

- Three months of rest and rehabilitation before sports activity can be resumed.
- After surgery for an upper arm fracture, four to six months of rehabilitation and conditioning is necessary before the athlete can return to contact sports or activities that require vigorous use of the injured arm.

BICEPS STRAIN

A biceps strain is a stretch or tear in the fibers of the biceps muscle. These strains usually occur in the main part of the muscle, known as the "belly."

Like all muscle strains, biceps strains are classified according to severity: first degree (mild), second degree (moderate), or third degree (severe).

For effective treatment of a muscle strain, refer to pages 155–157.

Symptoms:

- Pain and tenderness over the affected muscle.
- Pain with use of the muscle.
- Stiffness in the muscle.

Cause:

- Sudden, vigorous movement using the biceps muscle.

Athletes at risk:

- Biceps strains are especially common in athletes in throwing sports, and especially, weight lifters.

STRAIN OF THE CHEST MUSCLE *(Pectoralis Major)* ATTACHMENT TO THE UPPER ARM

Chest muscle strains are usually stretches or tears of the tendons where the chest muscles attach to the upper arm.

Like all strains, chest muscle-tendon strains are classified according to severity: first degree (mild), second degree (moderate), or third degree (severe).

Symptoms:

- Pain where the chest muscle inserts into the upper arm bone.
- Pain is especially acute when trying to lift objects.
- Strength limitations, especially when trying to pull the arm toward the chest, or rotating it inward against resistance.
- Difficulty tensing the chest muscles.
- Dramatic bruising over the entire outer chest area.
- Visible deformity and/or lack of definition in the chest muscle.

Cause:

- A single, extreme demand placed on the chest muscle.

Athletes at risk:

- Strains of the chest muscle attachment are especially common in weight lifters and athletes in field sports.

Concerns:

- Athletes often mistake these injuries for bruises and do not rehabilitate them properly. This puts them at risk for reinjury.

What you can do:

- In the case of a first-degree strain, use the RICE (page 46) prescription.

- Wait until the pain abates, then begin a progressive rehabilitation program.
- If the injury is a second- or third-degree muscle strain, seek medical attention.

Medication:

- For relief of minor pain and swelling, take acetaminophen as directed on label, or for relief of pain *and* inflammation, ibuprofen or aspirin if tolerated (see page 000).

What the doctor can do:

- For mild muscle strains, prescribe RICE.
- In the case of a second-degree muscle strain, prescribe relative rest (page 64) and early range-of-motion and strengthening exercises as often as pain permits. If the pain is severe, a sling may be worn for five to ten days to provide comfort.
- If the muscle has completely ruptured, surgery may be necessary. The ruptured muscle is stitched back to the upper arm bone from which it has detached.

Rehabilitation:

- In the case of a first-degree strain, level two or three rehabilitation exercises can start as soon as pain diminishes, and no later than forty-eight hours after the injury occurs. RICE should continue for seventy-two hours after the injury occurs. RICE should continue during this period.
- After a second-degree sprain, level two rehabilitation exercises can begin as soon as pain diminishes, and no later than seventy-two hours after the injury occurs. RICE should continue during this period.
- If surgery is necessary, the arm needs to be immobilized in a bandage for at least four weeks, after which level one rehabilitation exercises commence. Level two exercises can begin two weeks later.

Recovery time:

- First-degree strains: one week.
- Second-degree strains: three to six weeks.
- Third-degree strains: after surgery, six to twelve weeks.

Overuse Injuries of the Shoulder and Upper Arm

IMPINGEMENT SYNDROMES

Impingement syndromes are thought to be the main cause of chronic pain in the shoulder.

These disorders refer to a process in which the soft tissues that top the ball of the shoulder joint—the rotator cuff muscles and tendons, the subacromial bursa, and the biceps tendon—catch repetitively on the coracoacromial arch on the underside of the shoulder blade (this arch is made up of the coracoid process, acromion process, and coracoacromial ligament).

How do impingement syndromes develop? There are two sets of factors—internal and external.

External factors include both stresses placed on the shoulder joint from repetitive sports activities in throwing and racket sports, swimming, rowing, and weight lifting.

Internal factors mostly concern imbalances in strength between the rotator cuff muscles and other muscle groups. In a healthy shoulder, the powerful upward force of the deltoid muscle on the outside of the upper arm is counteracted by an intact rotator cuff. In that way, the ball at the end of the upper arm bone stays snug against the shoulder socket no matter what position the arm is in. However, if the stabilizing force of the rotator cuff is weakened by repetitive trauma, overuse, or age, during overarm activity the top of the upper arm bone is pulled upward and catches against the coracoacromial arch on the underside of the shoulder blade.

The first victims of this repetitive pinching are the rotator cuff tendons and bursae that lie between the top of the upper arm bone and the coracoacromial arch. The tendons and bursae get irritated, causing tendinitis and bursitis.

Gradually, the rotator cuff sustains more and more low-grade damage, leading to scarring and degeneration. As this is happening, a bone spur tends to form underneath the front of the acromion process. The vicious cycle continues as this bone spur makes tiny rips in the rotator cuff. Tears in the rotator cuff expose the biceps tendon, which in turn gets irritated, causing bicipital tendinitis.

Because of the space between the top of the upper arm bone and the coracoacromial arch is so small, and the supraspinatus tendon passes through this gap, that tendon is the structure exposed to maximum impingement stress.

Symptoms:

- Onset of symptoms is gradual.
- Pain when the arm is held outward and the athlete tries to make circular motions.
- Pain intensifies when the arm is held at a right angle at chest height (mimic looking at the watch face on top of the wrist), and the arm is moved downward so the fingers are pointing at the ground.

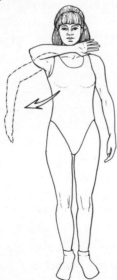

- "Impingement sign"—intense pain when the doctor holds the patient's arm straight out in front, and pushes it upward.
- Tenderness over the front of the upper arm bone.
- Pain may worsen at night.

Causes:

- Powerful, frequent overarm motions.
- Sudden increase in the frequency, intensity, or duration of the training or playing regimen.
- Relative weakness of or damage to the rotator cuff.
- Arthritis precipitated by an old A-C separation, calcification, or a genetic abnormality affecting the A-C joint, reducing the space through which the tendon must pass.

Athletes at risk:

- Those who participate in activities that require powerful overarm motions, especially swimmers. Also at risk: rowers, weight lifters, racket sports players, basketball players, and throwers.

What you can do:

- At the first signs of an impingement condition, ice the shoulder three to four times daily for twenty minutes at a time.
- Depending on the severity of the symptoms, reduce or avoid sports that aggravate the condition.
- Never render the shoulder completely inactive, as this may cause a condition known as "frozen shoulder" (see page 221). Perform the level two rehabilitation exercises.
- Begin a conditioning program for the shoulder, focusing on the rotator cuff muscles.
- Stretch out the rotator cuff muscles before vigorous exercise.
- Wear a neoprene heat retainer during activity (available at most drug stores).
- See a doctor when the condition has deteriorated to where it hurts at night.

Medication:

- For relief of minor pain, take acetaminophen as directed on label, or, for the relief of pain *and* inflammation, ibuprofen or aspirin if tolerated (see page 49).

What the doctor can do:

- Take a detailed medical history and perform a careful physical examination to confirm the diagnosis.
- Nonsurgical treatment options:

    Conditioning to strengthen and stretch the rotator cuff muscles is the cornerstone of treatment for this condition.

    Anti-inflammatories.

    Steroid injections are sometimes used to reduce the inflammation, though athletes are not able to do any vigorous overarm activities for two weeks afterward because of the weakening effect the steroid injection has on the tendon. Steroid injections are given too often for athletes with rotator cuff tendinitis, and are no substitute for physical therapy.

- In a worst-case scenario, surgery is necessary to repair torn rotator cuff muscles and tendons. The operation entails repairing the portion of damaged tissue from the tendon, and also removing the coracoacromial ligament and bone spurs to create more room for the tendon.

Rehabilitation:

- Strength and flexibility exercises are the key to correcting most impingement syndrome conditions. A carefully directed exercise program is needed to correct the strength and flexibility deficits contributing to the condition. Special focus should be on restoring "internal rotation."
- In conjunction with icing for twenty to thirty minutes three times daily, level two rehabilitation exercises should commence immediately and progress as quickly as possible.
- After surgery, level one rehabilitation exercises should begin after three to five days, except when major stitching is done, in which case a special brace is worn to hold the arm away from the body and protect the repair. For levels one, two, and three rehabilitation guidelines, refer to the sections on rehabilitation and conditioning at the end of this chapter.

Recovery time:

- With conservative treatment, improvement should be seen within two to four weeks, and the athlete can return to sports after six to eight weeks, if pain is gone and full range of motion is regained.
- When the condition is chronic and surgery is performed, patients with impingement syndrome can usually return to sports in three months, as long as pain is gone and full range of motion is regained.

ROTATOR CUFF TENDINITIS (*Supraspinatus Tendinitis*)

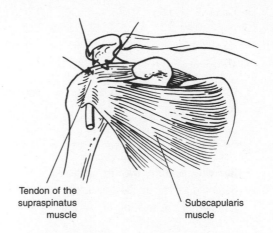

Tendon of the suppraspinatus muscle

Subscapularis muscle

Rotator cuff tendinitis is an inflammation of one or more of the muscle tendons that hold the ball of the shoulder joint tightly against the socket. Usually it affects the tendon of the supraspinatus muscle. Supraspinatus tendinitis, as it is properly known, is one of the most frequent causes of shoulder pain.

This tendinitis condition usually occurs in conjunction with an impingement syndrome (page 213).

Symptoms:

- Onset of symptoms is gradual.
- Pain and weakness during shoulder motion, especially when the arm is extended straight when raised and lowered between 80 and 120 degrees.
- Localized tenderness and sometimes swelling at the front and upper part of the shoulder.

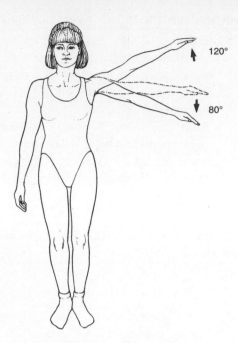

120°

80°

- In severe cases, the arm cannot be raised to shoulder height.

Causes:

- Powerful, repetitive overarm motions.
- Sudden increase in the frequency, intensity, or duration of the training or playing regimen.

Concerns:

- If neglected, rotator cuff tendinitis can deteriorate to the point where long layoffs and intense rehabilitation are necessary to correct the condition. Even then, conservative treatment may not work, and surgery may be the only way the athlete can return to sports. Rarely do athletes who require surgery regain their preinjury form.

What you can do:

- As soon as the symptoms of rotator cuff tendinitis surface, ice the shoulder three times daily for twenty to thirty minutes at a time.
- Continue to be active, but modify the overarm activity so it does not cause pain. If pain persists, cease the activity.

- Begin a conditioning program to stretch and strengthen the rotator cuff muscles, and return to sports in six weeks, but only when pain and range of motion have returned.
- If symptoms persist for more than two weeks, seek medical attention.

Medication:

- For relief of minor to moderate pain, take acetaminophen as directed on label, or, for the relief of pain *and* inflammation, ibuprofen or aspirin if tolerated (see page 49).

What the doctor can do:

- Take a detailed medical history and perform a careful physical examination to confirm the diagnosis.
- Direct the athlete to curtail or cease activities that caused the condition.
- Usually, nonsurgical treatment is sufficient to clear up rotator cuff tendinitis:
    RICE
    Anti-inflammatories
    Cortisone injections
- The cortisone will take forty-eight hours to relieve the tendinitis symptoms. Because of the weakening effect of cortisone, the athlete should not perform dynamic activity using the shoulder for two weeks. Cortisone usually takes three weeks to clear up the tendinitis. Even when the tendinitis remains chronic, no more than three cortisone injections are advisable because the drug may dangerously weaken the tendon.
- Surgery may be necessary when the tendinitis is so severe it does not respond to conservative treatment. The goal of surgery is to make more room for the tendon—removing the coracoacromial ligament, trimming off calcifications of the acromion of the shoulder blade, and excising the nearby bursa. If the tendons are significantly torn, the tears should be stitched together during the operation. Once a major surgical procedure, this operation is now done on an outpatient basis, thanks to the advent of arthroscopic surgery.

- When no stitching is done during the surgery, isometrics and physical therapist–assisted range-of-motion exercises can start as soon as pain allows—usually twenty-four to forty-eight hours after the operation. Strength training with weights and active range-of-motion exercises can begin in three to five days.

Rehabilitation:

- In cases of mild to moderate rotator cuff tendinitis, begin level two rehabilitation exercises immediately, working up to level three exercises within a week.
- After surgery, start level one rehabilitation exercises within three to five days.
- Following completion of rehabilitation, it is crucial to begin a rotator cuff conditioning program to prevent reinjury. For levels one, two, and three rehabilitation guidelines, refer to the sections on rehabilitation and conditioning at the end of this chapter.

Recovery time:

- If caught early, one to three weeks of shoulder activity modification and rehabilitation exercises are enough to clear up the condition.
- If the tendinitis deteriorates to where it is moderately severe, it may take up to six weeks of rest and rehabilitation for the condition to heal.
- After surgery, six to twelve weeks of rest and rehabilitation is needed before returning to sports, and at least twelve weeks before starting activities that require vigorous use of the shoulder.

SHOULDER BURSITIS *(Subacromial Bursitis, Calcific Bursitis)*

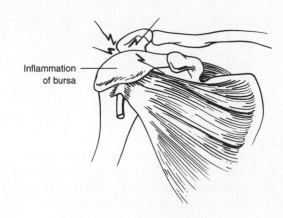

Inflammation of bursa

Shoulder bursitis is an irritation and swelling of the bursa sac that lies between the rotator cuff tendons and the shoulder blade.

This form of bursitis rarely occurs in isolation. The condition is usually brought on by impingement syndromes or damage to the rotator cuff tendons (see "Rotator Cuff Tendinitis" and "Impingement Syndromes," pages 215 and 213). In athletes older than thirty to thirty-five, it may be precipitated by calcium deposits that have developed around the rotator cuff tendons, which irritate the bursa and sometimes actually enter the bursa sac.

Symptoms:

- Onset of symptoms is gradual.
- Pain in the front and upper part of the shoulder.
- Pain when performing the same motions as in the "Symptoms" section of "Shoulder Tendinitis."
- Loss of motion.
- Localized tenderness and swelling over the bursa.

Causes:

- Repetitive overarm motions that trap the subacromial bursa between the rotator cuff tendons and the underside of the shoulder blade.

- Sudden increase in the frequency, intensity, or duration of training or playing regimen.
- Inflammation of the rotator cuff tendons, especially the supraspinatus tendon.
- Calcific tendinitis of the supraspinatus tendon that causes irritation to the bursa sac.
  Note: Shoulder bursitis may be caused by a single blow to the shoulder that causes bleeding into the bursa. In such cases it is an acute injury.

What you can do:

- Depending on pain, curtail or cease the activity that caused the condition, but do not render the shoulder completely inactive as this can cause "frozen shoulder" (see page 221).
- Apply ice immediately for twenty to thirty minutes at a time, as often as possible for three days.

Medication:

- For relief of pain and swelling, take acetaminophen as directed on label, or, for the relief of pain *and* inflammation, ibuprofen or aspirin if tolerated (see page 49).

What the doctor can do:

- Take the medical history and perform a physical examination to confirm the diagnosis. Sometimes arthography, bursography, and/or MRI is done to assist with the diagnosis.
- Direct the athlete to curtail or cease activities that caused the condition.
- Usually, conservative treatment is sufficient to clear up shoulder bursitis:
  Anti-inflammatories
  RICE
  Heat treatment
  Draining the bursa with a syringe
  Steroid injections into the bursa sac (followed by immediate rehabilitation exercises to restore strength and mobility)
- In severe cases, immobilize the shoulder in a sling or splint for a few days, but no longer

than this, as prolonged immobilization can cause "frozen shoulder."
- If conservative measures fail, surgery may be necessary. Bursa sac is removed with an arthroscope or through a small incision. Usually, the coracoacromial ligament is also removed during this operation.
- If the bursitis is caused by associated conditions such as torn or calcified rotator cuff tendons, these conditions are surgically addressed.
- After surgery, the arm is immobilized in a sling for ten days.

Rehabilitation:

- As soon as the first symptoms of bursitis are felt, level two rehabilitation exercises should start.
- After surgery, level one range-of-motion exercises should begin within seven days. Level two exercises should begin two weeks after surgery. For levels one, two, and three rehabilitation guidelines, refer to the sections on rehabilitation and conditioning at the end of this chapter.

Recovery time:

- With appropriate treatment, mild to moderate shoulder bursitis conditions clear up in two to three weeks.
- After surgery, six to eight weeks of rehabilitation before athletes can return to full sports activity.

INFLAMMATION OF THE LONG TENDON OF THE BICEPS (*Bicipital Tendinitis*)

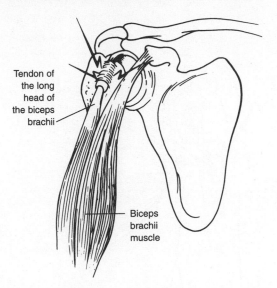

Tendon of
the long
head of
the biceps
brachii

Biceps
brachii
muscle

Bicipital tendinitis is an inflammation of the tendon that connects the biceps muscle with the shoulder joint. This tendon is especially vulnerable to irritation because it passes through a narrow groove in the top of the upper arm bone.

This tendinitis condition often occurs in conjunction with impingement syndromes, which, in their advanced stages, may damage the rotator cuff and expose the biceps tendon to irritation (see "Impingement Syndromes," page 213).

Symptoms:

- Onset of symptoms is gradual.
- Discomfort over the front of the shoulder.
- Pain increases when the elbow is held at a right angle (mimic looking at a watch face on the top of the wrist) and when the wrist is rotated outward against resistance.
- A crackling sensation (crepitus) over the top of the shoulder when bending or straightening the joint.

Causes:

- Repetitive, powerful overarm motions.
- Sudden increase in the intensity, frequency, or duration of the training or playing regimen.

- Damage to the rotator cuff caused by an impingement syndrome (rotator cuff damage exposes the biceps tendon to irritation).
- Deformity in the bicep groove: it is so shallow that the tendon slips out, or it has rough edges that irritate the tendon.

Athletes at risk:

- Seen most often in racket sports players, weight lifters, rowers, golfers, swimmers, gymnasts, and athletes in throwing sports such as baseball, javelin, shot put, and discus.

Concerns:

- If caught early, conservative treatment is usually enough to take care of this condition. However, if allowed to deteriorate, the tendon will tend to slip out of the groove more and more frequently, leading to a chronic condition. When the condition becomes chronic, surgery may be necessary.

What you can do:

- For mild cases of tendinitis, rest and ice are the most effective treatment.
- Level two rehabilitation exercises should begin as soon as pain goes away—usually within a few days. For levels one, two, and three rehabilitation guidelines, refer to the sections on rehabilitation and conditioning at the end of this chapter.
- Gradual return to sports can begin within two to three weeks.
- If the pain continues for more than ten days, seek medical attention.

Medication:

- For relief of minor to moderate pain, take acetaminophen as directed on label, or, for the relief of pain *and* inflammation, ibuprofen or aspirin if tolerated (see page 49).

What the doctor can do:

- Conservative treatment is almost always sufficient to clear up this condition:

Ice in the initial stages

Heat after seventy-two hours

Anti-inflammatories

Cortisone injections around the tendon

- If conservative measures fail, surgery may be necessary. An incision is made in the front of the shoulder and the tendon is removed from its attachment at the top of the shoulder. The tendon is then stitched to the front of the shoulder, where it is not as subject to the same degree of irritation. With proper rehabilitation, strength or mobility in the shoulder joint is not affected.

Rehabilitation:

- In mild cases of bicipital tendinitis, level two rehabilitation exercises can begin as soon as pain dissipates, usually within twenty-four to forty-eight hours.
- For moderate cases, level two exercises should start within a week. For levels one, two, and three rehabilitation guidelines, refer to the sections on rehabilitation and conditioning at the end of this chapter.

Recovery time:

- Mild cases usually clear up in a week.
- Moderate cases of bicipital tendinitis may take between two and three weeks of treatment to resolve.
- After surgery, the athlete can usually return to full activity after twelve weeks of rehabilitation.

INFLAMMATION OF THE PECTORAL MUSCLE INSERTION

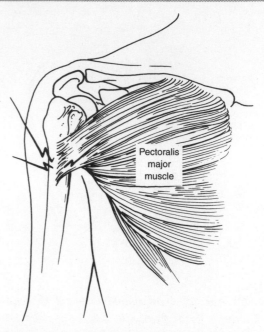

Pectoralis major muscle

Inflammation of the pectoral muscle insertion is caused by a series of microtears in the fibers of the tendon that attach the chest muscle to the upper arm.

Symptoms:

- Onset of symptoms is gradual.
- Pain where the chest muscle attaches to the upper arm, just below the armpit.
- Pain intensifies when trying to draw the arm inward toward the chest while applying resistance.

Causes:

- Powerful, repetitive throwing, lifting, or swinging motions.
- A sudden increase in the frequency, intensity, or duration of training or playing regimen.

Athletes at risk:

- Weight lifters who do an excessive amount of chest exercises using heavy weights, as well as racket sports players, swimmers, rowers, golfers, and gymnasts.

Concerns:

- If caught early, conservative treatment is usually enough to take care of this condition. However, if allowed to deteriorate, the tendinitis can become chronic, and surgery may be necessary so the athlete can return to normal activity.
- In older athletes, frequent microtears can result in complete rupture of this tendon.

What you can do:

- For mild cases of tendinitis, rest and ice are the most effective treatment.
- Level two rehabilitation exercises should begin as soon as pain goes away—usually within a few days. For levels one, two, and three rehabilitation guidelines, refer to the section on rehabilitation and conditioning at the end of this chapter.
- Gradual return to sports can begin within two to three weeks.
- If pain continues for more than ten days, seek medical attention.

Medication:

- For relief of minor pain, take acetaminophen as directed on label, or, for relief of pain *and* inflammation, ibuprofen or aspirin if tolerated (see page 49).

What the doctor can do:

- Conservative treatment is almost always sufficient to clear up this condition:
  Ice in the initial stages
  Heat after seventy-two hours
  Anti-inflammatories
  Cortisone injections around the tendon
  Initiate a strength and flexibility program
- Surgery is almost never done for bicipital tendinitis.

Rehabilitation:

- In mild cases of pectoral insertion tendinitis, isometric strengthening and gentle range-of-motion exercises can start immediately. Level two rehabilitation exercises can begin as soon as pain dissipates, usually within ten to fourteen days.
- For moderate cases, two to three weeks may be required before level two exercises start. For levels one, two, and three rehabilitation guidelines, refer to the section on rehabilitation and conditioning at the end of this chapter.

Recovery time:

- Mild cases usually clear up in a week.
- Moderate cases may take between two and three weeks of treatment to resolve.
- After surgery, the athlete can usually return to full activity after at least twelve weeks of rehabilitation.

"FROZEN SHOULDER" (Adhesive Capsulitis)

Frozen shoulder is a condition in which portions of the joint capsule stick together and form adhesions. Adhesive capsulitis, as it is properly known, can be potentially disabling and cause dramatic loss of mobility in a relatively short time, even as little as two to three weeks.

Because frozen shoulder is exacerbated by inactivity, rehabilitation of this condition is one of the few instances when exercises should be done beyond *the pain threshold—but only when supervised by a physical therapist.*

Symptoms:

- Reduced shoulder mobility.
- Extreme pain on movement, especially with throwing motions.
- An ache when the shoulder is not being used.

Cause:

- Nonuse of the shoulder due to discomfort from an injury such as tendinitis or bursitis.

Athletes at risk:

- Those who sustain overuse shoulder conditions such as tendinitis or bursitis.
- Frozen shoulder is especially common among diabetics, smokers, and menopausal women.

Concerns:

- If a frozen shoulder is allowed to persist, two years of intensive, continual physical therapy may be necessary to correct the condition.

What you can do:

- In conjunction with RICE therapy (page 46), immediately begin a shoulder range-of-motion program within the pain threshold. Because a carefully directed rehabilitation program is necessary to correct this condition, athletes with a suspected frozen shoulder should seek medical attention from a qualified sports doctor as soon as possible.

Medication:

- For relief of minor to moderate pain, take acetaminophen as directed on label, or, for the relief of pain *and* inflammation, ibuprofen or aspirin if tolerated (see page 49).

What the doctor can do:

- A complete medical history and thorough physical examination to confirm the diagnosis and rule out other possible causes for the complaint.
- Nonsurgical treatment options:

  Prescribe an intensive exercise program to restore range of motion to the shoulder. The program should begin immediately, and should consist of high-repetition, low-weight exercises to the point of pain and slightly beyond—as much as can be tolerated. Pain *should not* persist after the session.

  Depending on the degree of shoulder pain, over-the-counter and prescription anti-inflammatories are liberally prescribed.

  Range-of-motion exercises and medication are usually sufficient to promote recovery. If, however, the pain persists or worsens, and range of motion does not improve, deep heat therapy and the prescription drug prednisone should be used for a limited time.
- If physical therapy and medication have not cleared up the condition in four to six months,

the best choice may be surgery. To break the adhesions, the patient is placed under anesthetic, and the shoulder is physically manipulated through its maximum range of motion. This procedure must be followed by a comprehensive exercise program to ensure that range of motion is maintained.
- Alternatively, the doctor may perform an arthroscopy to inspect the inside of the joint and remove any accumulated scar tissue.

Rehabilitation:

- Frozen shoulder is exacerbated by inactivity, and for this reason, rehabilitation should begin *immediately*. In addition to prescribed exercises, patients should not hold back from using their shoulders for daily activities, even when pain is extreme.
- Rehabilitation of frozen shoulder is one of the few instances when patients should be encouraged to exercise beyond the pain threshold. This is necessary to break up the adhesions that have formed through inactivity. However, pain should not persist after the session.
- Athletes with frozen shoulder can usually begin their rehabilitation with level two exercises, and should try to progress as quickly as possible in the program. For levels one, two, and three rehabilitation guidelines, refer to the sections on rehabilitation and conditioning at the end of this chapter.

Recovery time:

- Usually, at least two to three months are necessary to loosen a frozen shoulder. However, in more severe cases it can take as long as two years for the shoulder to regain full range of motion. It is crucial that daily exercises continue—backsliding may be swift and discouraging.

Shoulder Rehabilitation

Shoulder rehabilitation involves exercises to promote healing, relieve inflammation and pain, and restore strength and range of motion to the joint.

Rehabilitation exercises serve to

- Promote blood flow to the area, which speeds the healing process
- Relieve stiffness in the joint caused by immobilization
- Prevent atrophy and tightening of the muscles resulting from inactivity.*

Because the shoulder is such a complex structure—with three major joints and twenty different muscles that control their movements—it is essential that athletes take a comprehensive approach to rehabilitation. In particular, athletes who perform powerful overarm movements need to pay attention to rehabilitating the rotator cuff muscles deep inside the shoulders, and not just the large muscles on top.

Rehabilitation should begin as soon as possible to prevent loss of range of motion and strength. Protracted inactivity after injury causes inordinate range of motion and strength deficits that need to be restored before return to sports activity. Delays in rehabilitation spell delays in an athlete's return to sports readiness.

After an injury that does not require surgery or prolonged splinting, range-of-motion exercises should begin as soon as pain and swelling diminish—usually no more than forty-eight hours after the injury symptoms begin, and often as early as twenty-four hours.

When surgery is necessary, range-of-motion exercises should begin as early as five days after surgery, and no more than two to three weeks later. The patient should be put in a sling or a splint that can be removed for physical therapy.

Exercise is the most effective way to restore an injured athlete to sports readiness. A physical therapist may also employ ice, superficial heat, deep heat, massage, electrical stimulation, and physical manipulation of the shoulder joint to promote healing and make performing the exercises more comfortable.

*For more on the importance and general principles of rehabilitation, refer to chapter 5, "Rehabilitating Your Sports Injury."

The starting intensity level of the rehabilitation depends on the severity of the injury. Postsurgery range-of-motion exercises usually begin at level one. At this level, range of motion is "active assisted"—the physical therapist helps the patients use their arm strength to move their shoulders through allowable ranges of motion. If the injury is too severe for active assisted exercises, the patient may have to rely on "passive assisted" exercises—the physical therapist moves the injured shoulder through allowable ranges of motion. Continuous passive motion machines (CPMs) can be taken home by the patient so he or she can do passive range-of-motion exercises at home.

After surgery, muscle atrophy is prevented by using isometric exercises. With the direction of a physical therapist, these exercises can usually begin immediately after surgery. Isometrics help maintain strength in the important muscles around the shoulder without compromising the healing process by changing the length of the muscle or the angle of the shoulder joint.

Athletes who have sustained only mild or moderately severe shoulder injuries can begin with level two exercises.

In the initial stages of the rehabilitation program, the primary goal is to restore range of motion; the secondary goal is to prevent atrophy in the surrounding muscles. As the rehabilitation program progresses, more strengthening exercises are included in the program.

Range-of-motion and strength exercises should always be done within the pain threshold. Any exercise that causes pain should be discontinued (with the exception of exercises for frozen shoulder).

The following are the most common and effective exercises used to rehabilitate the shoulder after injury.

Level One

After surgery, active assisted or passive assisted range-of-motion therapy is used as a starting point of rehabilitation. The physical therapist should move the patient's shoulder through its six major motions: flexion, extension, abduction, adduction, external rotating, and internal rotation. The shoulder should be moved only through those ranges of motion that do not compromise the stability of the surgery.

Isometrics and assisted range-of-motion therapy should

continue only until patients are capable of using their own strength to do level two exercises.

Level Two

When patients are able to move their injured shoulders themselves, level two "pendulum" range-of-motion exercises can begin.

Level two exercises can also be used as a starting point for rehabilitating moderate to severe shoulder injuries that do not require surgery. They primarily develop range of motion in the joint but through isometrics also help prevent atrophy in the important muscles around the shoulder.

Exercise 1: Pendulums (flexion, extension, abduction, adduction, internal rotation, external rotation)

Stand and lean forward, using good arm to hold chair for support. Let injured arm hang down. Swing arm—a) in clockwise and anticlockwise circles, starting with small circles and increasing the circumference as pain allows, b) forward and backward, as pain allows, c) side to side, as pain allows.

Do the pendulum exercises three times a day, starting with fifteen repetitions of each exercise, and building up to thirty.

Exercise 2: Lying arm raise (flexion, extension)

Lie on floor, holding light stick, hands shoulder width apart. Raise arms so they are pointing straight up, then return to starting position.

Exercise 3: Lying elbow raise (abduction, adduction)

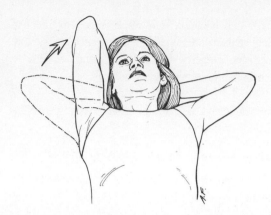

Lie on floor, hands clasped behind neck, elbows on the floor. Raise the elbows alternately toward ear.

Exercise 4: Shoulder roll (internal/external rotation)

Stand with hands touching tops of shoulders, and trace circles with elbows.

Exercise 5: Lying chop (internal/external rotation)

Lie on floor with injured arm stretched out to the side at 90 degrees to body, palm up. Bend elbow to form right angle so fingers are pointing straight up. Lower hand forward to hip. Hold thirty seconds. Return to starting position. Lower hand back toward ear. Hold thirty seconds. Return to starting position.

Do these exercises three times a day, starting with ten repetitions and building up to fifteen.

Level Three

When the patient can do the level two exercises without difficulty or pain, level three exercises can begin. Level three exercises can also be used as a starting point for rehabilitating mild shoulder injuries.

Level three exercises continue to promote range of motion in the shoulder and introduce resistance to strengthen the often-neglected rotator cuff muscles.

Besides promoting range of motion in the shoulder, level three exercises start using dynamic exercises to strengthen the large shoulder muscles, as well as the important rotator cuff muscles deep inside the shoulder, which hold the ball of the shoulder joint against the socket.

Exercise 1: Weighted pendulums
Exercise 2: Weighted lying arm raises
Exercise 3: Weighted lying elbow raises
Exercise 4: Weighted shoulder rolls
Exercise 5: Weighted lying chop

These exercises involve the same motions as the level two range-of-motion exercises, except that resistance is introduced in the form of light weights.

Repeat these exercises three times a day, starting at ten repetitions and gradually building up to thirty. You should be able to do ten repetitions with ease and without pain before moving onto eleven, and so on.

When you can comfortably do thirty repetitions three times a day using the starting weight, increase the weight by one pound or so, but reduce the number of repetitions back to ten, and gradually build back up to thirty.

Each time you can comfortably do thirty repetitions, increase the weight by one or two pounds, reduce the number of repetitions to ten, and build back up to thirty.

When the strength of the injured shoulder is 95 percent of the uninjured side (and, by association, 95 percent of its original strength), ease back into sports.

Before going back to sports, however, the athlete who has been injured should be able to do daily activities without pain and simulate the arm motions of his or her sport without pain.

To reduce the chance of reinjury, begin the strength and flexibility conditioning program that follows.

Conditioning Program for the Shoulder and Upper Arm

Conditioning to prevent shoulder injuries requires that you improve the strength and flexibility of all the major muscles of the shoulder—the large muscles that protect the shoulder structure and allow it to perform major pushing, pulling, and throwing motions as well as the important rotator cuff muscles deep inside the shoulder, which hold the ball of the shoulder joint against the socket.

Exercises to stretch and strengthen the muscles around the shoulder often incorporate exercises used to improve flexibility and strength in the back, chest, and elbow.

Incorporate into your workout at least one set of the following exercises for each muscle group mentioned. The exercises are described in chapter 3, "Strength and Flexibility: The Key to Injury Prevention."

Make these exercises part of an overall strength and flexibility program, and do them before any activity that will stress the muscle around the shoulder.

Shoulder Strengthening Exercises

Rotator cuff (internal rotators): Lying dumbbell raise
Rotator cuff (external rotators): Lying dumbbell curl
Deltoid (front): Dumbbell front raise, behind-the-neck-press, bench press
Deltoid (middle): Dumbbell front raise, behind-the-neck press, bench press
Deltoid (back): Bent-over dumbbell row
Trapezius: Shoulder shrug, upright barbell row
Latissimus dorsi: Bent-over dumbbell row
Pectoralis major: Bench press, incline barbell press, dumbbell flies
Biceps: Seated dumbbell curl, barbell curl
Triceps: Standing dumbbell triceps extension, lying barbell triceps extension, bar dips

Shoulder Flexibility Exercises

Rotator cuff (underside): Underside cuff stretch
Rotator cuff (front): Front cuff stretch
Rotator cuff (back): Back cuff stretch

CHAPTER FOURTEEN

Elbow Injuries

Injuries to the elbow joint and its surrounding structures, especially overuse injuries, are a growing scourge among recreational athletes. The explosion in the popularity of activities such as tennis, racquetball, squash, golf, and strength training, which put considerable stress on the elbow area, have precipitated a dramatic rise in overuse elbow injuries.

Injuries of the Elbow

Overuse elbow injuries may cause discomfort and layoffs from sports, but they are rarely emergencies. Treatment usually consists of RICE (page 46) and anti-inflammatory medication. Strength and flexibility exercises and a review of technique and equipment usually prevent recurrence of the condition. One notable exception is overuse elbow injuries in children and adolescents. Because their bones are not yet formed, overuse elbow injuries can distort the growth process in children, which may in turn cause long-term dysfunction (see "Little League Elbow," page 241).

Acute elbow injuries, on the other hand, are absolute emergencies. Swelling and disruption of the elbow structure can damage one or more of the major nerves that pass over the elbow joint, which control the forearm, wrist, hand, and fingers.

In addition, even partial damage to the blood supply that travels over the elbow can cause a very serious condition in the forearm called compartment syndrome. Failure to recognize this condition and receive immediate treatment can result in permanent loss of function in the muscles of the forearm, wrist, hand, and fingers.

Due to the potentially severe consequences of delayed treatment, emergency room professionals are well aware that patients with elbow injuries accompanied by severe pain, swelling, and loss of function must receive immediate medical attention.

Following initial treatment, athletes with acute elbow injuries such as fractures should seek the most expert form of medical care for treatment and rehabilitation, preferably the services of an expert orthopedist. Unless highly experienced in treating joint injuries, general practitioners and family physicians are simply not qualified to manage a serious elbow injury.

Elbow Injury Prevention

Acute elbow injuries are often caused by freak accidents and are therefore difficult to prevent. There are, however, several preventative measures athletes can take. First, learn to fall properly in a "tuck and roll" fashion, not on an elbow or outstretched arm. Also, wear protective elbow pads in sports where frequent impact may occur, such as volleyball.

Overuse injuries of the elbow can be minimized by observing a slow, progressive training regimen and not doing "too much too soon." this is especially important for athletes in throwing and racket sports.

Anyone who participates in sports that stress the elbow should participate in an exercise program that develops strength and flexibility in the structures surrounding the joint. Sometimes there is a tendency to focus too closely on the muscles at the front of the upper arm, the biceps, at the expense of the opposing triceps muscles behind

ELBOW ANATOMY

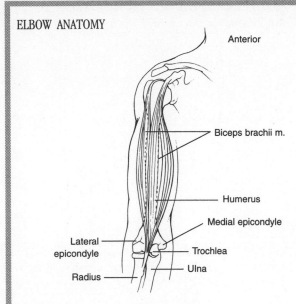

Anterior

- Biceps brachii m.
- Humerus
- Medial epicondyle
- Lateral epicondyle
- Trochlea
- Ulna
- Radius

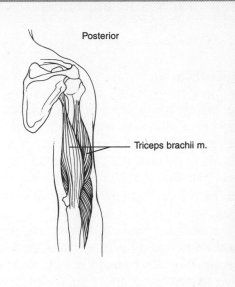

Posterior

- Triceps brachii m.

Bones and joints: The elbow joint is at the meeting place of the three major arm bones: the *humerus, ulna,* and *radius.* The humerus, the upper arm bone, extends from the shoulder joint to the elbow. At the elbow joint the bottom end of the humerus serves as a fixed point where the two bones of the forearm, the ulna and radius, rotate. Like all joints, the elbow is held together by ligaments, both around and inside the joint.

Muscles and nerves: The two main muscles in the upper arm are the *biceps* in front and the *triceps* behind. Both these muscles converge at the elbow joint. The biceps joins the radius bone in the forearm, and provides the ability to bend, or flex, the arm,

and rotate the wrist counterclockwise. The triceps muscle attaches to the ulna bone in the forearm, and makes it possible to straighten, or extend, the arm, and turn the wrist clockwise.

There are two main sets of muscles in the forearm. The *flexors,* those that make it possible to bend the wrist and fingers, attach to the inner side of the elbow, to a bony knob called the *median epicondyle.*

The nerves that operate the muscles of the arm, wrist, hand, and fingers originate in the neck and travel down the arm and over the elbow to the wrist, hand, and fingers. Over the elbow joint they have very little protection and are susceptible to both impact and repetitive stress.

the upper arm. Doing so can create a strength imbalance between these two sets of opposing muscles, which can itself be a contributing factor to both acute and overuse injuries. In addition, both the extensor and flexor muscles in the forearm should be developed through "wrist curl" exercises. These exercises are especially important in preventing overuse conditions such as tennis elbow and pitcher's elbow. For more on elbow flexibility and strengthening exercises, refer to the final section of this chapter.

Proper technique also has a role in preventing overuse injuries of the elbow. Incorrect form is a common cause of overuse injuries such as tennis elbow, pitcher's elbow, and entrapment of the ulnar nerve.

Equipment and environment also play a part in overuse injuries of the elbow, especially in racket sports, where the racket, balls, and court surface can put excessive stress on the joint. See "Preventing Tennis Elbow" (page 240) for a full description of preventing injuries in the lateral humeral epicondyle area.

Acute Injuries of the Elbow

Fractures

A fracture is a break in a bone. Fractures of the bones in the elbow area may be tiny hairline cracks, complete breaks, or traumatic shatterings of the bone. Fractures of the elbow result in a very painful, swollen elbow joint that is difficult to move. More than any other fracture site, improperly treated elbow area fractures pose grave risks of long-term disability.

Even when the fracture is relatively mild, permanent loss of elbow function may occur if the elbow is immobilized too long after treatment or given insufficient or improper rehabilitation. The fracture may indeed heal and X rays may reveal complete rejoining of the broken ends of the bones, but even so, the patient may no longer be able to straighten the elbow and may have decreased function for the rest of his or her life.

It is for this reason that athletes who sustain fractures around the elbow joint—however mild seeming—should seek the most qualified medical advice available, preferably that of an expert orthopedist. Do not be satisfied with a general practitioner or family physician who says that simple splinting of the fracture will suffice.

The second danger involving fractures to the bones around the elbow is their potential, unless treated promptly, to cause damage to the nearby nerves and blood vessels. In about 20 percent of all elbow fractures, one of the major nerves is affected. Surgery is always required to correct the effects of nerve damage. All fractures in the elbow area, then, should be considered emergencies.

Fractures in the elbow area primarily affect three arm bones—the humerus, radius, and ulna.

FRACTURE OF THE LOWER HUMERUS
(Supracondylar Fracture)

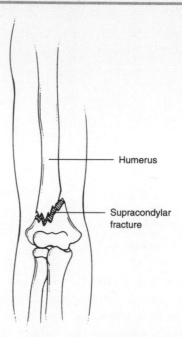

Humerus

Supracondylar fracture

A fracture is a crack, break, or complete shattering of a bone. Fractures of the lower humerus occur in the upper arm bone just above the elbow.

Because of the strength of the biceps and triceps muscles, displacement of the broken bones is quite extreme—these powerful muscles can pull the ends of the broken bones apart. For this reason, surgery is usually necessary for supracondylar fractures.

Symptoms:

- Obvious deformity just above and behind the elbow joint.
- Extreme pain when trying to move the elbow, tenderness to the touch, swelling, and bruising.

Causes:

- A fall onto the elbow.
- Direct impact to the elbow.

Athletes at risk:

- Supracondylar fractures are most often seen in athletes in contact sports and in activities with the potential for falling accidents.

Concerns:

- The immediate danger of this injury is that the ends of the broken bones can damage important nerves and blood vessels in the elbow joint, causing long-term dysfunction in the arm, hand, and fingers. The injury is an absolute emergency if there is loss of range of motion, tingling, numbness, or pain in the forearm, hand, wrist, or fingers. Delayed treatment dramatically increases the potential for damage.

What you can do:

- Send for emergency medical assistance.
- Splint the arm and secure it to the body with an elastic wrap.
- Gently apply ice over the area for twenty minutes at a time until medical assistance arrives.
- After initial treatment, seek the services of an expert orthopedist.

What the doctor can do:

- Rule out damage to the nerves and blood supply.
- If there is trouble straightening the wrist and fingers, or if there is numbness in the thumb and index finger, damage to the radial nerve or median nerve is suspected.
- If there is significant increase of compartment pressures in the muscles in the forearm, immediate release of these structures may be necessary. This is done by cutting through the compartments. If action is delayed beyond even a couple of hours, permanent loss of function in the forearm muscles can occur.
- When increased compartment pressures are developing, the doctor should immediately realign the ends of the broken upper arm bones to alleviate twisting of the arteries, nerves, or veins above the elbow.
- If examination reveals no disruption in the nerves and arteries, X rays will be taken to gauge the damage.
- Surgery is usually necessary to repair a displaced supracondylar fracture.

    An incision is made over the back of the elbow. If there is damage to the joint surface, this is repaired with screws and pins. Then the bones themselves are aligned and are held in place with plates.

    In children, surgery is usually not done. The bones are realigned manually by the doctor, and are held in place with pins inserted through the skin. These are removed three weeks after the procedure.

- Following surgery, the arm will need to be in a removable splint or sling for three weeks. This will be removed regularly so isometrics and physical therapist–assisted range-of-motion exercises can start.

Rehabilitation:

- Level one rehabilitation exercises can start within a week of the injury.
- After two or three weeks of protective immobilization at the most, level two rehabilitation can begin, with the emphasis on range of motion, not strengthening.
- After six to eight weeks of splinting, the bone will be healed. However, there will still be some joint stiffness and muscle atrophy. These need to be corrected by using the level three rehabilitation exercises, and then a conditioning program of strength training with weights and flexibility exercises. For levels one, two, and three rehabilitation guidelines, refer to the sections on rehabilitation and conditioning at the end of this chapter.

Recovery time:

- Six to eight weeks before heavy lifting can be resumed.
- For sports that stress the elbow, or where there is potential for further impact, three to six months for adults, eight to twelve weeks for children.
- Once bone healing is complete, patients should begin to ease back gradually into sports after completing a conditioning program that restores 95 percent strength and flexibility.

FRACTURE OF THE RADIAL HEAD

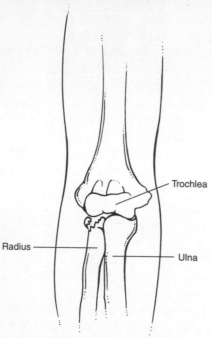

Trochlea

Radius

Ulna

A fracture is a crack, break, or complete shattering of a bone. A radial head fracture affects the mushroom-shaped knob at the top of the radius bone in the forearm, where it forms part of the elbow joint. Frequently, the radial head shatters in several places.

Symptoms:

- Extreme pain on the outside of the elbow, which quickly worsens as bleeding causes the joint to swell on its outer aspect.
- As swelling worsens, loss of range of motion.
- The only comfortable position to hold the elbow is at an angle of 90 degrees.

Cause:

- A fall onto the arm or hand, which transmits the impact up through the hand and forearm to the elbow joint.

Athletes at risk:

- Radial head fractures are most often seen in contact sports and in activities with a potential for falling accidents.

Concerns:

- As with any joint fracture, treatment of a radial head fracture requires the services of an expert orthopedist. If the bone heals improperly, there is the high probability joint function will be affected and the athlete may suffer loss of mobility in the forearm, hand, and fingers.
- Nerve and artery damage is extremely rare in the case of radial head fractures.

What you can do:

- Send for emergency medical assistance.
- Splint the arm and secure it to the body with an elastic wrap.
- Gently apply ice over the area for twenty minutes.
- After initial treatment, seek the services of an expert orthopedist.

Medication:

- For relief of minor to moderate pain, take acetaminophen as directed on label, or, for the relief of pain *and* inflammation, ibuprofen or aspirin if tolerated (see page 49).

What the doctor can do:

- Order X rays or sometimes a CAT scan to determine the extent of the damage to the radial head.
- If the radial head is only cracked, and there are no displaced fragments, surgery is usually not needed. Even when the radial head has broken into two or three fragments, surgery may not be necessary so long as there is not significant displacement of the pieces.
- The arm should be splinted with the elbow at a 90 degree angle for between one and three weeks. Isometrics and physical therapist–assisted range-of-motion exercises can start within a week of the injury to promote reattachment of the displaced bone chips.
- If reattachment of the fragments appears unlikely, such as when large portions of bone have broken off or the radial head has completely shattered, surgery may be necessary.

An arthroscope is inserted through a small incision behind the elbow. This device helps locate the fragments. Only small fragments can be removed with the arthroscope, and then, only if they will likely interfere with elbow function.

If the arthroscopy reveals that the entire radial head is smashed or that there are large displaced fragments, these need to be removed through an incision made over the elbow joint.

In certain cases, if the radial head is completely smashed but will not likely interfere with function because there are no fragments blocking motion, no surgery is done. Early range-of-motion exercises are done to promote reattachment of the displaced fragments.

- After surgery, the athlete wears a removable splint with the elbow positioned at 90 degrees. Isometric strengthening and physical therapist–assisted range-of-motion exercises usually begin five days after surgery, or when some healing has taken place and there is diminished pain and swelling.
- Even after removal of the entire radial head, full return of elbow function is expected after proper rehabilitation.

Rehabilitation:

- Rehabilitation for radial fractures follows the same course and schedule as therapy for supracondylar fractures (page 229).

Recovery time:

- Undisplaced fractures take about four to six weeks to heal completely with immobilization and well-directed rehabilitation exercises.
- After surgery on a displaced fracture, it takes at least two months before the patient can begin vigorous athletic activity, and up to three months before returning to contact sports.

FRACTURE OF THE ELBOW POINT
(Olecranon Fracture)

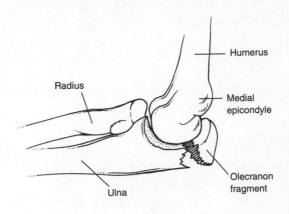

A fracture is a crack, break, or complete shattering of a bone. A fracture of the elbow point is a break in the ulna bone at the top of the rear of the forearm. It is usually caused by a fall onto the arm or elbow, which results in a break across the point of the elbow, called the olecranon. The ends of the fractured bone are usually displaced.

Symptoms:

- Pain and swelling at the back of the elbow.

Cause:

- A fall onto the arm or the point of the elbow.

Athletes at risk:

- Olecranon fractures are most often seen in athletes in contact sports and in activities with the potential for falling accidents.

Concerns:

- Because olecranon fractures affect the joint, they have to be realigned exactly to ensure that joint function isn't compromised. However, the break is usually clean and therefore realignment is quite straightforward.

- Nerve damage and compartment syndromes are quite rare in the case of olecranon fractures.

What you can do:

- Send for emergency medical assistance.
- Splint the arm and secure it to the body with an elastic wrap.
- Gently apply ice over the area for twenty minutes.
- After initial treatment, seek the services of an expert orthopedist.

What the doctor can do:

- Order X rays to determine the nature and severity of the fractures.
- If there is no displacement of the bones, the arm should be splinted at 90 degrees. Three to six weeks later, range-of-motion exercises should begin.
- Usually there is displacement—a piece of the elbow point is knocked off. Because the triceps muscle attaches to the point of the elbow, surgery is almost always required to ensure return of triceps function.

    Using a combination of pins or screws with wires, the pieces of displaced bone are carefully rejoined.

    After surgery, the arm is put in a sling or removable splint so isometrics and physical therapist–assisted range-of-motion exercises can begin—preferably within five days, if pain permits.

Rehabilitation:

- Rehabilitation for olecranon fractures follows the same course and schedule as therapy for supracondylar fractures (page 229).

Recovery time:

- Six to eight weeks before heavy lifting can resume, and twelve weeks before athletes can return to sports.

ELBOW SPRAINS

Sprains of the elbow occur when the ligaments of the joint are stretched or partially torn.

Elbow sprains may be mild (first degree), moderate (second degree), or severe (third degree). In some cases of third-degree elbow sprains, the joint may also dislocate (see "Elbow Dislocations," page 233).

Symptoms:

- Depending on the sprain's severity—first, second, or third degree—symptoms are: immediate pain, and within half an hour swelling, tenderness, and stiffness; difficulty straightening the arm; obvious deformity if there is an associated dislocation.

Cause:

- Violent straightening of the elbow beyond its normal range of motion, known as hyperextension.

Athletes at risk:

- Elbow sprains are most often seen in athletes in contact sports and in activities with the potential for falling accidents.

Concerns:

- Never underestimate an elbow sprain. Permanent loss of arm function may result from a serious elbow sprain that isn't managed properly because the ligaments don't fully heal. Careful rehabilitation in the hands of a skilled physical therapist is necessary.
- Also, the symptoms of sprains can mimic those of more serious conditions, particularly fractures. Seek immediate medical attention if there is any persistent pain or extreme swelling in the elbow area, loss of sensation, alteration in motor skills, or pain, numbness, or tingling in the forearm, wrist, and hand.

What you can do:

- To minimize early swelling for mild to moderate sprains, apply RICE (page 46) as soon as possible. Continue icing for twenty minutes at a time for the first forty-eight hours, and keep the arm elevated and the injury compressed.

- To avoid joint stiffness, start gentle range-of-motion exercises after twenty-four to forty-eight hours.
- Avoid the motion that caused the injury for three weeks.
- Elbow sprains are not emergencies, though athletes with second- or third-degree sprains should seek medical attention by the day after the injury occurs, at the latest.

Medication:

- For relief of minor to moderate pain, take acetaminophen as directed on label, or, for the relief of pain *and* inflammation, ibuprofen or aspirin if tolerated (see page 49).

What the doctor can do:

- Check blood supply and nerve function in the forearm to rule out neurovascular damage, and take X rays to rule out any possible fractures.
- RICE is the primary therapy for sprains. This should continue for forty-eight to seventy-two hours after the injury, in conjunction with range-of-motion exercises as soon as pain permits.
- If the pain is severe, a sling should be worn for relief.

Rehabilitation:

- Range-of-motion exercises should begin as soon as possible and, ideally, right after the swelling goes down and pain diminishes—usually after forty-eight hours.
- Ten days to two weeks may be necessary for an elbow sprain to heal before conditioning can begin. After a return of 95 percent of strength and flexibility in the elbow, athletes can return to sports.
- For levels one, two and three rehabilitation guidelines, refer to the sections on elbow rehabilitation and conditioning at the end of the chapter.

Recovery time:

- Mild and moderate sprains (first and second degree): two or three days for the ligament to heal. Avoid any possibility of hyperextending the elbow for three weeks.
- Severe (third-degree) sprains: from ten days to two weeks of rest and rehabilitation before the athlete is ready to go back to sports. Avoid the possibility of hyperextending the elbow for six weeks.

ELBOW DISLOCATIONS

A dislocation of the elbow occurs when the head of the radius or the ulnar bone in the forearm comes out of its socket at the bottom of the upper arm bone.

Symptoms:

- Deformity in the elbow joint.
- Intense pain, swelling, tenderness, and loss of mobility.

Causes:

- Trying to break a fall with the hand while the elbow is bent.
- Forceful straightening of the elbow beyond its range of motion (hyperextension).

Athletes at risk:

- Elbow dislocations are most often seen in athletes in contact sports and in activities with the potential for falling accidents.

Concerns:

- Elbow dislocations sometimes occur in conjunction with fractures of the midshaft of the ulna bone in the forearm, or of the ulna at the wrist.
- Dislocations always involve damage to the surrounding soft tissues—in particular the ligaments—so even when the joint is realigned, extra time is needed for joint stability to return.
- There is also grave risk of injury to important nerves and arteries after a dislocation, and especially after a complete dislocation, when the

ulna as well as the radius separates from the humerus. The injury is an absolute emergency if there is any pain, numbness, or loss of function in the forearm, wrist, or hand, because of the possibility of nerve damage or developing compartment pressures.

- If treatment and rehabilitation of an elbow dislocation are insufficient or improper, there may be residual damage to the ligaments, which will make the joint more susceptible to recurrent dislocations.

What you can do:

- Elbow dislocations need to be realigned as soon as possible.
- Send for emergency medical assistance.
- Splint the arm and secure it to the body with an elastic wrap.
- Gently apply ice over the area for twenty minutes at a time until medical assistance arrives.
- After initial treatment, seek the services of an expert orthopedist.

What the doctor can do:

- Rule out damage to the nerves and blood supply.
- Realign the dislocated bones.
- Take X rays to look for additional injuries—in particular, fractures of the humerus.
- Treatment for the dislocation itself will depend on the extent of the ligament damage.
- Nonsurgical treatment: Most commonly, dislocated elbows are immobilized in a sling or splint for comfort and protection for as short a time as possible. When the dislocated bone pops back in easily, immobilization may be necessary for only three to five days, after which rehabilitation can start.
- If the joint is extremely unstable because of severe ligament damage, surgery may be necessary. Depending on whether the ligaments are torn through or completely missing, they may be either repaired or replaced.
- After the operation, the elbow is immobilized in a removable splint for two to three weeks at the

most, during which time isometric strengthening and physical therapist–assisted range-of-motion exercises are done, followed by strength training with weights and active range-of-motion exercises.

Rehabilitation:

- Within two to three weeks at the most (and ideally, within five days), level one rehabilitation exercises can begin.
- Once some muscle function returns, patients can do level two exercises.
- When mobility is almost completely restored—usually within six to eight weeks—the patient should begin rehabilitation at level three.
- For levels one, two, and three elbow rehabilitation guidelines, refer to the sections on elbow rehabilitation and conditioning at the end of this chapter.

Recovery time:

- If nonsurgical treatment is successful, heavy lifting can begin within three to six weeks, and a return to sports that require vigorous use of the elbow can take place in twelve weeks. The same timetable applies to surgical treatment.

ELBOW BURSITIS *(Olecranon Bursitis)*

Underneath the skin at the point of the elbow lies a bursa sac that can swell up if the elbow receives a single violent blow or is subject to repeated impact. The swelling is caused by synovial fluid flooding the bursa in response to irritation of the sac.

Symptoms:

- An egg-shaped swelling on the elbow point, which may sometimes spread into the back of the forearm.
- Pain, and reddening of the skin over the bursa.
- In severe cases, loss of mobility in the elbow.

Cause:

- A single violent blow to the elbow, or repeated impact.

Athletes at risk:

- Those whose elbows make frequent contact with the ground, such as soccer goalkeepers, volleyball players, and wrestlers.

Concerns:

- Frequently, the impact that causes the bursitis also punctures the skin surface. Bacteria may enter this highly sensitive area. If there is increased pain or redness around the bursa, this could be a sign the bursa is infected. In such a case, see a doctor immediately.

What you can do:

- Apply RICE (page 46) until the swelling goes down. When not using RICE, wrap an Ace bandage around the elbow.
- *Never* use heat for a bursitis caused by a single impact; this will make the bursa sac swell further. (Heat may be prescribed, however, by the physician or physical therapist for chronic bursitis conditions).
- Start gentle range-of-motion exercises when pain and swelling permit.
- See a doctor if the pain becomes severe or the condition keeps recurring. If there is excessive swelling, redness, and/or pain, see a doctor as this might signal an infection.

Medication:

- For relief of minor to moderate pain, take acetaminophen as directed on label, or, for the relief of pain *and* inflammation, ibuprofen or aspirin if tolerated (see page 49).

What the doctor can do:

- Nonsurgical treatment:
  Initial treatment includes RICE, gentle range-of-motion exercises, and anti-inflammatories. If this course is unsuccessful, the doctor may use a syringe to puncture and drain the bursa sac.
  Steroid injections are sometimes used to treat bursitis.
- If the bursitis keeps recurring, X rays of the elbow may be done to check if there is a bone spur on the tip of the elbow that is causing the irritation.
- If the bursa becomes infected, oral antibiotics may be prescribed. When the infection is severe, intravenous antibiotics and occasionally surgery are used to remove the bursa. An incision is made behind the elbow, the bursa is cut open, and all the fluid inside is removed. If a bone spur has developed, it too is removed.

Rehabilitation:

- As soon as pain and swelling allow, gentle range-of-motion exercises should be done to avoid joint stiffness. Mobility exercises are especially important after surgical removal of a bursa.
- For levels one, two, and three rehabilitation guidelines, refer to the sections on elbow rehabilitation and conditioning at the end of this chapter.
- An elbow pad should be worn to protect against reinjury during daily activities.

Recovery time:

- Athletes can usually return to action within one to three weeks, or when the condition clears up.

RUPTURE OF THE TRICEPS TENDON

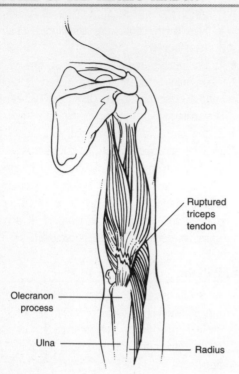

Olecranon
process

Ulna

Ruptured
triceps
tendon

Radius

Ruptures of the triceps tendon usually occur at the point where the triceps muscle attaches to the tip of the elbow. In order to restore triceps function, which allows straightening of the arm, surgery is almost always necessary in the case of a complete rupture of the triceps tendon at the elbow.

Symptoms:

- Pain at the elbow point.
- A gap may be felt above the elbow point where the tendon is supposed to attach.
- Dramatic loss of strength in the arm, especially with elbow-straightening motions.

Cause:

- A forceful blow or a fall on the elbow.

Athletes at risk:

- Ruptures of the triceps tendon are most often seen in athletes in throwing sports, contact sports, and activities with the potential for falling accidents.

Concerns:

- The triceps muscles enable extension the elbow. Therefore, unless a rupture of the triceps tendon is managed effectively, ability to straighten the arm may be affected.

What you can do:

- Put the arm in a sling.
- Apply ice for twenty minutes at a time.
- Seek medical attention.

What the doctor can do:

- Complete ruptures of the triceps tendons require surgical repair. An incision is made above the elbow; the torn tendon is located, then re-attached to the muscle with suture stitches.
- After surgery, the am is put in a sling or removable splint for six weeks.

Rehabilitation:

- Isometric strengthening and physical therapist–assisted range-of-motion exercises may begin five days after surgery.
- For levels one, two, and three rehabilitation guidelines, refer to the sections on elbow rehabilitation and conditioning at the end of this chapter.

Recovery time:

- Heavy lifting can usually be done after six weeks, while contact sports and those activities that require vigorous use of the triceps muscles should be avoided for at least twelve weeks.

Overuse Injuries of the Elbow

TENNIS ELBOW (Lateral Humeral Epicondylitis)

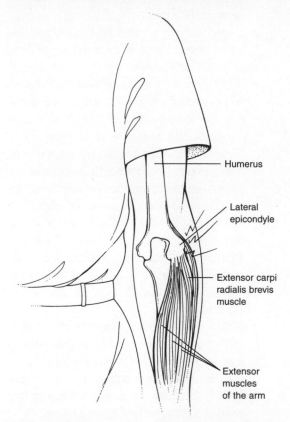

Humerus

Lateral epicondyle

Extensor carpi radialis brevis muscle

Extensor muscles of the arm

Tennis elbow refers to an inflammation of the tendon of the forearm extensor muscles where they insert into the bony knob on the outside of the elbow.

Tennis elbow is one of the most common overuse injuries of all, and is certainly the most frequently seen sports injury of the upper body. According to studies, up to half of tennis players who play every day and 25 percent of those who step on the court once or twice a week get this condition. But tennis elbow doesn't just affect tennis players alone. It is also seen in other racket sports—squash and racquetball, especially—as well as in golf.

Tennis elbow is caused by repetitive stress to the forearm muscles; that stress transmits up to where the muscle tendon inserts into the outer elbow knob, the lateral humeral epicondyle. The stress can be aggravated if the player is not properly conditioned, or if he or she uses

improper equipment or inappropriate technique. Often it's a combination of several factors. Faulty backhand techniques (too "wristy" a stroke) is the main culprit when it comes to form. There are a host of external factors that can cause tennis elbow, including:

- *Racket: the heavier the racket, the smaller the grip, and the tighter the string tension, the more stress on the arm.*

- *Court surface: hard, fast surfaces—grass and concrete especially—increase the speed at which the ball hits the racket strings, and increase the amount of stress transmitted to the elbow.*

- *Balls:. older and heavier balls increase the amount of stress absorbed by the arm.*

The risk factor in tennis elbow that is most often overlooked is conditioning, specifically lack of strength and flexibility in the shoulders. A weak shoulder is often the first stage in a sequence of ailments that culminates in tennis elbow. Often the athlete starts off with an irritation of the rotator cuff, which, as we have discussed, causes weakness in the entire arm. The weakness in the arm may affect technique, which may in turn cause tennis elbow.

Tennis elbow is especially prevalent in the over-forty set, because the older a person gets, the slower the body heals. In middle-aged or older athletes, the microtears where the muscle tendon inserts into the outer bony knob of the elbow do not have the time to heal between matches. See below for additional tips on preventing tennis elbow.

Symptoms:

- Onset of symptoms is gradual.
- Pain directly over the outer elbow knob, the lateral humeral epicondyle.
- Pain increases when the wrist is rotated against resistance, as in trying to turn a doorknob or shake hands.

Cause:

- Repetitive stress to the extensor muscles in the forearm that transmits to where the extensor tendon inserts into the outer elbow knob.

Athletes at risk:

- Primarily racket sports players and golfers.

Concerns:

- Tennis elbow needs to be addressed early. Otherwise, scar tissue builds where the muscle tendon inserts into the outer bony knob and makes the condition difficult to alleviate. Because this area heals so poorly (the blood supply here is extremely poor), prevention and early intervention are the key to management.
- If the pain on the bony knob on the outside of the elbow is severe, there may be a complete rupture of the tendon attachment to the lateral numeral epicondyle due to chronic weakening of the structure.

What you can do:

- Ice the area as soon as symptoms are felt. Ice massage is an especially effective technique for tennis elbow. Compression and elevation are not necessary because there is no swelling.
- After seventy-two hours, use a moist heating pad to promote healing.
- Cease all activities that caused the condition until the pain goes away and the cause or causes of the injury have been addressed (see "Preventing Tennis Elbow," page 240).

Medication:

- For relief of minor to moderate pain, take acetaminophen as directed on label, or, for the relief of pain *and* inflammation, ibuprofen or aspirin if tolerated (see page 49).

What the doctor can do:

- A physical examination will confirm the diagnosis of tennis elbow.
- X rays will be taken to rule out other possible causes of pain, such as a fracture or loose body in the joint. In addition, the doctor should investigate the possibility of other conditions, including rheumatic arthritis, a trapped radial or ulnar nerve, or referred pain from a pinched nerve in the neck.
- Surgery is rarely required for tennis elbow. Initial treatment consists of frequent icing, and use of anti-inflammatories.
- If the condition has been allowed to deteriorate before medical attention is sought, the doctor may give the patient a steroid injection. Steroid injections have proven to be a quick, highly effective means of clearing up the pain from tennis elbow. The injection is made near the point where the muscle tendon inserts into the bony knob on the outside of the elbow, not directly into the tendon. Each injection should be followed by one to two weeks of rest and then a gradual conditioning program. It is not advisable to give more than two to three steroid injections for tennis elbow, as this can weaken the tendon.
- If the condition hasn't cleared up after conservative treatment and steroid injections, surgery may be necessary. Surgery involves scraping the scar tissue out, then drilling a hole into the bone to stimulate blood supply. This drilling procedure promotes healing of the tissue.

Rehabilitation:

- The crux of the rehabilitation program for tennis elbow is to develop strength and flexibility in the entire arm, including the shoulder.
- Special attention should be paid to strengthening the tendon insertion into the lateral humeral epicondyle. To accomplish this most effectively, refer to conditioning program on page 247.

Recovery time:

- Depending on the extent to which the condition has deteriorated, tennis elbow can take anywhere from between two weeks to a couple of years to heal.

- In the case of mild tennis elbow, after addressing the cause of the condition athletes can return to action when the arm has regained full strength and range of motion, and there is no pain. In the initial stages, though, the activity level should be no more than half of the preinjury level. This can be increased by 10 percent each session.
- After surgery, it may take two to three months before a full playing schedule can be resumed.

INNER-SIDE ELBOW KNOB PAIN *(Medial Humeral Epicondylitis; "Pitcher's Elbow")*

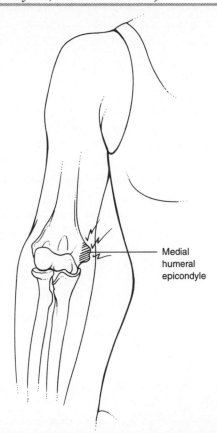

Medial humeral epicondyle

The other epicondylitis condition—medial humeral epicondylitis—refers to inflammation of the attachments of the forearm flexor tendons to the bony knob on the inside of the elbow joint. It is much rarer than tennis elbow, accounting for only about 10 percent of overuse injuries of the elbow.

Again, the key to managing pitcher's elbow successfully is early intervention.

Symptoms:

- Onset of symptoms is gradual.
- Pain over the inner bony elbow knob, the medial humeral epicondyle.
- Pain when trying to rotate the forearm inward or flex the wrist toward the body.

Cause:

- Repetitive stress to the flexor muscles in the forearm that transmits to where the flexor tendon inserts into the inner elbow knob.

Athletes at risk:

- This condition affects athletes who powerfully snap their wrists downward and inward as part of a motion required in their sport. The exaggerated motion that causes medial humeral epicondylitis is most common in baseball pitchers, hence its colloquial name, but is also seen in golfers, rowers, and javelin throwers. Another sport where it is common is high-level tennis, especially in players with powerful serves or those who use a lot of topspin on their stroke (the exaggerated rotation of the forearm as they play the stroke stresses the flexor muscles that attach to the inner bony knob).

Concerns:

- If the injury is allowed to deteriorate, loose chips can break off and scar tissue develops on the tendon. Another eventual outcome may be arthritis on the inside of the elbow tip.
- Nerve damage is seen in more than half of all athletes with medial humeral epicondylitis.
- If the pain persists for more than two weeks, seek medical attention.

What you can do:

- Applying it to the inside of the elbow joint, follow the same self-treatment program as the one for tennis elbow—rest and icing. Begin a strengthening program for the elbow and its surrounding musculature.

Medication:

- For relief of minor to moderate pain, take acetaminophen as directed on label, or, for the relief of pain *and* inflammation, ibuprofen or aspirin if tolerated (see page 49).

What the doctor can do:

- Do a bone scan or MRI to establish exactly what's wrong, ruling out other possible conditions such as ulnar nerve irritation and ligament damage.
- If the condition is caught early, nonsurgical measures may suffice: withdrawal from the activity that caused the condition for two weeks, followed by a month of active range-of-motion exercises and progressive strengthening.
- If bone fragments have been ripped off the inner aspect of the elbow, surgery may be necessary. Bone fragments are removed with an arthroscope or with open surgery.

Rehabilitation:

- After a two-week rest period, level two rehabilitation exercises can begin and progress as directed (see "Elbow Rehabilitation," page 245), with special emphasis on rehabilitating the flexor muscles.

Recovery time:

- It usually takes two weeks for the symptoms of mild to moderate pitcher's elbow to go away. A six- to eight-week rehabilitation program is necessary before the athlete can return to vigorous overarm activities.
- After surgery, about eight to ten weeks of recovery time and rehabilitation.

PREVENTING TENNIS ELBOW

If you suffer from tennis elbow, review the following possible causes of this condition, consider which may apply to you, and address them before returning to play.

Technique
- Your forearm muscles should be used for control, not power. Most of the power should come from your shoulders, torso, and leg muscles, coordinated with rotation of your hips.
- Focus on hitting the "sweet spot" as often as possible.
- Follow through on your stroke; don't "brake" after hitting the ball.
- Learn proper footwork so you approach the ball correctly.

Equipment
- Use a light racket (12–12.5 oz) made of graphite which provides good impact absorption.
- Use the largest grip that's comfortable. The optimal grip size is the distance from the tip of your ring finger to the bottom horizontal palm crease at the point between your ring and middle fingers.
- To minimize impact, your racket should have an approximate string tension of 52–55 lb. on 16-gauge nylon.
- Ensure that the balls you use are not old or wet.

Court Surface
Play on a court with a slower surface, thus reducing the impact of the ball on your racket.

Conditioning
Develop strength and flexibility in the arm, shoulder, and back muscles.

Tennis elbow straps may provide relief from tennis elbow, while at the same time allowing the injury to recover. However, never use a tennis elbow strap unless you are *positive* your injury is tennis elbow. Tennis elbow straps may worsen conditions such as medial elbow instability in adults and growth plate fractures in children, whose symptoms resemble tennis elbow but require very different treatment.

LITTLE LEAGUE ELBOW

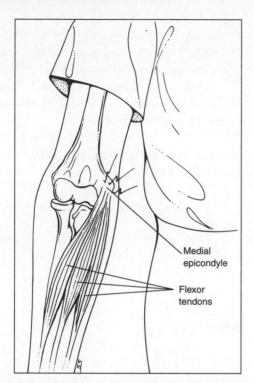

Medial epicondyle

Flexor tendons

Little League elbow is the colloquial term for damage to the growth cartilage on the inner aspect of the elbow of children and adolescents. Sometimes, the outer ball of the humerus, the capitellum, is also injured.

The mechanism of Little League elbow is the same as pitcher's elbow—it is caused by the powerful downward and inward snap of the wrist performed in throwing motions. In adults this motion causes microtears where the muscle tendon attaches to the bony knob on the inside of the elbow, which may in turn lead to pain and disability. But in children, whose bones are still growing, the muscle tendons attach to a relatively soft substance called "growth cartilage" at the ends of the growing bones. Known scientifically as an epophysis, this material is actually an unformed bone. Because it is often weaker than the muscle tendons, portions of growth cartilage on the inner aspect of the elbow may gradually be pulled off due to repetitive throwing motions.

If caught early enough, the separated growth cartilage can reattach. Unfortunately, Little League elbow is sometimes allowed to deteriorate to the point where surgery is necessary.

Symptoms:

- Onset of symptoms is gradual.
- Pain over the bony knob on the inside of the elbow joint.
- Stiffness when trying to straighten the arm, or inability to fully straighten it.
- If the pain develops suddenly, it can mean the end of the growth cartilage has been ripped off. Such an incident is always accompanied by extreme pain.

Cause:

- Repetitive throwing motions.

Concerns:

- Little League elbow is a very serious condition. Anytime a child's growth cartilage is damaged, bone growth is interrupted. Thus, unless treated properly, Little League elbow causes the elbow to grow abnormally and may create long-term disability. For this reason, any elbow pain in a growing child or adolescent should be treated very seriously, and preferably by an orthopedist who specializes in pediatrics.

What you can do:

- Any child who experiences elbow pain should immediately be removed from sports and taken to a pediatric orthopedic specialist.
- In the interim, frequent icing should be done according to the RICE prescription (page 46).

What the doctor can do:

- The physical examination will reveal tenderness directly over the child's inner bony knob, the median epicondyle.
- To get a better look at the injury, the doctor will order an MRI, arthrogram, or X ray of the child's joint. A comparison X ray of the uninjured side will also be done to assess the extent of damage to the injured elbow joint.
- If the diagnosis reveals only mild displacement of the growth cartilage from the main part of the bone, nonsurgical measures are appropriate. Six weeks of splinting is done to promote reat-

tachment of the bone chips. After two weeks of immobilization, the splint can be removed regularly for range-of-motion exercises.

- Where there is significant displacement of the growth cartilage from the bone, surgery may be needed to ensure the proper positioning of the detached growth cartilage during the healing process.
- Surgical treatment:

  An incision is made over the detached piece of growth cartilage, and it is reattached using pins and screws, or sometimes, suture stitches.

  If the assessment reveals chips of growth cartilage have broken off and are floating around in the joint, they should be surgically removed using an arthroscope. Several holes are drilled into the end of the bone to promote regrowth of bone cartilage in the damaged area.

Rehabilitation:

- After the two-week relative rest period, level two exercises can begin, building up to level three exercises within six to eight weeks of the initial symptoms. For levels one, two, and three rehabilitation guidelines, refer to the sections on rehabilitation and conditioning at the end of this chapter.

Recovery time:

- Children with Little League elbow must wait at least six to nine weeks before returning to action, and until they are pain free and have normal strength and flexibility in their arms. Premature return to throwing usually causes immediate reinjury of the elbow.
- If surgery is necessary, throwing is usually prohibited for up to six months.

Prevention:

- The main culprit in Little League elbow is allowing children to throw too much. Kids must be prevented from overthrowing. Young baseball players who perform more than 350 skilled

throws a week dramatically increase the likelihood of developing Little League elbow. The Little League's restrictions on pitching more than six innings a week needs to be revised to include practice throwing. Under no circumstances should children be allowed to make more than 250 skilled throws per week. Throws should be tracked using a hand counter operated by coaches and parents.

LOOSE/DETACHED BODIES IN THE JOINT
(Osteochondritis Dissecans)

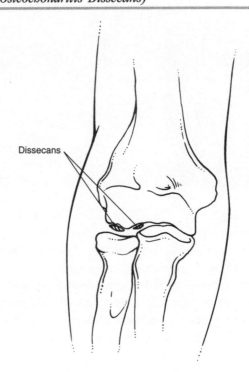

Dissecans

Loose or detached bodies inside the elbow structure are portions of bone and joint cartilage created by the bumping and grinding of the ends of the forearm and upper arm bones.

This injury is usually seen in children aged twelve to seventeen whose growing bones are more vulnerable to this repetitive stress.

Symptoms:

- Onset of symptoms is gradual.
- Pain and tenderness on the outside of the elbow.
- Joint locking accompanied by a sudden stab of pain, as well as muscle spasms and swelling.
- Difficulty fully straightening the arm.

Cause:

- Powerful, repetitive overarm throwing motions.

Athletes at risk:

- Primarily baseball pitchers and gymnasts.

Concerns:

- If joint locking is experienced, seek medical attention. These symptoms indicate that surgery is required to remove the detached pieces of joint cartilage.

What you can do:

- Rest and ice the elbow. In particular, cease the activity that caused the condition.
- Seek medical attention.

Medication:

- For relief of minor to moderate pain, take acetaminophen as directed on label, or, for the relief of pain *and* inflammation, ibuprofen or aspirin if tolerated (see page 49).

What the doctor can do:

- The medical examination will usually reveal a loose or detached piece of joint cartilage.
- If the condition is severe and a piece of joint cartilage has broken off, the patient will complain of locking in the elbow three or four times a day, and it will be difficult to straighten the arm fully (though bending and rotating the arm usually pose no problem). Just touching the joint causes pain.
- To confirm the diagnosis of osteochondritis dissecans in the sore elbow, as well as assess its severity, X rays are usually taken of *both* elbow joints. The view inside the uninjured elbow is needed as a comparison to tell the extent to which the bone cartilage on the injured side has been displaced. What is normally seen is either a piece of bone cartilage about to dislodge with further activity, or pieces that have already broken off.
- Because X rays do not allow doctors to see the actual joint surface, which is made of cartilage, sometimes an MRI or arthrogram is used to get a better look at the damage. These diagnostic tools allow doctors to examine the actual joint surface and, if the piece of joint cartilage has not yet detached, see the outline of the loose piece lying in its crater.
- Adults who have osteochondritis dissecans almost always require surgery to repair the damaged joint. (In children, immobilization and rest may allow the body's healing process to help the loose chip fully rejoin the joint. Three months of limited activity is usually necessary.)
- Surgical options:

  The surgeon will make two puncture holes in the skin over the elbow and, using an arthroscope, enter the joint and remove the loose piece of joint cartilage from the crater. Several tiny holes in the crater will be made with a bone drill. The blood supply created by these drilled holes creates hard scar tissue. Occasionally, the surgeon may pin the loose piece of bone back in place.

  If the initial diagnosis reveals that the injury has already deteriorated and a bone chip has come loose, it may be pinned back in place or, more commonly, the piece of bone is removed arthroscopically.

  If the chip has lodged in a portion of the joint where an arthroscope cannot reach, an incision will be made over the elbow and it will be removed.

Rehabilitation:

- If nonsurgical treatment is employed, level two rehabilitation exercises can start after a brief rest period—between seven and fourteen days—

and progress as directed (see "Elbow Rehabilitation," page 245).

- After surgery for osteochondritis dissecans, rehabilitation can begin at the same time—seven to fourteen days afterward—because there is no instability in the elbow. Usually after surgery, patients start with level two exercises.

Recovery time:

- When rest is used to promote healing, three to six months without surgery is sufficient to heal the injury.
- If surgery is necessary, two to three months before full activity can commence.

SLIPPAGE/ENTRAPMENT OF THE ULNAR NERVE (Ulnar Neuritis)

Ulnar neuritis is an inflammation of the ulnar nerve caused by repetitive stretching and pulling of the nerve out of its groove behind the elbow.

Symptoms:

- Onset of symptoms is gradual.
- Initially, discomfort on the inner side of the elbow after strenuous activity. Frequently, the pain comes and goes.
- Unless treated, pain intensifies and begins to radiate down the forearm to the fourth and fifth fingers.
- Numbness in the forearm may occur, and loss of mobility in the little finger and ring finger.
- "Pins and needles" effect makes the arm feel as if it has "fallen asleep."
- Localized pain directly over the "funny bone" nerve on the inside of the elbow. In advanced cases, tapping the ulnar nerve sends pain down the forearm to the ring finger.
- Usually, symptoms come on slowly, though some athletes report a sudden "twang" on the inside of the elbow that signifies the onset of a constant problem.

Cause:

- Powerful, repetitive elbow motions.

Athletes at risk:

- Those in throwing or racket sports, as well as golfers and weight lifters.

Concerns:

- If ulnar neuritis is allowed to progress to where it becomes chronic, cessation of nerve function can occur, which results in loss of much of the function of the forearm, wrist, and hand.

What you can do:

- If the condition is caught in its early stages, two weeks of rest will allow the condition to settle down.

Medication:

- For relief of minor to moderate pain, take acetaminophen as directed on label, or, for the relief of pain *and* inflammation, ibuprofen or aspirin if tolerated (see page 49).

What the doctor can do:

- A nerve conduction study is done to confirm that the problem is with the ulnar nerve in the elbow, and is not originating with a pinched nerve in the neck.
- Nonsurgical measures are successful in controlling about half of all ulnar neuritis conditions.
- Nonsurgical treatment consists of rest and anti-inflammatories.
- In the remaining cases that do not respond to nonsurgical measures, the nerve has been pinched so much there is scarring, or is stretched to the extent that it repeatedly slips out of the groove. In such cases, surgery is usually necessary.
- Surgical options:
  The surgical procedure involves moving the ulnar nerve from the back of the elbow to the front, just below the inside of the biceps. After moving the nerve surgically, athletes are almost always able to return to their preinjury level of activity without any decline in athletic performance.

The elbow is splinted for two to three weeks to prevent the stitches holding the ulnar nerve in place from tearing loose.

Rehabilitation:

- As soon as pain permits—preferably within five days of surgery—level one exercises should start. After two or three weeks of splinting, level two exercises can begin.
- Four weeks after the surgery, the patient starts a program of strength exercises using progressively heavier weights. For levels one, two, and three rehabilitation guidelines, refer to the sections on rehabilitation and conditioning at the end of this chapter.

Recovery time:

- If caught early, ulnar neuritis can clear up in two weeks.
- If it deteriorates to stages two or three, however, athletes can expect a layoff of a month or, often, a season.
- If surgery becomes necessary, normal activity can be resumed after two to three months of rehabilitation.

Elbow Rehabilitation

Rehabilitation exercises serve to
- Promote blood flow to the area, which speeds the healing process.
- Relieve stiffness in the joint caused by immobilization.
- Prevent atrophy and tightening of the muscles resulting from inactivity.*

The elbow responds especially poorly to immobilization after injury because splinting too long can result in long-term dysfunction and loss of range of motion, so rehabilitation needs to begin as soon as possible. Athletes whose elbows are immobilized for more than three weeks are at high risk of long-term elbow dysfunction.

*For more on the importance and general principles of rehabilitation, see chapter 5, "Rehabilitating Your Sports Injury."

After an injury that does not require surgery or lengthy immobilization, range-of-motion exercises for the elbow can begin as soon as pain and swelling diminish—usually no later than twenty-four to forty-eight hours after the surgery.

When surgery is necessary, range-of-motion exercises can begin as early as five days after the operation and certainly no more than two or three weeks later. To accomplish this, the patient should be put in a sling or splint that can be removed for rehabilitation sessions.

Exercise is the most effective way to restore an injured athlete to sports readiness. A physical therapist may also employ ice, superficial heat, deep heat, massage, and electrical stimulation to promote healing and make performing the exercises more comfortable.

The starting intensity level of the rehabilitation exercises depends on the severity of the injury. Postsurgery range-of-motion exercises usually begin at level one. At this level, range-of-motion exercises are "active assisted"—the physical therapist helps patients use their own strength to move the elbow through allowable ranges of motion. If the injury is too severe for active assisted exercises, the patient may have to rely on "passive assisted" exercises—the physical therapist moves the injured elbow through allowable ranges of motion. Continuous passive motion machines (CPMs) can be taken home by the patient so he or she can do passive range-of-motion exercises at home.

After surgery, muscle atrophy is prevented by using isometric exercises. With the direction of a physical therapist, these exercises can usually begin immediately after surgery. Isometrics help maintain strength in the important muscles of the elbow without compromising the healing process by changing the length of the muscle or the angle of the joint.

Athletes who have sustained only mild or moderately severe injuries can begin with level two exercises. The primary goal at this stage is to restore range of motion; the secondary goal is to prevent atrophy in the surrounding muscles. As the rehabilitation program progresses, more strengthening exercises are included.

Range-of-motion and strength exercises should always be done within the pain threshold. Any exercise that causes pain should be discontinued.

The following are the most common and effective exercises used to rehabilitate the elbow after injury.

Level One

After surgery, active assisted or passive assisted range-of-motion exercises are used as a starting point of rehabilitation. Within the limitations of the injury, the athlete should work on the elbow's four main ranges of motion: flexion, extension, supination, and pronation.

Isometrics and assisted range-of-motion therapy should continue only until patients are capable of using their own strength to do level two exercises.

Level Two

When patients are able to move their injured elbows themselves and can do isometric exercises without pain, level two exercises can begin.

Level two exercises can also be used as a starting point for rehabilitating moderate to severe elbow injuries that do not require surgery. They primarily develop range of motion in the joint but also help prevent atrophy and tightening in the muscles of the upper arm and forearm.

Exercise 1: elbow range of motion (flexion/extension)
Bend and straighten elbow through full range of motion.

Exercise 2: elbow range of motion (pronation/supination)
Sit with forearm flat on a table, palm facing tabletop. Turn forearm so back of hand is against the table.

Repeat the above exercises fifteen to thirty times each, three times a day.

Level Three

When the patient can do the level two exercises without difficulty or pain, level three exercises can begin.

Level three exercises can also be used as a starting point for rehabilitating mild elbow injuries.

Besides continuing to promote range of motion in the elbow (flexion and extension; pronation and supination), level three exercises start using dynamic exercises to strengthen the main muscles surrounding the elbow—the biceps and triceps in the upper arm, and the flexors and extensors in the forearm.

Exercise 1: elbow range of motion; biceps strength
Holding a small weight, bend and straighten elbow through full range of motion.

Exercise 2: elbow range of motion; triceps strength

With elbow pointing up and hand dropped back holding a small weight, straighten arm upward.

Exercise 3: wrist range of motion; forearm strength

Holding a towel between your hands, twist it forward and backward.

Repeat these exercises three times a day, starting at ten repetitions and gradually building up to fifteen. You should be able to do ten repetitions with ease and without pain before moving on to eleven, and so on.

When you can comfortably do fifteen repetitions three times a day using the starting weight, increase the weight by 10 percent, but reduce the number of repetitions back to ten, then gradually build back up to fifteen.

Each time you can comfortably do fifteen repetitions, increase the weight by 10 percent, reduce the number of repetitions to ten, and build back up to fifteen.

When the strength of the injured elbow is 95 percent of the uninjured side (and, by association, 95 percent of its original strength), ease back into sports.

Before going back to sports, however, the athlete who has been injured should be able to do daily activities without pain and stimulate the arm motions of his or her sports without pain.

To reduce the chance of reinjury, begin the strength and flexibility conditioning program that follows.

Conditioning Program for the Elbow

Conditioning to prevent elbow injuries involves improving the strength and flexibility of all the major muscles surrounding the joint, primarily the biceps and triceps of the upper arm and the flexors and extensors of the forearm.

Exercises to stretch and strengthen the muscles around the elbow often incorporate exercises to improve flexibility and strength in the shoulder and wrist/hand. Effective conditioning to prevent elbow injuries must also include exercises to improve strength and flexibility in the surrounding joints, especially the shoulder.

Incorporate into your workout at least one set of the following exercises for each muscle group mentioned. The exercises are described in chapter 3, "Strength and Flexibility: The Key to Injury Prevention."

Make these exercises part of an overall strength and flexibility program, and do them before any activity that will stress the muscles around the elbow.

Elbow Strengthening Exercises

Biceps: Seated dumbbell curl, barbell curl
Triceps: Standing dumbbell triceps extension, bar dips, lying barbell triceps extension
Forearm extensors: Wrist curl, wrist roll
Forearm flexors: Reverse wrist curl, wrist roll

CHAPTER FIFTEEN

Wrist Injuries

Injuries to the wrist are quite common in sports and are especially prevalent in children and young adults. Younger athletes are especially susceptible to *acute* wrist injuries and, in particular, fractures.

In adults, whose fully formed bones are less vulnerable to acute trauma, and who are less likely to be involved in the kinds of rough-and-tumble activities than children, overuse injuries are more common. That is not to say adult recreational athletes do not sustain acute wrist injuries. They do. And because wrist fractures are among the most frequently misdiagnosed sports injuries, many do not receive proper treatment, due to the subtlety of many acute wrist injury symptoms.

Unfortunately, undiagnosed or mismanaged wrist fractures may have serious long-term consequences—most significantly, loss of wrist mobility. For that reason, any confirmed bone fracture or wrist pain that persists after two weeks of rest should be seen by an orthopedist, and preferably by a wrist and hand specialist.

Injuries of the Wrist

Acute wrist injuries include fractures, dislocations, and sprains.

These injuries can result from a fall onto an outstretched arm, as in horseback riding, biking, skiing, or in-line skating, or from a sudden twisting motion that subjects the wrist to sudden forward or backward bending. Direct impact to the wrist, the kind sustained in a fall or collision, or from impact against the wrist such

as a bat, stick, or racket handle, is another cause of acute wrist injuries.

Depending on the nature and severity of the acute injury, symptoms can range from obvious deformity and excruciating pain to low-grade discomfort and swelling. Fractures of the wrist bones themselves—the carpals—are frequently misdiagnosed as sprains because the symptoms may not be severe, and the damage often does not show up on initial X rays.

Overuse injuries of the wrist include tendinitis, nerve conditions (neuropathies), and, in children, fractures of the growth plates at the end of the radius and ulna bones in the forearm.

Overuse injuries of the wrist develop over time from the kind of repetitive stress seen in sports that require frequent snap-and-twist motions of the wrist. Tendinitis of the wrist, for example, may be caused by frequent swinging at an object, as in baseball, tennis, golf, lacrosse, or by powerfully releasing an object with a sudden twist-and-snap action, as in bowling, weight lifting, pole vault, javelin, discus, shot put, or rowing.

Tendinitis of the wrist is especially prevalent because of the narrowness of the sheaths through which the tendons in this area travel. Even slight irritation to the tendons causes tightness in the sheath and symptoms of tendinitis is a crackling sensation in the tendons known as crepitus.

Nerve injuries such as ulnar neuritis and carpal tunnel syndrome are caused by repetitive external stress to nerves that pass through the wrist, such as the pressure exerted by bicycle handlebars or the handle of a racket, stick, or bat. Characteristic symptoms of nerve injuries are pain, tingling, and numbness in the hands and fingers.

The key to managing overuse injuries is early detection and treatment. Otherwise, the outcome may be long layoffs, extended pain, and wrist dysfunction, problems that sometimes only surgery can alleviate.

The consequences of mismanaged overuse injuries are especially serious for children. Growth plate stress fractures at the lower end of the forearm bones are becoming increasingly common in young gymnasts. The damage is caused by frequently landing on hands (impact radiates to the wrist), and by repetitive bending and straightening of the wrist. Injuries to the growth plates may disturb the normal growth process in growing children, leading to stunted or abnormal growth at the ends of the forearm bones and therefore disrupted joint function.

Wrist Injury Prevention

Acute wrist injuries are often caused by accidents and are difficult to prevent. There are, however, some preventive measures athletes can take. First, learn to fall properly in a tuck-and-roll fashion, not on the wrist or outstretched arm. Also, it is recommended that athletes wear protective forearm and wrist pads in sports where frequent impact may occur, such as in-line skating, hockey, and football.

Overuse injuries of the wrist can be minimized by observing a slow, progressive training regimen and not doing "too much too soon." This holds true especially for athletes in sports that involve dynamic snap-and-twist motions—baseball, tennis, golf, lacrosse, bowling, weight lifting, javelin, discus, shot put, and rowing.

Proper technique also has a role in preventing wrist overuse injuries. Incorrect technique is a common cause of overuse injuries such as ulnar neuritis and handlebar palsy.

Do not overstress sensitive nerves in the wrist. Gloves are available for bikers that help prevent leaning pressures that cause an overuse nerve disorder in the wrist known colloquially as "handlebar palsy."

Strength and flexibility exercises for the forearm and wrist help prevent both acute and overuse injuries. They are especially important for athletes engaged in sports that repeatedly stress the wrist. For more on wrist flexi-

bility and strengthening exercises, refer to the final section of this chapter.

Acute Injuries of the Wrist

Wrist Fractures

A fracture is a break in the bone. Fractures of the bones in the wrist area may be tiny hairline cracks, complete breaks, or traumatic shatterings of the bone.

Fractures in the wrist area often have subtle symptoms. Swelling, tenderness, and displacement may be minor. For that reason, they are frequently misdiagnosed as sprains and don't receive appropriate treatment. This happens frequently with fractures of the forearm bones.

Often, fractures of the wrist bones themselves—the carpals—cannot be detected on X rays, particularly fractures of the scaphoid bone. The problem is that blood supply to these bones is poor, and they often do not heal by themselves unless they receive proper treatment. This can lead to degenerative changes in the joint with pain during use, as well as impaired function. Unless they are identified and managed properly from the start, fractures of the scaphoid often need surgery.

All this points toward the need for vigilance on the part of athletes who sustain wrist injuries, and the need to seek out expert care.

A fall onto an outstretched arm is the most common cause of a wrist fracture. Where the wrist fracture occurs is closely associated with the age of the athlete. Older adult athletes—in their thirties and over—tend to sustain fractures of the lower end of the forearm bones, the radius and ulna. Because their bones are more brittle, the fracture tends to be "comminuted," which is to say, the ends of the broken bones are shattered.

Among young adults whose growth is almost completed, fractures generally occur in the scaphoid bone in the wrist itself.

In youngsters who are in a growth spurt, fractures usually occur at the vulnerable growth plates in the lower end of the radius bone.

Prepubescent children usually sustain fractures right through the physis at the radius and/or ulna at the bottom of the forearm.

WRIST ANATOMY

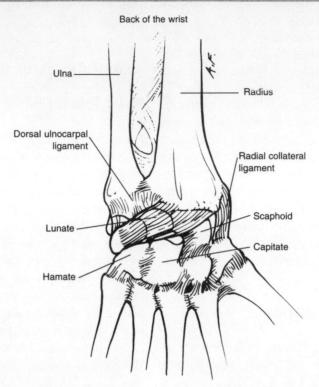

Back of the wrist

Ulna

Radius

Dorsal ulnocarpal
ligament

Radial collateral
ligament

Scaphoid

Lunate

Capitate

Hamate

Bones and joints: The wrist joint connects the forearm and wrist bones. It lies between the end of the two forearm bones, the ulna and radius, and the eight bones of the wrist, the *carpals,* the most important being the *scaphoid, lunate, lamate,* and *capilate.*

Muscles and nerves: A network of muscles and nerves traveling from the forearm controls the wrist as well as the hand and fingers.

Most wrist movement comes from the flexor and extensor muscles in the forearm.

Three nerves send impulses from the brain that produce movement in the wrist, hand, and fingers. They also provide sensation in these areas. These nerves are the *median, ulnar,* and *radial.* The median nerve passes through a bony arch on the palm side of the wrist called the *carpal tunnel,* while the radius and ulnar nerve run along the radius and ulnar bones in the forearm.

FRACTURE OF THE LOWER RADIUS BONE IN THE FOREARM *(Colles' Fracture)*

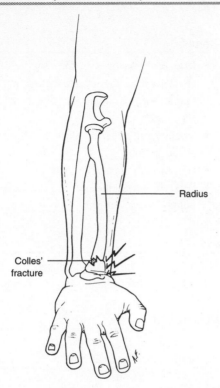

Radius

Colles' fracture

A fracture is a crack, break, or complete shattering of a bone. In adults thirty years and older, fractures of the lower radius bone in the forearm are the most common wrist fractures. These fractures often result in a shattering of the ends of the broken bones—a comminuted fracture. Often the ulna bone also gets broken.

Symptoms of a mild lower radius fracture may be quite innocuous because there is only minor displacement of the broken bones. Swelling may be mild, and pain felt only when trying to use the wrist. Consequently, mild lower radius fractures are often mistaken for sprains. Any pain in the wrist area should be seen by a doctor and X-rayed.

Displaced and comminuted fractures of the lower radius are more common, and their symptoms are more obvious.

Symptoms:

- Deformity on the thumb side of the lower forearm.
- Pain, swelling, and tenderness around the wrist.

Cause:

- A fall onto the outstretched arm that forcefully bends the hand upward and backward.

Athletes at risk:

- Forearm fractures are most often seen in athletes in contact sports and in activities with potential for falling accidents.

Concerns:

- Unless a comminuted fracture of the lower radius heals back to its original status, it will shorten relative to the length of the other forearm bone, the ulna. Efficient function of the wrist depends on the delicate relationship between these two bones. Therefore, shortening of the radius bone after a fracture may compromise wrist rotation as well as "ulnar deviation" (turning the wrist downward toward the little finger).

What you can do:

- Seek or call for emergency medical assistance.
- Splint the forearm and wrist in the injured position.
- Gently apply ice over the injury until medical attention is available.

What the doctor can do:

- Rule out damage to the nerves and blood supply.
- Order X rays to determine the nature and severity of the fracture.
- If possible, nonsurgically realign the broken ends of the broken bones ("closed reduction").
- When successful closed reduction is not possible (as in the case of a comminuted fracture), surgical intervention may be necessary to prevent radius shortening relative to the ulna and compromising long-term wrist function.
- Surgery involves placing two pins into the thumb area and two more pins above the broken end of the radius, then "stretching out" the radius, using a rod that runs between the pins.

- Although lengthy immobilization of the wrist is often necessary for this kind of fracture—between four to six weeks—the cast leaves the thumb and fingers free so the muscles and joints of the hand, fingers, and forearm can be exercised.

Rehabilitation:

- Within a week of surgery, level one exercises for the hand, fingers, and forearm can begin, and should continue throughout the time the wrist is immobilized. When the cast is removed, level one exercises for the wrist should begin, and progress according to the prescription in the rehabilitation section at the end of this chapter.

Recovery time:

- After surgery, a minimum of twelve weeks before athletes can return to vigorous athletic activities and, depending on the severity of the injury, up to six months.

FRACTURE OF THE SCAPHOID BONE (Carponavicular Fracture)

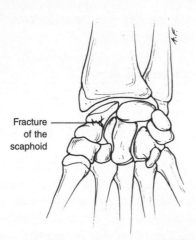

Fracture of the scaphoid

A fracture is a crack, break, or complete shattering of a bone. Among young adults whose growth is almost completed, a fall onto an outstretched arm may fracture the scaphoid bone in the wrist itself. The impact drives the scaphoid bone into the lower end of the radius bone

in the forearm, which may then break the scaphoid into two parts. This kind of injury is also known as a carponavicular fracture.

Symptoms:

- Pain and tenderness in the "snuffbox" portion of the wrist—the crater created by the two thumb tendons when the thumb is extended backward.
- Specific pain when pulling back the long bone of the thumb.
- Loss of wrist range of motion.
- Hand weakness, mild swelling, bruising over the thumb side of the wrist.

Cause:

- A fall onto the outstretched arm that forcefully bends the hand upward and backward.

Athletes at risk:

- Fractures of the scaphoid bone are most often seen in young adult athletes in contact sports and in activities with potential for falling accidents.

Concerns:

- This fracture is often misdiagnosed as a sprain because initially it doesn't show up on X rays. Even if X rays show no signs of a fracture but the symptoms are suspicious, this injury should be treated as a fracture. This precaution is taken because blood supply to the scaphoid is extremely poor, and unless it receives early treatment, the bone will probably not heal by itself, and the outside portion of broken bone may die. When a fracture of the scaphoid doesn't heal, there is the potential for long-term wrist dysfunction.

What you can do:

- Seek or call for emergency medical assistance.
- Splint the forearm and wrist in the injured position.
- Gently apply ice over the injury until medical attention is available.

What the doctor can do:

- Order X rays to determine the nature and severity of the injury.
- Nonsurgical treatment options:

    Even if X rays are negative, the wrist and hand should be put in a cast for seven to ten days if symptoms are suspicious, because undisplaced fractures of the scaphoid may not show up on initial X rays.

    A second set of X rays should be taken after this period of immobilization, by which time any bone damage will be visible, because degeneration around the fracture line will have occurred. If the second set of X rays uncovers an undisplaced fracture, eight weeks of continued casting will be necessary to allow union of the fractured bone. Whether an above-elbow or below-elbow cast is used, the thumb should always be immobilized so thumb notion doesn't prevent union of the broken scaphoid bone.

    If the second set of X rays is again negative, the athlete can return to action after a brief rehabilitation program.

    If union hasn't been achieved after three or four months of conservative treatment, or if initial X rays reveal a displaced fracture of the scaphoid, surgery should be done.

- Surgical options:

    The two broken portions of the bone are joined with screws or wires. If the scaphoid is badly out of position or completely broken apart, a bone graft may be necessary. Chips of bone are taken from the pelvis and packed into the fracture site, where their presence will promote healing. After surgery, the wrist is immobilized in a long arm cast for six weeks, followed by casting in a short arm cast until X rays reveal healing has occurred. At this time, the screws or wires are removed, and rehabilitation for the wrist can begin.

Rehabilitation:

- Within a week of the injury, level one exercises for the hand and fingers can start (no thumb movement can be done because this digit is completely immobilized). After bone union takes place, the cast is removed and the athlete should begin level one range-of-motion and strengthening exercises for the wrist. For levels one, two, and three rehabilitation guidelines, refer to the sections on rehabilitation and conditioning at the end of this chapter.

Recovery time:

- Properly treated, an undisplaced fracture of the scaphoid may take three months to heal, while displaced fractures may take as long as four months. Sometimes, bone grafting may be necessary for the bone to heal. The wrist should be protected with a rigid removable splint during sports until strength and range of motion are almost equal to those of the uninjured wrist.
- Studies have shown that it is best to protect the wrist for three months after the cast is removed.

WRIST SPRAIN

A wrist sprain is a stretch or tear of the ligaments around the wrist. Sprains are classified according to severity: first, second, or third degree. First-degree sprains involve slight stretches of the ligaments, with the possibility of a few fibers being torn. Second-degree sprains are when the ligaments are partially stretched and torn. Third-degree sprains are total ruptures of the ligaments.

Wrist sprains usually affect either the ligaments that hold together the lower ends of the two forearm bones, the radius and ulna, or the ligaments that link the eight wrist bones—the carpals.

Symptoms:

- Immediate pain on injury, especially over the wrist joint.
- Swelling within an hour of the injury—the more severe the sprain, the more extreme the swelling.
- Range of motion may be restricted, and the wrist may feel weak.
- Difficulty in grasping objects.
- No specific point of pain.
- More serious sprains cause joint instability.

Cause:

- Forceful backward bending of the hand.

Athletes at risk:

- Wrist sprains are often seen in athletes in contact sports and activities with potential for falling accidents.

Concerns:

- If a sprain is ignored or mismanaged—even a moderate one—the consequences may be serious. Efficient wrist function depends on the ligaments in this area, especially those that control rotation, the radius and ulna in the lower forearm. If a serious sprain is ignored, surgery may eventually be necessary to regain full function.
- More serious injuries may mimic the symptoms of sprains, especially fractures of the scaphoid bone in the wrist and fractures of the lower radius and ulna bones in the forearm. Therefore, any doubt about whether the wrist injury is a sprain or fracture should be cause to consult a physician.

What you can do:

- Treat first-degree sprains with RICE (page 46). Immobilize the wrist in a brace (available at most drug stores) for three days, then start range-of-motion exercises on the fourth day.
- For second- and third-degree sprains, use RICE and seek medical attention.
- If pain and loss of range of motion are severe, immobilize the wrist and put the arm in a sling.

What the doctor can do:

- Try to rule out a possible fracture with X rays, as well as a physical examination for points of localized tenderness—especially above the scaphoid bone in the wrist, and the lower forearm bones, the radius and ulna.
- Nonsurgical treatment options:
  Place the wrist in a cast if in any doubt whether there is a fracture (see above, "Fracture of the Scaphoid Bone.")

If a sprain can be confirmed, the wrist should be immobilized in a brace that can be removed for RICE. Anti-inflammatories may be prescribed to control swelling.
Second- and third-degree sprains may require up to four weeks of splinting before athletes can return to sports.

Rehabilitation:

- After a first- or second-degree sprain, level one or level two exercises can begin as soon as pain permits, usually within four days of the injury, and progress accordingly.
- For third-degree wrist sprains, which require splinting, the splint can be removed within a week, so level one rehabilitation exercises can begin. Because of the tendency for swelling to take place, individual rehabilitation sessions for wrist sprains should be short and done frequently every day. Icing should be done after each session to reduce swelling. For levels one, two, and three rehabilitation guidelines, refer to the sections on rehabilitation and conditioning at the end of this chapter.

Recovery time:

- After a mild sprain, the athlete may be ready to go back to sports in a week. Moderate to severe sprains may rule out sports for six to twelve weeks.
- Note: Upon return to action after a wrist sprain, wear a support bandage to help prevent reinjuring the ligaments.

WRIST DISLOCATIONS

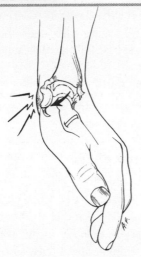

Dislocations of the wrist usually affect the lunate bone in the wrist. There are three main types of dislocations that affect the lunate: posterior dislocation of the lunate; anterior dislocation of the lunate; and perilunate dislocation.

Symptoms:

- Deformity in the palm side or knuckle side of the hand near the wrist crease, especially a lump where one of the eight wrist bones, the carpals, may have popped up or down.
- Swelling, pain, tenderness in the wrist area, accompanied by loss of range of motion.

Causes:

- A fall onto an outstretched arm in which the hand bends backward or forward, or impact that compresses one wrist bone against another.

Concerns:

- Like other acute wrist injuries, dislocations may be difficult to recognize. It is important to diagnose and treat these injuries early because delayed or improper treatment can lead to poor recovery.

What you can do:

- Immobilize the wrist and put the arm in a sling.
- Seek medical attention.

What the doctor can do:

- Order X rays to confirm the diagnosis.
- Nonsurgical treatment:
  If possible, return the dislocated bone to its original position ("closed reduction"), followed by splinting for six to ten weeks.
  If this is not successful (often the ligaments are torn so badly that the bone remains unstable), the doctor may do an "open reduction."
- Surgical treatment:
  The doctor will make an incision, enter the joint, and remove the blocking area, then stitch the ligaments back together. A pin is used to keep the lunate in place. After surgery the wrist is immobilized for six to ten weeks, though rehabilitation for the hand, fingers, thumb, and forefingers can start within a week.

Rehabilitation:

- Within a week of the injury, level one exercises for the hand, fingers, thumb, and forearm can start, and should progress accordingly while the wrist is immobilized. When the splint and pins are removed after six weeks, level one exercises for the wrist should begin and progress according to the prescription in the rehabilitation section at the end of this chapter.

Recovery time:

- It may take three to six months before an athlete with a dislocated wrist is able to go back to sports that stress this joint. The wrist should be strapped or protected with a store-bought splint for several months after return to sports.

FRACTURE OF THE HOOK OF THE HAMATE

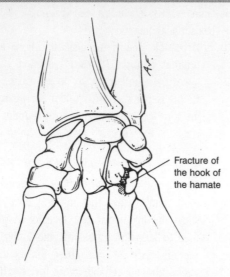

Fracture of the hook of the hamate

A fracture is a crack, break, or complete shattering of a bone. Fractures in the wrist often affect the hamate bone, the bony prominence located just over the wrist crease on the outside of the wrist. The hamate has a vulnerable "hook" that can get broken if it gets crushed against the bone next to it, the capitate. This compression may be caused by single impact from an object such as the handle of a bat, racket, or stick. It may also be damaged due to repetitive impact in sports that place frequent stress on this part of the wrist, such as cycling, golf, baseball, and tennis.

Symptoms:

- Pain and tenderness over the heel of the hand ("karate chop" area).
- Weakness when trying to grip.
- Numbness in the little finger.

Causes:

- Impact from an object such as the handle of a bat, racket, or stick.
- Repetitive impact to the heel of the hand.

Athletes at risk:

- From a single blow, participants in softball, baseball, racket sports, lacrosse, and hockey.
- From repetitive impact, cyclists, golfers, and baseball, softball, and tennis players.

Concerns:

- Because blood supply to the hamate is poor, a fractured hamate rarely heals unless it is recognized and treated immediately.

What you can do:

- Immobilize the wrist and put the arm in a sling.
- Seek medical attention.

What the doctor can do:

- X rays to verify the diagnosis. The pictures will show a crack or gap between the hook of the hamate and the rest of the bone.
- Because blood supply to this bone is so poor, conservative treatment rarely succeeds in achieving union of the two broken pieces of bone.
- Surgical options:

    An incision is made over the hamate, and the entire hook is removed. (This procedure should be done by a hand surgeon because of the proximity of the ulnar nerve, which could easily be damaged by a surgeon unfamiliar with this area.)

    After surgery, four weeks of casting is necessary, after which time the athlete wears a removable custom-molded splint with a protective bubble over the hamate.

Rehabilitation:

- Level one exercises for the hand, fingers, thumb, and forearm can begin one week after surgery, and progress accordingly. When the cast is removed four weeks after the surgery, level one exercises for the wrist can start and should progress according to the prescription in the rehabilitation section at the end of this chapter.

Recovery time:

- Six to twelve weeks of rest and rehabilitation is necessary before athletes with a fractured hook of the hamate can go back to sports that stress the wrist. Four to six weeks before returning to sports where the wrist is not subjected to excessive impact or bending (as long as the protective splint is worn).

Overuse Injuries of the Wrist

CARPAL TUNNEL SYNDROME

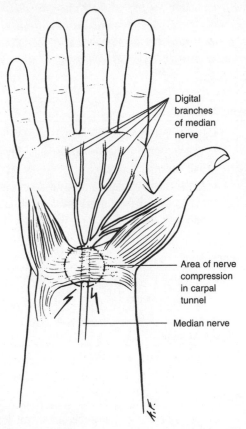

Digital branches of median nerve

Area of nerve compression in carpal tunnel

Median nerve

Carpal tunnel syndrome refers to a buildup of pressure in the carpal tunnel on the underside of the wrist. The pressure compresses the median nerve that travels through this narrow channel. Carpal tunnel syndrome is the most common nerve entrapment problem in sports.

Symptoms:

- Symptoms develop gradually and may first be felt at night.
- Most often, numbness and tingling in the thumb, index finger, middle finger, and half the ring finger. In its most severe form, there is aching pain in the wrist and sharp, burning pain, tingling, and weakness in the four digits mentioned above.
- Shaking the hand may relieve the symptoms.

Cause:

- Excessive inversion of the wrist.

Athletes at risk:

- Primarily cyclists and, increasingly, those who use stairclimber machines.

Concerns:

- If allowed to deteriorate, carpal tunnel syndrome can cause permanent hand weakness and compromise function, especially with pinching motions.

What you can do:

- In mild cases, use RICE (page 46).
- Cease the activities that caused the condition.
- Use a wrist splint with a rigid underside and Velcro straps on top (available at most drugstores) that will prevent further inversion of the wrist. Wear the brace at night and as much as possible during the day.

Medication:

- For relief of minor to moderate pain, take acetaminophen as directed on label, or, for the relief of pain *and* inflammation, ibuprofen or aspirin if tolerated (see page 49).

What the doctor can do:

- A nonsurgical approach is usually taken to treat carpal tunnel syndrome:
    An electromyograph (EMG)—a nerve conduction study—to confirm the diagnosis.
    RICE
    Anti-inflammatories
    Splinting
    Cortisone injection
- If conservative treatment fails, surgery may be necessary:
    A "carpal tunnel release" is performed, in which the surgeon cuts through the heavy fascial tissue that crosses the wrist and compresses the carpal tunnel.
    Alternatively, the doctor may choose to trim

the scar tissue off the inflamed nerves. Both these surgical procedures are done on an outpatient basis.

If the ulnar nerve is also irritated, a procedure to release pressure on this nerve will be done at the same time.

After surgery, the wrist is immobilized for ten to fourteen days, at which time the stitches are removed.

Rehabilitation:

- When nonsurgical treatment is used, level two exercises can begin as soon as the symptoms are gone.
- After surgery, the patient can begin gentle range-of-motion exercises for the hand, fingers, thumb, and forearm within a week. Level one exercises for the wrist itself can begin as soon as the stitches are removed—usually ten to fourteen days after the operation. By the fourth to sixth week after surgery, level three exercises should have commenced. For levels one, two, and three rehabilitation guidelines, refer to the sections on rehabilitation and conditioning at the end of this chapter.

Recovery time:

- When nonsurgical treatment is used, return to sports can take place when the symptoms have gone—usually after two weeks of RICE, anti-inflammatories, and splinting.
- After surgery, it will be at least six weeks before sports are possible.

ULNAR TUNNEL SYNDROME *(Ulnar Neuropathy, "Handlebar Palsy")*

Ulnar neuropathy is an irritation of the ulnar nerve that runs along the heel of the hand—the side used to "karate chop" a piece of wood. The most frequent cause of ulnar neuropathy is gripping bicycle handlebars for extended periods, hence its colloquial name, "handlebar palsy."

Symptoms:

- Onset of symptoms is gradual.
- Tingling and numbness in the little finger and half the ring finger.
- As the condition deteriorates, weakness when trying to spread the fingers and loss of coordination with wrist, hand, and finger movement.

Cause:

- Direct and frequent pressure to the tissues over the ulnar nerve.

Athletes at risk:

- Cyclists.

Concerns:

- The longer the nerve becomes irritated, the more scar tissue builds up, and the more it disrupts electrical function in the nerve. This will compromise motor control and sensation in the hand. When ulnar neuropathy becomes chronic, conservative treatment is too late, and surgery may be the only remedy. The key to effective management, then, is early detection and treatment.

What you can do:

- Use RICE (page 46) in early stages.
- Avoid the activity that caused the condition.
- When the symptoms go away, return to biking, but take steps to prevent recurrence of the condition: wear padded gloves, change grip position, and adjust the height of the handlebars.

Medication:

- For relief of minor to moderate pain, take acetaminophen as directed on label, or, for the relief of pain *and* inflammation, ibuprofen or aspirin if tolerated (see page 49).

What the doctor can do:

- Treatment prescriptions—both nonsurgical and surgical—are the same as for carpal tunnel syndrome (see page 257).

Rehabilitation:

- Rehabilitation is the same as for carpal tunnel syndrome (page 258).

Recovery time:

- Recovery times are the same as for carpal tunnel syndrome.

WRIST GANGLION CYST *(Tenosynovitis Cyst)*

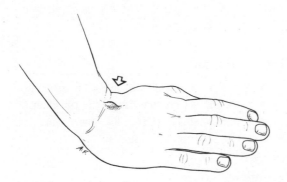

A ganglion is a concentration of synovial fluid just below the skin. In the wrist, ganglia are usually seen just forward of the wrist crease on top of the hand. They are triggered by irritation of the tendons that run across the top of the wrist joint. Ganglia may follow another injury, especially to the wrist tendons.

Symptoms:

- Onset of symptoms is gradual.
- A small lump just forward of the wrist crease on top of the hand, ranging in size from a pea to a marble and sometimes larger.
- In the early stages, little pain. If allowed to progress, pain and loss of range of motion in the wrist.

Cause:

- Repetitive pressure to the tendons over the top of the wrist joint.

Athletes at risk:

- Any athlete in a sport that subjects the wrist to repetitive loading, especially gymnastics and rowing.

Concerns:

- No matter what the treatment, ganglia frequently recur.

What you can do:

- In the early stages use RICE (page 46).
- Gentle compression can be applied using a small foam pad.
- Avoid stressing the joint through overuse or impact.
- If the condition persists, seek medical attention.

Medication:

- For relief of minor to moderate pain, take acetaminophen as directed on label, or, for the relief of pain *and* inflammation, ibuprofen or aspirin if tolerated (see page 49).

What the doctor can do:

- X rays to rule out a more serious condition, such as a fracture.
- If the ganglion diagnosis is confirmed, prescribe RICE in conjunction with splinting to avoid aggravating the condition.
- If the ganglion persists or worsens, drain the fluid with a syringe. Sometimes cortisone may

be injected into the ganglion to get rid of the inflammation; then the wrist is splinted to prevent further irritation of the tendons. A last resort will be surgical removal of the cyst.

WRIST TENDINITIS

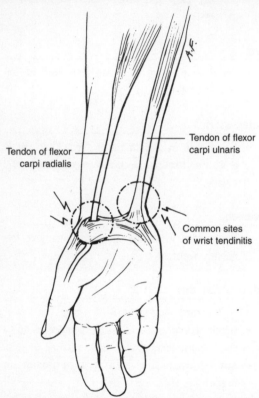

Tendon of flexor carpi radialis

Tendon of flexor carpi ulnaris

Common sites of wrist tendinitis

Wrist tendinitis most commonly refers to an inflammation of the two flexor tendons that pass over the wrists from the forearms to the hands and fingers. Because of the narrowness of the sheaths through which the tendons in this area must pass, the wrist is very susceptible to tendinitis conditions. In fact, it is thought that wrist tendinitis conditions are the most common in sports medicine.

Symptoms:

- Onset of symptoms is gradual.
- Localized pain that worsens with activity.
- A crackling sensation (crepitus) in the tendons over the wrist.
- Difficulty gripping objects.
- The area may be warm to the touch.

Causes:

- Repetitive bending and straightening of the wrists through large ranges of motion—frequent swinging at an object or powerfully releasing an object with a sudden twist-and-snap action.
- The condition is usually brought on by a sudden increase in the frequency, intensity, or duration of training or playing activity.

Athletes at risk:

- Those in sports that demand repetitive bending and straightening of the wrists through large ranges of motion—rowers, kayakers, bowlers, weight lifters, pole vaulters, and tennis, golf, baseball, and lacrosse players, as well as participants in javelin, discus, and shot put.

Concerns:

- When allowed to worsen, wrist tendinitis may become chronic, and often requires surgery to alleviate the problem. For this reason, early intervention is crucial.

What you can do:

- At first sign of tendinitis, use RICE (page 46).
- Cease the activity that caused the condition.
- If the condition persists for longer than two weeks, seek medical attention.

Medication:

- For relief of minor to moderate pain, take acetaminophen as directed on label, or, for the relief of pain *and* inflammation, ibuprofen or aspirin if tolerated (see page 49).

What the doctor can do:

- Nonsurgical treatment is usually successful in treating wrist tendinitis:
  RICE
  Anti-inflammatories
  Splinting (the splint should maintain the wrist in a neutral or dorsiflexed position)

Immobilization in a short-arm cast for two weeks

- In rare cases, surgery may be necessary:

A tendon sheath release involves cutting the openings of the tendon sheaths so the tendon has more room to move within.

In some cases where the tendinitis has gone untreated, calcium deposits that have built up on the tendons may have to be trimmed off. After surgery, the wrist is immobilized in a cast for two weeks, after which time the cast and stitches are removed, and wrist rehabilitation exercises can begin.

Rehabilitation:

- When nonsurgical treatment is used, level two exercises can begin as soon as the pain is gone.
- After surgery, range-of-motion and strengthening exercises for the hand, finger, thumb, and forearm can begin within a week. Level one exercises for the wrist itself should start as soon as the cast is removed two weeks after the operation. For levels one, two, and three rehabilitation guidelines, refer to the sections on rehabilitation and conditioning at the end of this chapter.

Recovery time:

- Mild cases: seven to ten days.
- When surgery is required: six to twelve weeks.

DE QUERVAIN'S DISEASE *(Tendinitis of the Abductor and Extensor Tendons Linking the Wrist to the Thumb)*

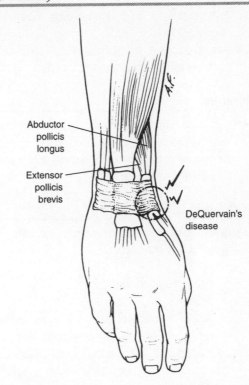

Abductor pollicis longus

Extensor pollicis brevis

DeQuervain's disease

De Quervain's disease refers to an inflammation of the abductor and extensor tendons that run across the wrist and into the thumb.

Symptoms:

- Onset of symptoms is gradual.
- A low-grade ache on the thumb side of the wrist.
- Local swelling and tenderness on the thumb side of the wrist.
- It hurts to move the thumb into a 90 degree angle (the "thumb's up" signal).

Cause:

- Repetitive snapping of the wrist in throwing and racket sports.

Athletes at risk:

- Those engaged in throwing or racket sports.

What you can do:

- Early detection is crucial.
- Use RICE (page 46), over-the-counter anti-inflammatories, and a thumb splint to alleviate the condition.
- See a doctor if the symptoms are severe or if they persist for more than two weeks.

Medication:

- For relief of minor to moderate pain, take acetaminophen as directed on label, or, for the relief of pain *and* inflammation, ibuprofen or aspirin if tolerated (see page 49).

What the doctor can do:

- Nonsurgical treatment is usually successful in treating this condition:
  RICE
  Anti-inflammatories
  Splinting
  Cortisone injections (never into the tendon itself, but into the surrounding sheath)
- For athletes whose tendons have become so thickened that nonsurgical treatment is insufficient, surgery may be necessary:
  The doctor performs a tendon release by cutting open the tendon sheath and giving the tendon within more room to move.
  If the tendons have become so irritated that calcium deposits have accumulated, the doctor may choose to trim off the deposits at the same time.
  After surgery, the wrist is immobilized in a cast for two weeks, following which rehabilitation for the wrist can begin.

Rehabilitation:

- When nonsurgical treatment is used, level two exercises for the wrist can begin within a week of initial treatment.
- After surgery, start level one exercises after the cast is removed (two weeks after the operation). For levels one, two, and three rehabilitation guidelines, refer to the sections on rehabilitation and conditioning at the end of this chapter.

Recovery time:

- When nonsurgical treatment is used to correct this condition, five days to two weeks of care is usually sufficient before athlete can return to action.
- After surgery, the athlete can usually expect to be back in action four weeks after the operation.

KIENBÖCK'S DISEASE *(Softening of the Lunate Bone)*

Kienböck's disease refers to a condition in which blood supply to the lunate bone in the wrist is disrupted, causing the bone to soften and eventually die. The lunate bone is located just forward of the wrist crease on the little finger side.

Symptoms:

- Onset of symptoms is gradual.
- Pain, stiffness, weakness, and loss of range of motion in the wrist and hand.
- Tenderness in the hand over the lunate bone, just forward of the wrist crease on the little finger side.

Cause:

- Repetitive microtrauma to the lunate bone.

What you can do:

- Use the RICE prescription (page 46).
- Seek medical attention.

Medication:

- For relief of minor to moderate pain, take acetaminophen as directed on label, or, for the relief of pain *and* inflammation, ibuprofen or aspirin if tolerated (see page 49).

What the doctor can do:

- Order X rays or a bone scan to confirm the diagnosis. Visible shrinkage of the bone is evidence of death of bone cells of the lunate.

- There is no standardized treatment for this condition. No one treatment has proven universally successful.
- Rest and immobilization in a cast for six weeks has in some cases worked, though surgery is the usual course of action.
- Surgical options:

    Usually, in severe cases of Kienböck's disease, the doctor removes the lunate and replaces it with a silicone implant. After surgery, the wrist is usually immobilized for six weeks, after which rehabilitation for the wrist can begin. A removable protective splint is worn during sports for three months after the operation.

Rehabilitation:

- After surgery, level one rehabilitation exercises for the hand, fingers, thumb, and forearm can begin within a week. Level one rehabilitation for the wrist itself can begin when the cast and stitches are removed, six weeks after surgery. For levels one, two, and three rehabilitation guidelines, refer to the sections on rehabilitation and conditioning at the end of this chapter.

Recovery time:

- The athlete can return to sports that stress the wrist when the strength and range of motion in the injured wrist are 95 percent of that on the opposite side, and earlier if the sport does not place great demands on the wrist joint.

Wrist Rehabilitation

Wrist rehabilitation involves range-of-motion and strengthening exercises to relieve inflammation and pain, restore full mobility to the joint, and develop overall strength and flexibility. Rehabilitation should begin as soon as possible, because joints respond poorly to immobilization and prolonged casting can lead to long-term dysfunction and loss of mobility.

After an injury that does not require surgery or lengthy splinting, range-of-motion exercises for the wrist can begin as soon as pain and swelling diminish—usually no later than forty-eight hours after the injury and often as early as twenty-four hours.

When surgery is necessary, range-of-motion exercises begin as early as five days after the operation. To accomplish this, the patient should be put in a sling or splint that can be removed for rehabilitation sessions. Even when wrist movement cannot be done, hand and finger as well as forearm exercises should be performed.

The starting intensity level of the rehabilitation program depends on the severity of the injury. Postsurgery range of motion usually begins at level one. At this level, range-of-motion exercises are "active assisted"—the physical therapist helps patients use their own strength to move the wrist through allowable ranges of motion. If the injury is too severe for active assisted exercises, the patient has to rely entirely on the physical therapist to move the wrist through allowable ranges of motion. This form of rehabilitation is known as "passive assisted" range of motion.

Whether active assisted or passive assisted exercises are used, it is absolutely crucial that patients with severe elbow injuries begin rehabilitation as soon as possible.

Athletes who have sustained only mild or moderately severe wrist injuries can begin with level two exercises.

In the initial stages of the rehabilitation program, the primary goal is to restore range of motion; the secondary goal is to prevent atrophy in the surrounding muscles. As the rehabilitation program progresses, more strengthening exercises are included in the program.

Range-of-motion and strength exercises should always be done within the pain threshold. Any exercise that causes pain in the wrist should be discontinued or curtailed.

The following are the most common exercises used to rehabilitate the wrist after injury.

Level one

After surgery or a severe injury, passive assisted, active assisted, or, preferably, active exercises (the patient does all the movement) are used as a starting point of rehabilitation.

Physical therapist–assisted range-of-motion therapy should continue only until patients are capable of using their own strength to do level two exercises.

Level two

When you are able to move your injured wrist yourself, level two exercises can begin. Level two exercises can also be used as a starting point for rehabilitating moderate to severe elbow injuries that do not require surgery. They primarily develop range of motion in the joint but also help prevent atrophy in the muscles of the forearm, hand, and fingers, and prevent adhesions from developing around the tendons.

For maximum benefit, keep your elbow tucked into your side while doing the exercises (that way, you avoid "cheating" by using your elbow to do the work, not your wrist).

The exercises promote the wrist's five ranges of motion: dorsiflexion, palmar flexion, ulnar deviation, radial deviation, and rotation, as well as finger strength and range of motion.

Exercise 1: wrist range of motion (dorsiflexion/palmar flexion)

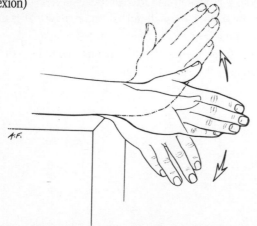

Place forearm on a table with wrist hanging off edge, palm down, fingers relaxed. Bend hand as far as possible downward, then upward.

Exercise 2: wrist range of motion (radial deviation/ulnar deviation)

Place forearm on table with wrist hanging off edge, palm facing in, fingers straight. Turn hand as far as possible downward, then upward.

Exercise 3: wrist range of motion (pronation/supination)

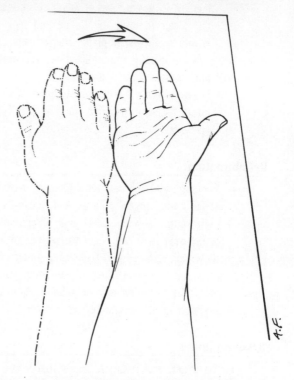

Sit with forearm flat on table, palm facing tabletop. Turn wrist so back of hand is against table.

Exercise 4: wrist range of motion (rotation)
Rotate wrist in circles one way, then the other.

Exercise 5: hand/finger range of motion and strength
Make a fist, then straighten fingers and spread them out.

Exercise 6: hand/finger range of motion and strength
Squeeze an elastic Ace bandage, Silly Putty, or other suitable object.

Exercise 7: hand/finger/thumb range of motion and strength

With thumb, touch tip of each of the other fingers on same hand and exert as much pressure as possible.

Exercise 8: hand and finger strength and range of motion

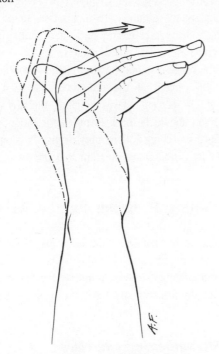

Touch top of palm with tips of fingers of same hand, then make a right angle with fingers.

Work your way up to being able to repeat these exercises fifteen to thirty times a day, and do these exercises at least three times a day (and as often as possible).

Level three

When you can do the level two exercises without difficulty or pain, level three exercises can begin.

Level three exercises can also be used as a starting point for rehabilitating mild wrist injuries.

Besides promoting range of motion in the wrist, level three exercises start strengthening the main muscles surrounding the wrist—the flexors and extensors in the forearm, and the muscles of the hand and fingers.

Exercises 1 and 2: wrist range of motion; forearm strength

Perform exercises 1 and 2 from level two, now using a small weight (anything from a can of tuna to a half-pound weight).

Exercise 3: wrist range of motion; forearm strength

Holding a towel out in front of you horizontally between hands, twist it forward and backward. Change grip so hands are one on top of each other, and the towel is vertical, and twist back and forward again.

Exercise 4: wrist range of motion; forearm strength

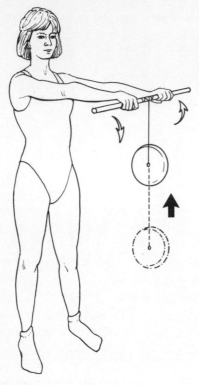

Tie light weight (maximum two pounds) to the end of a rope, and attach rope to cane or broomstick. Grasp shaft with palms down, then raise weight by bending wrists upward.

Lower weight by bending wrists downward. Repeat exercise, this time with palms up.

Exercise 5: hand/finger range of motion and strength
Repeatedly squeeze hand strengthener or deflated tennis ball.

Exercise 6: hand/finger/thumb range of motion and strength
Do exercise 5 of level two, now with elastic band wound around fingers.

Repeat these exercises at least three times a day, starting with ten repetitions and gradually building up to thirty. You should be able to do ten repetitions with ease and without pain before moving on to eleven, and so on.

When you can comfortably do fifteen repetitions three times a day using the starting weight, increase the weight by 10 percent but reduce the number of repetitions back to ten, then gradually build back to thirty.

Each time you can comfortably do thirty repetitions, increase the weight by 10 percent, reduce the number of repetitions to ten, and build back to thirty.

When the range of motion and strength of the injured wrist are about 50 percent of the uninjured side, you can start doing sports-specific training ((bouncing a tennis ball against the ground with your racket; miming a golf swing), then start easing back into sports (play doubles; golf nine holes, not thirty-six).

When the range of motion and strength of the injured wrist are 95 percent of the uninjured side (and, by association, 95 percent of its original mobility and strength), you should be back to full participation.

To reduce the chance of reinjury, begin the strength and flexibility conditioning program that follows.

Conditioning Program for the Wrist

Conditioning to prevent wrist injuries requires that you improve the strength and flexibility of all the major muscles surrounding the joint, primarily the flexors and extensors of the forearm and the muscles of the hands and fingers.

Wrist Strengthening Exercises

Incorporate into your workout regimen at least one set of the following exercises for each muscle group listed. The exercises are found in chapter 3, "Strength and Flexibility: The Key to Injury Prevention."

Make these exercises part of an overall strength and flexibility program, and do them before any activity that will stress the muscles around the wrist.

Forearm extensors: Wrist curl, wrist roll
Forearm flexors: Reverse wrist curl, wrist roll

CHAPTER SIXTEEN

Hand and Finger Injuries

Hands and fingers are the body parts most commonly damaged in competitive team sports, and the site of a significant portion of the accident-related injuries in recreational sports. Injuries to the hands and fingers are especially prevalent in recreational sports with a potential for falling accidents, such as skiing, biking, in-line skating, and gymnastics.

Overuse injuries of the hand and finger are rare. Repetitive stress in the hands and fingers usually transmits upwards, resulting in overuse conditions in the wrist and forearms, not the hands and fingers themselves.

Efficient hand and finger function is crucial to daily living. A minor injury to one of our fingers—or, worse, a thumb—reminds us how important each of our digits is. Unfortunately, the diagnosis, treatment, and rehabilitation of hand and finger injuries is a very complex field, and it is troubling that so many athletes with such injuries are treated by someone with little knowledge of the area. Return to full function after a hand or finger injury is extremely important. Injuries to the hand and fingers, then, should be diagnosed, treated, and rehabilitated by experts in the highly specialized field of hand orthopedics.

Injuries of the Hand and Fingers

Acute hand and finger injuries include fractures, dislocations, and sprains. They can result from a fall, direct impact to the hand and fingers, or from a twisting or bending motion.

Acute hand and finger injuries are very common in contact sports such as football, lacrosse, and hockey, usually as a result of the athlete's falling to the ground, getting hit on the hand or the fingers by an opponent or an opponent's equipment, colliding with an opponent or their equipment, or twisting a finger in a tackle. Acute hand and finger injuries are also seen in sports with a potential for falling accidents.

Overuse injuries of the hand and finger are limited almost exclusively to inflammation of the flexor tendon in the finger, known as flexor tendinitis.

Hand and Finger Injury Prevention

Acute hand and finger injuries are usually caused by freak accidents and thus quite difficult to prevent. There are, however, several preventive steps athletes can take. The most important of these is to wear appropriate protective equipment. Padded gloves that lessen impact in falling accidents are especially important.

In both downhill and cross-country skiing, preventing the most common hand and finger injury—ruptures of the ulnar collateral ligament at the base of the thumb—may be a matter of *not* using a particular piece of equipment, namely, the strap on the ski pole. In a backward fall, ski pole straps have the tendency to force the thumb into a position that predisposes it to this serious injury. Skiers should use poles without straps or avoid using the pole straps.

In tackling sports, proper tackling techniques need to

HAND AND FINGER ANATOMY

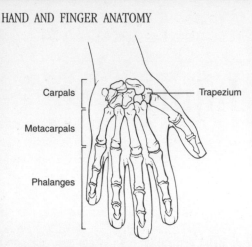

Carpals

Metacarpals

Phalanges

Trapezium

Bones and joints: Attached to the wrist bones are five strong bones called the *metacarpals*. Four of these bones form the palm and extend onward to form the four finger bones. Each of the fingers is a separate unit made up of three shorter and stronger bones. The fifth metacarpal, the shortest and strongest of all, splits off the wrist to form the first bone in the thumb.

Compared to the ligaments and joint capsules in the rest of our body, those that hold the joints of our hands and fingers together are quite loose to give the structure the flexibility it needs.

Muscles, tendons, and nerves: The forearm muscles provide for powerful wrist, hand, and finger movement. Forearm muscle power reaches the hand and fingers through a series of muscle-tendons that pass both over and under the wrist, then split off and join the fingers.

In the hand and fingers themselves there are twenty-seven muscles, eight in the thumb alone. The large number of muscles in such a small area explains the versatility of this structure.

To operate the muscles in the hand and fingers, messages are sent to them from the brain. These messages are transmitted through nerves, primarily the *median, radial,* and *ulnar.* To help the fingers perform intricate functions, these highly sensitive nerves also send information back to the brain concerning sensation and touch.

be learned. Athletes should not try to grasp their opponents' shirts with their fingers, as this can quite easily cause a sprain. Instead they should learn to wrap their arms around their opponents' legs to immobilize them.

Finally, athletes with preexisting finger conditions should tape their injured finger to the one next to it to provide stability and avoid aggravating the condition.

Acute Injuries of the Hand and Fingers

BENNETT'S FRACTURE; BOXER'S FRACTURE (Metacarpal Fractures)

A fracture is a crack, break, or complete shattering of a bone. The most common metacarpal fracture—a Bennett's fracture—occurs at the base of the thumb and often causes damage to the joint surface at this site. The second most common of these fractures affects the metacarpal on the side of the little finger and is known as a Boxer's fracture, because it is often caused by punching.

Symptoms:

- Bennett's fracture: extreme pain when trying to move the thumb; swelling and discoloration at the base of the thumb.
- Boxer's fracture: deformity of the fifth knuckle. The athlete may be unable to make a fist.

Causes:

- Bennett's fracture: forceful backward bending of the thumb that causes a portion of the bone to be torn off.
- Boxer's fracture: violent impact to the fifth knuckle of the fist, forcible backward bending of the little finger, or impact to the end of the little finger that transmits to the metacarpal shaft.

Athletes at risk:

- Boxers, contact sport athletes, and those engaged in sports with the potential for impact to the hand and fingers from a ball—basketball, volleyball, baseball, and softball. Metacarpal injuries are also frequently seen in athletes engaged in sports with the potential for falling accidents, such as skiing, in-line skating, biking, and gymnastics.

Concerns:

- Inadequate or improper treatment of Bennett's fracture can result in long-term loss of strength and mobility in the thumb.

What you can do:

- Immobilize the hand and fingers.
- Secure the hand to the body with an arm sling.
- Seek medical attention.
- Gently apply ice over the injury for twenty to thirty minutes at a time until medical attention arrives.

What the doctor can do:

- Order careful X rays to determine extent and severity of the fracture.
- Realign the ends of the broken bones.
- Keep the ends of the bones in place using a splint as part of a short-arm cast.
- When conservative treatment is used, immobilization of the finger/thumb for three to four weeks is usually adequate.
- Surgical realignment of the thumb metacarpal is often necessary because damage is done to the joint surface where the thumb metacarpal meets the wrist. Usually, the dislodged joint surface has to be pinned back in place in order to achieve good realignment. The thumb is immobilized for six weeks after surgery.

Recovery time:

- When conservative treatment is used to address a fractured metacarpal, the athlete can generally return to contact sports six to eight weeks after the injury occurs, and sooner when the sport does not involve stress to the hand.

- After surgery, three to six weeks of healing and rehabilitation before the athlete can return to sports that place stress on the fingers.

THUMB SPRAIN *(Tear of the Ulnar Collateral Ligament; Skier's Thumb, Gamekeeper's Thumb)*

A sprain is a stretch, tear, or complete rupture of a ligament. Most thumb sprains involve the ulnar collateral ligaments, the ligaments that connect the metacarpal bone to the first thumb bone. Frequently, the ligament is completely ruptured, and the detached end of the ligament rips off a portion of bone from the joint. This is known as an avulsion fracture. Ironically, when a piece of bone is torn off, it is easier to restore this important structure surgically to its original state.

A rupture of the ulnar collateral ligament is known colloquially as skier's thumb because it is seen so frequently in downhill skiers (in a fall, ski pole straps have the tendency to force the thumb backward). In fact, about one in ten of all skiing injuries seen by doctors is a rupture of the ulnar collateral ligament.

Symptoms:

- Pain and localized tenderness in the joint between the first thumb bone and the metacarpal.
- Bruising and swelling around the joint.
- If the rupture is complete, the first thumb bone will move freely against the metacarpal bone.

Cause:

- A fall that forces the thumb backward and away from the index finger.

Athletes at risk:

- Skiers especially, but also anyone who engages in an activity with a potential for falling accidents—in-line skaters, bikers, and gymnasts.

Concerns:

- Unless treated properly, a thumb sprain can involve long-term instability and/or dysfunction in this important digit.

What you can do:

- If pain and loss of mobility are severe, immobilize the thumb and seek medical attention.
- Gently apply ice over the injury for twenty to thirty minutes until medical attention is available.

Medication:

- For relief of minor to moderate pain, take acetaminophen as directed on label, or, for the relief of pain *and* inflammation, ibuprofen or aspirin if tolerated (see page 49).

What the doctor can do:

- First- and second-degree ulnar collateral sprains are treated by immobilizing the thumb in an aluminum splint for three weeks, after which time specialized therapy begins.
- Third-degree sprains—complete ruptures of the ligament—are usually treated surgically. If the ligament has ruptured into two pieces, it is sewn back together. If the ligament has not torn in two but has "ruptured" by tearing off a piece of bone where it attached to the joint—an avulsion fracture—the detached portion of bone is pinned back in place. After surgery, the thumb is immobilized in an aluminum splint for three weeks.

Recovery time:

- First- and second-degree sprains: six to eight weeks.
- After a surgical ligament repair, it will be eight to twelve weeks before the athlete can return to sports. For the first six weeks after returning to sports, the athlete should wear a protective thumb splint.

MALLET FINGER (*Rupture of the Long Extensor Tendon of the Finger; Jersey Finger, Tendon Avulsion Injury*)

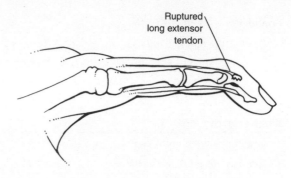

Ruptured long extensor tendon

A "mallet finger" describes a condition in which a tendon that extends to the end of one of the fingers rips completely away. Often a small portion of bone comes off, too, making it a tendon avulsion injury.

Symptoms:

- Pain at the last finger joint.
- Inability to straighten the finger. The tip of the injured finger will be permanently bent.

Cause:

- Forceful impact to the end of the finger that causes it to be driven back toward the hand.

Athletes at risk:

- Those who engage in sports in which they might be hit on the tip of the finger by a ball—football, basketball, baseball, softball, water polo, and volleyball players.

Concerns:

- If untreated, a mallet finger can become permanently dysfunctional, painful, and deformed. A mismanaged tendon avulsion can cause arthritis in later life.

What you can do:

- If pain and loss of mobility are severe, immobilize the finger and seek medical attention.
- Gently apply ice over the injury for twenty minutes at a time until medical attention is available.

What the doctor can do:

- Immobilize the finger in a plastic splint that keeps the finger in a fully straightened position. The splint should be worn for six to eight weeks.
- If a portion of the bone has been torn off (a tendon avulsion injury), surgery is necessary to pin the piece of detached bone back in place.

Recovery time:

- Six to twelve weeks of rest and rehabilitation is needed before the athlete can return to sports that put the finger at risk. To minimize the risk of reinjury, athletes should tape the injured finger to the adjoining ("buddy tape") as long as there is pain.

FINGER SPRAIN/DISLOCATION (Jammed Finger)

A finger sprain is a stretch or tear of the ligaments holding the finger bones together. Finger sprains are classified according to severity. First-degree sprains generally involve tearing of up to 25 percent of the ligaments; second-degree sprains damage between 25 and 75 percent of the fibers; third-degree sprains are complete ruptures of the ligaments. In third-degree sprains, the ruptured ligament sometimes tears off a portion of bone from the joint (an avulsion fracture).

Symptoms:

- Pain and swelling in the immediate area of the sprain.
- Loss of mobility.
- Significant instability when the ligaments are completely ruptured.

Causes:

- Forceful bending of a finger joint beyond its normal range of motion.
- A direct blow to the end of the finger.

Athletes at risk:

- Athletes in contact sports and in sports where they might be hit on the tip of the finger by a ball—football, basketball, baseball, softball, water polo, and volleyball. Finger sprains are also common in activities with the potential for falling accidents—skiing, in-line skating, and biking.

Concerns:

- If severe finger sprains do not receive adequate treatment, the consequences may be long-term loss of function and instability. In such circumstances, a complex surgical procedure is needed to correct the condition.

What you can do:

- If pain and loss of mobility are severe, immobilize the finger and seek medical attention.
- Apply ice for twenty to thirty minutes at a time until medical attention is available.

What the doctor can do:

- In the case of mild, moderate, or even severe sprains, treatment may consist of immobilization of the finger in a splint for one or two weeks to allow healing. After this, the injured finger will be "buddy taped" to the finger next to it until full strength and range of motion are regained through rehabilitation.
- If the injury is an avulsion fracture, surgery may be necessary to pin the detached portion of bone back in place. After surgery, the finger is immobilized in a splint for three weeks, at which time the pin is removed and rehabilitation exercises can start. A protective splint is worn for a further three weeks.

Recovery time:

- A sprained finger may take up to six weeks to heal. If the finger has dislocated, other tissues will likely be damaged, and twelve weeks of rest and rehabilitation may be necessary before the athlete can return to sports requiring strenuous use of the fingers.
- After surgery, at least twelve weeks.

FINGER DISLOCATIONS

In finger dislocations, a finger bone is forced out of position at the joint. When a finger dislocates, there is always significant disruption in the ligaments of the joint.

Symptoms:

- Pain, tenderness, and loss of mobility in the finger.
- Deformity in the joint.
- A popping sensation when the injury occurs.

Causes:

- Forceful bending of a finger joint beyond its normal range of motion.
- A direct blow to the end of the finger.

Athletes at risk:

- Athletes in contact sports and in sports where they might be hit on the tip of the finger by a ball—football, basketball, baseball, softball, water polo, and volleyball. Finger sprains are also common in activities with the potential for falling accidents—skiing, in-line skating, and biking.

What you can do:

- Immobilize the finger in the injured position.
- *Do not* try to realign the finger, as the finger may be fractured, and moving it can cause further displacement of the fracture.
- Seek medical attention.
- Ice the area for twenty to thirty minutes at a time until medical attention is available.

What the doctor should do:

- Order X rays to rule out a possible fracture.
- Realign the joint, then take further X rays to ensure the bone is properly realigned.
- Splint the joint for three weeks in the same way a sprain is immobilized.

Recovery time:

- The athlete can return to noncontact sports in six to eight weeks, and to sports with the potential for collisions with opponents and/or equipment in eight to twelve weeks.

Overuse Injuries of the Hand and Fingers

TENDINITIS OF THE FINGER AND HAND
(Flexor Tendinitis)

Flexor tendinitis is an inflammation of the tendons that run from the forearm across the wrist and the hand to the fingers. These tendons flex the fingers toward the palm. Irritation of these tendons through overuse causes them to swell in their narrow sheaths, which produces the symptoms of tendinitis.

Symptoms:

- Onset of symptoms is gradual.
- Pain, soreness, swelling, and stiffness in the index and/or long finger/s.
- Pain along the length of the tendon from the palm to the finger.
- Difficulty touching the palm with the finger.
- In severe cases, difficulty straightening the finger.

Cause:

- Repetitive, powerful bending of the hand and fingers toward the palm.

Athletes at risk:

- Those who repetitively and forcefully bend their

fingers—baseball pitchers, hockey and racket sports players, and golfers.

Concerns:

- If mismanaged, flexor tendinitis can cause chronic stiffness that requires long-term rehabilition to correct.

What you can do:

- In the early stages, rest and ice.

Medication:

- For relief of minor to moderate pain, take acetaminophen as directed on label, or, for the relief of pain *and* inflammation, ibuprofen or aspirin if tolerated (see page 49).

What the doctor can do:

- If rest and ice are not successful, immobilize the finger in a splint for three to five days and prescribe anti-inflammatories.
- If the inflammation does not respond to this treatment, inject cortisone into the area.
- Usually, conservative treatment is sufficient to resolve this condition.

Recovery time:

- In mild cases, when the tendinitis is caught early, three to five days.
- If allowed to deteriorate, it may take anywhere from a week to a month for this condition to clear up.

Hand and Finger Rehabilition

Rehabilitation exercises serve to

- promote blood flow to the area, which speeds the healing process

- relieve stiffness in the joint caused by immobilization

- prevent atrophy and tightening of the muscles resulting from inactivity.*

Because the hand and fingers are highly complex, diagnosis, treatment, *and* rehabilitation should be done by an expert in the field. As with the wrist, most hand surgeons work with physical therapists who are themselves specialists in rehabilitating this part of the human anatomy.

After an injury that does not require surgery or lengthy immobilization, range-of-motion exercises for the hand and fingers can begin as soon as pain and swelling diminish—usually no later than forty-eight hours after the injury occurs and often as early as twenty-four hours.

When surgery is necessary, range-of-motion exercises can begin as early as five days after the operation, and certainly no more than two or three weeks later. To accomplish this, the patient should be put in a splint that can be removed for rehabilitation sessions.

The starting intensity level of the rehabilitation exercises depends on the severity of the injury. Postsurgery range-of-motion exercises usually begin at level one. At this level, range-of-motion exercises are "active assisted"—the physical therapist helps patients use their own strength to move the hand or fingers through allowable ranges of motion. If the injury is too severe for active assisted exercises, the patient may have to rely on "passive assisted" exercises—the physical therapist moves the injured hand or fingers through allowable ranges of motion.

After passive assisted or active assisted exercises, athletes who have had surgery for a hand or finger injury can usually progress to gentle range-of-motion exercises using their own strength. The primary goal at this stage is to restore range of motion to the injured joint; the

* For more on the importance and general principles of rehabilitation, see chapter 5, "Rehabilitating Your Sports Injury."

secondary goal is to prevent atrophy in the surrounding muscles. As the rehabilitation program progresses, more strengthening exercises are included in the program.

Range-of-motion exercises should always be done within the pain threshold. Any exercise that causes pain should be discontinued.

Because the hand and fingers are so complex, injuries to them are extremely difficult both to treat and to rehabilitate. An entire subspecialty has developed in orthopedics to treat injuries to the hand and fingers, and most hand surgeons work with physical therapists who are themselves specialists in the field. Their work is highly specialized and technical, so specific hand and finger injury prescriptions are not given here.

Hand and Finger Conditioning

Conditioning to prevent hand and finger injuries involves improving the strength and flexibility of all the major muscles surrounding the joint, primarily the flexors and extensors of the forearm. Refer to the conditioning section at the end of the chapter on "Wrist Injuries" for those exercises.

CHAPTER SEVENTEEN

Head and Neck (Cervical Spine) Injuries

Head and neck (cervical spine) injuries can be among the most serious in sports, because they involve the brain, spinal cord, or surrounding nerves, which are responsible for thought, movement, and sensation. Severe injuries to the head and/or neck can cause death or permanent disability.

Adult recreational athletes can take some comfort in the knowledge that serious head and neck injuries are rare in their sports. However, injuries to these areas are seen in those who participate in the so-called adventure sports, such as mountain climbing and skydiving, whose popularity is on the rise.

SPORTS MOST LIKELY TO CAUSE SERIOUS HEAD AND SPINE INJURY

Maximal Risk	High Risk
Automobile/motorbike racing	Gymnastics
Diving	Horseback riding
Football	Mountain climbing
Hang gliding	Parachuting
	Ski jumping
	Skydiving
	Snowmobiling
	Trampolining

There will be little self-treatment possible in the event of a serious head and/or neck injury. But for the sake of others, and so others will be able to help them if they suffer such an injury, all Americans should know how to act in such situations.

Head Injuries

Knowing how to recognize head injuries is important, because a seemingly benign injury can quickly deteriorate into a life-threatening situation. Multiple minor head injuries can lead to permanent brain damage, sometimes known as the "punch drunk" syndrome.

It should always be assumed that a head injury accompanied with loss of consciousness also involves a neck injury.

Neck Injuries

Being alert to the possibility of a neck injury is extremely important. The consequences of an untreated or improperly handled neck injury can be devastating.

When a neck injury is suspected, DO NOT MOVE THE INJURED PERSON. Because neck injuries are usually caused by impact involving the head, there is usually an associated head injury. Therefore, it should always be assumed that the athlete needs to be treated for both a head and cervical spine injury until one or both have been ruled out.

Injuries of the Head and Neck

Acute injuries of the neck include sprains, fractures, contusions, and strains. Any of these can result in serious injury to the spinal cord.

A *sprain* is when any of the spinal ligaments is stretched or torn. The stability of the neck is affected, and a sprain may allow the vertebrae to shift on top of each other and possibly pinch or injure a nerve or the spinal cord.

A *fracture* of one or more vertebrae can pinch a nerve or injure the spinal cord.

A *contusion*, or bruise, to the bone, muscle, or spinal tissue can cause bleeding and swelling, which in turn can constrict or pinch the spinal cord or branch nerves.

A *strain* is when the muscles or tendons in the neck are stretched or torn, which can affect the stability of the neck.

As a result of a fall, a direct blow, or twisting motion, the neck can be injured in a variety of ways, including compression, flexion, hyperextension, flexion/rotation, hyperextension/rotation, and lateral flexion.

Irrespective of the type, mechanism, and site of a neck injury, and because it is very difficult to differentiate between a sprain, fracture, contusion, and strain, management of the injury should be the same. Always suspect a serious head and/or neck injury in an unconscious athlete. Never move the athlete unless the athlete is in danger of further injury.

If an athlete complains of pain anywhere along the neck after impact to the head or neck, he or she should seek immediate medical attention.

Acute injuries of the head involve injuries to the brain tissue or skull. Four types of injuries fit this definition: concussions, contusions (bruises), hemorrhages and hematomas, and fractures.

A *concussion* is a temporary malfunction of the brain that involves actual brain damage.

A *contusion*, or bruise, involves bleeding and possible swelling of the brain tissues.

A *hemorrhage* or *hematoma* is bleeding or pooling

HEAD AND NECK ANATOMY

Bones and joints: The skull and the seven vertebrae of the neck, or cervical spine, are the major bones in the head and neck area.

The neck is made up of seven vertebrae connected by joints and ligaments. Between each vertebrae is a disc that acts as a shock absorber and increases flexibility. The structure of the neck allows for independent movement of the head as well as movement of the head with the neck.

Muscles and nerves: The spinal cord is the thick trunk of nerves that runs from the brain, down the neck, and to the tailbone. This vital component of the central nervous system sends electrical signals from the brain to the various tissues to make them function. Digestion, breathing and heart rates, muscle contractions, and most other body functions depend on signals from the brain that are sent using the spinal cord and its many branches. The brain also receives feedback from the rest of the body through the nerves. As in the rest of the spine, the spinal cord is protected in the neck area because it runs through a passageway within the vertebrae.

The head and neck are moved by the muscles in the upper back and neck. The role of the muscles in the head and neck area is twofold: their "static" function, to hold the head and neck up when the body is upright, and an "active" function, head and neck movement.

of blood between the tissue layers covering the brain or inside the brain.

A *fracture* is a crack or break in the skull.

Nearly all head and neck injuries are caused by direct impact. The impact may cause either a skull injury at the point of contact or a brain injury on the side opposite to where the blow occurred. Head injuries may also occur when the head is shaken vigorously, as in a whiplash injury.

Though acute head and neck injuries are rare in recreational sports, they do occur in contact sports such as football, ice hockey, lacrosse, and rugby. They are also seen in sports with a potential for falling accidents, such as biking, skiing, in-line skating, and gymnastics.

For both head and neck injuries, the response should be virtually identical. Except in the case of an athlete with a head injury who is conscious, athletes with head injuries who are unconscious and all athletes with neck injuries require EMERGENCY MEDICAL ATTENTION.

Overuse injuries of the head and neck are uncommon.

Head and Neck Injury Prevention

Acute head and neck injuries can be prevented by developing strength and flexibility in the neck, adopting an appropriate state of readiness when contact is anticipated (known as "bulling" the neck), learning proper technique for the sport, and using appropriate protective equipment. These comprehensive preventive measures are especially important for athletes engaged in full-contact, or "collision" sports such as football, hockey, and rugby, where violent impact is part of the sport.

For recreational athletes, it is usually sufficient to pay attention to the last two components of the head and neck injury prevention guidelines: learning proper technique for the sport and using appropriate equipment. It is especially important to learn proper technique in sports with a potential for falling accidents, which may range from mountain climbing to downhill skiing and biking.

Acute Injuries of the Head and Neck

When faced with a serious head or neck injury, do not spend time trying to ascertain the cause or type of injury. All are caused by similar events and have similar symptoms and signs. The key to managing a serious head or neck injury is to minimize the immediate damage and call for qualified assistance.

HEAD INJURIES: *Concussion, Contusion, Hemorrhage/Hematoma, Fracture*

A concussion *is a temporary malfunction of the brain that involves actual brain damage.*

A contusion, *or bruise, involves bleeding and possible swelling of the brain tissues.*

A hemorrhage *or hematoma is bleeding or pooling of blood between the tissue layers covering the brain or inside the brain.*

A fracture *is a crack or break in the skull.*

Symptoms:

- A conscious athlete with a head injury may complain of
  Dizziness
  Ringing in the ears
  Headache
  Nausea
  Blurred vision
  More severe symptoms: extended memory loss, slurred speech, seizures, breathing irregularity. These indicate the need for immediate notification of emergency medical personnel.
- In addition, the athlete with a head injury may exhibit the following symptoms:
  Blood or clear fluid draining from the nose, mouth, or ears
  A bump or deformity at the point of impact
  Bleeding or a wound at the point of impact
  Unequal pupil size or inappropriate response to light (they may not constrict when exposed to light)
  Confusion, disorientation
  Convulsions, seizures
  Slurred speech

Breathing or pulse irregularities

Memory loss—determine by asking questions such as the following: "What is your phone number?" "How did you get here?" "What day is it?"

The eyes do not track a moving object— such as the finger—as a unit; one eye is slower than the other.

- When the athlete is unconscious, he or she may exhibit

  Irregular breathing or respiratory arrest

  Leaking blood or clear fluid from the mouth, nose, or ears

  Pulse irregularities

  Pupils unequal in response or unresponsive to light

Causes:

- All the above injuries are caused by impact to the head, from a fall, a blow, or forceful shaking of the head in a whiplash motion.

Athletes at risk:

- Serious head and neck injuries are most often seen in athletes in contact sports and in sports with a potential for falling accidents.

Concerns:

- Any significant head injury has a potential for death or permanent disability.

What to do:

- DO NOT:

  Remove an athlete's head protection until a spine injury has been ruled out.

  Try to revive the athlete or clear an athlete's head by using smelling salts or ammonia, as the strong smell may cause the athlete to jerk his or her head.

- When the athlete is conscious:

  Send for medical assistance.

  Move the athlete out of harm's way.

  If qualified, monitor the ABCs (airway, breathing, and circulation), provide rescue breathing or CPR as necessary, and treat for shock.

- When the athlete is unconscious:

Send for emergency medical assistance.

Stabilize the athlete's head and neck.

If qualified, monitor the ABCs (airway, breathing, and circulation), provide rescue breathing or CPR as necessary, treat for shock, control any heavy bleeding, and immobilize any fractures or unstable injuries.

NECK INJURIES: *Strains, Fractures, Contusions, and Sprains*

A fracture of a vertebrae can pinch a nerve or injure the spinal cord.

A contusion, or bruise, to the bone, muscle, or spinal tissue can cause bleeding and swelling, which in turn can constrict or pinch the spinal cord or branch nerves.

A strain is when the muscles or tendons in the neck are stretched or torn, which can affect the stability of the neck.

Symptoms:

- Numbness or tingling in the toes, feet, fingers, or hands. (This can safely be checked by asking the athlete to name the finger or toe being touched.)
- Inability to move the fingers or toes.
- Dramatically different hand grip strength. Ask the athlete to perform a comparative grip test.
- Muscle spasms near the spine.
- Possible breathing difficulties.

Cause:

- All the above injuries are caused by impact to the head or neck, from a fall, a blow, or forceful whiplash motion.

What to do:

- Send for emergency medical assistance.
- If qualified, provide rescue breathing or CPR to an unconscious athlete, *using "jaw thrust" method only*.
- Immobilize the athlete's head and spine.
- Treat for any heavy bleeding.
- Monitor the pulse and heart rate.
- Stabilize any other fractures, dislocations, sprains, or strains.

RECOGNIZING DIFFERENT
CATEGORIES OF CONCUSSIONS

A concussion is a disturbance in consciousness, usually caused by a blow to the head that "shakes up" the brain inside the skull cavity. Concussions are one of the most common sports injuries, especially among younger athletes engaged in contact sports.

Because even minor concussions can have serious consequences, it is important to know how to recognize the varying degrees of severity of concussions (and what to do in different situations).

Concussions are generally classified as mild, moderate, and severe, depending on the symptoms:

Mild
- No loss of consciousness
- Slight confusion
- Momentary memory loss with full memory return
- Mild headache
- Mild dizziness but no unsteadiness
- Tinnitus (ringing in the ears)
- All symptoms clear in one minute

Moderate
- Second mild concussion at same event
- Recurrent mild concussions within seven days
- Loss of or disturbance in consciousness less than two minutes in duration
- Loss of memory (amnesia) less than thirty minutes in duration
- Moderate headache
- Tinnitus
- Dizziness with minimal unsteadiness
- Visual disturbances (blurred or double vision)
- Hallucinations

- Nausea
- Most symptoms clear up in five minutes (mild headache, amnesia, tinnitus, or dizziness may remain longer)

Severe
- Loss of or disturbance in consciousness more than two minutes in duration
- Amnesia more than thirty minutes in duration
- Severe headache, nausea, tinnitus, dizziness, or hallucinations
- Marked unsteadiness
- Vomiting
- Any symptoms recur or suddenly worsen with passage of time

Other life-threatening brain injuries are depressed skull fracture, brain bruise, and bleeding within the skull. These events are usually accompanied by a mild to moderate concussion, followed by an apparently normal, lucid period. The injured person then experiences a rapid deterioration in condition. ANY SUDDEN CHANGE IN CONDITION OR INDICATION OF PARALYSIS, PHYSICAL WEAKNESS, OR MARKED MENTAL CONFUSION IS AN EXTREME MEDICAL EMERGENCY. A skull fracture may cause blood or fluids to flow from the ears, nose, or mouth. THIS IS ALSO AN EMERGENCY SITUATION.

Any degree of concussion should result in medical evaluation. Brain injury may not be apparent until hours after the trauma occurs. The athlete may have to be observed closely throughout the night and be awakened about every one to two hours to check the level of consciousness and orientation.

Nonemergency Head and Neck Injuries

CERVICAL NERVE STRETCH SYNDROME
("Burner"/"Stinger")

When the head is hit and forcefully bent sideways, a nerve in the neck can be pinched near the bones, muscles, or other neck tissues.

Symptoms:

- Numbness, tingling, or burning in the neck, shoulder, or arm.
- Stinging or shocking sensation in the back of the neck and shoulder.
- Slight weakness and/or loss of sensation in the arm or hand on the injured side.

Cause:

- Impact that forces the head sideways and downward.

Athletes at risk:

- Burners and stingers are most often seen in athletes in contact sports, especially football and wrestling.

Concerns:

- Scar tissue that builds up as a result of recurrent injuries of this kind creates scar tissue buildup that makes the nerves less pliable, and therefore creates a vicious cycle in which the nerves become more susceptible to being pinched. Permanent nerve damage can result from recurrent burners and stingers.

What you can do:

- If sensation and strength do not return within five minutes, or the injury becomes recurrent, seek medical attention.

What the doctor can do:

- Rule out nerve damage; then, if the athlete intends to subject himself to the same forces that caused the condition, recommend a protective device to prevent recurrence of the condition (for example, padding between the head and shoulder that prevents sideways bending).

Rehabilitation:

- Rehabilitation is unnecessary. However, the athlete should focus on strengthening the muscles around the neck to help prevent the injury's recurrence.

Recovery time:

- Symptoms are usually only momentary. If they persist longer than five minutes, seek medical attention.

NECK SPRAIN *("Whiplash")*

A neck sprain, commonly referred to as whiplash, is a condition in which the ligaments that link the vertebrae are stretched or torn.

Symptoms:

- Immediate pain on one side of the neck.
- Pain usually diminishes within thirty minutes, after which time a dull ache develops, worsening into a sharp pain.
- Spasm in the neck muscles.
- Limitation of head movement.
- For comfort's sake, the athlete may hold the head in an unusual position.

Cause:

- A single violent impact that forces the neck into an extreme position.

Athletes at risk:

- Neck sprains are most common in athletes in contact sports and activities with a potential for falling accidents.

What you can do:

- Apply RICE (page 46), and seek medical attention.

Medication:

- For relief of minor to moderate pain, take acetaminophen as directed on label, or, for the relief of pain *and* inflammation, ibuprofen or aspirin if tolerated (see page 49).

What the doctor can do:

- Take X rays to rule out a fracture, dislocation, or disc injury.
- Perform a neurological examination to rule out a spinal cord or nerve root injury.
- Prescribe a soft collar to reduce muscle spasm.
- Prescribe icing for forty-eight to seventy-two hours.
- For severe injuries, recommend bedrest for two to three days, in combination with analgesics and anti-inflammatories.

Rehabilitation:

- Range-of-motion exercises should start as soon as possible and, ideally, as soon as pain diminishes, usually within forty-eight to seventy-two hours.
- Ten days to two weeks may be necessary before conditioning can begin.
- After a return of 95 percent of strength and flexibility in the neck, athletes can return to sports.
- For levels one, two, and three rehabilitation guidelines, refer to the section at the end of this chapter.

Recovery time:

- Depending on their severity, neck sprains may take anywhere from a few days to several months to recover fully.

ACUTE TORTICOLLIS *(Wryneck)*

One of the most common medical conditions suffered by athletes; a stiffness in the neck commonly referred to as wryneck.

Symptoms:

- Vicelike pain in the neck, usually just on one side.
- Head movement is limited.
- The neck muscles are tender and tense.

Cause:

- Holding the neck in an unusual position for a prolonged period, or exposure to a cold draft.

Athletes at risk:

- Any athlete can develop this condition.

Concerns:

- Wryneck may be a symptom of a more serious underlying problem, such as disc degeneration.

What you can do:

- Use a moist heating pad.
- Wear a soft neck collar.
- If there is no improvement after one week, seek medical attention.

Medication:

- For relief of minor to moderate pain, take acetaminophen as directed on label, or, for the relief of pain *and* inflammation, ibuprofen or aspirin if tolerated (see page 49).

What the doctor can do:

- Order X rays to rule out nerve damage.
- Prescribe moist heat, a soft collar, and traction.

Rehabilitation:

- It is important to begin early range-of-motion exercises to restore mobility to the neck.
- For levels one, two, and three rehabilitation

282 • HEAD AND NECK (CERVICAL SPINE) INJURIES

guidelines, refer to the section at the end of this chapter.

Recovery time:

- Wryneck may take anywhere from two days to several months to clear up.

ACUTE CERVICAL DISC DISEASE *("Slipped Disc")*

Commonly known as a slipped disc, this condition actually occurs when one of the discs that lies between the vertebrae in the neck breaks up, and the fragments impinge on the nerves in the area.

Symptoms:

- Neck and arm pain, though the arm pain is almost always on only one side.
- Degree of pain depends on the extent of the nerve impingement. Pain may be mild, moderate, or severe.
- Arm movement is affected. Arm reflexes slow down, and sensation in the arm may also be compromised. Pins and needles in the affected arm.

Causes:

- A degenerative condition, slipped discs develop in older people as their discs dry up and get more brittle. This makes them more susceptible to the wear and tear associated with sports, as well as daily activity.
- Although fragmentation takes place over several years, a sudden incident may cause a fragment to dislodge, pinch the nerve, and cause pain.

Athletes at risk:

- Any athlete may suffer from disc degeneration, but this condition is especially common among those who have at one time or another participated in contact sports.

Concerns:

- If the fragment of disc compresses the root of

the nerve for long enough, permanent arm weakness may result.

What you can do:

- Use a heating pad to reduce muscle spasm.
- Seek medical attention.

Medication:

- For relief of minor to moderate pain, take acetaminophen as directed on label, or, for the relief of pain *and* inflammation, ibuprofen or aspirin if tolerated (see page 49).

What the doctor can do:

- Perform a physical examination to confirm disc degeneration and associated nerve impingement, testing arm reflexes, arm muscle strength, and skin sensation in the arm.
- Order X rays to further confirm the diagnosis, and rule out other problems such as an infection or tumor.
- Treatment for cervical disc disease is usually nonsurgical:
  A soft collar to splint the neck
  A strong narcotic drug and muscle relaxant such as Valium
  A heating pad
  Cervical traction, which separates the vertebrae, thus relieving the pressure of the disc fragments on the nerve. Traction is done twice a day for two weeks.
- If after six weeks aggressive nonsurgical treatment is unsuccessful (a rare occurrence), then surgery may be done:
  Remove the disc fragment surgically, followed by hospitalization for two or three days.
  After surgery, the patient wears a soft collar for up to three months.

Rehabilitation:

- As soon as the neck is pain free, level one rehabilitation exercises can begin. Restoration of range of movement is the priority in the initial stages.

- Once normal range of movement is restored, the patient can start level two exercises.
- When full range of motion and moderate strength have been restored, the athlete can begin the more intense neck stretching and strengthening program of the level three exercises.
- For levels one, two, and three neck rehabilitation guidelines, refer to the rehabilitation section at the end of this chapter.

Recovery time:

- This is a degenerative condition that recurs every two or three years. Symptoms usually clear up within two or three weeks when proper treatment is used.
- After surgery, three months of recovery time and rehabilitation are necessary before the athlete can go back to activities that subject the neck to stress.

CERVICAL SPONDYLOSIS (*Spur Formation*) AND CERVICAL RADICULITIS (*Pinched Nerve in the Neck*)

As discs lose their height and plumpness, vertebrae move closer together and spurs form, causing a condition known as spondylosis. *These spurs may grow and start impinging on nerves in the neck, creating a condition known as* radiculitis.

Symptoms:

- Limited neck motion.
- Deep ache in the neck that worsens over a period of two or three days. As pain worsens, it spreads over the top of the shoulder blades.
- Sometimes the pain moves into the chest, mimicking the symptoms of a heart attack.
- Stiffness in the neck may cause headaches, dizziness, and sleep difficulties.
- In severe cases, there may be numbness and weakness in the arm and fingers.

Cause:

- Repetitive impact and bending of the neck.

Concerns:

- If condition goes untreated, neck mobility may be impaired, there may be chronic pain, and swallowing may become difficult.

What you can do:

- Use a heating pad.
- Sleep on an orthopedic pillow.
- Seek medical attention.

Medication

- For relief of minor to moderate pain, take acetaminophen as directed on label, or, for the relief of pain *and* inflammation, ibuprofen or aspirin if tolerated (see page 49).

What the doctor can do:

- Treatment for this condition is usually nonsurgical:
  Anti-inflammatories
  Soft collar when neck movement is difficult
  Cervical traction (twice daily for two weeks)
  Cortisone injections into the painful "trigger points," usually located in the shoulder
- Occasionally, surgery may be required for this condition. The procedure is usually very successful:
  Fusion of the vertebrae above and below the affected disc to make a permanent bony connection between the two. To take the pressure off the nerve, the disc and associated spurs are also removed during the procedure.
  A soft collar must be worn by the patient for up to three months after the surgery.

Rehabilitation:

- Level one rehabilitation exercises should begin as soon as pain allows, and preferably, as soon as possible after the acute stages of pain. For levels one, two, and three rehabilitation guidelines, refer to the sections on rehabilitation and conditioning at the end of this chapter.

Recovery time:

- Episodes of this condition are recurrent, usually months apart. When the athlete learns to recognize the early symptoms of an episode, he or she can usually circumvent a full-blown attack by early management: medication, a soft collar, and perhaps traction.
- After surgery, three months of rehabilitation before the athlete can go back to sports that place excessive demands on the neck.

DENTAL INJURIES

Injuries to the teeth are not common in adult recreational athletes but are extremely prevalent in children. A tooth that is injured is usually cracked, chipped, loose, or completely knocked out.

Usually the front teeth in the upper row are affected, and in about half of all cases, more than one tooth is damaged.

Symptoms:

- Possibly pain as well as sensitivity to heat, cold, or pressure if the tooth is chipped down to the dentin or pulp.
- A tooth that is damaged may be extremely painful if the nerve is affected.

Causes:

- Collision with another athlete or a direct blow from a piece of equipment—hockey stick, squash/racquetball racket, softball, etc.

Athletes at risk:

- Any athlete engaged in a sport where forceful facial contact with another athlete or equipment may occur.

Concerns:

- In growing children, tooth injuries that are not properly managed may lead to long-term dental deformity.
- Fractures affecting the dentin and pulp may predispose the tooth to infection and tooth death.

What you can do:

- Seek immediate medical attention from a dentist for a cracked tooth, a tooth that is loose and bleeding, or a tooth that is knocked out.
- In the meantime, initial actions on the part of the athlete can mean being able to save the injured tooth:

    Exposure to the air for more than thirty minutes can cause tooth death and make it impossible to rescue the tooth.

    If the tooth is loose, try to realign it into its original position. If it is completely knocked out, rinse it with water and replace it into the tooth socket. If this is not possible, keep the tooth in the mouth—under the tongue, for instance—until a dentist can be consulted.

EYE INJURIES

Although the eyes are naturally well protected from injury, eye injuries are not unknown in sports. Those that do occur need to be taken extremely seriously because of the potential for long-term damage to the athlete's sight, the most important sense. It is very important for athletes to wear protective eyewear where appropriate.

The most common eye injuries are orbital hematoma ("black eye"), abrasion of the cornea, hyphema (bleeding in the anterior chamber of the eye), and detached retina.

Symptoms:

- Orbital hematoma: this bruise to the soft tissues around the eye usually results in swelling, discoloration, and, in severe cases, bleeding into the white of the eye or deformity, signifying a fracture of the bones around the eye.

- Corneal abrasion: when the cornea is scratched by material that has entered the eye, the athlete will experience some or all of the following symptoms: pain, a burning sensation, a red, watery eye, swelling, decreased vision, blurred vision, and sensitivity to light. It may be possible to see a foreign object in the eye and/or a scratch or cut on the eye.
- Hyphema: when the eye is hit by a blunt object smaller than the eye socket, bleeding can occur in the pupil. The blood pools in the bottom of the eye.
- Detached retina: a blow to the eye may result in retinal detachment, in itself painless, but afterward the athlete may complain of specks floating in the vision, flashes of light, blurred vision, or decreasing quality of vision.

Cause:

- Eye injuries are usually caused by direct impact to the eye or from the intrusion of a foreign body, such as a piece of dirt or glass.

What you can do:

- Apply ice to the soft tissues around the eye (*without putting pressure on the eye*).
- *Seek medical attention in all cases of eye injuries, especially when there are signs of bleeding or sight is impaired.*

EAR INJURIES

Ear injuries may be categorized as either outer ear or inner/middle ear injuries.

Injuries to the *outer ear* are rarely seen in adult recreational sports. They were traditionally seen in boxing and wrestling, where repetitive blows to the ear caused the condition known as cauliflower ear. Equipment improvements have made this condition rare even in athletes in those sports. When a blow to the ear does take place, it should be treated with ice and firm compression with an elastic bandage. If the fluid does not disperse, the athlete should consult a doctor to have the ear drained with a syringe.

HOW TO REMOVE FOREIGN PARTICLES FROM INSIDE THE EYE

There are established ways to get a particle of dirt or glass out of the eye. Usually, it is better to have someone else try to remove the particle.

Do not try to remove the particle with the fingers, rub the eye, or try to remove any object lodged in the eye.

Instead, have the person lie down with the eye closed until the initial pain diminishes. This should enable them to determine whether the particle is under the upper or lower lid.

If it is under the lower lid, the particle can usually be removed by applying pressure with the finger to the lower lid, thus exposing the surface under the lid. The particle can then be removed by wiping this inner membrane with a sterile cotton applicator ("Q-tip").

Particles under the upper lip are much more difficult to remove. There are two ways to try to remove the particle—one simple, the other less so. The more simple method should be tried first. While the person is looking downward, pull the upper lid over the lower lid. This causes the ducts to produce tears, which may wash the particle onto the lower lid.

If this procedure does not work, use the second method. Materials needed: applicator stick, sterile cotton-tipped applicator ("Q-tip"), eyecup, and eyewash.

1. Gently pull down the upper eyelid and lay an applicator stick horizontally across the base.

2. Have the person look down, then grasp the eyelashes and fold the eyelid back over the stick.

3. Holding the lid and applicator stick ("Q-tip") in place with one hand, use the sterile cotton swab to remove the particle.

After the particle has been removed, the person should use the eyecup and eyewash to cleanse the eye. Use soothing ointment if there is irritation.

If it is difficult to remove the particle, apply a patch to the eye and have the person seek medical attention.

If a blow to the side of the head is followed by *inner ear* pain, slight bleeding, or impaired hearing, the athlete should suspect a damaged eardrum. In such cases, always seek medical attention because of the potential for long-term hearing loss.

To protect their ears against loud noises, athletes who shoot guns should wear ear protection.

Air pressure injuries of the inner ear (otitic barotrauma) are sometimes seen in athletes who subject themselves to dramatic changes in air pressure—e.g., scuba divers, sky divers, and paragliders.

Usually, athletes in these sports learn to resolve air pressure changes by "equalizing," whether by swallowing, yawning, chewing, or, most commonly, blowing through the nose while clamping the nostrils shut with the thumb and forefinger.

With otitic barotrauma the person cannot perform air pressure equalization, often as a result of nasal passage congestion from a cold, allergy, or other infection. The increased pressure can cause bleeding in the middle ear and even a burst eardrum. For this reason, athletes engaged in sports that subject them to dramatic air pressure changes should avoid these activities if they have nasal passage congestion.

NOSE INJURIES

In these injuries, there is a break in the cartilage or bone of the nose. Broken noses are among the most common facial injuries in sports.

Symptoms:

- Pain
- Grating feeling in the nose (crepitus)
- Swelling
- Discoloration
- Possible deformity
- Bleeding
- Difficulty breathing through the nose

Cause:

- A blow to the front or side of the nose.

Athletes at risk:

- Those engaged in contact sports or activities with a potential for collisions with other athletes or a direct blow from a piece of equipment.

Concerns:

- This is not usually a serious injury, though for cosmetic reasons, athletes are advised to seek medical attention to set the nose properly.

What you can do:

- Apply ice.
- With the thumb and forefinger, pinch the nostrils shut to stop the bleeding.
- Sit with the head tilted *forward*.
- Seek medical attention to have the nose set.

HOW TO STOP A BLEEDING NOSE

Impact to the nose in sports can cause bleeding from the nostrils. A bloody nose may also be caused by high blood pressure, dry nasal passages, or impact to the head.

An athlete with a bleeding nose should do the following:

- Sit with the head leaning *forward*.
- Clamp the nostrils shut with the fingers to apply direct pressure.
- Apply ice to the bridge of the nose if the bleeding does not stop.
- *Do not blow the nose.*

Seek medical attention if the bleeding does not stop or if there is deformity (signifying a broken nose).

Neck Rehabilitation

Rehabilitation exercises serve to

- promote blood flow to the area, which speeds the healing process

- relieve stiffness in the joint caused by immobilization

- prevent atrophy and tightening of the muscles resulting from inactivity.*

After an injury that does not require surgery or lengthy immobilization, range-of-motion exercises for the neck can begin as soon as pain and swelling diminish—usually no later than twenty-four to forty-eight hours after the injury.

When surgery is necessary, range-of-motion exercises may begin as early as five days after the operation. (The patient may be put in a neck brace that can be removed for rehabilitation sessions.)

Exercise is the most effective way to restore an injured athlete to sports readiness. A physical therapist may also employ ice, superficial heat, deep heat, massage, electrical stimulation, and traction to promote healing and make performing the exercises more comfortable.

The starting intensity level of the rehabilitation exercises depends on the severity of the injury. Postsurgery range-of-motion exercises usually begin at level one. At this level, range-of-motion exercises are "active assisted"—the physical therapist helps patients use their own strength to move their necks through allowable ranges of motion. If the injury is too severe for active assisted exercises, the patient may have to reply on "passive assisted" exercises—the physical therapist moves the neck through allowable ranges of motion.

After surgery, muscle atrophy is prevented by using isometric exercises. With the direction of a physical therapist, these exercises can usually begin immediately after surgery. Isometrics help maintain strength in the important muscles of the neck without compromising the healing process by changing the length of the muscles or the angles of the joint.

Athletes who have sustained only mild or moderately severe injuries can begin with level two exercises. The primary goal at this stage is to restore range of motion; the secondary goal is to prevent atrophy in the surrounding muscles. As the rehabilitation program progresses, more strengthening exercises are included in the program.

Range-of-motion and strength exercises should always be done within the pain threshold. Any exercise that causes pain should be discontinued.

The following are the most common and effective exercises used to rehabilitate the neck after injury.

Level one

After surgery, active assisted or passive assisted range-of-motion exercises are used as a starting point of rehabilitation. Within the limitations of the injury, the athlete should work on the neck's four main ranges of motion: forward flexion, extension, lateral flexion, and rotation.

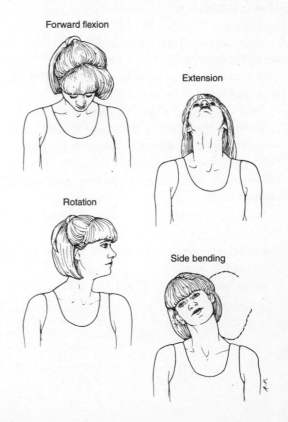

Forward flexion

Extension

Rotation

Side bending

* For more on the importance and general principles of rehabilitation, see chapter 5, "Rehabilitating Your Sports Injury."

Isometrics and assisted range-of-motion therapy should continue only until patients are capable of using their own strength to do level two exercises.

Level two

When patients are able to move their injured necks themselves and do isometric exercises without pain, level two exercises can begin.

Level two exercises can also be used as a starting point for rehabilitating moderate to severe neck injuries that do not require surgery. They primarily develop range of motion in the joint but also help prevent atrophy and tightening in the muscles of the upper arm and forearm.

Exercise 1: neck range of motion (flexion, extension, lateral flexion, and rotation)

Tilt head left and right, forward and backward, then left and right again.

Level three

When the patient can do the level two exercises without difficulty or pain, level three exercises can begin. Level three exercises can also be used as a starting point for rehabilitating mild neck injuries.

Besides continuing to promote range of motion in the neck, level three exercises start using dynamic movements to strengthen the main muscles in the neck.

Exercise 1: neck range of motion; neck strength (flexion)

Lying on back, lift head up off floor to look at feet.

Exercise 2: neck range of motion; neck strength (extension)

Lying facedown, lift head and look upward.

Exercise 3: neck range of motion; neck strength (lateral flexion)

Lie on right side, right arm outstretched, left arm placed on floor in front of chest for balance. Lift head off floor. Change sides and repeat.

Exercise 4: neck range of motion; neck strengthening (rotation)

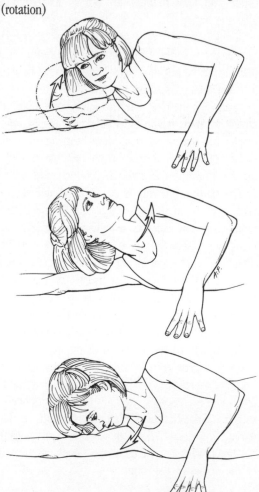

Lie on right side (same position as start of previous exercise). Raise head so left ear is moving toward left shoulder. Return head to horizontal position (not resting position), then rotate neck to look at ceiling. Return head to horizontal position, then rotate neck to look at floor.

Repeat these exercises three times a day, starting at ten repetitions and gradually building up to fifteen. You should able to do ten repetitions with ease and without pain before moving on to eleven, and so on.

When the strength of the injured neck is 95 percent better, ease back into sports.

Before going back to sports, however, the athlete who has been injured should be able to do daily activities without pain and simulate the neck motions of his or her sports without pain.

To reduce the chance of reinjury, begin a strength and flexibility conditioning program for the neck.

Conditioning Program for the Neck

Conditioning to prevent neck injuries involves improving the strength and flexibility of all the major muscles in the area.

Incorporate into your workout regimen at least one set of the following exercises for each muscle group mentioned.

The exercises are described in chapter 3, "Strength and Flexibility: The Key to Injury Prevention."

Make these exercises part of an overall strength and flexibility program, and do them before any exercise that will stress the muscles around the neck.

Neck Strengthening Exercises

Neck flexors: Neck machine
Neck extensors: Neck machine
Upper back (trapezius): Seated row, dumbbell bent row, chin-up

Neck Flexibility Exercises

Neck muscles: Seated neck stretch

CHAPTER EIGHTEEN

Skin Problems in the Athletic Population

Skin problems are common in sports. The skin is the body's largest organ, so the risk of damage is ever present. Whether indoors or outdoors, athletic activity has a potential to cause a variety of problems, from sunburn to frostbite, from cuts to allergic contact dermatitis.

Athletes can successfully treat most common sports-related skin problems, and they can also avoid these conditions through a variety of preventive measures.

Skin problems affecting the foot are covered in chapter 6, "Foot Injuries."

Abrasions ("Turf Burns," "Strawberries")

An abrasion is a scrape of the superficial layer of skin, the epidermis. Abrasions are commonly referred to as turf burns or strawberries because of their appearance and symptoms. Abrasions commonly result in pain, a burning sensation, and a gradual tightening sensation as the injury heals.

These injuries usually occur when an athlete slides or falls against a rough or hard surface. They are commonly seen in cyclists, skateboarders, football and soccer players who play on AstroTurf or a dry natural surface, and participants in any sport with a potential for falling or sliding accidents.

Abrasions are usually not serious. However, if the damage affects a large area of skin, or if any dirt, grit, or other foreign matter gets embedded in the skin, there

is the risk of infection, scarring, and what plastic surgeons call tattooing (when the skin becomes permanently discolored because dark-colored foreign matter lodges in the skin and new skin heals over it).

Abrasions need to be cleaned with cold water from a fast-running source such as a tap or hose. Use a washcloth to get rid of any debris. If the foreign matter is deeply embedded, it will be necessary to scrub the injury vigorously to avoid permanent tattooing. To do this, apply ice cubes or an ice pack to the area for several minutes. When the area is numbed, use a clean, moist, soapy washcloth to scrub the area forcefully.

Blood will seep from the wound and pain may be intense. When all the dirt is gone, reapply the ice to relieve pain and minimize bleeding. Apply over-the-counter antibacterial cream and cover with a nonstick pad.

After cleaning, care needs to be taken in dressing the abrasion. Do not make the mistake of covering the injury with a bandage so a scab forms. Contrary to popular perception, encouraging a scab to form does nothing to promote healing. Instead, keep the abrasion moist using petroleum jelly or a thin layer of over-the-counter antibiotic cream (bacitracin and Polysporin are two effective brands). Use these medicated ointments for only two to three days, as they are a frequent cause of allergic reactions.

Protect the abrasion with a nonadherent gauze pad

held in place with tape. Ointment needs to be reapplied two or three times a day. Either replace the entire bandage or simply detach one side of the bandage and apply fresh ointment to the injury under the original bandage.

Within twenty-four hours, remove the bandage and clean the area with mild soap and water. *Do not take a bath to clean the wound, because the unclean, soapy water can cause infection.*

If the pain is extreme, or if the abrasion is quite deep, seek medical attention at a hospital emergency room. The doctor may administer a local anesthetic, then use a surgical scrub brush or toothbrush to clean the injury. If the athlete has not had a tetanus injection within the previous five years, a booster shot will be administered to immunize against *Clostridium tetani*, a bacterium found in dirt. If this organism gets into the body through an abrasion, an infection may develop that involves painful muscle spasms, lockjaw, and eventually death if left untreated.

Abrasions are unavoidable in some circumstances, but one can be protected by wearing low-friction clothing or by padding over the elbows, knees, and hips during athletic activity with a potential for falling accidents— especially biking, and in-line skating.

Cuts *(Lacerations)*

Cuts, or lacerations in medical parlance, are extremely prevalent in sports. Facial cuts and cuts in the extremities, especially the fingers, are very common.

The most common symptoms of cuts are pain, rapid bleeding, and possibly, bruising of the skin.

No matter how small, and no matter where they occur, cuts need to be treated immediately because of the potential for infection, scarring, and "tattooing" (see above, "Abrasions").

Initial treatment should be directed at controlling bleeding and preventing infection. Pressure should be applied to the site for as long as it takes to stop the flow of blood—usually five to ten minutes. Gauze or a clean cloth are both effective materials to apply pressure to the wound (when either the gauze or cloth become soaked with blood, do not replace it; simply place another clean dressing directly over it and reapply pressure).

If a cut is deep, long, or jagged, or if there is numb-ness and/or an adjoining muscle cannot be moved properly (a sign of nerve damage), seek emergency medical attention.

An effective home remedy for minor cuts is to place a water-soaked tea bag over the cut and apply gentle pressure. Hold it there until bleeding stops. The tannic acid of tea mixes with blood from the wound and helps the blood coagulate quickly.

Do not apply a tourniquet of any kind to a cut, unless a major artery has been severed and there are massive amounts of blood gushing from the wound. Applying a tourniquet to even a minor cut may result in severe nerve and tissue damage.

After bleeding stops and the wound has been cleaned with soap and water, apply a sterile rectangular adhesive bandage so there is gentle pressure holding the cut together. It is not necessary to use antiseptic creams or sprays, as these are no more effective than the body's immune system in resisting infection. If the cut is severe enough that stitches are needed, apply a dressing (see "Abrasions," above), and seek medical attention at a hospital emergency room within four hours of the injury to avoid risk of infection.

The athlete should not return to athletic activity until given the go-ahead by a doctor. After healing, cuts should be protected from the sun to prevent scarring. Applying vitamin E or castor oil also helps minimize scarring.

Return to activity should be judged on an activity-by-activity basis. Wearing helmets, face protectors, and mouthpieces may allow an athlete to return to full participation before the cut has fully healed. To prevent cuts, athletes should always wear protective helmets, goggles, and face masks where appropriate.

Sunburn *(Actinic Dermatitis)*

Sunburn, or dermatitis, is the destruction of skin cells caused by the sun's ultraviolet radiation.

The symptoms of a sunburn usually show up two to three hours after exposure. Sunburns are classified according to their severity, first, second, or third degree, and the symptoms vary accordingly. With a first-degree sunburn, the skin turns pink to bright red. Sufferers of a second-degree burn will develop blisters. In third-degree sunburns, the skin may turn black or white, and there

HOW TO RECOGNIZE SKIN CANCER

Excessive, unprotected exposure to the sun can cause nonmelanoma skin cancers: these are squamous cell skin cancer and basal cell skin cancer, both of which are curable but whose treatment can be disfiguring.

A much greater concern is that repeated episodes of severe sunburn during childhood and youth can cause malignant melanoma, a potentially fatal form of skin cancer. Melanomas cause approximately 6,000 deaths a year in the United States.

Melanoma develops around pigmented areas of skin, such as moles and freckles. It usually occurs after the age of forty. Usually the melanoma is a very dark brown or black mole, often with a ridged surface and red-and-white coloring inside. It is important to be able to know how to rule out which skin blemishes are dangerous and which are not.

The "ABCD" method is used to detect a melanoma.

A—asymmetry (an irregular shape). Draw a line through the mole's center and the two halves will not be equal. A benign mole is round and symmetrical.

B—irregular border. Noncancerous growths have regular borders. Cancerous growths have craggy edges.

C—color. Cancerous lesions are multicolored, ranging from tan to brown to black, often with red, white, and pink mixed in. Noncancerous growth are usually a single color.

D—diameter. If the growth measures more than a quarter of an inch across, it may be cancerous.

If there is any suspicion of melanoma, contact a dermatologist immediately.

mild to moderate sunburn. Not only does the aspirin provide pain relief, it also blocks a biochemical reaction that causes the skin to redden, and shuts down the sun's damage to the skin. *As soon as the burn is felt* (it does not work the day after), take two aspirin and take two more every two to three hours to a maximum of eight. Children with sunburn can be given pediatric aspirin.

Aloe vera cream sold in drugstores provides effective, natural relief from sunburn. Do not use the anesthetic sprays available in drugstores. They provide temporary pain relief but dry out the skin and delay recovery.

For more moderate burns, symptoms can be relieved by bathing in water to which a pound of cornstarch has been added. Severe burns or infected burn sites should be treated by a doctor or dermatologist.

Seek medical attention from a dermatologist when skin is bright red, tender, and covered with blisters that weep and ooze. These are the signs of a second-degree burn. The doctor may remove the fluid from the blisters and prescribe a steroid cream such as prednisone to be used for several days.

Sunburn is one of the most easily prevented skin problems. Any athlete who participates in outdoor sports needs to use a sunscreen with a sun protection factor (SPF) of between 25 and 45.*

It is absolutely essential that the sunscreen is waterproof so it does not wash off when you perspire, swim, or use water to cool off during a workout. Apply the sunscreen to dry skin before the athletic activity, and reapply it just before exercising.

A sunburn can potentially cause a malfunctioning of the organs below the skin, which can result in an infection of hair follicles or sweat glands. Incontrovertible evidence now shows that long-term, low-intensity exposure to strong sun can cause thickening of the skin, permanent damage, and, most serious, skin cancers that may be disfiguring or even fatal.

may be little pain. Fortunately, second-degree sunburns are rare, and third-degree sunburns are even rarer.

Any athlete who exercises out of doors is susceptible to sunburns. Especially at risk are those who exercise outdoors for prolonged periods and athletes who participate in water sports.

Burns should be treated according to the degree of inflammation. Mild burns can be treated with the topical application of a soothing lotion containing anesthetic. Boric acid may also be used as a soothing agent.

Aspirin is an extremely effective means of treating

---

*All sunscreens now come with sun protection factor (SPF) ratings, from 2 to 45. These ratings let consumers know how long they can stay in the sun before burning when using the sunscreen versus no protection at all. For example, someone who would normally start to turn pink in twenty minutes can use an SPF 10 sunscreen and withstand up to 200 minutes of sun exposure without getting burned.

An SPF of 15 provides enough protection for most people. But for people who are fair-skinned, have blue eyes, freckles, and either blond or red hair, a higher SPF may be appropriate.

Frostbite/Frostnip

Frostbite is the freezing of skin tissues caused by excessive exposure to cold. Frostbite varies in intensity and is classified according to how deep the freezing penetrates. Mild frostbite, sometimes called frostnip, is freezing of the superficial layers of skin without blister formation. The characteristic symptoms of mild frostbite are itching, tingling, and numbness. If the condition worsens, the pain begins to abate and may even disappear. Skin also changes color when it is frostbitten. It whitens, then turns red, and finally has a white-purple hue when it is completely frozen. Severe frostbite may involve complete numbness in the area, stiffness, blistering, and, in some cases, tissue death that causes gangrene.

The parts of the body at greatest risk of developing frostbite are the tip of the nose, earlobes and rims, fingertips, and toes.

Frostbite (though rare) is seen in athletes who are not used to exercising in cold weather and those who participate in winter sports, winter camping, high-altitude climbing, and hunting.

At the first signs of frostbite, come out of the cold immediately and rewarm the affected area as quickly as possible.

The most effective way to thaw frozen skin is to immerse it in a bath kept at a constant temperature of 100–105 degrees Fahrenheit for up to an hour. Because rapid rewarming is an extremely painful process, take two aspirin, ibuprofen, or acetaminophen tablets to relieve the pain.

If the hands and/or fingers are affected, and there is no access to hot water, tuck the affected body part under an armpit, between the thighs, or in the groin.

If there is a chance the area may refreeze, do not attempt to warm it until you know you will be out of the cold for a significant period. Once skin has frozen, been rewarmed, then refrozen, the likelihood of damage is drastically increased.

Once the skin has thawed and returned to its normal temperature, bandage the area and seek medical attention at a hospital emergency room.

After the doctor has carefully examined the area, pain medication and antibiotics are given, in addition to a tetanus booster if needed. During the following week(s), the doctor should monitor the athlete for any signs of infection.

Frostbite can be prevented by wearing proper protection for the face, neck, and extremities during outdoor winter exercise. Winter athletes should wear multiple layers of lightweight, nonrestrictive clothing (see page 000).

Prickly Heat (Miliaria)

Prickly heat, or miliaria, is a common sports-related skin disorder. It affects athletes who sweat profusely during sports or who wear heavy athletic equipment. Common symptoms include itching and burning caused by moisture retention in the sweat glands, and a rash of red bumps. The areas commonly affected are the arms, torso, and "creases" in the body that allow for bending motions.

Prickly heat is generally not serious, but it can be highly uncomfortable. Treatment involves bathing the area with hypoallergenic products. The athlete should avoid overheating and wearing constrictive clothing during sports. In general, athletes can participate in activities in the heat if they spend sufficient time at rest in cool, dry area.

Jogger's Nipples

Jogger's nipples describes a condition characterized by painful chafing of the areolae and nipple caused by friction. The most common cause is friction from coarse running shirts. It is more prevalent in men, because women usually wear bras during exercise.

To prevent this condition, athletes should wear shirts made of smooth material. To minimize irritation, the athlete can also apply petroleum jelly (Vaseline) over the nipples or cover them with Band-Aids.

Skin Chafing (Intertrigo)

Chafing, or intertrigo, is extremely common in athletes. This condition begins with a combination of heat and moisture that causes the skin to soften. Then friction and repeated rubbing, especially between the thighs, causes the skin to become rubbed raw, or chafed. Chafing describes an area that oozes, then develops lesions that quickly form a crusty, crackling surface.

To treat the affected area, the athlete should use medicated wet packs containing an over-the-counter solution such as Burows. The area should be treated for approximately twenty minutes, three times a day. Following each treatment, a prescription-strength hydrocortisone cream (1 percent) should be applied topically.

Chafing can be prevented by wearing loose-fitting clothing made of natural fibers. Any susceptible areas should be kept as dry and clean as possible during exercise. Male athletes should wear loose cotton boxer shorts under their athletic supporter.

Allergic Contact Dermatitis

Allergic contact dermatitis is common in sports environments. Allergic reactions can be caused by any number of factors, including certain types of equipment, deodorants, topical analgesics, the resin in athletic tape, and the rubber used in certain sneakers and heat retainers.

Symptoms develop within a day to a week of exposure. They include itching, redness, swelling, and a rash that initially oozes, then forms a crusty surface.

For immediate relief in the acute phase of the condition, cool, wet dressings of Burow's solution may be applied for half an hour at a time, three times a day. Topical corticosteroids may be applied to help relieve the symptoms.

In all cases of contact dermatitis, consult a dermatologist as soon as possible to avoid a chronic condition. The doctor will probably prescribe steroidal creams and oral medication.

In addition, if the precipitating agent can be determined, contact with it should be immediatley discontinued.

If the cause of the dermatitis is unknown, the dermatologist may perform "patch tests" to ascertain the cause.

Insect Bites

Athletes frequently come into contact with stinging insects such as bees, wasps, and hornets during outdoor activity. The effects of an attack from one of these insects are usually temporary but painful. However, under certain circumstances, there may be serious consequences associated with insect stings.

When a bee stings a human, it leaves its stinger and venom sac embedded in its victim's skin, then dies shortly thereafter. To prevent more venom being injected into the skin, it is important to remove the stinger and venom sac immediately. Do not try to extract the stinger with fingers or tweezers, as this usually causes more venom to be squirted into the skin. Instead, try to flick out the stinger by quickly scraping a fingernail, knife blade, or credit card over the stinger.

Wasps and hornets, on the other hand, do not lose their stingers, and so they continue to be a threat after an attack. After being stung by either a wasp or hornet, leave the area to avoid another attack.

After a bee, wasp, or hornet sting, wash the area with soap and water to prevent bacterial infection (these insects often scavenge in garbage). To reduce pain and swelling, apply cold to the sting, preferably an ice cube, but if one is not available, a cold can of soda will suffice. Continue to apply cold for at least half an hour to forty-five minutes.

The symptoms of an insect sting may continue for an hour or so. If pain, swelling, and itching continue for longer than that, taken an over-the-counter antihistamine such as diphenhydramine (Benadryl) as directed on label. Aspirin is also an effective means of minimizing swelling and itching.

To minimize attraction to the stinging insect, athletes who engage in outdoor sports should avoid scented products such as soaps and colognes, as well as brightly colored or very dark clothing.

Warning: Approximately 1 in 150 people is allergic to beestings. In these hypersensitive individuals, a beesting can trigger anaphylactic shock, a severe reaction that can begin within minutes. Symptoms of anaphylactic shock may include the following: nausea; wheezing and difficulty breathing (bronchospasm); cool, clammy, and pale skin; rapid pulse; diarrhea; cramps; extreme thirst; dizziness; loss of consciousness; and, if not treated immediately, death.

A warning sign that anaphylactic shock may be developing is swelling in the back of the throat that inhibits breathing and swallowing. Anyone with these symptoms after a beesting should seek immediate emergency room attention.

A person with known hypersensitivity to beestings should seek immediate medical attention when stung. It is recommended that these persons—if they engage in frequent outdoor athletic or recreational activity—carry with them a special emergency kit containing a syringe and the drug epinephrine to counteract the bee venom.

Jock Itch *(Tinea Cruris)*

Jock itch, or tinea cruris, is a frequent complaint among male athletes; it rarely affects females. Characteristic symptoms include itchy, red scaly patches on the groin, thighs, and buttocks. Pus-filled blisters may also develop.

Poor hygiene, inadequate ventilation of the groin area, and friction are the primary causes of jock itch. If left untreated, this condition can become chronic, spreading to the thighs and torso.

Prime candidates for jock itch are athletes who wear an athletic supporter (jock strap), athletes who do not bathe soon after exercising, athletes who wear tight, constricting apparel or jockey shorts made of synthetic materials, and athletes who are overweight or who have heavily muscled thighs that rub together during exercise.

Proper hygiene, antifungal medication, and minimizing excessive warmth and moisture in the groin area are the fundamentals of treatment for this condition.

Gently wash the affected area with soap and water, making sure to rinse the soap off completely to prevent irritation. Dry the area thoroughly. Twice daily apply a thin coating of over-the-counter clotrimazole (Lotrimin). Results should be seen in three to five days. Continue to use the medication for three to five days after the condition clears up. For several weeks after the condition resolves, use a cornstarch-free powder (Zeasorb AF) after showering to keep the groin dry.

After exercise, do not linger in damp clothing, including swimsuits. Wear loose-fitting boxer shorts as underwear and change it daily. Always wear clean athletic clothing for exercise—especially shorts and undergarments. Overweight athletes who sweat heavily and whose thighs rub together should lose weight. If these measures are unsuccessful, consult a dermatologist.

The doctor may use a scalpel to remove a tiny sample from the area. Examination under a microscope should reveal the exact cause of the condition.

To clear up the condition, the doctor will usually recommend continuing the above regimen and prescribe oral antifungal medication, generally ketoconazole (Nizoral), or griseofulvin (Fulvicin-U/F, Gris-PEG, Grifulvin V) if the condition is caused by a dermatophyte (such as ringworm or eczema). Almost always, such treatment will clear up the jock itch.

CHAPTER NINETEEN

Sports Medicine Concerns of Female Athletes

Women have made extraordinary strides in sports and fitness activities. The greatest boost for women's participation in sports and fitness activities occurred in 1971 with the passage of Title IX of the Educational Assistance Act. This legislation decreed that all institutions receiving federal funds had to offer equal opportunities for women in all programs, including athletics. Significantly, passage of Title IX dovetailed with societal interest in health fitness, especially its emphasis on achieving well-being through exercise. Thus began women's massive entrance into sports and health fitness activities. The statistics reflecting women's growing interest in exercise are impressive.

In the few short years since women entered the sports and fitness arena in force, sports medicine clinicians and researchers have learned much more about the sports medicine concerns of the female athlete, in particular how they relate to injuries and to gynecological and reproductive issues and, most recently, the relationship between eating disorders, premature osteoporosis, and stress fractures (the "female athlete triad").

Female-specific Sports Injuries

The increased participation of women in sports and fitness activities raises a number of important concerns. For sports-active women, the two most contentious issues are: Do women sustain particular types of injuries? and Do women get injured more often than men?

8. FEMALE SPORTS PARTICIPANTS IN 1992 (Age Seven and Older)

Among sports participants aged seven or older, females constitute a majority of participants in 11 of 50 activities surveyed for 1992 by the National Sporting Goods Association (NSGA).

SPORT	PERCENT FEMALE
Aerobic dance	81.8%
Exercise walking	65.8
Ice/Figure skating	62.2
Traditional roller skating	62.1
Horseback riding	61.5
Croquet	56.9
Calisthenics	56
Badminton	54.4
Swimming	52.7
Exercising with equipment	51.6
In-line skating	50

"Female" Injuries?

For female athletes, the evidence relating to the first issue is paradoxically reassuring: women appear to suffer the same kinds of injuries as men. There is no such thing as a "good" injury, but the fact that "sex-specific" injuries are a rarity allays outdated and erroneous concerns about women and sports.

The primary female organs are better protected from serious athletic injury than the male organs. Serious sports injuries to the uterus or ovaries are extremely rare.

Breast injuries, a commonly heard argument against women's participation in vigorous sports, are among the rarest of all sports injuries. "Jogger's nipples," an abrasion of the nipples, can be taken care of by placing tape or a Band-Aid over the area before exercising. A well-fitted bra should also help resolve this condition (it may also help correct shoulder and back problems caused by large breast size).

Pelvic infections, most commonly vaginal and urinary tract infections, may occur slightly more often in female athletes than in nonactive women. Symptoms of vaginitis include a pus-colored, odorous discharge. The slightly higher incidence of vaginal infections can probably be explained by the accentuation of the same factors that predispose all women to infections of this kind—prolonged exposure to wet shorts and underwear, increased warmth and sweat in the area, and frictional irritation. Urinary tract infections, particularly of the bladder, are seen more often in women than men. To minimize the risks of infection, female athletes should drink plenty of fluids, especially water, which increases urine flow, promoting bacterial "washout."

More Injuries?

The second issue, whether women sustain a higher rate of injuries than men, is more complex. There has been concern that females are at greater risk of injury from sports training than their male counterparts because of the physiological differences between the sexes. The limited medical evidence available seems to show that women sustain more injuries than men, but that this higher rate is not due to physiological differences.

CHOOSING A SPORTS BRA

Excessive breast motion during exercise can be painful, and may cause sagging and stretch marks. To prevent these undesirable consequences, female athletes should get proper breast support by using either a compressive or support bra.

Women with B or C breast cup size should use *compressive* bras (those that act like a binder). For women with C cup size or larger, a firmer, more supportive bra is needed, one that holds each breast in its own cup, the *encapsulating* bra.

Some suggested features of a good sports bra:

- Seams should be padded, and there should be no seam over the nipples.

- The fabric should be absorbent and nonallergenic.

- Fifty percent or more of the fabric should be cotton, to allow for ventilation and to reduce chafing.

- Hooks and other metallic parts should be covered. Rear closure hooks are preferred.

- The use of elastic should be minimized, since its constant expansion and contraction can lead to chafing.

- The straps should be wide, comfortable, and constructed to prevent slipping from the shoulders.

Male and female athletes sustain many of the same acute injuries, including fractures, dislocations, and contusions. These injuries do not discriminate between men and women—they occur in the same way and should be managed identically. However, overuse injuries may be more common among female athletes. The constantly repeated movements in running, jumping, or racket sports can lead to stress fractures, knee complaints, certain kinds of tendinitis and bursitis, and shinsplints.

Female athletes are especially susceptible to these problems because they often lack long-term preparation for vigorous sports training. In general, women begin their participation in competitive sports later than their male counterparts, without the benefit of conditioning

SKELETAL DIFFERENCES BETWEEN WOMEN AND MEN AND THEORETICAL CONSEQUENCES	
Body part	Possible result
Size: usually smaller, shorter	Lower center of gravity Lighter body frame Different running mechanics
Pelvis: wider	Injury *theoretically* more likely because of knee instability
Thighs: slant inward toward knees	
Lower leg bones: less "bowed"	
Limbs (relative to body length): shorter	Shorter lever arm for movement—important for use of sports equipment
Shoulders: narrower, more sloped	Different mechanics of upper limb motion
Upper arms: do not hang straight	
Elbows: marked "carrying angle"	Important in throwing pattern

from lifelong athletic activity or the conditioning for endurance, strength, and flexibility. Society still prescribes different roles for men and women after puberty. Girls who are climbing trees or jungle gyms with boys at age nine will stop before their teenage years. At thirteen it is quite common for boys to continue playing sports and engaging in fitness activities while girls shun such "unladylike" activities.

Inadequate preparation increases the chance of injury. It takes many years of preparation to condition the bones and soft tissues for vigorous athletic activity. Classical ballet, with its long tradition of physical training, requires three or more years of progressive training before a student is allowed to practice advanced techniques such as *en pointe*. Ballet instructors understand that bones and muscles take a long time to become stronger in response to increased physical demands.

For this reason it is especially important for female athletes to work themselves gradually into sports and fitness programs if they have not done much sports activity as children.

Among female athletes in childhood the likelihood of overuse injuries may be exacerbated by tightness caused by growth. Girls frequently begin sports training at the height of the growth spurt (between eleven and thirteen). At this stage bone growth creates tightness in the muscle-tendon units and in soft tissues, resulting in loss of flexibility in the joints and, consequently, overuse injuries.

Two overuse injuries are especially prevalent among female athletes. These are stress fractures in the back, lower leg, and foot, and disorders of the knee. Both conditions are also seen in male athletes, but they are more common in female athletes.

Stress fractures result from a series of microfractures that are unable to heal because of the frequency or intensity of the repetitive trauma. The normal response of bone to increased stress is for the microfractures to heal over and the bone to rebuild itself. In addition, bone exposed to recurrent microtrauma may also increase in size, as in a tennis player's arm or the shins of a runner. But stress fractures will develop if certain types of activities are constantly repeated and bones are denied the opportunity to heal. Athletes of all skill levels are susceptible to stress fractures; the most common cause is a sharp increase in the intensity or frequency of training.

Female athletes who are not menstruating regularly may be at greater risk of stress fractures. The decreased estrogen levels associated with menstrual irregularities may cause bone thinning. Thin bones are weaker, and are thus more susceptible to stress fractures. Among young female athletes whose periods have stopped entirely for up to a year, there is an almost tripled incidence of stress fractures. In female recreational athletes, many of whom are runners and aerobic dancers, the most common sites of stress fractures are the pelvis, hip, lower leg, and foot. For more on the relationship between menstrual irregularities and stress fractures, refer to the section on the "female athlete triad" (page 299).

The second condition seen more frequently among female athletes is knee pain, especially kneecap pain (see chapter 8).

Although the onset of these complaints may be associated with an error in training or a minor injury to the kneecap, evaluation of an athlete with this condition usually reveals a combination of problems, including muscle-tendon imbalances across the knee and one or more anatomical malalignments, such as patella alta (when the kneecap rides too high and bumps against the bottom of the thigh bones), knock-knee, and bowlegs.

One suggested explanation for the frequency of these complaints in female athletes is the width of the female pelvis. Combined with knock-knee this physiological feature is said to cause the kneecaps to slip from side to side. However, there is little hard evidence for this theory and scientific studies show no significant biochemical relationship between the width of the female pelvis and these problems. It is more likely that cultural deconditioning and strength and flexibility imbalances are the cause of knee problems in female athletes (usually the quadriceps muscles are weaker than the hamstring muscles, and the hamstrings tighter than the quadriceps).

Usually these knee problems respond well to a simple exercise program involving static straight-leg raises and a flexibility regimen. Also, shoe inserts (orthotics) that alter the foot-ground relationship often help compensate for anatomical malalignments and at the same time increase impact absorption. The vast majority of female athletes respond well to these treatments. As their level of straight-leg weight resistance increases to 12 or 15 pounds with the repetitions, symptoms steadily subside.

The available evidence suggests that women are not inherently more likely to be injured than men, and their participation in sports is not jeopardized by gender-specific injuries as once feared. Injuries that do occur are often due to sociological factors that make women's conditioning levels lower than men's. As social attitudes change and women begin to participate in sports and fitness activities from a younger age, it is expected that their improved fitness levels will lessen their incidence of injuries.

What remains of great concern to sports medicine experts studying the female athlete, however, is the newly established relationship between eating disorders, menstrual irregularities, and stress fractures.

The Female Athlete Triad: Eating Disorders, Menstrual Irregularities, and Stress Fractures

The relationship between three distinct but interrelated conditions—eating disorders, menstrual irregularities, and stress fractures—has puzzled sports professionals for as long as women have participated in vigorous exercise. The sports medicine profession has only recently come to understand how these phenomena are interrelated. In 1993, an American College of Sports Medicine task force on the special problems of female athletes coined a term to describe the relationship: the female athlete triad.

Female athletes have more eating disorders than sedentary women. The combination of poor eating habits and high activity level can cause a woman's body fat level to drop below the level necessary for normal menstrual function. When women stop having their periods (amenorrhea) or have periods irregularly (oligomenorrhea), they lose much of the estrogen necessary for the bone rebuilding that normal bodies perform on a continuous basis. This causes premature osteoporosis, a disease that causes the bones to become thinner and more brittle, which in turn predisposes the athlete to stress fractures.

Female athletes and their family, friends, colleagues, and exercise partners should know of the potential serious consequences of this phenomenon, which may include death. The key to treating the female athlete triad is prevention and early intervention.

Eating Disorders Among Female Athletes

Eating disorders are a significant problem among female athletes. Studies show that from 15 to 62 percent of female athletes have eating disorders severe enough to meet the criteria for anorexia nervosa and bulimia nervosa as defined by the *Diagnostic and Statistical Manual of Mental Disorders—IV* (DSM-IV). By comparison, only 1 percent of the general female population meet these criteria. Moreover, the current research may underrepresent the problem. Although their behaviors may not fit the DSM-IV criteria for anorexia or bulimia, many athletic women exhibit eating habits and nutritional status that put them at risk for developing serious psychiatric, endocrine, and skeletal problems.

Among elite athletes, eating disorders are especially prevalent in performance-oriented sports where leanness is perceived to be an advantage: gymnastics, diving, ballet, and figure skating. Eating disorders are also common among recreational athletes who engage in sports and exercise primarily for weight control. These athletes participate in activities as wide-ranging as aerobic dance, distance running, cross-country skiing simulation, and stationary biking. The female athlete's focus on exercise, diet, and body composition may become an obsession when thinness rather than health fitness becomes the overriding objective. Many reach the point when no amount of exercise is enough, and no weight loss is too much.

The dangers of anorexia nervosa and bulimia nervosa in the general population are well known. These two eating disorders can lead to many psychiatric, endocrine, and orthopedic problems, which may, in their most extreme cases, cause death. Among anorexic nonathletes who do receive treatment, there is a mortality rate of between 10 and 18 percent. The sooner intervention starts, the better the chance for recovery.

Among the possible consequences of vigorous exercise and low body weight on menstruation are delay of menarche (when females begin having their periods), amenorrhea, and oligomenorrhea.

Amenorrhea and oligomenorrhea: Amenorrhea means the cessation of menstrual periods. Oligomenorrhea means infrequent menstruation (fewer than six periods in a year).

Evidence suggests that one of the principal reasons women stop having their periods is that when body fat level drops below a certain percentage of body mass (17 percent, it is estimated), estrogens also decrease and androgens increase, disrupting the balance of hormones that ordinarily keeps menstruation going.

Because vigorous exercise causes body fat levels to decrease, this condition is much more common among athletic women. Depending on which study is used, the reported incidence of amenorrhea in young female athletes ranges from 3.4 percent up to 66 percent. In contrast, the reported prevalence of amenorrhea in the nonathletic female population is 2 to 5 percent.

There are factors other than low body fat levels that may cause amenorrhea or oligomenorrhea, which explains why female athletes with normal body fat levels still suffer menstrual irregularities more than the general population, and why many female athletes with low body fat levels menstruate regularly.

Psychological stress is one such factor. Sports can lower stress, but they can also be a source of heightened stress, particularly in solo sports such as gymnastics, ballet dancing, and figure skating. Stress can cause a woman to stop menstruating. Psychological sports stress is uncommon in recreational athletes, but stress in other areas of life may cause menstrual irregularities.

Other reasons a woman may stop menstruating include pregnancy, hypothyroidism, pituitary adenoma, polycystic ovarian disease, and androgen excess syndromes.

Delay of menarche: Menarche refers to the time when a female first starts having her periods. In the United States, the average age of menarche is about twelve and a half years. Yet girls participating in sports such as running, gymnastics, ballet dancing, and figure skating start their periods close to sixteen years of age. Again, the percentage of body weight as fat seems to be the key factor in starting periods, as well as the psychological and physical stress experienced by elite female athletes. The typical athlete who experiences delay in menarche is a young female athlete who is driven to excel in her sport, and who is obsessed with her appearance because she believes or has been told that performance is linked to thinness.

It is understood that females who participate in vigorous exercise are more likely to have menstrual irregularities than those who do not. What is not as well understood is whether there are dangers associated with menstrual irregularities. Until recently it was thought that the dangers were minimal. In fact, many top female athletes found it desirable not to have the inconvenience of menstruating during important competition. More significantly, studies showed that athletes with menstrual irregularities had not experienced long-term impairment of gynecological and reproductive function. No permanent impairment was found in a survey of 107 of the women champions in the 1952 Olympic Games. A 1972 study of former elite international female athletes revealed that these women had fewer complications during pregnancy and easier deliveries than was recorded for a group of normally active women and a less physically active group.

Usually periods resume after vigorous exercise is discontinued, and at that stage many women report favorable changes: lighter flow, less cramping and discomfort, and shorter duration of flow.

Effects of Menstrual Irregularity on Bone Density and the Risk of Skeletal Injuries

Although such reports are reassuring, during the last decade researchers have raised a troubling concern: the relationship between menstrual irregularities and bone density.

Regular exercise is known to combat the effects of osteoporosis. However, in certain circumstances exercise has been shown to hasten the onset of osteoporosis and increase the likelihood of conditions such as stress fractures.

Osteoporosis is a bone disease that causes bones to thin and weaken. Though osteoporosis can affect men, it is much more likely to affect women, especially after menopause. With osteoporosis, bone minerals—mainly calcium—are lost, and bones become so brittle that a minor injury can break a wrist, hip, or spine.

Osteoporosis can occur in young women, too. Decreased estrogen levels associated with delayed menarche, infrequent periods, or complete cessation of periods may cause premature osteoporosis. Premature osteoporosis is often seen in very athletic young women who exercise or diet so strenuously that they exhibit these menstrual disturbances. Untreated, these young women may lose up to 20 percent of their skeletal mass, and may end up in their twenties with the bone density of a fifty-year-old woman. Current research shows that some bone loss is *irreversible*. Not only do these women lose bone mineral density and become osteoporotic, but they may never regain their previous bone densities.

Unlike older women with osteoporosis, who are susceptible to complete fractures, younger women with menstrual irregularities are more likely to sustain stress fractures. Among young female athletes with amenorrhea,

> ### CHOOSING A HEALTH CLUB
>
> Joining a health fitness facility is an important decision and one that involves many factors, the most important of which are health and well-being. Here are the major areas you should consider:
>
> - Is the staff qualified?
> - Are the facilities and equipment adequate?
> - Does the facility offer adequate programming?
> - Is the facility staff concerned about user safety?
> - Does the facility operate in an ethical business manner?
>
> Visit several facilities. Ask questions, not only of the staff but of the users as well. Contact the local Better Business Bureau (or similar organization) for any information it can provide regarding health fitness facilities in your area. Make an honest attempt to identify what you really want and expect from a health fitness facility. Compare your answers with the information collected on the different facilities, and only then make a decision.
>
> For a comprehensive guide to what to look for in a health club, consult the American College of Sports Medicine book, *ACSM's Health Fitness Facility Standards and Guidelines*, available from Human Kinetics Publishers by calling 1-800-747-4457.

there is an almost tripled incidence of stress fractures. A study of female college athletes showed that only 9 percent of those who had their periods regularly experienced stress fractures, as compared to 24 percent of athletes with irregular or no periods. The most common sites of stress fractures in female athletes are the back, hip, pelvis, lower leg, and foot.

Resuming Periods and Avoiding Problems Associated with Menstrual Irregularities

If a female athlete stops menstruating and believes that poor eating habits are primarily to blame, she should have a nutrition checkup with a registered dietitian or a sports nutritionist. (American Dietetic Association's National Center for Nutrition and Dietetics referral service: 800-366-1655.)

Nutritionist and author Nancy Clark has the following tips for women seeking to regain their periods:

Cut back on exercise by between 5 and 15 percent and eat a little more. Athletes who stop training altogether, as may happen if they are injured, often resume their periods within two months. Some amenorrheic athletes resume their periods with just reduced exercise and no weight gain or after gaining less than five pounds. This amount of weight gain is small enough not to cause a drastic weight change, but it may be crucial in achieving better health.

Rather than striving to achieve an artificially low weight, female athletes should let their bodies have a greater "say" in determining a more natural weight. The female athlete should look at her weight history (highest, lowest, "normal" weight), percentage of body fat, physiques of family members, and the weight at which she feels good and that she can comfortably maintain without constant dieting. Her physician or dietitian can provide unbiased professional advice.

Do not crash diet. If she has weight to lose, the female athlete should moderately cut back on food intake (20 percent). Severe dieters commonly stop menstruating. By following a healthy weight reduction program, female athletes will not only have greater success with long-term weight loss but will also have enough energy for their exercise.

When she reaches an appropriate weight, the female athlete should practice a simple rule for eating: Eat when hungry, stop when content. If hungry all the time and obsessed with food, chances are the athlete is eating too few calories. Athletes should remember to eat enough calories to support their exercise program. As evidence suggests, amenorrhea may in part be caused by irregular eating habits (eating little at breakfast and lunch, then overeating at night; restricting diet Monday to Thursday, then gorging on weekends). Female athletes should try to consume calories on a regular schedule of wholesome, well-balanced meals.

Eat adequate protein. Research suggests amenorrheic athletes tend to eat less protein than other women. It is unclear why meat seems to have a protective effect on women's periods. Nutritionists have theorized that women who eat meat eat fewer calories from fiber-rich foods, and high fiber can affect hormones and calcium absorption.

A safe intake of protein for female athletes is about .5 g. to .75 g. per pound of body weight, higher than the current RDA for sedentary women. For a 120-pound woman, this comes to 60 to 90 g. of protein (13 to 20 percent of an 1,800 calorie diet) and is the equivalent of three or four 8-ounce servings of low-fat milk or yogurt and one 4- to 6-ounce serving of meat.

Eat at least 20 percent of calories from fat. Amenorrheic athletes often avoid meat because they are afraid of eating fat. Some have an exaggerated perception that if they eat fat, they will get fat. Although excess calories from fat are easily fattening, some fat (20–30 percent of total calories) is an appropriate part of a healthy sports diet. Athletes can eat between 40 and 60 g. of fat a day, allowing them to balance out their diet with such foods as beef, peanut butter, cheese, and nuts.

Maintain a calcium-rich diet to help maintain bone density. Because women build peak bone density in their early adult years (twenties and thirties), the goal should be to protect against future problems of osteoporosis by eating calcium-rich foods today. A safe target is 800 to 1,200 mg. of calcium a day—three to four servings of low-fat milk, yogurt, or other dairy or calcium-rich foods.

If the athlete is eating a very high-fiber diet (i.e., lots of bran cereal, fruits, and vegetables), there may be a greater need for calcium because fiber may interfere with calcium absorption.

And remember, food is *health*, not just fattening calories.

TREATING THE FEMALE ATHLETE TRIAD

Treating the female athlete triad is largely a question of education and early intervention. Female athletes who exercise primarily for weight control must be wary of their susceptibility to eating disorders. Vigilance should also be exerted by family members, friends, and colleagues. The typical athlete with an eating disorder is somewhat obsessive, introverted, reserved, self-denying, overcompliant, and rigid in her views.

If a woman answers yes to any of the following questions, she should seek medical counsel:

- Do you use or have you ever used laxatives? Diuretics? Diet pills?

- Have you ever made yourself vomit to lose weight or to get rid of a big meal?

- Do you skip meals or avoid certain foods?

Through the medical history and physical examination, an experienced doctor should be able to ascertain whether the female patient is suffering from any components of the triad. The existence of one of the disorders in the triad should be a red flag to the doctor to determine whether the other two are also present.

To break the cycle of eating disorders, which may include binging and purging behaviors (eating large meals, then, when feelings of guilt and shame set in, using laxatives, diuretics, or self-induced vomiting to void

them from the body), experts recommend that athletes stop restricting their diet and start eating frequent, small, low-fat meals that are rich in complex carbohydrates. Small meals eaten often will quell hunger pangs, provide fuel and fluid for exercise, and increase the metabolic rate. If the athlete is incapable of doing this, she should seek nutritional counseling.

The following are some guidelines for female athletes on losing weight safely and effectively:

- With a nutritionist, establish a reasonable weight goal and a realistic amount of time in which to achieve it. Do not attempt weight loss during the sports season (this may result in a loss of lean body mass). During the off-season, athletes should try to lose no more than one pound per week.
- Eat a diet that meets maximum performance needs: 60–70 percent complex carbohydrates; 15–20 percent protein; and 15–20 percent fat.
- Learn about proper nutrition and weight loss strategies.
- Eliminate ''empty'' calories: foods containing simple sugars, hidden fats, and alcohol. This usually means avoiding sweet snacks, and switching to healthy snacks like carrots and fruit.
- Join a weight management group, ideally one comprised chiefly of exercisers. Be sure the group includes discussion of food fads, behavioral modification techniques, and stress management.

Exercise During Pregnancy and Postpartum

Exercise during pregnancy continues to be a controversial topic. The most modern evidence suggests that women in low-risk pregnancies not only can exercise safely, carrying healthy children to term, but also can actually experience many benefits as a result of the exercise.

After delivery, women who have exercised throughout their pregnancy regain their prepregnancy weight sooner than do women who have been sedentary. Weight gain

during pregnancy is generally less in athletic women than in nonathletic women. Exercise during pregnancy may also have a beneficial psychological effect, particularly on the mother's self-image.

Nevertheless, precautions should be taken to safeguard the health of both mother and fetus. Exercise regimens should take into consideration the pregnant woman's prepregnancy fitness level, her medical profile, any past or current obstetrical or gynecological complications, and physical changes associated with the pregnancy. Common sense, proper precautions, and the recommendations of

9. HEART RATE GUIDELINES FOR POSTPARTUM EXERCISE

	BEATS PER MINUTE	
AGE	LIMIT*	MAXIMUM
20	150	200
25	146	195
30	142	190
35	138	185
40	135	180
45	131	175

*Each figure represents 75 percent of the maximum heart rate that would be predicted for the corresponding age group. Under proper medical supervision, more strenuous activity and higher heart rates may be appropriate.

the obstetrician are key components in any exercise program during pregnancy.

The American College of Obstetricians and Gynecologists (ACOG) has developed guidelines on exercise in pregnancy and the postpartum period. These guidelines outline general criteria for safe home exercises, considering the altered physical and physiological conditions that exist during pregnancy.

No single set of recommendations will meet the needs of all women. Based on their pregnancy level of activity, some women may be able to tolerate more strenuous exercise whereas others may need to adopt less vigorous activity.

Exercise Guidelines for Pregnancy Only

- Maternal heart rate should not exceed 140 beats per minute.
- Strenuous activities should not exceed fifteen minutes in duration.
- No exercise should be performed in the supine position after the fourth month of gestation is completed.
- Exercises that employ the Valsalva maneuver (breath holding) should be avoided.
- Caloric intake should be adequate to meet not only the extra energy needs of pregnancy but also of the exercise performed.

- Maternal core temperature should not exceed 38 degrees centigrade.

Exercise Guidelines for Pregnancy and the Postpartum Period

- Regular exercise (at least three times per week) is preferable to intermittent activity. Competitive activities should be avoided.
- Vigorous exercise should not be performed in hot, humid weather or during a period of febrile illness.
- Ballistic movements (jerky, bouncy motions) should be avoided. Exercise should be done on a wooden floor or a tightly carpeted surface to reduce shock and to provide sure footing.
- Deep flexion or extension of joints should be avoided because of connective tissue laxity. Activities that require jumping, jarring motions, or rapid changes in direction should be avoided because of joint instability.
- Vigorous exercise should be followed by a five-minute period of muscle warm-up. This can be accomplished by slow walking or stationary cycling with low resistance.
- Vigorous exercise should be followed by a period of gradually declining activity that includes gentle stationary stretching. Because connective tissue laxity increases the risk of joint injury, stretches should not be taken to the point of maximum resistance.
- Heart rate should be measured at times of peak activity. Target heart rates and limits established in consultation with the physician should not be exceeded (see Table 9 for recommended postpartum heart rate limits).
- Slowly rise from the floor to avoid orthostatic hypotension that causes fainting. Some form of activity involving the legs should be continued for a brief period.
- Drink liquids liberally before and after exercise to prevent dehydration. If necessary, activity should be interrupted to replenish fluids.
- Women who have led sedentary lifestyles should begin with physical activity of very low intensity and advance activity levels very gradually.
- Activity should be stopped and the physician consulted if any unusual symptoms occur. These include pain, bleeding, dizziness, faintness, shortness of breath, pal-

pitations, tachycardia (irregular heartbeat), back or pubic pain, or difficulty walking.

Women and Strength Training

As a result of the health fitness boom, millions of women have taken up aerobic conditioning in the form of running, aerobic dancing, stairclimber machines, bicycling, and cross-country skiing. More slowly, women are also coming to realize the sports-specific and health fitness benefits of strength training with weights.

Women make the same relative gains in strength as men when they undertake similar strength training programs. Yet women have tended to steer clear of strength training for fear they will develop the same large muscles men do when they lift weights regularly. This fear is unjustified. Very few women who strength train will experience unwanted increases in muscle size. Women lack the amounts of the male hormone, testosterone, necessary to build big muscles. For women, a more likely outcome of a strength training program is a *decrease* in the bulk of their arms or legs because fat is lost and in addition, muscle definition improves. Most women regard this as a desirable change.

Many of the existing myths about women and strength training derive from images of the oiled physiques of professional female bodybuilders. It is believed that many of these women take anabolic steroids, which can produce unusual muscle size and definition in women (and also have extremely harmful side effects). A small number of women have unusually high levels of testosterone, and their muscles may become rippled or large when they engage in a strength training program. Large muscle size is also determined by the number and size of the individual woman's muscle fibers.

Most of a woman's muscle mass is concentrated in the lower body. The upper body, by contrast, is where a woman's muscles are weakest and where they decondition the fastest. Therefore, a woman needs to focus on training her upper body to achieve balanced overall body strength. A woman's upper body strength training regimen should include the bench press, upright and seated rows, internal and external rotator cuff exercises, lateral and front raises, lateral pull-downs, shoulder press, and arm curls.

RUNNING SMART

The following safety tips for female runners were released by the Road Runners Club of America (RRCA) in October 1989.

- Carry identification or write your name, phone number, and blood type on the inside sole of your running shoe. Include any important medical information.
- Do not wear jewelry.
- Carry change for telephone calls.
- Run with a partner.
- Write down or leave word of your running alone. Inform your friends and family of your favorite routes.
- Run in familiar areas. In unfamiliar areas, contact a local RRCA club or running store. Know the location of telephones and open businesses and stores. Alter your route pattern so that someone cannot exactly predict it.
- Always stay alert. The more aware you are, the less vulnerable you are.
- Avoid unpopulated areas, deserted streets, and overgrown trails. Especially avoid unlit areas at night. Run clear of parked cars or bushes.
- Do not wear headphones. Use your hearing to be aware of your surroundings.
- Ignore verbal harassment. Use discretion in acknowledging strangers. Look directly at others and be observant, but keep your distance and keep moving.
- Run against traffic so you can observe approaching automobiles.
- Wear reflective material if you must run before dawn or after dark.
- Use your intuition about suspicious persons or areas. React on your intuitions and avoid the person or area if you feel unsafe.
- Carry a whistle or other noisemaker.
- Call the police immediately if something happens to you or someone else, or if you notice anyone out of the ordinary during your run.

Sports medicine experts agree: the benefits of sports and fitness activities by far outweigh the potential drawbacks. Exercise can promote physical and psychological well-being in women of all ages, including pregnant women. As seen, there may be dangers associated with obsessive participation in exercise, especially when combined with poor eating habits. In such cases athletes may experience diminishing returns on their participation. Therefore it is important that female athletes, young and old, be fully aware of the potential benefits and dangers of their involvement, and take steps to ensure that their athletic experience is as safe and successful as possible.

CHAPTER TWENTY

Exercise and the Elderly

Among the most enthusiastic fitness participants are our older citizens. Older athletes occupy a prominent place among the ranks of the recreational athlete. Participation in "masters" sports—those for the over fifty-five set— is growing steadily, according to *National Masters News*. Many of these older athletes are graying members of the late-seventies fitness boom, but increasing numbers of older Americans are brand new entrants into the sports and health fitness milieu.

The trend toward increased exercise participation in Americans over the age of fifty-five has a great deal to do with the growing body of evidence suggesting that exercise has special benefits for this group.

Effects of Exercise on the Aging Process

The undesirable consequences of aging are well known: aerobic capacity declines, muscular strength declines, lean tissue declines, fat tissue increases, skin thickness decreases, and bone density decreases.

Many of the undesirable consequences of aging are attributable not so much to growing old itself but to the decline in physical activity that accompanies this inevitability. Many seniors (particularly men) are in good health when they retire but soon begin to deteriorate. After an initial flurry of activity, these people tend to rise later than usual in the morning, watch more television, and eat as much (or more) food as during their working years. The result is often the onset of joint

10. SPORTS AND HEALTH FITNESS ACTIVITIES—PERCENT OF FREQUENT PARTICIPANTS OVER FIFTY-FIVE

	DAYS PER YEAR	PERCENT
Fitness walking	(100+)	38.1
R.V. camping	(15+)	37.8
Treadmill exercise	(100+)	33.7
Stationary cycling	(100+)	31.7
Golf	(25+)	26.3
Ski machine exercise	(100+)	24.5
Fishing (saltwater)	(25+)	23.3
Shooting (trap/skeet)	(25+)	20.6
Rowing machine exercise	(100+)	20.4
Bowling	(25+)	19.9
Fly fishing	(25+)	18.3
Fitness swimming	(100+)	18.1
Other freshwater fishing	(25+)	17.4
Hunting	(25+)	12.7
Hiking/Backpacking	(25+)	11.8
Low-impact aerobics	(100+)	11.3
Tennis	(25+)	11.1
Bicycling (fitness)	(100+)	10.7
Running/Jogging	(100+)	10.2
Skiing (alpine)	(15+)	9.8
Racquetball	(25+)	8.7
Step aerobics	(100+)	5.7
Mountain biking	(52+)	5.2

Source: American Sports Data, Inc. Study conducted in January, 1993.

stiffness, occasional loss of balance, breathlessness, fatigue, apathy, depression, tension, and weight gain. Experts agree: these symptoms are the consequences of decreased physical activity.

Many Americans think their later years are a time to slow down and do less, and that physical decline is an inevitable consequence of getting old. This is not true. Many of the problems associated with aging can be halted, or even reversed, through a regular exercise program.

Research on the effects of exercise on the elderly has yielded two profound conclusions: exercise provides direct physical benefits, and there are virtually no dangers associated with sensible exercising.

For older Americans especially, physical activity—even at moderate levels—provides direct medical benefits and serves as preventive medicine as well. The ultimate benefit of being active is not only a *longer life* but a much better *quality of life*.

Exercise helps maintain balance and agility, greatly reducing the risk of injury from a fall. Falls are a major cause of injury, disability, dependence, and death among elderly people. In 1991, the leading cause of death among people aged seventy-five and older was accidents, many of which were falls, according to the National Safety Council. Staying physically active improves muscular strength and thus reduces the chances of falling and the risk of injury when falls do occur. Studies done in nursing homes have shown that people at least seventy-five years old with low mobility levels were twice as likely to fall as those with high mobility levels.

An exercise program will keep the muscles, tendons, and ligaments from tightening and shortening, enabling older people to move around more easily. It makes the heart and lungs stronger, muscles stronger, and the body more flexible. Exercise may also slow the onset of arthritis, and can be used to control such life-threatening problems as diabetes and high blood pressure.

Being in shape also helps promote a healthier lifestyle among older people, as it does among their younger counterparts. Once they take up exercise, many older people adopt better eating habits, helping them combat heart disease, hypertension, some types of cancer, diabetes, and osteoporosis. Annoying conditions such as constipation may subside, making it easier to maintain a desirable, healthy diet.

As they become more aware of their bodies, those who take up exercise in later life often quit unhealthy habits such as smoking and excessive alcohol consumption.

Improving body awareness is not the only benefit of taking up exercise. It also improves mental health. Being active tends to lessen depression and gives an improved outlook on life. Older people who are active have more energy to pursue and fulfill hobbies, interests, and goals. Daily chores are less tiring, and people are able to pursue life's challenges with more enthusiasm and vigor. While exercising, older people make new contacts and make friends. Horizons are broadened, and the person feels more in control of his or her life.

Exercise is a way to attain, or maintain, good physical and mental health necessary for a mobile, independent lifestyle free of overreliance on relatives, friends, or institutional care. It equips a person to withstand the stresses of life and reduces mental fatigue, tension, strain, and boredom. It also helps a person look, feel, and act younger. Studies have shown that in societies where regular physical activity and proper diet are parts of the lifestyle, those who have passed the usual retirement age continue to be physically vigorous with strong muscles and bones and supple bodies.

Precautions for Elderly Exercisers

There are few drawbacks or dangers associated with exercise programs for older people, and certainly, the benefits of being active far outweigh the risks of sedentary behavior. Almost no reports exist of serious heart-lung problems for older people. Cardiac rehabilitation programs, enrolling many people over sixty-five with known artery disease, also report few heart-lung complications.

There are certain commonsense precautions that should be taken as the older person begins or continues to exercise, especially if they were not particularly active when they were younger. Before beginning an exercise program, anyone over thirty-five years old should receive medical clearance. Also, it is a good idea to have an annual physical. If someone has high blood pressure or other cardiovascular problems, he or she should consult a physician before beginning any kind of exercise program. It is a good idea for older athletes to have a maximal exercise stress test to determine how intensely

THE RELATIONSHIP BETWEEN
SPORTS AND OSTEOARTHRITIS

Arthritis, which means "joint inflammation," is not one disease but more than 100 conditions that often affect organs, muscles, skin, and the connective tissue that makes up tendons and ligaments as well as the joints. The most common form is osteoarthritis, or degenerative arthritis.*

Known as "the scourge of the older athlete," osteoarthritis affects an estimated 16 million Americans over fifty years old. It is often the reason older athletes give up sports.

Osteoarthritis involves damage to cartilage that covers the ends of any two bones that meet to form a joint. Many acute sports injuries cause such cartilage damage. It may also be caused by repetitive low-grade impact ("bumping and grinding").

The symptoms of osteoarthritis are aching, soreness, and a grating sensation when moving the weight-bearing joints of the body, especially the hips, knee, and spine.

Many young athletes who injure their joints will develop arthritis in middle and old age. Old fracture sites within joints are commonly involved, particularly at the ankle and knee joints. Football players and other athletes who engage in contact sports are often affected. Arthritis of the wrist is common among squash and racquetball players who use wrist shots, while arthritis of the acromio-clavicular joint in the shoulder is common among golfers, tennis players, baseball players, and hockey players, who use across-the-body arm movements. Tennis players, pitchers, and others who use a "whipping" arm motion may develop arthritis of the elbow. Recent evidence, however, suggests that distance running does not increase the likelihood of arthritis in the lower extremities.

The standard treatment for osteoarthritis is to take nonsteroidal anti-inflammatories (NSAIDs) such as ibuprofen and naproxen, or high-dose Tylenol (acetaminophen), all available without prescription. Another helpful over-the-counter remedy is capsaicin (sold as a generic or Zostrix cream).

Exercise can help, especially conditioning exercises that strengthen the muscles around the joint, so long as the particular exercise does not injure the joint. Too many osteoarthritis sufferers drastically cut back on activity, which can be counterproductive, since the surrounding muscles atrophy and even more stress is placed on the affected joint.

In severe cases, osteoarthritis may cause a person so much immobility and pain that the only option is surgery to replace the entire joint. Every year, 200,000 Americans have their knees replaced, and 300,000 have their hips replaced, almost all because of osteoarthritis.

For more information, call: Arthritis Foundation, 1-800-283-7800.

---

*The other main form is rheumatoid arthritis, a more serious illness that affects 2.5 million Americans. Unlike osteoarthritis, which is caused by injury to the joints, rheumatoid arthritis occurs when immune and inflammatory cells invade the joint. This condition destroys cartilage throughout the entire joint, not just one area, as in osteoarthritis. The bone underneath can also be eaten away.

he or she can train and, more important, whether he or she has any underlying heart disease that could be made worse by exercise. An athlete can be fit but still have some form of heart disease. Also, many older people have arthritis, and while that is no excuse to stop exercising (in most cases, appropriate exercise helps reduce arthritis symptoms), older athletes should be sure the aching joint is due to arthritis and not a sports injury that could get worse.

Older athletes must also pay close attention to training properly and avoid overtraining at all costs, especially as they increase speed or distance. They should not, for instance, increase their mileage by more than 10 percent per week, and never increase both speed and distance at the same time. They should go slowly at first if they are trying a new sport because new muscles need to be gradually adapted to training. Rest days should be taken after a hard or tiring workout. The same study that found that older athletes get injured less often found that once an injury does occur, it takes longer to heal in older people.

Training properly also includes thoroughly warming up, stretching, and cooling down after every workout. Stiff joints can be a problem for older athletes, so they should take special care to get the "kinks" out.

Exercise Tips

Although people of all ages begin and maintain exercise programs in almost the same way, here are some tips for older people from the American Running and Fitness Association.

Choose an activity or activities that you enjoy.

A complete physical examination (including a stress test) is crucial before starting an exercise program. The exam should include a risk-factor analysis to help determine susceptibility to developing cardiovascular disease.

Warm-up and cooldown should never be skipped. These activities help prevent injuries.

Become familiar with basic exercise terminology, like "target heart rate." Target heart rate is the rate at which your heart should beat while you exercise. Ask your doctor to explain what your target heart rate is.

You can also make sure you are not overexerting yourself by using the "talk test." If you can talk comfortably while exercising, you are probably exercising at the appropriate pace.

Start your exercise program *slowly!* If you become fatigued and feel you should stop, then stop for the day. You will not improve as fast as a younger person, so do not get discouraged. You will reach your goal—it just might take a few months instead of a few weeks. Do not overexert yourself.

Certain exercises are less stressful than others. Walking, for instance, may be a good alternative to running if you have not exercised in years. It burns about the same number of calories if the same distance is covered, and gives you a good workout—especially if you stay within your target heart rate range. Swimming and cycling are also good choices because they place less stress on the skeletal system while providing an excellent workout.

For all-around fitness, an aerobic exercise (one that works your lungs and cardiovascular system for at least twenty to thirty consecutive minutes) is best, but you should find other healthful, enjoyable activities to complement your aerobic program. These could include gardening, horseshoe throwing, bowling, golf, tennis, croquet, hiking or camping. Some individual or team sports may also be considered proper exercise, depending on how active you are while doing them. Activities like these are actually preferable if you cannot exercise aerobically because of a medical disability. You might also want to try some weight training with light weights or circuit weight training to help keep your bones strong.

Remember that you must allow your body to recover from any type of exercise. After a workout, older people and sedentary people of any age should allow their muscles to recover. A good guideline: exercise every other day. If you get injured or feel extra sore, take a break from your program. Gentle walking, though, may be done on a daily basis.

Try exercising with a partner or group of people who will help you get—and stay—motivated. You could, for example, get involved in a walking program sponsored by your local hospital or senior center.

Exercise regularly. An occasional missed workout should not affect fitness. However, studies have shown that people begin seeing a decline in physical fitness after just two weeks of missing workouts and are back to their original level of fitness as quickly as three to five months later.

The Importance of Flexibility Exercises and Strength Training

A well-rounded fitness program will improve flexibility, muscular strength, and endurance. Flexibility is highly specific to the individual joints, and exercises to improve flexibility should emphasize movement through a range of motion. Static stretching is the safest and least stressful way to achieve greatest joint flexibility. A well-rounded program also includes some form of resistance training, whether it be with weights, resistance machines, or calisthenics. In addition to the physical fitness benefits, strength training stimulates bone density and can enhance one's ability to perform everyday tasks.

Strength training programs can help you remain active and independent longer—and have a better quality of life. Increased strength leads to improved balance and mobility among older people, and increases bone density to combat osteoporosis.

After car accidents, falls are the leading cause of death in people aged fifty-five to seventy-nine, and the leading cause of death for those between eighty and eighty-nine. Scientists know that for those with a history of falls, knee and ankle strength was significantly lower. Studies show that seniors who increase their strength also improve their balance on 1. a stationary platform with their eyes opened, 2. a stationary platform with their eyes closed, 3. a moving platform with their eyes opened, and 4. a moving platform with eyes closed.

Researchers have also established a positive relationship between strength training and bone density. In one major study, elderly participants who did not engage in a strength training program lost 2 percent of their bone density, while those who were doing strength training did not lose any bone density. Loss of bone density is a major cause of the debilitating disease osteoporosis.

Guidelines

Establish goals. Most seniors are more interested in improving functional capacity than in having strong muscles, but whatever the goals are, it is always easier and more enjoyable to exercise if one has some measure of progress.

Train at a moderate intensity. Exercise all the major muscle groups *two to three* times a week for twenty to thirty minutes a session. Special emphasis should be given to the quadriceps and hamstrings of the upper leg and the muscles around the hip, as these groups of muscles are usually weak, and are important for balance.

At least initially, lift weights in a supervised setting. Start with a low weight (about 30 percent of maximum capacity) and work yourself up to heavier weights (80 percent of maximum capacity). Those who do lifts of between 60 and 80 percent of their maximum capacity will experience significant strength gains. These gains can be felt in only two or three weeks.

Proper breathing is especially important for elderly strength trainers. If exercisers hold their breath during

---

PREPARTICIPATION CHECKLIST

Has a doctor ever said you have heart trouble?
— Yes — No

Do you suffer frequently from chest pain?
— Yes — No

Do you often feel faint or have spells of severe dizziness? — Yes — No

Has a doctor ever said your blood pressure was too high? — Yes — No

Has a doctor ever told you that you have a bone or joint problem, such as arthritis, that has been or could be aggravated by exercise? — Yes — No

Are you over age sixty-five and not accustomed to any exercise? — Yes — No

Are you taking any prescription medications, such as for heart problems or high blood pressure?
— Yes — No

Is there a good physical reason not mentioned here that you should not follow an activity program?
— Yes — No

From the "PAR-Q Validation Report" (modified version) by the British Columbia Department of Health, D. M. Chisholm, M. I. Collins, W. Davenport, N. Gruber, and L. L. Lulak, *British Columbia Medical Journal*, 17 (1975).

---

a lift, blood pressure may increase and pulse rate may decrease; neither is safe.

Begin and end the strength training session with warm-up and cooldown exercises.

Equipment Recommendations

The safety and effectiveness of strength training for seniors has been enhanced by equipment advances. Not only are these machines now available at low cost but they have a number of features that make them well suited for these athletes.

- Balance—a common problem with seniors—is not a factor when weight machines are used.

- The lower back is protected because the user is seated and belted.

- The handles on the new machines are easier to grip, so users do not have to grasp them as hard and elevations in blood pressure are less likely.

- The machines offer low levels of resistance, so users can start at a low level.

- The weights increase in small increments.

- Many machines can be double pinned to limit ranges of motion that are too large. This is an advantage for older users with arthritis pain or previous injury, who want to limit the machine to the pain-free part of their range of motion.

Some sports medicine experts believe free weights are better for elderly exercisers because they are usually used while standing. According to these experts, the action of the muscles as they work to stabilize the upright body may help build bone density.

Those who do not have access to strength training equipment can improvise with sandbags, plastic bottles filled with water, even canned goods. Although a formal program gives better results, exercises with these improvised weights yield very similar health benefits.

Diet

An appropriate diet for the older athlete is much the same as for younger people (refer to chapter 21, "Nutrition for Sports," for a complete review of the special nutritional needs of athletes): breads and cereals, six to eleven servings; meat, poultry, fish, and eggs, two to three servings; fruits, two to four servings; vegetables, three to five servings; dairy, two to three cups of milk (or the equivalent).

However, there may be a few dietary considerations to be kept in mind as someone grows older. Increased calcium intake is important to strengthen bones. Older women need 1,000–1,500 milligrams of calcium daily. Fibrous foods such as whole grains, fruit, and vegetables can reduce constipation and other gastrointestinal problems associated with age.

Older people have slower metabolisms, and therefore require more nutrients with fewer calories than when they were younger (although exercise speeds up metabolism, allowing older athletes to consume more calories without risking weight gain). Therefore, it is a good idea to cut down on high-calorie "junk food" loaded with fats and sugars.

On the other hand, you may find you are eating too little and losing too much weight. There are a number of reasons why this might be. Senses of taste and smell could be less keen, so food is not as appealing; medication or illness might make food unappetizing; loneliness and depression may keep you from eating properly; or simply a lack of knowledge about good nutrition may lead to poor eating habits.

Determine what keeps you from eating healthfully, and then take steps to correct it. If you do not know how to eat well or whether your diet is appropriate, consult a registered dietitian (page 316). If you rely on a lot of prescription medication, ask your physician if they affect food nutrient absorption. If lack of interest is because of dulled senses, you can go out of your way to make food attractive and appealing by eating in a pleasant room, seasoning food with interesting spices, and eating with people who are enjoyable to be with.

The Competitive Older Athlete

Most older Americans say they work out to stay fit and look good. The advantages of strong muscles, increased energy, a trim physique, and a sense of control over the body are enough to make them stick to a regular exercise routine. But many older athletes are motivated by competition. To them, there are always laps to swim faster, races to conquer, and 10k times to improve.

Seniors who plan to compete should first receive a thorough physical to rule out cardiovascular disease and other medical disorders. Next, they must assess themselves and set realistic goals. While they cannot set the same goals they could if they were teenagers, they also know they would not want to be the same athletes. Masters athletes, it is said, are smarter athletes. They have made training mistakes in their lives, and learned from them. A study reported in the *American Journal of Sports Medicine* found that as age increased, the likelihood of injury decreased. This occurred in spite of the fact that the average mileage increased slightly after age forty-five.

Psychologically, as well, older athletes may have an edge over their younger counterparts. They are better able to handle the stresses of competition.

When embarking on a quest to become a competitive athlete, the senior must keep in mind that the more fit he or she is, and the longer he or she has participated in a particular sport, the harder it will be to improve performance. And what is more, it takes longer for older athletes to recover from a hard workout—forty-eight hours versus twenty-four hours for younger athletes. An effective way to get around this is for older athletes to add another sport to their routine. Runners, for example, should mix in some biking or stairclimbing. By alternating sports that work the muscles differently, the older athlete can reduce the chance of injury while maintaining a daily exercise regimen.

To help older athletes compete equitably with younger counterparts, many sports recognize winners in different age categories. This way, older athletes do not necessarily have to prove their mettle by beating teenagers. They can compete with their peers and excel within their own age group as they get older. The thrill of victory is a powerful motivational factor. For many seniors, it provides incentive to stay active and goes a long way to promoting longevity and improving quality of life.

An exercise program for persons over sixty years old has been developed by Dr. Richard Keelor for the President's Council on Fitness and Sports. To obtain a copy of this excellent program, "Pep Up Your Life," contact the American Association of Retired Persons at 601 E Street, N.W., Washington, D.C. 20049.

CHAPTER TWENTY-ONE

Nutrition for Sports

Athletes have long believed that "you are what you eat." Nutrition is one of the most important elements of improving sports performance, although the connection is often taken to illogical extremes. Americans are susceptible to bogus quick-fix solutions to dietary problems, and nowhere is nutritional quackery more prevalent than among athletes. Athletes are always seeking ways to improve performance in almost any way possible, and there are many people willing to take advantage of this desire.

Athletes' nutritional needs are almost identical to those of nonathletes. They require carbohydrates, fats, protein, vitamins, minerals, and water in quantities determined by age, body size, and activity level. These requirements can be met by a basic, well-balanced diet, not by magic foods, wonder diets, or dietary supplements that may actually be harmful.

It is true that *quantitatively*, athletes may have greater overall nutritional needs than nonactive people. Someone who exercises regularly places heavy demands on the body's reserves of fluid and energy. To assure optimal performance, the athlete should increase his or her ordinary diet to maintain these reserves. Most top athletes realize how important nutrition is and have professional advice in this area. Recreational athletes may not have this luxury. Although recreational athletes may have an interest in nutrition—especially how it affects their sports performance—sometimes it is difficult to make sense of the barrage of material cascading from television screens, magazine pages, and supermarket shelves.

There are moves afoot to change America's poor dietary habits. The most up-to-date advice from nutrition scientists has been synthesized by the U.S. Department of Agriculture and the Department of Health and Human Services. These are the USDA and HHS's Dietary Guidelines for Americans:

Eat a variety of foods to get the energy, protein, vitamins, minerals, and fiber needed for good health.

Maintain healthy weight to reduce the chances of having high blood pressure, heart disease, a stroke, certain cancers, and the most common kind of diabetes.

Make your diet low in fat, saturated fat, and cholesterol to reduce the risk of heart attack and certain types of cancer. And because fat contains over twice the calories of an equal amount of carbohydrates or protein, a diet low in fat can help in maintaining a healthy weight.

Eat plenty of vegetables, fruits, and grain products, which provide needed vitamins, minerals, fiber, and complex carbohydrates and can help lower fat intake.

Use sugars only in moderation. A diet with lots of sugars has too many calories and too few nutrients for most people and can contribute to tooth decay.

Use salt and sodium only in moderation to help reduce the risk of high blood pressure.

If consumed at all, alcoholic beverages should be consumed only in moderation. Alcoholic beverages provide calories but little or no nutrients. Drinking alcohol is also the cause of many health problems and accidents and can lead to addiction.

MENU PLAN FOR ACTIVE PEOPLE

	Male (2,800 kCal)	Female (2,000 kCal)
Breakfast	¾ cup bran cereal ½ banana 1 cup 1% milk 6 oz. orange juice 1 slice meat 1 tsp. margarine* 1 tsp. jam	½ cup bran cereal ½ cup banana 1 cup 1% milk 6 oz. orange juice

Lunch	1 cup minestrone soup
	roast beef sandwich:
	    large roll
	    3 oz. lean roast beef
	    2 tsp. mayonnaise*
	    lettuce, tomato
	raw vegetables
	1 apple
	2 small oatmeal raisin
	    cookies
	1 cup 1% milk
	1 oz. pretzels
		1 cup minestrone soup
		roast beef sandwich:
		    large roll
		    2 oz. lean roast beef
		    1 tsp. mayonnaise
		    lettuce, tomato
		raw vegetables
		1 apple
		1 small oatmeal raisin
		    cookie
		1 cup 1% milk

Afternoon
Snack
	6 oz. juice,
	1 candy bar** or 1
	    slice of devil's food
	    cake with frosting**
	    (average slice 2.5
	    oz.)
		6 oz. juice
		1 candy bar** or 1
		    slice of devil's food
		    cake with frosting**
		    average slice 2.5
		    oz.)

Dinner	green salad with 1
	    tbsp. low-cal dressing
	1 whole grain roll
	1 tsp. margarine*
	1 chicken leg, no skin
	1½ cups rice
	1 cup broccoli sauteed
	    in 1 tsp. olive oil*
	1 orange
	1 cup 1% milk
		green salad with 1
		    tbsp. low-cal dressing
		1 whole grain roll
		1 tsp. margarine*
		1 chicken leg, no skin
		¾ cup rice
		1 cup broccoli sauteed
		    in 1 tsp. olive oil*
		1 orange
		1 cup 1% milk

Evening
Snack
	1 cup vanilla low-fat
	    yogurt
		1 cup vanilla low-fat
		    yogurt

* Small amounts of fat are a necessary part of an overall low-fat diet.
** An overall wholesome diet can include some sweet snacks, such as cake or candy.

Proper and Improper Weight Loss Programs

An estimated 60 to 70 million American adults and at least 10 million American teenagers are carrying around too much fat on their bodies. Each year millions of these people embark on weight loss programs for esthetic reasons, often without medical supervision.

In addition, weight reduction is often recommended by physicians for medical reasons. It is well known that obesity is associated with a number of health-related problems, including overly straining the heart (added weight forces it to work harder), left ventricular dysfunction, high blood pressure, diabetes, kidney disease, gallbladder disease, respiratory dysfunction, joint diseases and gout, endometrial cancer, abnormal plasma lipid and lipoprotein concentrations, problems in the administration of anesthetics during surgery, and impairment of work capacity.

Because so many people are affected by the problem of obesity, the American College of Sports Medicine (ACSM) has determined that guidelines are needed for safe and successful weight loss programs.

In summary, a desirable weight loss program

- provides a calorie intake of at least 1,200 kCal per day for normal adults in order to meet their normal nutritional requirements

- includes foods acceptable to the dieter from the viewpoints of sociocultural background, usual habits, taste, cost, and ease in acquisition and preparation

- provides a negative calorie balance (but not more than 500 to 1,000 kCal per day lower than recommended intake), resulting in gradual weight loss without metabolic abnormalities. Maximal weight loss should be 2.2 pounds (1 kg.) per week.

- includes the use of behavior modification to identify and eliminate dieting habits that contribute to improper nutrition

- includes an endurance-exercise program of at least three days a week, twenty to thirty minutes per exercise session, at a minimum of 60 percent of maximum heart rate

- provides for new eating and physical activity habits that can be continued for life in order to maintain the achieved lower body weight.

Gaining Weight Healthfully

For athletes who want to gain weight to improve sports performance or simply change the way they look (gains of no more than 1–2 pounds per week should be attempted), sports nutritionist and author Nancy Clark offers these practical guidelines:

- *Eat consistently.* Every day, eat three hearty meals plus one or two snacks. Do not skip any meals.

- *Eat larger portions than normal.* Instead of having one sandwich for lunch, have two. Have a taller glass of milk, a bigger bowl of cereal, a larger piece of fruit.

- *Select higher-calorie foods.* Read food labels to determine which foods have more calories than an equally enjoyable counterpart. For example, 8 ounces of cranberry-apple juice has more calories (170) than 8 ounces of orange juice (110); a cup of split-pea soup has more calories (130) than a cup of vegetable soup (80).

- *Drink plenty of juice and milk.* Beverages are a simple way to increase calorie intake. Instead of drinking water, quench thirst with calorie-laden fluids. One high school soccer player gained 13 pounds over the summer simply by adding six glasses of cranberry-apple juice (about 1,000 kCal) to his standard daily diet.

- *Do resistance exercises.* Push-ups, free weights, and Nautilus-type machines stimulate muscle development, so that the athlete will *bulk up,* not *fatten up.* Athletes concerned that exercise will result in weight loss rather than gain should remember that vigorous exercise tends to stimulate appetite, so they will eat more and thereby gain even more weight.

Extra exercise, not extra protein, is the key to increased muscular development. Expensive protein drinks are effective only because they contain additional calories. These calories can be obtained much less expensively simply by substituting high-calorie conventional supermarket foods for others of low caloric value.

Nancy Clark is the author of two excellent books on sports nutrition, *The Athlete's Kitchen* (1981, $7.50) and

Nancy Clark's Sports Nutrition Guidebook (1990, $16.50), available from NE Sports Publishers, P.O. Box 252, Boston, MA 02113.

Sports Nutrition Basics

Eating well helps everyone have better health, stamina, and energy. Good nutrition is especially important for athletes who want to optimize their performance. This applies not only to professional athletes and the crème de la crème of our college and high school athletic departments—it goes for recreational athletes, too.

Even with the right combination of genes, training, and coaching, poorly fed athletes are unlikely to fulfill their potential, whether it be finishing a five-set tennis match on the weekend, jogging five miles during lunch break, or doing an aerobics class after work.

Athletes in both short-intensity sports and endurance sports perform best on a high-carbohydrate, low-protein diet.

A wholesome diet based on carbohydrates (between 55 and 65 percent of daily caloric intake) including meat or other protein-rich food as the "accompaniment" (10 to 15 percent of caloric intake) and fat for the remaining calories (about 25 to 30 percent of caloric intake) is appropriate for all athletes. This diet should include foods from all the main food groups (at least six to eleven servings of breads, cereals, rices, and pastas; three to five servings of vegetables; two to four servings of fruit; two to three servings from the meat, poultry, fish, dry beans, eggs, and nuts group; and two to three servings from the milk, yogurt, and cheese group) that not only taste good but are high in nutrients and are easy to digest.

Carbohydrates are the most important energy source during intense physical activity. "Carbs" come in two forms: simple and complex. Simple carbohydrates are found in fruits, juices, milk, frozen yogurt, and candy, while complex carbohydrates are found in whole grains, vegetables, pasta, rice, and breads. The body breaks down both forms of carbohydrates into glucose for immediate energy needs. Excess glucose is stored mainly in the muscles and, to a lesser degree, in the liver, as glycogen to fuel exercise. While it is the most important nutrient, carbohydrate is also the least abundant nutrient stored in the body. Just two hours of exercise or eight hours of fasting can significantly deplete carbohydrate stores. In athletes, depleted glycogen stores can cause fatigue and poor performance.

Sports nutritionists generally recommend a carbohydrate intake of about 3–4 grams of carbohydrate per pound of body weight per day, or a minimum of 500 grams of carbohydrates per day, particularly for endurance athletes. For example, a 180-pound athlete would need about 700 grams of carbohydrates (2,800 calories) per day. This means eating a great deal of pasta and vegetables: one baked potato is about 21 grams, an apple about 18 grams, and a bowl of Cheerios about 20 grams of carbohydrate.

In addition to consuming a high-carbohydrate diet as part of the daily health regimen, consuming carbohydrates soon after training maximizes recovery.

Protein is necessary to build and repair muscle, ligaments, tendons, and other tissue. It is not a particularly useful energy source. Less than 10 percent of the energy used during training comes from protein breakdown. Athletes need only about 1 or 2 grams of protein per kilogram (2.2046 pounds) of body weight per day. Only a limited amount of protein is needed for tissue building. Excess protein is turned into fat.

If the total intake of carbohydrates is insufficient, the body turns to protein to produce energy instead of using it to do its intended job—tissue building. In such cases, the body starts losing lean muscle mass.

A small serving of protein-rich food (lean meat, poultry, seafood, dairy products, and beans) at each meal is enough to support vigorous athletic activity and fulfill the body's basic requirements. Protein supplements are not necessary for athletes who are meeting their overall daily caloric needs.

Fat is the most concentrated energy source of the dietary nutrients. Fats may be classified as either saturated or unsaturated (polyunsaturated or monounsaturated). Saturated fatty acids (fat from beef, pork, lamb and poultry, dairy products, coconut oil, palm oil, hydrogenated oil, and chocolate) tend to increase blood cholesterol levels. Saturated fats should provide no more than 10 percent of the daily caloric intake. Polyunsaturated fats come primarily from vegetable oils (corn, cottonseed, safflower, soybean, and sunflower oils) and from fish oils. Monounsaturated fats are found in avocados, canola oil, olive oil, peanut oil, and most nuts.

Most Americans have plenty of fat, and need to consume only minimal amounts. The average person has sufficient fat energy available to jog 1,000 miles (but would run out of carbohydrates in 15 to 20 miles). In addition to providing energy, fat provides insulation and shock protection, transports certain vitamins through the system, and supplies essential fatty acids. Dietary fats should provide 10 to 30 percent of daily caloric intake—which would represent a major reduction in the typical American diet.

Consuming too little fat creates other problems for the athlete, in particular inadequate calorie intake. Some fat at each meal is appropriate, but avoid excessive amounts of fried, greasy, oily, and buttery foods, which will fill the stomach but leave the muscles unfueled.

Vitamins and minerals are important for a variety of metabolic reactions, but they provide no energy. There is a widespread misconception among athletes that vitamin supplements will enhance athletic performance.

Many athletes consume large quantities of vitamin-mineral supplements in the belief that these dosages will improve performance. However, medical science offers no evidence that performance is improved by consumption of these supplements. The American Medical Association states that healthy men and women who are not pregnant or breast-feeding do not require vitamin-mineral supplements as long as they are eating a varied diet.

The AMA's most recent report on the subject conceded that, due to the changing dietary habits of Americans (increased consumption of processed foods and meals "on the run"), there may be many people whose vitamin-mineral intake is insufficient. However, these individuals are urged to improve their diet before resorting to supplements.

When athletes use a supplement, the dose should never exceed 150 percent of the recommended dietary allowance (RDA). Although most nutritionists agree that no harm will come from taking this amount, they also state that there is no evidence this practice is helpful.

The AMA report states that supplements containing two to ten times the RDA of any vitamin should be taken only under medical supervision when an individual has a specific disease for which the vitamins are prescribed.

Taking "megadoses" of vitamins—an increasingly popular tactic among athletes—is condemned by the AMA. Megadose therapy is costly and builds false hopes. Of greater concern to medical professionals is evidence that massive consumption of vitamins and minerals can be toxic and/or impair the delicate metabolic relationships between vital nutrients.

The bottom line: Supplements of vitamins or minerals exceeding the RDA will not improve the performance of well-nourished athletes.

Fluids need to be emphasized as part of a healthy diet, especially by athletes. Proper hydration is the most frequently overlooked aid to athletic performance.

Fluids are necessary to regulate body temperature and prevent overheating. For example, if an athlete loses three to four pounds during practice or training, he or she will be less able to reduce body heat. This failure to regulate temperature will drastically hurt performance and can cause medical problems. Fluids also transport energy, vitamins, and minerals throughout the circulatory system and are necessary for all bodily functions. Everyone should drink at least six to eight glasses of water daily or until the urine is a clear color. Athletes should also drink copious amounts of fluid before, during, and after exercise. Frequent urination is a positive sign that enough fluids are being consumed. A simple way to determine how much fluid to drink is to get weighed before and after a workout or competition. The weight loss will be almost entirely fluids and should be replaced accordingly (one pound of lost sweat = two cups fluid). Drinking *more* fluids rather than fewer can help prevent dehydration and overheating. Fluids can include water, juices, or sports drinks.

For casual athletes, water is sufficient for fluid replacement. If the exercise lasts longer than 30 minutes (especially in high temperature or humidity), the participant should drink a cup of cool water every fifteen to twenty minutes. Athletes should not wait until they are thirsty before drinking, as the thirst drive lags behind actual needs. A drop in body weight of 2 to 4 percent will affect performance. For example, 10km race times may be decreased by 4 to 8 percent. Weight losses of more than 4 percent can raise temperature and cause heat cramps, heat illness, heat stroke, and even death.

For endurance activities lasting longer than two hours, sports performance does not just depend on water balance but blood sugar levels, too. In these cases, many sports drinks provide water and supply a small amount of sugar and sodium. Current research suggests that athletes in endurance sports benefit when sports drinks are consumed as compared to just water. Several types of sugar (glucose, sucrose, fructose, or maltodextrin) are contained in sports drinks. All have similar properties, except fructose, which may hamper water absorption and irritate the stomach if it is the prime energy source.

Some sports drinks use glucose polymers to boost the sugar content of the drink without affecting the rate of water absorption. These drinks offer about 20 percent sugar solution, providing a significant amount of sugar. This can be very beneficial during ultra-endurance events where muscle and liver glycogen stores are depleted. Several glucose polymer drinks are currently available, including Exceed, Bodyfuel, and MAX.

After exercise, rehydration occurs more quickly when the fluid contains small amounts of sodium as compared to plain water. Sports drinks provide this small amount of sodium (50 to 20 mg per 8 fluid ounces) for this purpose.

Making Sense of Nutrition Science: The Food Guide Pyramid

It is important for athletes to have a sound knowledge of nutritional concepts. Putting this knowledge into practice is a different matter. A simplified, systematic way to ensure an intake of adequate calories and all essential nutrients is to use a basic food guidance system instead of calculating exact amounts needed each day of protein, vitamins, minerals, and so on.

The latest food guidance system is the Food Guide Pyramid developed by the U.S. Department of Agriuculture and endorsed by the Department of Health and Human Services.

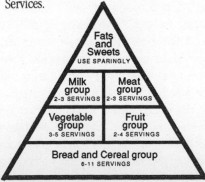

Source: U.S. Department of Agriculture, U.S. Department of Health and Human Services

---

ANABOLIC STEROIDS AND ATHLETES

Use of anabolic steroids is rare among recreational athletes. However, it is on the rise partly because of the increase in the popularity of strength training. It is estimated that 20 percent of people who use weight rooms use steroids. Use of steroids by amateur athletes seems to be growing fastest among young athletes. A study by researchers at the University of Pennsylvania revealed that 6.6 percent of adolescent boys have used anabolic steroids. A full quarter of the boys who admitted to taking steroids did it not to bulk up for football but to look more muscular.

All athletes should be familiar with the harmful effects of anabolic steroids in the event that they, their family members, friends, or colleagues are ever tempted to use these dangerous substances. The most serious include adverse effects on the liver, cardiovascular system, reproductive system, and psychological health.

Negative Side Effects of Steroids

Liver
Chemical hepatitis
Risk of benign and malignant liver tumors

Male reproductive system
Decreased sperm production
Testicle shrinkage
Prostate enlargement
Risk of testicle and prostate tumors

Psychological effects
Increased aggression
Mood swings, including " 'roid rages"
Sex-drive changes

Cardiovascular system
Increased blood pressure
Decreased HDL ("good" cholesterol)

Female-specific effects
Masculinization (irreversible), including clitoral enlargement, increased "hairiness," and deepening voice
Menstrual changes

Youth-specific effects
Premature closure of growth plates—stunted growth
Early maturation

Immune system
Inhibition of natural defenses against infection

Musculoskeletal system
Weakened tendons and ligaments, increasing risk of injury

Meal Timing: When and What to Eat

Top performance is possible only by maintaining adequate carbohydrate stores, and this is achieved by eating properly on a daily basis. However, having these stores requires planning for meals immediately before and after exercise and, sometimes, during the activity itself.

As described above, an athlete's daily diet should include 3–4 grams of carbohydrates per pound of body weight per day, or a minimum of 500 grams, to ensure adequate carbohydrate intake.

The body converts carbohydrates into blood glucose and glycogen. The latter is a form of carbohydrate that is stored in the muscles and liver in limited amounts. During exercise, the body draws on its glycogen stores for fuel; if the exercise is demanding, total glycogen reserves can be used up after two hours. If the reserves are not high enough to begin with, the result is early fatigue. The key to increasing performance in endurance events through nutrition is to begin with maximum levels of glycogen in the muscles, which allows athletes to perform at a higher pace for longer periods.

Besides the daily intake of carbohydrates, a "carbohydrate loading" technique can be incorporated into the training regimen when preparing for events requiring endurance beyond ninety minutes—a marathon, tennis/squash/racquetball tournament, or triathlon, for instance. Many endurance athletes use carbohydrate loading programs prior to competition.

The traditional method of carbohydrate loading, first developed by Scandinavian researchers about twenty-five years ago, involves severely depleting the glycogen stores through exercise a week or so before a major competition, and drastically reducing carbohydrate intake for the next several days. Then, three days prior to competition, the athlete dramatically reduces or cuts out training and increases carbohydrate intake to the point where it represents up to 90 percent of calories. The glycogen-starved muscles absorb the carbohydrates in an extremely concentrated form, which increases their endurance. Unfortunately, there are numerous undesirable side effects associated with the depletion phase of the traditional "carbo loading" regimen, including dizziness, muscle soreness, irritability, and fatigue.

An improved carbohydrate loading technique eliminates many of the problems associated with the traditional method and is more appropriate for the recreational athlete. In this method, the athlete eats a normal mixed diet for two days (about 50 percent of calories from carbohydrates) instead of cutting down on carbohydrates. Training is reduced during this period. Then, for three days prior to the event, the athlete eats a high-carbohydrate diet (70 percent of calories from carbohydrates) and rests on the day immediately before. This updated approach to carbohydrate loading creates glycogen stores equal to those of the traditional method.

Consumption of carbohydrates should be increased from a normal 350 grams to 550–600 grams. Any consumption in excess of 600 grams will not result in greater concentrations of glycogen in the muscles; the excess will probably be converted into fat.

The carbohydrates chosen should be of the complex variety, as these provide higher concentrations of glycogen than do simple carbohydrates such as candy. When most athletes think of carbohydrates, they automatically think of pasta, grains, or beans, not realizing that carbohydrates are concentrated in fruit and are the primary nutrient in most vegetables. Refer to Table 10 for a list of convenient carbohydrate-rich foods and their specific carbohydrate contents.

Precompetition meal and fluids: The precompetition meal and fluid intake should minimize hunger pangs, ensure proper hydration (equal to expected fluid loss), provide for prompt emptying of the gastrointestinal tract, and, to the extent possible, satisfy personal preferences.

Athletes should eat a light meal three to six hours before vigorous exercise. The meal should provide 75 to 150 grams of carbohydrate to supplement glycogen stores. As protein is virtually useless as a source of immediate energy, and contributes to dehydration because it increases the need to urinate, protein should constitute a very small part of the preactivity meal. For instance, if the preactivity meal is pasta, the sauce should contain little meat; if it is a sandwich, the bread slices should be thick and the amount of meat (preferably turkey or chicken) small. The meal should be low in fat, as fats take longer to digest. Fat slows emptying of the stomach and upper gastrointestinal tract, thereby impairing breathing and placing increased strain on circulation, eventually leading to nausea and vomiting.

Athletes should choose foods that are familiar and easy to digest. Liquid meals offer convenience and rapid absorption into the system but should be tried out during training, not before an important event.

As we have seen, preactivity meals need to be planned so the stomach is empty by the time the athlete begins to exercise so he or she does not suffer nausea and gastrointestinal upset. The larger the calorie content of the meal, the longer it takes to digest. The athlete should follow these guidelines for preactivity meals:

- four to six hours for a large meal to digest
- two to three hours for a smaller meal (less than 500 calories)
- one to two hours for a blended or liquid meal
- less than an hour for a light snack (piece of fruit, small bowl of cereal)

Sometimes these guidelines are not easy to follow. For instance, many endurance events begin first thing in the morning. Should the athlete who expects to run in a 10 A.M. marathon wake at 6 to consume three or four baked potatoes? What about the avid tennis player who has scheduled a Sunday morning match? For athletes who wish to exercise vigorously in the morning but do not want to wake early and eat a large meal, the best choice is to eat a large, carbohydrate-rich meal relatively late the night before, then a small breakfast two hours before the event.

For participants in endurance activities, drinking 8 to 12 ounces of cold water ten to fifteen minutes before exercising is advisable, especially if they are susceptible to dehydration. Cold drinks offer the advantage of emptying more rapidly from the stomach and at the same time enhancing body cooling.

The preactivity "sugar fix" is currently a subject of controversy. Athletes have long believed a candy bar or can of soda immediately before activity will give them a "sugar rush" and a boost of energy. However, until recently the common wisdom was that consuming sugar right before exercise actually *impairs* performance, because the quick energy lift athletes are seeking is brought on by a rapid rise in blood glucose and a release of extra insulin. The combined effect of insulin and exercise may cause the blood sugar level to plummet, a condition known as hypoglycemia, and make the athlete feel lightheaded, shaky, and uncoordinated. Gastric distress was thought to be another side effect of a sugar-intensive preexercise snack.

Recent evidence, however, suggests the sugar fix may not be so bad after all. Researchers at the University of Pennsylvania concluded that temporary hypoglycemia does not impair performance in high-intensity exercise. They also reported that in their studies of cyclists who had been given chocolate bars before a grueling race, none of the subjects suffered stomach problems. However, this study differs from the landmark research done in the late 1970s by David Costill and his colleagues at the Human Performance Laboratory at Ball State University in Indiana, in which the subjects were given highly concentrated glucose. (Candy bars, unlike glucose, contain fat and caffeine as well as sugar.)

What is the recreational athlete to make of the controversy? For now, most nutritionists are not changing their directives to athletes. They admit that the sugar fix provides energy but recommend that the energy come from a more nutritious source, such as yogurt, juice, soft pretzel, banana, or simple sandwich. The bottom line for recreational athletes is that relying on a sugar fix depends on insulin sensitivity and nutrition preferences.

During exercise: For events lasting longer than ninety minutes, athletes should eat carbohydrates during the event. Consuming these carbohydrates will improve stamina and performance. Carbohydrates also help maintain normal blood sugar levels as well as provide a source of energy for the muscles. The harder an athlete exercises, the more likely he or she will be to require food during the activity. Solid food snacks such as bananas, fig bars, and bagels can be eaten and digested during exercise and are ideal for participants in long-distance events such as cross-country skiing, running, and cycling.

As thirst is not an effective indicator of fluid needs for athletes during training and prolonged periods of exertion, athletes need to force themselves to drink more fluids than they think they require. Even partial rehydration can minimize the risks of overheating and stress on the circulation. There is also a well-known psychological lift associated with consuming liquids during competition. To be readily available for rehydration and cooling, fluids must quickly leave the stomach. For this reason, how much the athlete drinks, the temperature of what he or she drinks, and what type of liquid is consumed are of importance.

Although large qualities of fluid leave the stomach quickly, they can cause stomach upsets. For this reason, it is preferable to drink small volumes of fluid more frequently (200 to 300 ml every fifteen minutes).

As discussed in the previous section, cold drinks have the advantage of leaving the stomach more quickly and at the same time encouraging body cooling. In most situations, plain water is preferred.

After exercise: Carbohydrate intake is also important after vigorous physical exertion. Glycogen in muscles is replaced most rapidly during the hours immediately following exercise. In the first thirty minutes after exercising, athletes should consume at least 100 grams of carbohydrates, followed by a similar intake two to four hours later. This is especially important after intensive events when the athlete wants to return quite soon to a training schedule.

What form these carbohydrates take doesn't matter. Initially, liquid carbohydrate sources such as glucose polymer drinks may be more convenient and palatable and may contribute to rehydration. Juices are an especially effective source of liquid carbohydrates. Fruit, pasta, or other solid carbohydrates may taste better a little later. Refer to Table 10 for a list of the carbohydrate content (in grams) of a few liquid and solid foods.

To calculate how much fluid to drink after vigorous exercise, athletes should weigh themselves before and after the activity. This may not be practiced before every session, so the athlete should be familiar with approximately how much fluid weight he or she loses during exercise. For each pound of weight lost during exertion, the athlete should drink at least two cups of fluid. Another effective way to monitor hydration is through urination; the athlete is adequately hydrated if urine is clear; darker yellow urine is a sign that more fluids need to be consumed.

It is important for athletes to experiment with what nutrition and hydration suits them best during their *training* schedule, not an important event. Through experimentation athletes will learn what suits them best, and can then use those guidelines during competitive events to maximize performance.

10. CARBOHYDRATE CONTENTS OF LIQUID AND SOLID FOODS

FOOD	AMOUNT	CARBOHYDRATES (grams)
Fruit		
orange	1 medium	64
raisins	¼ cup	30
apricots	4	30
banana	1	25
apple	1 medium	20
grapes	1 cup	16
juice (apple/orange)	1 cup	30
Bread		
hero roll	8"	60
bran muffin	1	45
pancakes	3 medium	42
Vegetables		
baked potato	1 large	55
baked beans	1 cup	50
rice	1 cup	50
corn	1 cup	31
carrot	1 medium	7
Others		
commercial high-carbohydrate drink	12 ounces	70–90
yogurt (strawberry)	1 cup	43
egg noodles	1 cup	37

INDEX